CHURCH PEOPLE IN THE STRUGGLE

RELIGION IN AMERICA SERIES

Harry S. Stout, *General Editor*

CHURCH PEOPLE IN THE STRUGGLE

*The National Council of Churches and
the Black Freedom Movement, 1950–1970*

JAMES F. FINDLAY, JR.

New York   *Oxford*
OXFORD UNIVERSITY PRESS
1993

Oxford University Press

Oxford New York Toronto
Delhi Bombay Calcutta Madras Karachi
Kuala Lumpur Singapore Hong Kong Tokyo
Nairobi Dar es Salaam Cape Town
Melbourne Auckland Madrid

and associated companies in
Berlin Ibadan

Copyright © 1993 by James F. Findlay, Jr.

Published by Oxford University Press, Inc.
200 Madison Avenue, New York, New York 10016

Library of Congress Cataloging-in-Publication Data
Findlay, James F., 1930–
Church people in the struggle : the National Council of Churches
and the Black freedom movement, 1950–1970 / James Findlay.
p. cm. (Religion in America series)
Includes bibliographical references and index.
ISBN 0-19-507967-1
1. Afro-Americans—Civil rights.
2. Civil rights movements—United States—History—20th century.
3. National Council of Churches of Christ in the United States.
4. Afro-Americans—Civil rights—Mississippi.
5. Civil rights movements—Mississippi—History—20th century.
6. United States—Race relations.
7. Mississippi—Race relations.
8. Civil rights—Religious aspects—Christianity.
9. Race relations—Religious aspects—Christianity.
I. Title. II. Series: Religion in America series
(Oxford University Press)
E185.61.F47 1993   261.8'348'0097309045—dc20
92-27457

1 3 5 7 9 8 6 4 2

Printed in the United States of America
on acid-free paper

DEDICATED TO

Doris W. Findlay, James D. Findlay, Eileen J. Findlay,
and especially, Peter F. Findlay,
September 20, 1963–October 31, 1983

ACKNOWLEDGMENTS

I am deeply appreciative of the continuing support I have received throughout this project from the Lilly Endowment. Beginning with a small grant from Robert Lynn for the summer of 1986 that he repeated for several years thereafter and continuing with a much larger award from Craig Dykstra in 1990 to 1991, which assured the final drafting of this book, endowment officials have helped mightily to transform this work from dream into reality. The University of Rhode Island provided crucial assistance through summer stipends, extended released time, and emergency travel funds to conferences and research centers. The support of Beverly Swan, Douglas Rosie, and Peggy Brown was especially important in this regard. A small grant from the National Endowment for the Humanities made it possible to carry out the first phase of my research. My parents would also be happy to know that the money they bequeathed to their children made it possible for me to take a brief unpaid leave to finish the central research for this project. For all these sources of support I am most grateful.

As is usually the case in the creation of a work like this, a network of scholars and colleagues has provided me with critical readings of the evolving manuscript and personal support in times of frustration and discouragement. Of special significance have been John Dittmer of De-Pauw University and Leonard Sweet, president of United Theological Seminary in Dayton, Ohio, who read the entire manuscript and met with me twice at the Lilly Endowment offices in Indianapolis for intense half-day critique sessions. Scarcely less significant was the detailed assessment of the final two chapters prepared by James Washington of Union Theological Seminary in New York. Other scholars who read and offered criticisms of portions of the manuscript included Virginia Brereton, James Cone, Robert King (two helpful readings), John Mulder, James Patterson, Richard Taylor, David Thelen, and Norman Zucker. David Garrow read an early version of one chapter of the book and also assisted by introducing me to the procedures for securing FBI documents and by responding very precisely on short notice to cries for help. A number of colleagues at the University of Rhode Island, including Joel Cohen (especially supportive as my department chairperson), Frank Costigliola, Robert Gutchen, Joe McCartin, Sharon Hartman Strom, Gerry Tyler, Robert Weisbord, and Norman Zucker put up with my daily fears and enthusiasms about research and writing, served as sounding boards for my ideas, and cheered me on when things didn't fall into place quickly enough. I can never repay fully the help all of these people provided.

Because this study focuses on relatively recent events, many of the individuals involved are still alive. Some of these people have taken considerable interest in my project and have willingly agreed to respond, usually more than once, to my quest for information and personal reflections on the events of the sixties and earlier. I want to thank especially J. Martin Bailey, Rims Barber, Robert Beech, Harry Bowie, R. H. Edwin Espy, James Hamilton, Bruce Hanson, Donald McCord, Warren McKenna, Kenneth Neigh, Jack Pratt, Jon Regier, Roger Smith, and Lucius Walker for their special assistance and encouragement. Although I cannot name each of them, I also want to express my appreciation to the over one hundred ministers who responded to me at length about their experiences in Mississippi in the spring and summer of 1964 and to those persons who participated with me in lengthy oral interviews, which probed in depth their memories of the sixties and their recent reflections about the significance of those events of a quarter century or more ago. This book would not have been possible without their contributions.

Staff people at research libraries are unsung but essential collaborators with historians. At the Presbyterian Historical Society, Fred Heuser, Kristin Gleeson, Jerry Gillette, and especially Nora Robinson and Martha Thomas eased my way around a number of research pitfalls. At the University of Rhode Island library the staff in the interlibrary loan office, Vicky Burnett and Marie Rudd, were models of helpfulness and efficiency in the processing of endless requests, as was Marie Beaumont, coordinator of the library's microfilm and microfiche center. I also wish to note the superb assistance I received at the Library of Congress Manuscripts Division; at the presidential libraries of Herbert Hoover, John F. Kennedy, and Lyndon B. Johnson; at the Martin Luther King Center for Non-violent Social Change, especially the assistance of Louise Cook and Diane Ware; the State Historical Library at the University of Wisconsin; the Walter Reuther Center for Labor History and Urban Affairs, Wayne State University; the Minnesota Historical Society; the library of Tougaloo College; the library of Mississippi State University; the library of the University of Iowa; Lilly Library, Indiana University; Mugar Library, Boston University; the library of the Boston University School of Theology; the library of Princeton Theological Seminary; Disciples of Christ Historical Library; the Schomburg Library, especially the support of Diane Lachantanere; the Methodist Archives at Drew University; the library of DePauw University. The editor of the *Journal of American History* has given permission to reprint, especially in chapter 2, much of my article in the June 1990 issue of the *Journal* entitled "Religion and Politics in the Sixties: The Churches and the Civil Rights Act of 1964."

I also wish to express my appreciation to Cynthia Read, senior editor at Oxford University Press, for her steady hand on the entire process that converted my manuscript into a book, and to Catherine Clements, the manuscript editor for Oxford, for the many improvements she made in my writing. And finally I must take special note of the work of the History Department secretaries, Louise Hilliard and Elaine Wills, for their readiness to provide logistical support and their unfailing cheerfulness in responding to my requests. Ms. Wills, especially, typed literally hundreds of letters for me over half a decade with quickness and a remarkable lack of typing errors that noticeably sped the book-forming process along.

The dedication will never fully reveal the contribution my family has made to the creation of this book. Discussions with my oldest son, Jim, now a United Church of Christ minister in Cleveland, sharpened considerably my brief forays into theological issues. My daughter, Eileen, herself a budding historian of Latin America, pressed me constantly about women's issues; substantial additions to the manuscript were the result. I am much indebted to her for these suggestions. My wife, Doris, remained a tower of strength and support throughout the long period of gestation of and struggle over this book. She never hesitated in her belief that the book would be completed when the author had his doubts. For that, and for many other reasons, I am very grateful to her. In many ways the death in 1983 of my youngest son, Peter, of leukemia, provided the central inspiration and focus for this entire effort. The project became the principal means by which I put my shattered personal and professional life back together after Halloween day, October 31, 1983. A student at Brown University, twenty years old when he died, he knew about this project and enthusiastically endorsed it. That fact has both inspired and driven me onward throughout the past nine years. I know he would be immensely pleased that the project has been brought to closure.

CONTENTS

CHURCH PEOPLE IN THE STRUGGLE

Introduction

On June 7, 1963, the General Board of the National Council of Churches voted to establish immediately a Commission on Religion and Race to help initiate a new role for mainstream Protestant churches in the racial conflicts that increasingly engulfed the nation. "Up to now," asserted a council spokesperson, "there has always seemed to be time for gradual change, and modest tokens of progress in racial justice were accepted as the best we could do." But now, "the issue is being sharply focused in every corner of the nation," especially by the African American community "moving quickly and with great commitment to action that often means suffering, harrassment and sometimes death." The writer went on: "There is a growing consensus that this summer may be a decisive period in American history for beginning to deal with this haunting sin. The world watches to see how we will act—whether with courage or with fumbling expediency." Therefore, "in such a time the Church of Jesus Christ is called upon to put aside every lesser engagement, to confess her sins of omission and delay, and to move forward to witness to her essential belief that every child of God is a brother [sister?] to every other."[1]

Thus *nationwide* for the first time the Protestant churches became supporters of "direct action" and of direct involvement with the national black community in the struggle for racial justice. The sentiments and plans were not limited to people in the National Council of Churches. In May 1963 the United Presbyterian Church, U.S.A., and in July 1963 the United Church of Christ, two of the most influential Protestant denominations under the council's ecumenical umbrella, also established special commissions on race and voted to fund these new ventures with budgets of hundreds of thousands of dollars.

As in the National Council of Churches, a deep sense of urgency suffused denominational discussions concerning the creation of the new social action agencies. An observer at the Presbyterian national meeting in Des Moines noted that "without a dissenting vote the Assembly approved (more accurately, *acclaimed*) the proposal and seemed eager to have the Commission begin work before, let us say, lunch." Similar feelings animated the president of the United Church of Christ as he urged delegates to their General Synod meeting to *"end discrimination now,"* since the "struggle for racial equality is so much the over-riding moral issue of our time" that "our part in it must be the over-riding concern of our consciences and of our immediate acts."[2]

Adopting an appropriate biblical phrase, the churches and their allies seemed to be entering a *"kairos"* moment. *Kairos* is a word appearing frequently in the New Testament, a Greek word for "time," but a very special kind of time. In contrast to *chronos*—regular, normal, or "clock" time—the New Testament writers used *kairos* to describe a "right" time, or moment of heightened expectations, when unusual events of great importance were happening, or about to happen, which were determined by God. *Kairos,* then, was "a time of opportunity demanding a response: God offers us a new set of possibilities and we have to accept or decline."[3] Or, as Jesus stated at the beginning of his public ministry: "The *kairos* [time] is fulfilled, and the Kingdom of God is at hand. Repent and believe the gospel" (Mark 1:15).[4]

This special New Testament perspective has influenced the attitudes and perceptions of church people at historical moments other than the 1960s.[5] But it seems especially apt as a powerful word image to describe the work of mainstream Protestants during much of the sixties in the tangled forest of American racial relations. This book is an attempt to describe that special historical era, that "moment in time especially favorable for an undertaking."[6]

Chapter 1 consists, first, of an attempt to trace the rather tepid efforts in the 1950s of ecumenical church people to deal with racial matters. Between 1960 and 1963 there emerged a sense of the imminence of a *kairos* among church people, of the growing need to act or to participate publicly *as the church* in the great racial struggles that were so deeply affecting the nation. At the end of Chapter 1 and in succeeding chapters, the narrative suggests that this special moment of church involvement in racial affairs appeared decisively in mid-1963, that it did not fully dissipate until about 1970, and that the National Council of Churches played a central role in all of these activities. Chapters 2 through 7 represent an attempt to lay out many of the historical contours of that extended "moment," to suggest some of the reasons for its gradual disappearance, and to delineate a few of the consequences that resulted. Admittedly *kairos* has been applied in a historical context that does not match exactly that of New Testament times, but the word remains a powerful metaphor drawn from biblical sources that helps to illuminate the recent past, and thus its use here seems appropriate.

Until recently there has been surprisingly little interest among professional historians in the history of mainstream Protestantism during much of the twentieth century. The Social Gospel movement and its chief spokesman, Walter Rauschenbusch, have continued to attract attention, and in the past three decades there has been some historical research done on the Protestant churches in the twenties, especially focused on Prohibition and the Fundamentalist-Modernist controversy. Excellent biographies of Harry Emerson Fosdick and Reinhold Niebuhr provided some sense of mainstream church life in the thirties and forties, but until recently, serious historical studies of the period after World War II remained almost nonexistent. One had to rely on the chapters in Sydney Ahlstrom's magisterial *A Religious History of the American People,* published in the 1970s, to secure any sort of a synoptic view of mainstream Protestantism in the interwar and post-World War II eras.[7]

Perhaps this was a reflection of the seeming decline of the public role of the Protestant churches during these years. American religious historians during the same period often seemed captivated both by the towering figure of Perry Miller, his critics, and those who extended in new directions his vision of New England Puritanism, and by the fascinating historical problems and interpretations associated with the cultural phenomenon known as nineteenth-century evangelicalism.[8] Both the colonial era and the nineteenth century were lengthy moments in time when religion, especially the Protestant version, still played a significant role in American life and culture. Historians seemed to respond accordingly.

Throughout the 1970s and 1980s the mainline churches experienced noticeable declines in membership and public influence. This provoked an identity crisis of sorts that in turn sparked interest in the history of these churches earlier in the twentieth century. One purpose of this new historical writing, perhaps, was to serve as a basis for inner renewal.[9] The large gaps that existed in the historiography of the Protestant churches in the twentieth century also meant that eventually historians simply recognized that fact and began to try to change the situation. Whatever the explanations, in the past few years there have appeared several important studies that have focused on people or events or movements especially related to the history of recent mainstream Protestantism, often viewed as an informal national religious "establishment" existing at least through the first half of this century.[10] This study fits into that historiographical context.

In at least two ways, however, the concerns of this book move beyond the current evaluation of the Protestant establishment. First, it examines in depth a portion of the history of a key *ecumenical* organization associated with the mainline churches, not the individual churches themselves. There has been relatively little historical study of the ecumenical movement in this country, even though it is now recognized as a major expression of mainstream Protestantism throughout the twentieth century. The principal institutional manifestations of ecumenism have been the Federal Council of Churches, established in 1908, and the National Council of Churches, which replaced the Federal Council and expanded organizationally beyond it, beginning in 1950.[11] The history of these two councils provide many openings to those who might wish to study the ecumenical tradition within American Protestantism, as well as the two organizations for their own sake.[12] Both the Federal Council of Churches before 1950 and the National Council of Churches after that date were guardians and advocates of the Social Gospel. Indeed, this study views the racial policies of the National Council and of some of its constituent denominations in the 1960s as strongly reasserting the Social Gospel tradition, even though the founders of that tradition seemed more concerned with economic than with racial issues.[13]

Second, this work focuses on race relations in the predominantly white churches in the 1950s and 1960s, a topic recognized but not strongly emphasized in the recent studies of mainstream Protestantism and in the secular histories of the civil rights movement covering much of the same time period.[14] I began this project naively intending to discuss and explain the responses of several of the mainline churches to the national civil rights movement. It quickly became apparent that this was a large and very complex task I could not complete in what remained of my allotted "threescore and ten." I settled on a more limited study of the National Council of Churches. In part this was possible because the central archives of the National Council and other manuscript collections related to the council and the black freedom movement of the sixties already were available to scholars (see "Sources"). I also came to see that the council's policies on racial issues usually were representative of the mainline churches. In its actions it reflected rather well the beliefs of those who shaped similar agendas in the denominations under the ecumenical umbrella. Moreover, the very nature of the council—it was a *federation* of church groups pooling resources to deal especially with domestic and foreign issues of public significance—pointed to the constant need to consult, listen to, and stay relatively close to diverse constituencies. This federated, or conciliar, characteristic insured that the National Council was, most of the time, "representative" of its member denominations.

In the first chapter of this book I suggest that, on racial matters, from 1950 to 1963 the National Council of Churches did little more than follow or keep abreast of its constituents. After June 1963, however, it led much more often than it followed. Interesting consequences were the result. Gradually diverging visions of the role of the council in American life developed, which the racial struggle accentuated and which deeply divided the council's constituencies.[15] Moreover, elitist leadership practices (present both in the council and in certain of the denominations) accented differences between national leaders and local followers; by the end of the decade the most creative national church ventures in race relations were failing. (National events and forces over which the churches had little or no control also helped to insure these failures of the late sixties and early seventies.) It is both an exhilarating and sad tale to try and recapture.

Finally, we must be careful not to overstate the contribution of the white churches to the freedom movement simply by focusing so intently on those efforts. Behind everything discussed in these pages rests the mostly unspoken assumption of the central, indispensable role that the African American community, secular and religious, played in shaping and directing events. Edler Hawkins, the first black moderator of the United Presbyterian General Assembly, stated it all succinctly in May 1963 even as he urged his white church brothers and sisters to help:

> the Negro has accepted primary responsibility in his push for freedom, rather than delegate that responsibility to others. . . . [Also] he is saying now what he has for so long withheld, . . . and saying it with an honesty and integrity that was not characteristic of an earlier period when he just didn't say what he really felt, even to his friends. And because of the inevitability of the issue, he is staking almost his life on it, as he realizes . . . that a freedom that is so necessary is also a freedom for which he must suffer and perhaps even die.

Hawkins concluded with this challenge:

> for the church *not* to speak and *not* to act—this kind of silence is terror ro the hearts of us who being Negroes were yet born into the life of the church, and will die in it, and, one hopes we could add, die for it.[16]

Words like these were both a goad and an inspiration to white church people through much of the rest of the sixties.

Notes

1. "A Report of the President's Temporary Committee of Six on Race," National Council of Churches (NCC) June 7, 1963, pp. 1, 2; news release, NCC June 7, 1963; both items in box 115, folder 125, Student Non-Violent Coordinating Committee Papers, Martin Luther King Center for Non-Violent Social Change, Atlanta (hereafter cited as SNCC Papers).

2. *Presbyterian Life,* June 15, 1963, p. 6; Ben M. Herbster to "the Churches and Ministers . . . and to the Delegates to the General Synod," June 18, 1963, box 18, folder 16, United Church of Christ Board of Homeland Ministries Archives, Amistad Center, New Orleans (hereafter cited as UCCBHM Archives). All italicized words are in original. See also Norman J. Baugher to Harold D. Fasnacht, August 1, 1963; Robert Spike to Baugher, August 6, 1963; both items in folder "Emergency Commission on Race: Brethren Agencies, Correspondence with, 1963," Norman J. Baugher files, Church of the Brethren History Library and Archives, Elgin, Illinois (hereafter cited as BHLA Archives). *Presbyterian Life,* June 15, 1963, pp. 5–7, 17; *Minutes,* 175th General Assembly, United Presbyterian Church, U.S.A., May 20, 1963, pp. 130, 141–143; *Minutes,* Fourth General Synod, United Church of Christ, July 4–11, 1963, pp. 22–26, 94, 132–135; *United Church Herald,* July 4, 1963, p. 6, and July 25, 1963, pp. 6, 7–8; and especially "General Board Discussion of the Report of the President's Temporary Committee of Six on Race," June 7, 1963, record group RG 6, box 48, folder 1, National Council of Churches Archives, Presbyterian Historical Society, Philadelphia (hereafter cited as NCC Archives).

3. Robert McAfee Brown, ed., *Kairos: Three Prophetic Challenges to the Church* (Grand Rapids, Mich., William Eerdmans, 1990), p. 3.

4. For similar concerns in the letters of Paul, see 2 Corinthians 6:2, Ephesians 5:16, and Colossians 4:5. There are also passages in the New Testament that stress the *imminence* of *kairos,* not that it was already at hand or present. This understanding underscored the necessity to be prepared both to discern and then to respond to that special moment, for example, Luke 19:44, 21:8, John 7:3–6, Matthew 26:18. The baseline discussion of *kairos* within recent New Testament scholarship is in Oscar Cullman, *Christ and Time: The Primitive Christian Conception of Time and History* (Philadelphia, Westminster Press, 1964), especially pp. 39–44. See also James Barr, *Biblical Words for Time,* rev. ed. (Naperville, Ill., Alec R. Allenson, 1969), pp. 53–57.

5. Brown, *Kairos,* pp. 4–12, notes how church people in Germany in the 1920s and recently in South Africa have utilized the concept to interpret immediate events and to suggest how the churches should act in response. Paul Tillich utilized *kairos* extensively in his theological writings, and the concept served to justify his involvement in the German Socialist movement immediately after World War I. See his *The Protestant Era* (Chicago, University of Chicago Press, 1941), pp. 32–51, and R. Allan Kitten, *The Ontological Theology of Paul Tillich* (Kamper, J. H. Kok, 1956), pp. 50–52, 201–202, 222–231.

6. The phrase is Cullman's in *Christ and Time,* p. 39.

7. Donald Gorrell, *The Age of Social Responsibility: The Social Gospel in the Progressive Era, 1900–1920* (Macon, Ga., Mercer University Press, 1988); Ronald C. White, Jr., *Liberty and Justice For All: Racial Reform and the Social Gospel* (San Francisco, Harper and Row, 1990); Ralph Luker, *The Social Gospel in Black and White: American Racial Reform, 1885–1912* (Chapel Hill, University of North Carolina Press, 1991); Paul Minus, *Walter Rauschenbusch: American Reformer* (New York, Macmillan, 1988); Robert M. Miller, *American Protestantism and Social Issues, 1919–1939* (Chapel Hill, University of North Carolina Press, 1958); George M. Marsden, *Fundamentalism and American Culture, 1870–1925* (New York, Oxford University Press, 1980); Donald Meyer, *The Protestant Search for Political Realism, 1919–1941* (Berkeley, University of California Press, 1960); Richard Fox, *Reinhold Neibuhr: A Biography* (San Francisco, Harper and Row, 1987); Robert T. Handy, "The American Religious Depression, 1925–1935," *Church History* (March 1960), pp. 3–16; Robert M. Miller, *Harry Emerson Fosdick: Preacher, Pastor, Prophet* (New York, Oxford University Press, 1985); Sydney Ahlstrom, *A Religious History of the American People* (New Haven, Yale University Press, 1972), especially chaps. 52–56.

8. David D. Hall's "On Common Ground: The Coherence of American Puritan Studies," *William and Mary Quarterly,* XLIV (April 1987), pp. 193–229, demonstrates that Perry Miller's influence still flourishes in scholarship on colonial America. The full range of historical studies of nineteenth-century evangelicalism appears (slightly dated) in Leonard I. Sweet, ed., *The Evangelical Tradition in America* (Macon, Ga., Mercer University Press, 1984), chap. 1.

9. An example of this type of writing, focused on a single denomination, is the volumes in the series The Presbyterian Presence: The Twentieth Century, edited by Milton J. Coalter, John M. Mulder, and Louis B. Weeks, published by Westminster/John Knox Press, Louisville. The final volume, written by the editors, entitled *The Re-Forming Tradition: Presbyterians and Mainstream Protestantism* (1992), ably sums up the series and places the wealth of data collected into a

meaningful historical context. Essays especially relevant to this study are in two other parts of the series, *The Presbyterian Predicament: Six Perspectives* (1990), and *The Diversity of Discipleship: The Presbyterians and Twentieth-Century Christian Witness* (1991). A parallel though less detailed analysis of the Disciples of Christ is in D. Newell Williams, ed., *A Case Study of Mainstream Protestantism: The Disciples' Relation to American Culture, 1880–1989* (Eerdman's, Grand Rapids, Mich., 1991). A more broadly conceived work, which has strongly influenced discussions of the recent history of the Protestant churches, is Wade Clark Roof and William McKinney, *American Mainline Religiom: Its Changing Shape and Future* (New Brunswick, Rutgers University Press, 1987).

10. Robert Wuthnow, *The Restructuring of American Religion: Society and Faith Since World War II* (Princeton University Press, 1988); Robert M. Miller, *G. Bromley Oxnam: Paladin of American Liberal Protestantism* (Nashville, Abingdon Press, 1991); Martin E. Marty, *Modern American Religion,* vol. I, *The Irony of It All, 1893–1919* (Chicago, University of Chicago Press, 1986), vol. II, *The Noise of Conflict, 1919–1941* (1991); Bradley J. Longfield, *The Presbyterian Controversy: Fundamentalist, Modernists, and Moderates* (New York, Oxford University Press, 1991); and especially William R. Hutchison, ed., *Between the Times: The Travail of the Protestant Establishment in America, 1900–1960* (New York, Cambridge University Press, 1989). *Between the Times* has done much to set the initial parameters of discussion about the history of mainstream, "establishment" Protestantism prior to 1960. The first chapter, for example, authored by editor Hutchison, provides a good definition of mainstream Protestantism and offers clues as to how its leaders functioned as an informal religious "establishment" for at least the first half of the twentieth century. Marty, in his yet more recent *The Noise of Conflict,* p. 11, acknowledges the influence of the Hutchison-edited book in shaping his interpretations of part of the same time period.

11. For a good discussion of the founding of the National Council of Churches, in part suggesting how it differed from the Federal Council, see *Christian Century,* December 13, 1950, pp. 1473, 1476, 1479–1480, 1483, 1486.

12. A comprehensive history of the ecumenical movement within American Protestantism has yet to be written. Probably the best survey currently available is Samuel McCrea Cavert, *The American Churches in the Ecumenical Movement, 1900–1968* (New York, Association Press, 1968). Cavert, not a trained historian, was the last executive secretary of the Federal Council of Churches and continued in that position in the National Council from 1950 to 1954. Two essays in Hutchison, *Between the Times,* make clear, although only in brief outline, the importance of the ecumenical movement in defining mainline Protestantism, especially in carrying forward the concern of advocates of the Social Gospel that the churches be involved publicly in many of the major social and economic issues confronting the nation. Robert A. Schneider, "Voice of Many Waters: Church Federation in the Twentieth Century," pp. 95–121, and David W. Wills, "An Enduring Distance: Black Americans and the Establishment," pp. 168–192. Erskine Clarke, "Presbyterian Ecumenical Activity in the United States," in Coalter, Mulder, and Weeks, *The Diversity of Discipleship,* pp. 149–169, also contains suggestive comments.

13. Luker, *The Social Gospel in Black and White,* p. 314, makes clear that there was at least a limited interest in racial matters in the Federal Council of Churches from the time of its founding in 1908.

14. In Wuthnow, *The Restructuring of American Religion* there are only three

pages dealing directly with the civil rights movement. The superb histories of the civil rights movement already available have explored only superficially the role the predominantly white churches played in those dramatic events. But see Julian Bond's suggestive essay, "The Politics of Civil Rights History," in Armstead L. Robinson and Patricia Sullivan, eds., *New Directions in Civil Rights Studies* (Charlottesville, Va., University of Virginia, 1991), pp. 10, 13–14. Hutchison, *Between the Times,* includes an examination of black-white relations prior to 1950 within the "establishment" in David W. Wills's previously cited essay, "An Enduring Distance." On the Presbyterians, see Gayraud Wilmore, "Identity and Integration: Black Presbyterians and Their Allies in the Twentieth Century," in Coalter, Mulder, and Weeks, *The Presbyterian Predicament,* also reprinted in *The Diversity of Discipleship,* pp. 209–233. See also David Wills's suggestive "The Central Theme of American Religious History: Religious Pluralism, Puritanism, and the Encounter of Black and White," *Religion and Intellectual Life,* 5 (Fall 1987), pp. 30–41.

15. See especially Clarke, "Presbyterian Ecumenical Activity in the United States," pp. 166–167.

16. *Presbyterian Life,* June 15, 1963, p. 7.

1

The Origins of Activism,
1950–1963

On October 12, 1958, before 30,000 people, the President of the United States, Dwight Eisenhower, laid the cornerstone of the Interchurch Center, the permanent home of the National Council of Churches at 475 Riverside Drive in New York City. The outdoor ceremony, on land donated by John D. Rockefeller, Jr., directly across the street from the "Cathedral of Protestantism," Riverside Church, was a moment charged with symbolism, partly obvious, partly hidden. The presence and active participation of President Eisenhower suggested strongly the powerful cultural role the National Council and the Protestant churches it represented continued to play in American life. This moment was almost a classic manifestation of the "civil religion" of the nation in operation. A long procession of robed clerics and academicians, which formed at Riverside Church and then moved slowly to the construction site a block away, "read like a Who's Who of American Protestantism." At the back of the ceremonial platform fluttered large varicolored banners representing thirty-seven Protestant and Eastern Orthodox denominations, almost all members of the National Council of Churches. The presence of the ecumenical movement overarching those denominations seemed almost palpable. It was, one observer noted, "the largest gathering [to date] to pay tribute to the developing solidarity of Protestant and Orthodox churches in the United States."

There were grass-roots participants, too—a massed choir of 500 to sing for the president, bell-ringers from nearby churches, even several hundred of the construction workers building the Interchurch Center joined the procession to the construction site. Perhaps these people served as an unconscious counterbalancing image to the suprachurch connotations the National Council of Churches could never avoid entirely. Finally and appropriately, the benediction was rendered by Harry Emerson Fosdick, pastor emeritus of Riverside Church and since the 1920s a key leader and personal symbol of the forces of liberal Protestantism that underlay and animated the celebration. Looking back one might surmise that for many of the participants the celebration itself and the permanent, material reminder of the day—the growing steel shell of national Protestant headquarters in Morningside Heights—left them with a sense of self-satisfaction, faith in the continuing institutional success of key religious bodies of the nation, and even some feelings of cultural triumphalism.[1]

Indeed, the historical record that remains of mainline Protestantism in the 1950s seems tinged with similar attitudes and feelings. The National Council of Churches again provides reminders of those tendencies. From the time of Harry Truman on, leaders from the two major political parties regularly addressed the biennial (after 1954 triennial) general assemblies and other special convocations of the National Council. These were opportunities for policymakers in Washington, especially those in the executive branch and the State Department, to utilize a relatively neutral but sympathetic platform to explain and defend their programs. Conversely, these appearances usually provided politicians and government officials with an implicit sense of support from a powerful and important opinion-shaping portion of the general public.[2] John Foster Dulles was directly involved in the work of both the Federal Council of Churches and the National Council before becoming Secretary of State in 1953. Arthur Flemming, Eisenhower's appointment as first head of the Department of Health, Education and Welfare, was also deeply involved in the activities of the council in both the fifties and the sixties.[3] All these events provided further confirmation of the many informal ways church and state reinforced each other and that in the 1950s mainstream Protestantism was still a part of the informal national religious "establishment."

Even the seemingly uninspired fact of the publication of a new edition of the Bible highlighted the mainstream Protestants who produced it. The Revised Standard Version of the Bible, published in 1952, was the product of fifteen years of scholarly endeavor and the first comprehensive update of the scriptures in half a century. Clearly this was an ecumenical effort widely acclaimed throughout a nation historically deeply attached to Bible study and Bible-related religious faiths. Eventually, in 1963, the "RSV" was accepted, with minor additions, as the official Roman Catholic Bible, a further ecumenical triumph. The National Council of Churches, representing the Protestant denominations who made the scholarly reevaluation possible, held the copyright. Inevitably this meant a continuous windfall of publicity (and profits) for ecumenical and mainstream Protestantism from the moment the first copy of the new Bible, bound in Moroccan leather, was presented to President Truman in the Oval Office on September 26, 1952.[4]

The widespread Protestant sense of well-being in the fifties also rested on a set of statistics that conveyed very positive images. These were the numbers, published on an annual basis, that established precise levels of church membership, church benevolences, monies invested in new church buildings, even Sunday School enrollments. Throughout the fifties all of these data produced a steadily upward curve that delighted church leaders and were widely publicized. By 1960 the official estimate was that over 63 percent of the American public were church members, a fourteen-point increase in twenty years. Over 35 percent were Protestants, by far the largest religious grouping.[5]

The increase in church membership in the decade was sufficiently dramatic to cause church publicists to proclaim the presence of a widespread "religious revival."[6] There were questions, though, to be raised about these claims. Looking closely at the relevant long-term data, one quickly noticed that church membership as a percentage of the total population increased 8 percent in the decade of the forties versus 6 percent in the fifties, yet no one talked about a "religious revival" occurring in the earlier ten-year period.[7] Even more serious questions were raised by people wondering how deep and lasting the so-called revival was (a perennial issue in previous revivals in this country, extending back to the colonial era). In late 1956 members of the news staff of the National Council of Churches circulated a questionnaire to "a representative cross-section of the nation's leadership in religious and civic affairs," which asked "Is there a religious revival?," and then printed many of the replies. Liston Pope, Dean of Yale Divinity School and a specialist in race relations and social ethics, forcefully expressed the concerns of some of the doubters:

> At this time of the greatest need, the influence of religion on human affairs appears to be indirect and, all told, rather minimal. . . . The religious agencies [have not] been of very much importance in bridging over the gaps between economic classes and racial groups; indeed the churches and other Christian bodies have largely adapted themselves to these divisions. Even with respect to the values by which men live and judge their social institutions, religious forces for the most part have been relegated to the sidelines and secular values are elevated to positions of supreme importance.[8]

Pope's early life as a southerner and the fact that professionally he was a close student of the intractable racial puzzles of this country probably helped to endow him with a strong streak of realism. And our study of the National Council of Churches—one of those "other Christian bodies" to which Pope so delicately referred—and its work in race relations in the 1950s make his generalizations even more apropos. Perhaps, then, our initial description of the fifties was wrong. Better to say that the churches possessed *disparate* tendencies—not just the triumphant mood that so many church people sensed and spoke about, but other attitudes and practices that conveyed less dynamic and positive images.

Throughout the 1950s the National Council of Churches expressed itself on racial matters primarily in two ways. First, by means of resolutions adopted by the key governing bodies of the council—some in the large general assembly meetings held every two or three years, but most at sessions of the General Board, a much smaller but representative "executive committee" that was the true policymaking organ of the council. Second, the Department of Racial and Cultural Relations was responsible for the creation and implementation of ongoing programs designed as specific, tangible expressions of the National Council's broad public statements regarding racial prejudice and segregation. Because of the far-reaching impact of race on American life, other agencies of the council (for example, the migrant ministry program, the Department of Town and Country, or the Division of Christian Education) occasionally directly, and sometimes indirectly, also dealt with racial issues. But over the years the council's thought and action on race were revealed most clearly in the general policy resolutions mentioned above and in the work of the Department of Racial and Cultural Relations.

Between 1950 and 1958 the National Council adopted as official policy two dozen resolutions on racial issues connected to broad societal concerns and specific historical events.[9] Probably the most important of these was the "Statement on the Churches and Segregation" adopted by the General Board in June 1952. The resolution was important for several reasons. First, it reasserted an official policy regarding racial discrimination that had been announced by the Federal Council of Churches in March 1946, which had influenced a number of Protestant denominations to pass similar resolutions in the intervening years.[10] Second, it focused specifically on the churches, made clear their deep complicity in the nation's practice of racial discrimination and segregation,[11] and stated that because "the pattern of segregation is diametrically opposed to what Christians believe about the worth of men," "we must take our stand against it." The statement then went on to suggest specific ways in which the churches at all levels could begin to end their own and the larger society's discriminatory practices, to work for "a non-segregated church and a non-segregated community."[12]

As significant as the contents of the Statement on Segregation was the manner in which it was finally adopted. The General Board intended to approve the proclamation at its regular quarterly meeting on March 21, 1952, but southern churchmen, distressed by the uncompromising nature of the document, helped to secure a postponement of the vote for three months to provide "more time for study" of the statement. On March 23, a Sunday, two thousand members of Adam Clayton Powell's Abyssinian Baptist Church, urged on by their leader ("How can we expect the legislators of America to be more Christlike than their clergymen?"), voted to secede from the National Council of Churches. The same day seventy-five African Methodist Episcopal Church ministers in New York City met and adopted a resolution calling for "reconsideration" of the NCC's statement before the June 11 meeting of the General Board.[13]

When the board finally approved the strongly worded document in June (fears that it would be substantially modified did not materialize), some observers claimed outside pressure like that of the black churches had kept the National Council on a steady course.[14] Both publicly and in letters to some of the critics before and after the June vote, Samuel Cavert, the executive director of the National Council, strongly denied such claims, asserting that the delay from March to June reflected a desire to allow a "really democratic process" to take place "in dealing with real differences," and to handle those differences "in a Christian spirit," which eventually produced "much better results" than if the southerners had been given the opportunity "to claim that their point of view had not been understood or faced."[15]

Clearly the incident had stirred considerable public interest, both within and outside the churches.[16] The issue of race stirred deep emotions; for the churches this moment was but a tiny harbinger of the whirlwind of racial change that, beginning in the mid-fifties, was to sweep across the land, touching church people just as much, and in some cases more, than other Americans. Moreover, the on-and-off approach of the National Council to the enactment of its strong statement on segregation, however well intentioned and probably ultimately correct, suggested a certain hesitancy that was also revealing. This debate occurred just two years after the formation of the council in 1950; cautiousness in leadership probably was affected by that fact as the council sought to move slowly against its southern constituencies, who were always its most hesitant supporters.[17] The council was continuing the social activism of its predecessor, the Federal Council of Churches, but under different circumstances. In addition to the uncertainties inherent in a large, new ecumenical agency still struggling to define itself, between 1946 and 1952 the cold war had emerged and the intense anticommunism that accompanied it was already creating a national climate of opinion that was different, and much more cautious, than that of 1946. Indirectly at least the growing conservative temper of the fifties, even as early as the spring of 1952, probably served as a further cautionary note.

Finally, the events in 1952 served as a reminder that two years before the *Brown* decision, almost four years before Montgomery, at least some black religious leaders did not hesitate to attack their white counterparts for "moving so slowly in taking a firm stand against racial segregation," as a young, white Episcopalian priest from Baltimore described it in a letter to the executive director of the National Council of Churches. Belying the passive image too often projected of them in that day and later, Reverend Adam Clayton Powell and certain ministers of the AME Church in New York City would have applauded the young priest and probably would have agreed when he said that "of course, the matter [of segregation] is a most difficult one. It will only be solved, in my opinion, as we all admit at least the philosophy of equality, [then] putting equality into practice as much as our feeble courage allows us to do."[18]

"Putting equality into practice"—that was the nub of the matter. Unfortunately, for most of the rest of the decade the National Council of Churches (and most of the mainstream Protestant churches) found it difficult to advance very far beyond the techniques and positions they had adopted in 1952 regarding segregation and racial discrimination. As noted earlier, resolutions and proclamations remained one of the principle means by which the National Council of Churches expressed itself about discrimination—in support of the Supreme Court's *Brown* decision in 1954, commending President Eisenhower's handling of the Little Rock crisis in 1957, announcing in 1957 that no meetings of National Council bodies were to be held in cities where public accommodations discriminated because of race.[19] But these were little more than slight slaps on the wrist to those institutions and people practicing segregation and had little or no long-term practical effect.

Indeed, the Council's support of the *Brown* decision was actually a pulling back from policies followed in the late 1940s by the Federal Council of the Churches. In December 1949, the Federal Council submitted an *amicus curiae* brief before the Supreme Court in support of Heman Sweatt's suit against the University of Texas Law School that as an African American he had been denied equal access to advanced education in Texas. *Sweatt v. Painter* was an important legal forerunner of *Brown* in 1954; the Federal Council of Church's *curiae* brief was a small but significant venture at the time into political activism. Officials of the Federal Council justified the brief as a logical outgrowth of the statement of 1946 on segregation and noted that lawyers from the NAACP handling the case urged that the brief be prepared since "such briefs are of enormous value because of the moral, social and public policy issues involved."[20]

As might be expected, there was considerable opposition to this move among southern churches. In an almost exact parallel with the results of the debate over the second Statement on Segregation in 1952, the southern Presbyterian Church, U.S., eventually "disassociated" itself from the Federal Council's actions. Some southern Methodist conferences were pressed (but did not act) to withdraw from the council.[21] In this situation leaders of the ecumenical organization could take some small comfort from the support extended them by Judge J. Waties Waring, member of the United States District Court in Charlestown, South Carolina, native of that state, and even then a widely recognized champion of African American civil rights. In January 1950, following the filing of the Federal Council's brief with the Supreme Court, Judge Waring wrote to the executive director of the Council offering his congratulations. In his letter the judge also commented about the role he felt the churches should play in helping to end segregation.

> For a long time, I have been thinking that one of the most important approaches to the goal for ending racial segregation is through the churches. The defenders of segregation can deal in much sophistry and put up many arguments based on practice and custom and erroneous legal decision. But their weakest line of defense is in the religious area. And there is really no semblance of an argument when the approach is made from that standpoint. And, therefore, I am of the belief that the cheif burden for ending segregation should be thrown upon the decent thinking churchmen of the country.

Judge Waring proceeded with a practical suggestion—that the Federal Council of Churches communicate its position on the Sweatt case down through the various levels of church organization until "eventually ministers . . . press upon their congregations the idea of militant action to end segregation." Waring believed that "such a course of action may arouse the religious people of this country and bring sufficient pressure to influence our vacillating government in Washington." When senators, for example, "begin to realize there is a great wave of religious backing to the abolition of segregation, they will stop playing petty politics and wipe out the bane of segregation."[22]

Given the advantage of hindsight, we know that Judge Waring was far too optimistic about the willingness of his fellow southerners and supporters in the north to relinquish segregation and was naive about the ease with which national Protestant leaders might "arouse the religious people of this country" to take a new path in racial attitutdes and practices. But his vision did bear a strong resemblance to the programs of action the National Council of Churches and its religious and secular allies finally undertook in 1963, almost a decade and a half later. In 1949 the time was not yet ripe. Neither were the churches ready to follow Waring's suggestions in 1954 at the time of the *Brown* decision. The leaders of the National Council of Churches then were more cautious than their fathers. On May 19, 1954, two days after the Court rendered its verdict, the General Board of the National Council passed a resolution expressing its support of *Brown*.[23] But another *amicus curiae* brief was never prepared to buttress this most fundamental of legal blows to the national system of segregation.

In the case of both the curiae brief and the segregation statement of 1952, initial pressure for action by the council came from the Department of Racial and Cultural Relations (using here its post-1950 title). These were perhaps unusual instances of the work of this agency, which most of the time seemed almost determinedly conventional and unspectacular.[24] Reflecting its origins in the era of the Social Gospel, the Federal Council of Churches established a Department of Race Relations in 1921. The FCC did not create a full-time executive secretary for the department until 1934. Then officials placed in that position an existing staff person, Dr. George Haynes, a nationally recognized black activist and scholar, one of the founders of the Urban League and also the creator of the Sociology Department at Fisk University. Haynes stayed with the Federal Council until his retirement in 1947. He was replaced then by J. Oscar Lee, his principal assistant, who remained the executive secretary of the department when the National Council of Churches began in 1950 and continued in that position throughout the fifties and on into the sixties.[25]

Born in Washington, D.C., Lee grew up in Philadelphia and was educated in predominantly black and predominantly white institutions in both the north and south—Lincoln University in Pennsylvania, Yale and

Union (New York) seminaries, Union Seminary in Richmond, Virginia. He secured a doctoral degree in Virginia in 1946. From 1943 to 1946 Lee also served as an assistant director of the Connecticut Council of Churches, spending much of his time with migrant workers in the tobacco fields located in the Connecticut River valley. This early career seemed almost a model of preparation for his eventual work with the Federal Council and National Council of Churches. By late 1946, when he joined the staff of the Federal Council, Lee already possessed considerable experience as a black person dealing with racial issues in an ecumenical, nearly all-white church context. Clearly, too, he had prepared himself well professionally, securing degrees from among the best seminaries in American Protestantism at the time, North and South. Lee also recapitulated characteristics of his mentor George Haynes. Like Haynes, he was a specialist in the field of social ethics and the sociology of religion. Also like Haynes, by the time he became director of the Department of Race Relations in 1947, Lee was an experienced church administrator.[26] Thus it was understandable why he continued in his position after 1950 (in a renamed Department of Racial and Cultural Relations) as the Federal Council was merged into the National Council of Churches. Continuity was of paramount importance in 1950 and immediately after, and no one seemed better qualified than Lee to provide such reassurance as the person in charge of the National Council of Church's program on race relations. This also implied that "boat rocking" on racial issues should be kept to a minimum. Lee seems to have recognized this fact and acceded to it.[27]

Thus, not too surprisingly, Lee continued throughout most of the decade of the fifties to promote activities he or Haynes had initiated earlier. A good example was the annual meeting of "interdenominational institutes" on race relations, begun in 1948 and held throughout the 1950s on college campuses nationwide. Interracial groups, drawn from local churches, state and regional ecumenical agencies, and national church-related organizations like the YMCA and YWCA, gathered for several days for worship, lectures, field trips, and recreation together. They sought to become "laboratories in practical Christian brotherhood," to learn methods and techniques "to improve race relations in the local community, and to develop inclusive churches and Church-related institutions." By the mid-fifties over five hundred people were participating each year.[28] Beginning in 1934 the department also published a bimonthly newsletter, *Interracial News Service,* which provided information about the work of the department and the activities of local African American, Native American, Hispanic, and Asian groups throughout the country. This publication was mailed to thousands of clergy nationwide.[29]

Probably the best-known and most widely observed event sponsored by the Department of Racial and Cultural Relations was Race Relations Sunday. Initiated in the 1920s, its long-standing success and increasing popularity in the postwar era probably were because it required so little of local churches—a once-a-year reminder, usually in February, that problems of race still existed in the country. By 1950, and after, preparations for this annual event occupied a large amount of the staff time of the department. Nevertheless, in regular reports to his executive board Lee enthusiastically recounted many details of these preparations and pointed to the vast number of reprints (close to a hundred thousand annually) of the official race relations "Message" from the National Council of Churches sent each year to Protestant clergy and local church groups throughout the country.[30]

These various elements of the department's program underlined the fact that its primary purpose was *educational*. One intent was simply to disseminate information, which if used properly at the local level might begin to dispel prejudice. This was the logic behind the publication of *Interracial News Service* and the celebration of Race Relations Sunday. It was also one justification for holding the annual "institutes" on race relations for local church people and administrators of national social action programs in the various denominations. These institutes were also designed not only to study the problems of race in local settings but to allow church people to develop solutions, through mediation and conciliation, to the local problems of racial discrimination.[31] Finally, the institutes simply brought black and white people together, often for the first time, for worship, fellowship and face-to-face discussion of the knotty issues of race that confronted them all.

From the perspective of the 1990s, these tactics now seem rather naive and not likely to change much the deeply rooted practices of racial discrimination in the United States. All of these efforts of the Department of Racial and Cultural Relations emphasized a cautious, evolutionary, go-slow approach to the solution of racial problems. That approach left the decisions about the pace of change in the hands of whites, which usually meant little or no change. It was also a point of view fully in tune with the public temper of the early fifties. Education and face-to-face discussion could be useful first steps toward change, but in themselves offered no long-term solutions to such deeply entrenched structural problems in the society as poverty or segregated housing and public schooling, all of which inevitably accompanied discrimination and enabled the latter to remain deeply rooted in our national life.

In its early years the top leadership of the National Council of Churches seemed content to let the Department of Racial and Cultural Relations move unchallenged along its well-worn path. During the early fifties, J. Oscar Lee was the only African American on the entire professional staff of the National Council (there were several African American secretaries, which perhaps implicitly reinforced his sense of isolation and relative powerlessness). Later Lee recalled that it "took a lot of doing" even to integrate his own staff during the rest of the decade. There was no overt opposition, "just inaction" when he recommended other blacks for openings. He also felt that for many whites in those days, even staff people of the NCC, to work for a black person was "in some degree to lose face." Thus often subtle discouragement occurred *after* a person was hired.[32] These comments point strongly to the conclusion that the department and its programs, even in the cautious way in which they nearly always were framed, were not a major priority of the NCC leadership for much of the fifties.

A similar lack of urgency about racial issues even among the members of the executive board of the Department of Racial and Cultural Relations revealed itself in the spring of 1956. In April of that year, five months after the brutal lynching of young Emmett Till in Mississippi and just a few weeks after Till's murderers were acquitted of all charges by all-white juries of Mississippians, Oscar Lee presented to his board a strong statement of condemnation he had drafted, hoping that it "might be released as the position which the Department held regarding this subject." Members of the executive committee hesitated, knowing that the General Board of the National Council had just passed a resolution only indirectly recognizing the Till incident, because the General Board "did not want to criticize the verdict of a jury." Afraid to disagree publicly with the primary governing body of the National Council, Lee's statement was referred "to a sub-committee for re-working."[33] One can barely imagine the feelings of Lee and those of the African American permanent secretary, Olivia Pearl Stokes, as she recorded the committee's decision. Hesitancy and caution compounded were rendering the National Council of Churches a near moral cipher, unable even to pass a resolution adding its voice to the national outcry against another vigilante murder in Mississippi of an innocent young black person.[34]

The sense of frustration and moral impotence this incident pointed to was spreading among church leaders in the denominations under the umbrella of the National Council. Many Americans recognized that the Supreme Court's momentous action favoring integration in the *Brown* decision in 1954 opened up new possibilities in race relations. Religiously committed activists felt that the churches should be at the forefront in pressing for an end to segregation and worried because the national leadership of the mainstream Protestant churches seemed so reluctant to take on such a role. This sense of urgency was accentuated by the emergence in 1955 and 1956 of Martin Luther King, Jr., a young black Baptist minister who, along with his supporters, linked profound moral criticism of segregation with the use of new, much more dynamic protest tactics of mass rallies (centered in the African American churches) and economic boycotts, which quickly energized an entire African American community in the Deep South to effective resistance. The success of the bus boycott in Montgomery, and the crucial role that the black churches and their leaders played in that event, only made clearer the inaction and moral hesitancy of the leaders of the major white church groups.

In March 1956, Ralph Smeltzer, a top official in the Church of the Brethren, articulated many of the worries of some of the mainline church leaders in a letter to Arvild Olsen, the head of the Division of Christian Life and Work of the National Council, and J. Oscar Lee's immediate boss. Claiming that his concern was "shared by a number of other persons in denominational leadership with whom I have conferred," Smeltzer spoke of the "racial revolution" facing the country and of the need for the churches to provide greater leadership in order to assure that the revolution is "kept in non-violent channels." "Our churches reach into every local community. We have a gospel of love, good will, and non-violence. We can make a distinctive contribution . . . which will further integration" throughout the country. Thus

> "there is a great need just now for the churches . . . to develop a nation-wide strategy for meeting the present need and opportunity, for develping common objectives and methods; for the developing of a feeling of unity and common approach by the denominations."

Smeltzer went on to urge that the National Council respond by calling a national conference to begin discussing the issues and to decide how specifically to respond, then hold similar regional or state conferences "to encourage and strengthen local churches and local pastors as they face the specific problems of integration in their local communities." It had been his experience, Smeltzer argued, the "larger conferences" such as those he proposed were "more prophetic and courageous in their statements and approaches than . . . local ones." Such meetings, he believed, could "give real encouragement to local pastors and local congregations and help them to be more courageous than they otherwise would." Smeltzer ended by once again urging that the National Council of Churches and its Department of Racial and Cultural Relations provide the necessary leadership to enable the churches to "embark upon a bolder and broader program toward racial integration." The denominations "need this leadership" from the council, he said, as a part of doing "more individually and also together."[35]

Smeltzer was urging the National Council of Churches to exercise vigorous national moral leadership in the mushrooming debate and conflict over race just as Judge Waring had done six years earlier. The Church of the Brethren official's proposal for implementing a "bolder and broader program toward racial integration" may or may not have worked since it was never tried. What was significant was his belief that the churches could and should play a major role in determining the nation's course in the great struggle over racial change. Like Judge Waring before him, he was pressing the Protestant church "establishment" to live up to some of its highest ideals, to implement in public in a historical moment unusually alive with possibilities the biblical injunction to "seek justice and walk humbly with thy God."[36] He was seeking a *kairos* moment, but the churches were not yet quite ready to respond to such a vision.

Interestingly, even as Smeltzer was writing his letter, officials of the

National Council of Churches moved a bit beyond passing resolutions to a more activist stance regarding racial matters. In December 1955, more than a year after the *Brown* decision, the General Board authorized an "experimental" program to respond to the many crises, large and small, precipitated in communities throughout the South by the Supreme Court's edict that segregated public schools be ended. As one participant put it later, the council sought "a formula" that would utilize the "particular strengths" of the churches in "a human situation of [great] complexity" without "appearing to be intervening from 'the outside.' We knew," the writer continued, "that our principal asset was the existence of churches in all the communities affected and we were hopeful . . . that this channel of community life could be effectively used for the amelioration of interracial tensions."[37] The Department of Racial and Cultural Relations was authorized to add a full-time staff person to implement this program—but not until funds for the program had been secured outside the department's existing budget! Thus not until late 1956 did the "Southern Project" become fully operational.[38] Although it was an innovative program for its time, it was limited in scope and suggested how relatively unprepared the mainstream churches still were to affect in any lasting way the course of the racial struggle in the late 1950s and early 1960s.

The success of the Southern Project rested almost entirely on the shoulders of a shrewd young southern Baptist minister named Will D. Campbell, who became the first director on November 1, 1956. Born in 1924 in rural Amite County, deep in the southern part of Mississippi, Campbell, a veteran of World War II, had received his advanced educational training in the immediate postwar years and became the Director of Religious Life (Protestant chaplain) at the University of Mississippi in 1954. Underneath Campbell's earthy, down-home, almost "red-neck" exterior existed a thoughtful, sophisticated minister and preacher. He was intimately acquainted with the nuances of southern life, especially its complex system of race relations. But through a combination of factors—probably early family influences, certainly his experiences in the war and outside Mississippi afterward as well as the possession of a critical intelligence and a strong religious faith—by the mid-1950s Campbell had transcended many of the parochial, deeply prejudiced views of southern (and northern) whites toward their black fellow Americans.[39] His liberal views on race and his willingness to speak out about these views both endangered his position at Ole Miss and attracted the attention of people in the national church bodies. He seemed almost ideally suited to become the director of the Southern Project when it was created in 1956.[40]

Campell felt his way carefully in the early months of the project, crisscrossing the South and establishing contacts with interested and strategically placed black and white church people in such states as Georgia, Mississippi, Louisiana, Texas, Alabama, and Tennessee. He opened an office in Nashville, centrally located to both the Border States and the

Deep South. When local outbursts of racial violence occurred, such as in Clinton, Tennessee, in late 1956 and early 1957 over school desegregation, or in Birmingham, Alabama, in December 1956 where the bombing of the home of Rev. Fred Shuttlesworth anticipated similar acts in that city in the 1960s, Campell appeared. By January 1957, he had established close contacts with Martin Luther King, Jr., and the Montgomery Improvement Association (he attended King's first trial, in Montgomery, in 1956). Later in 1957 he worked unsuccessfully with church people in Little Rock to defuse the extreme racial tensions there during Governor Faubus's attempt to prevent school desegregation.[41] In 1960 and 1961 he was in Nashville, New Orleans, Dallas, and Fayette County, Tennessee, and in 1962, in Macon, Georgia, each time in the midst of community crises over school desegregation and voter registration.[42] Twenty-five years later Campbell himself summed up this work. He was an "itinerant missioner," moving "from place to place encouraging white participants in the struggle, acting as propagandist to friendly and unfriendly media, occasionally infiltrating the established structures of power, offering solace and sanctions to black [and white] victims of bigotry."[43]

In Little Rock, for example, Campbell made two lengthy visits to the city between early September and late November 1957, helping to organize ministers statewide to meet and then to protest publicly Governor Faubus's efforts to prevent the desegregation of the local schools. Liberal church leaders issued public proclamations condemning the governor's intervention, and J. Oscar Lee as well as Campbell maintained a steady stream of encouragement to their clerical contacts in the city.[44] In the face of powerful, intransigent opposition, however, these efforts at moral suasion were quite inadequate. Campbell observed in a letter to Lee in late September, "the whole atmosphere is depressing . . . but I must admit the sight of the U.S. troops made me feel better. . . . Guess that's why I could never quite be a pacifist."[45] These churchmen were receiving a dose of social reality regarding race that was a mere harbinger of what was yet to come.

When he could, Campbell also tried to take a longer view of the struggle over racial issues. This was especially evident in his new hometown of Nashville, where he worked hard with both religious and secular leaders in the extended and eventually successful struggle to integrate the local school system. He was a perceptive observer; his long memos written to church leaders all over the South served both to educate his readers and to maintain a growing network of civil rights advocates both within and outside the church.[46]

And almost immediately he was in demand as a speaker and participant in workshops, "institutes," and training sessions on race relations throughout the South. Especially important were his frequent "consultations" with national and local church leaders in many different spots, intense one or two-day meetings designed to shape specific strategies to respond to the ever-increasing racial unrest. All of these gatherings enabled him steadily to expand his contacts, to keep informed about racial problems throughout the region, and to serve as an astute and extremely knowledgeable general advisor and even as an important reference source about other people able to help in local crisis situations.[47]

Campbell was subtle in his approach to people and hardworking. His work soon attracted the attention of individuals and organizations with more power than the churches to facilitate change. By 1958 he was in frequent contact with the staff of the Southern Regional Council, a major civil rights organization throughout the late fifties and early sixties. In 1961 he participated in some of the earliest discussions about conditions in the South held by both the Justice Department and the Civil Rights Commission under the new Kennedy administration. Eventually he became a part-time consultant to the commission.[48] And throughout the Southern Project's existence, first the Fund for the Republic and then Stephen Currier and his wife, young millionaire activists who funded many of the early ventures in civil rights activities, provided at least half of Campbell's financial support.[49]

The Southern Project represented an important departure of mainstream Protestantism from previous approaches to the race problem. Goaded to act because of the brushfires of racial conflict igniting everywhere in the South in the middle and late 1950s, the project represented the first time that any of these national church bodies officially intervened directly in these conflicts. The era of expressing good intentions by passing resolutions was coming to an end. Although, as Will Campbell himself noted, "the religious forces were a bit late at the gate,"[50] the mainline churches were beginning to commit their considerable moral weight, their substantial resources both human and economic, and a far-flung and potentially very useful network of supporters to the struggle for racial change.

Yet in hindsight one must also observe how limited and hesitant these first steps were. The project had a staff of *one person* and essentially had to raise its own money to survive. Given the magnitude of the problems to be dealt with, the annual budget of $25,000, although relatively easily secured,[51] seemed a ridiculously low sum to be gathered from churches representing thirty-two million people. Black civil rights leaders like Martin Luther King, Jr., and his assistants in the Southern Christian Leadership Conference, or people like James Lawson in Nashville or even John Lewis of SNCC, were all nurtured by the total black religious community in intimate, direct ways that never seemed quite possible in the mainline churches, especially for someone who was a southern churchman who represented a liberal ecumenical organization like the National Council of Churches.[52]

Campbell also probably personally preferred working by himself since he was very independently minded and harbored considerable suspicions of large organizations like the National Council. Working alone enabled him to remain somewhat free of normal bureaucratic constraints, although J. Oscar Lee demanded of him regular and very detailed reports of his daily activities. Thus in working mostly with white groups, he had to rely primarily on personal persuasion and the power of the Christian gospel "to convict" people in the white power structure grudgingly to make even small changes in public practice or the basic institutions that shaped the relations between the races. His special effectiveness as a pastoral counselor of sorts to dozens of ministers throughout the South who had experienced harassment for being outspoken in support of racial change (a "handholding" operation some called it) further underscored the individuality of his approach and also his fundamental humaneness.[53] But there were inherent limitations in all these efforts. Ultimately Campbell's efforts could not affect very substantially the white-dominated institutions, attitudes, and practices that shaped race relations so powerfully in the South and elsewhere. Individual negotiations and personal counseling at numerous flash points by a single individual were in the long run not a very effective institutional policy, especially when most of the people Campbell talked to, including many church people, refused voluntarily to make substantive changes in their daily acts of discrimination.

He had relatively little to say to the African American community, even though he worked hard at maintaining connections with King and the SCLC, key southern chapters of the NAACP, and other parts of the African American churches.[54] Campbell was tolerant and nonjudgmental toward people with views different from his, but at bottom he was a moderate, even on racial issues. As late as 1959 he professed he didn't "know much about" the Highlander School nearby in Tennessee, then being viciously attacked for alleged Communist tendencies because of its interracial workshops and conferences. He decided to stay aloof from Myles Horton and his associates and admitted half-jokingly to his friends in New York City that "I'm getting old and conservative—don't want to go too far out on a limb." In the early sixties he seemed never terribly interested in CORE and SNCC, the most militant of the civil rights groups, and at Albany, Georgia, in 1962, watched with considerable disdain (and perhaps with some justification) the dozens of Protestant ministers from the North who joined King's demonstrations there, knowing they would be arrested and then released quickly and relatively painlessly ("hypocrites" Campbell and others dubbed these outsiders).[55]

By 1963 it was becoming clear that the Southern Project was losing some of its effectiveness and its reason for being. The lack of long-range planning was being questioned by other staff of the Department of Racial and Cultural Relations, and Campbell's intensely personal style seemed somewhat less appropriate.[56] Newer, more militant civil rights groups were pushing forward and accelerating demands within the black community beyond school desegregation to include sit-ins at lunch counters, "freedom rides" on interstate buses, and mass demonstrations in certain southern cities in support of comprehensive economic boycotts, especially of downtown businesses. Much more than in the fifties the federal government was being pushed to intervene more directly, and a more liberal Democratic administration seemed likely to do so. These forces, and changing conditions within the National Council of Churches, were pushing that organization toward the establishment of yet more activist racial policies and even the creation of new organizations. In the early part of 1963 the Southern Project began to be phased out, and in August 1963, Will Campbell left the employ of the National Council of Churches, eventually to become a free-lance writer and nationally recognized essayist, novelist, and laypersons' theologian.[57]

Pointing to weaknesses in the Southern Project should not, however, obscure the historical significance of that program, a largely unknown part of the story of the civil rights movement. The Southern Project and the work of Will Campbell *were* an important starting point for the social activists in the churches, offering one of the first inklings of the constructive possibilities inherent in widespread white church involvement in the national struggle to improve race relations. With very limited resources in 1956, the National Council of Churches developed a role for itself in the continuing racial struggle—to offer moral support and a skilled outside negotiator and mediator to blacks and whites groping toward a new social order in local communities throughout the South. Eventually it became clear that these aims and tactics of the project were too limited, but it was also clear that this program of the National Council of Churches had played an important role in preparing the churches for yet more comprehensive and direct involvement in the racial revolution from 1963 onward.

And perhaps Will Campbell's least recognized but most important contribution in the late fifties and early sixties was to assert through his *words,* as well as in his daily acts, the powerful moral understandings that a biblical faith could inject into the debate over race. One of those moments was in December 1959 when he tried to explain the Southern Project to the General Board of the National Council. Inevitably he had to speak theologically about what he was doing. Campbell made clear that his mission was primarily to the white people of the South, or as he phrased it, to the "segregationists." His and the National Council's task was not to say to white southerners that they were breaking the law with their discriminatory practices, or that violence must be ended, for southerners remembered all too well, it "is still fresh in [our] very genes," the violence and imposed law of the conquering North in the Civil War. Instead, using biblical categories, Campbell spoke to the segregationist of "grace," and "redemption," and when applied to race these words meant that "by this grace we are no longer Negro or white . . . but we are a part of a community which asks only one question and that has to do with redemption, not with color." And the southerner "understands these words."

But, Campbell went on, work in race relations also involved the "judgment" of God, on both black and white southerners. And out of the experience of God's judgment southerners must work out their own solutions to the race problem. All whites as well as blacks are involved in those solutions, and it was the task of church leaders (like Campbell and the NCC) "to bring as many of our fellow Christians . . . to the point of saying with us from our knees regarding our inescapable involvement in this insidious thing called racial discrimination: 'Lord have mercy upon us, Christ, have mercy upon us.'" Or, as one white southerner commented as to how she had changed once she saw the relevance of the Gospel to the matter of race—"now my heart is broken," a reply that Campbell felt was "quick and close to the kingdom."[58]

Perhaps it was possible that such words about grace, redemption, and judgment, along with Campbell's daily actions, might speak frequently with special force to southern church people, many of whom were struggling to escape the terrible snares of racial practices that seemed to hold them captive forever. Campbell's words were also a reminder to northern churchmen of the humility *they* needed in abundance as they gathered increasingly to "help" in the great national effort to alter relations between black and white. This unique combination of words and actions caused one long-time and shrewd observer of race relations in the South to write aptly about Campbell in 1963: "No one has spoken more tellingly . . . to the churches and church-goers in the South. For those of us engaged actively in race relations work, Will has been a beloved pastor."[59] If what Leslie Dunbar said was true, then both the National Council of Churches and Will Campbell might experience a bit of quiet satisfaction from the Southern Project they had conceived and tried to implement from 1956 to 1963.

Still, even in the late fifties, this project, once vividly described by Campbell as the work of "a bootleg preacher and freelance civil rights activist,"[60] barely sufficed as a response from the churches to those caught up in the great national racial struggle. As early as 1959 Campbell himself believed that "there is a level yet to be reached" in the struggle, a time "when those responsible for implementing legal gaims will turn to the moral forces and say, 'We are convinced it must be done. Now show us how.'" Events did not develop exactly the way Campbell thought they would, but his words showed he understood that the mainline churches and the NCC still needed to broaden their response to the racial crisis, to work more fully and effectively "with the real power structure in the various communities [and nationally]."[61] It took a while for the black community, principally in the South, and people within the churches, both black and white, to create such an opportunity, a moment of *kairos,* but that moment did come.

Within the National Council of Churches a new generation of leaders also was beginning to emerge around 1960, people who were fully conscious of the revolutionary implications of the racial changes occurring, cognizant of the powerful moral implications of those changes, and more willing than some earlier officials to risk the churches' prestige by involving them more directly in efforts to support those changes. As noted earlier, throughout most of the fifties the council had been run by people who had also been key leaders in the Federal Council of Churches or in one of the other ecumenical organizations that joined in 1950 to form the new umbrella organization, the National Council of Churches. The first General Secretary of the National Council, for example, was Samuel Cavert, who held the same position (with the same title) in the Federal Council. Cavert retired early in 1954 and was replaced Roy B. Ross, since 1950 his principal administrative assistant and earlier an important ecumenical leader in the field of Christian education. J. Oscar Lee and the Department of Racial and Cultural Relations represented a similar pattern in the area of race relations. For everyone in the National Council the decade of the fifties was primarily a time of consolidation and knitting together of eight previously separate national ecumenical bodies. The need to maintain a strong sense of continuity, not entirely unlike the secular pressures for "consensus" in this same era of McCarthy and Eisenhower, was a powerful motivation, which explained much about leadership patterns in the council in the fifties and about the organization's general cautiousness about racial matters.

A seldom publicly recognized yet powerful factor helping to create a general "go-slow" environment were persistent anti-Communist attacks made upon the National Council of Churches throughout the decade. Because of its liberal views on unions, segregation, nuclear war, and the recognition of Communist China (especially after 1959), the council was viewed as "socialistic" by a variety of right-wing people—businessmen, author John Flynn, radio commentator Fulton Lewis, Jr., and especially evangelical church groups, which had been jousting theologically and on social issues with "liberal Protestants" since the 1920s. There is no direct evidence that the public positions of the council were modified to accommodate specific right-wing attacks, but general worries existed throughout the fifties. Perhaps the clearest sign for ecumenically inclined church people that the McCarthy era was ending occurred in 1960. That year some of the most blatant charges leveled by conservative groups against the National Council were incorporated into a frequently used Air Force training manual. The council responded angrily, demanding immediate withdrawal of the offending document. Apologies from the Secretary of Defense and the Air Force, withdrawal of the manual, and widespread public support enabled the council, almost for the first time, to educate the general populace about its long-standing harassment by right-wing groups.[62]

The successful minimizing of conservative attacks upon the National Council in 1960 pointed to other changes that were taking place internally. A new generation of leaders was assuming control, shaped primarily by their experiences in the council or in other ecumenical organizations *after* 1950. In 1958, for example, R. H. Edwin Espy became associate general secretary, second in command administratively in the council and viewed by many as heir apparent to the top administrative post. He did become the general secretary in 1963 and remained in that crucial position throughout the sixties. With long experience in the student ecumenical movement both nationally and internationally before he joined the National Council in 1955, Espy arrived unencumbered by previous commitments within that organization. Thus he possessed a flexibility and openness to new ideas and perspectives that was important. Espy also began his work in New York as a principal staff person of the Division of Christian Life and Work, one of the most socially conscious departments of the council.[63] By the early sixties, Espy had become a top administrator who played an important enabling role in the council's moves toward greater social activism.

Jon Regier, another key figure in the council's involvement in race relations in the sixties, became the director of the Division of Home Missions in 1958, a department that like the Division of Christian Life and Work, was weighted heavily toward programs with strong Social Gospel overtones. Regier's previous experience had been in social settlement work in Detroit and Chicago. He came to New York from Howell House, a Presbyterian-sponsored inner-city community center on the south side of the Windy City. Thirty-six years old, he was already well versed in the problems of race in major midwestern urban centers. He was another refreshing new face among the top staff people of the National Council.[64]

Finally, as one further hint of change, at its General Assembly in San Francisco in 1960 the delegates elected as president of the council J. Irwin Miller, a highly successful midwestern businessman and a layman—the first such person to be selected. Each president served a three-year term, representing the council in many public capacities and serving often as its unofficial spokesman. It was one of the highest honors the council could convey on a non-staff church person. And informally the president possessed considerable influence, both within and outside council meetings. As a socially conscious manufacturer, a biblical scholar, and patron of the arts from Columbus, Indiana, Miller was another interesting new figure among the top officials of the National Council.[65]

Miller had strong things to say as the mainline churches entered the sixties. He remarked in the first general board meeting over which he presided that he perceived the new decade as a moment when the world was "most violently upset" because of "the changes which are now rushing upon us from all sides. . . . We are changing" he asserted, "from the simple to the complex, from the familiar to the strange, with a speed which exceeds all experience, and in a direction which we do not yet seem to have calculated." No longer would conventional responses suffice, "consumer surveys" advising the council to do "more or less of what [it] . . . has been doing for ten years." By following such a path, "we may somehow miss serving the clear need of our time, and the church can find itself running well behind the pack, shouting hysterical advice to correct situations and conditions of body and spirit which (at least in their familiar forms) have now ceased to exist." Special qualities were required of the council in order to respond properly. This included having the sensitivity to gauge "quickly and accurately the direction and significance of present changes," it involved the use of imagination to be "capable of altering and adjusting our actions and programs to make them serve the times," and it embraced a sense of excitement, for if plans and programs do not "fire the hearts and spirits of men and women" they will "come to nothing." And they "cannot strike such a blaze if we, the servants of the Council, are not ourselves on fire."[66] Although couched in generalities, Miller's thoughts could be applied quite easily to the rapidly changing national scene of race relations, the continuing need for the churches to reshape their role in response, and a hint of some of the qualities needed to bring about that change. These were the kinds of words that could serve as a catalyst for *kairos*.[67]

Colin Williams, a young theologian who came to "475" (the National Council's headquarters on Riverside Drive) in 1962, eventually expressed in two brief but widely read essays ideas that could justify the shifts in social programs Miller and others seemed to suggest were needed. Williams was an Australian; during the fifties he became deeply involved in the worldwide ecumenical movement while he was a student and later as a seminary instructor in Australia and in the United States. He was deeply affected by D. T. Niles, a widely admired Indian theologian who in the 1950s pressed the fledgling World Council of Churches to under-take a comprehensive study of "the missionary role of the church" in the comtemporary world. Williams, possessing both theological and ad-minstrative gifts, helped to conceive and implement this analysis for the World Council of Churches and joined the staff of the National Council in 1962 as director of the Department of Evangelism, to oversee directly its implementation in the United States.[68] By 1963 this work of theo-logians, ethicists, and sociologists from Europe and the United States was far enough advanced to require someone to summarize their conclu-sions in a brief essay, which was then to be used widely in American churches as a study guide or a means toward church self-examination at the local level. Williams assumed this task and quickly wrote *Where in the World* (1963) and then *What in the World* (1964), both published by the National Council of Churches. The essays, widely distributed and dis-cussed within the mainline churches,[69] challenged thousands of lay peo-ple and clergy to think in new ways about the church's position in the world and the activist roles it ought to undertake in contemporary American life.

Williams argued that in America (and in Europe) industrialization, modern technology, and urbanization had created a society in which the church was no longer at the center of daily life. God was still at work in the world, but He revealed Himself as much in the work place or other secular spots as in local churches, which were too residential and too much centered on the home, which now represented only a small slice of people's daily existence. The old, nineteenth-century evangelical perception (still widely accepted even in the mainline churches) was that God manifested Himself first within the churches and from there His message was carried to the world, hopefully to convert and transform the world (God-Church-World). Now, by necessity, the churches had to try and discern God working in the secular world, had to move out into that world and work within it through new missionary enterprises and in alliance with appropriate secular groups and forces (God-World-Church).[70] Williams summarized his arguments this way:

> This viewpoint insists that the present structures of the church are so dominated by the church's surrender to its own worldly security, and that the church is so imprisoned within the expensive facades of buildings that relate to men [and women?] only in a very limited portion of their life, that she can find renewal only as she surrenders these securities and pours herself out upon the world, careless of her own safety or reputation or wealth, allowing the forms of her renewed life to grow around all the shapes of worldly need.[71]

This was an attitude that by 1963 had gained considerable acceptance in church circles, especially in the mainline seminaries, among the clergy who were recent graduates of those seminaries, and within a rather large body of national and regional denominational and ecumenical leaders who drew on the seminaries for ideas and hired their graduates to aid them in their work. The writings of the martyred German theologian Dietrich Bonhoeffer, and American seminary faculty like Martin Marty, Gibson Winter, and Peter Berger, as well as the study papers of European scholars participating in the World Council of Churches' examination of church mission, influenced not only Colin Williams but also the most forward-looking persons, lay and clerical, throughout the mainstream Protestant denominations.[72]

Clearly for Williams and like-minded church people there had to be a search for new methods of mission. Utilizing national church boards or special commissions to confront a major social issue like racial segregation was to be applauded and encouraged, for this could be an example of one of the new forms of missionary activity. As *Where in the World* noted, action such as this by the National Council "could possibly represent a major breakthrough in the way the Church responds to God's missionary call from the world."[73] *Where in the World* reflected the near-readiness of many church leaders in New York and in other parts of the country to break with past practices in responding to the black struggle for freedom. Only a few more jolts were needed to push these people onto a new path of vigorous and direct involvement.

Between 1960 and 1963 a rapidly ascending curve of major challenges to the national racial status quo occurred, principally in the southern states, to which in one way of another the churches were going to have to respond. There had been a number of unheralded local demonstrations in different parts of the South prior to 1960, but the famous college student sit-ins at five-and-ten-cent stores, beginning in the spring of 1960 in Charlotte, North Carolina, and quickly spreading throughout the upper South and the Border States, signaled national recognition of sit-ins and boycotts as a new pressure tactic being used by the black community. This was in addition to action through the courts, initiated chiefly by the NAACP, which had begun the process of school desegregation in the middle and late 1950s.[74] The student sit-ins were soon followed by CORE-sponsored "Freedom Rides" on interstate buses into the Deep South in May 1961, which resulted in severe violence in Alabama and Mississippi. These events also forced the Kennedy administration to intervene, rather hesitantly, for the first time in the escalating crisis.

In 1962 mass demonstrations and legal tests of segregation in the Deep South continued, especially at Albany, Georgia, and at the University of Mississippi. (The campaign in Albany began in November 1961 and lasted almost a year; the crisis at Ole Miss occurred chiefly in the fall of 1962.) The demonstrations in "Al-*benny*" ultimately failed and constituted a major defeat for Martin Luther King, Jr., and the Southern Christian Leadership Conference, which sponsored them. But Albany was the first spot where predominantly northern white church people (principally ministers) marched with the SCLC. Although Will Campbell had reservations about this particular church activity, it was a sign of stirrings in the mainline churches, which would soon lead to much deeper and more direct involvement of the National Council of Churches, and other denominations, in the racial struggle.[75]

Other pressures for direct action by the churches were developing. In January 1963 a national Conference on Religion and Race convened in Chicago. It represented the first major ecumenical effort—Protestants, Catholics, and Jews joining together—to focus attention on the racial crisis. The three-day gathering attracted several hundred religious leaders, but rhetoric still outweighed the ability to mount concrete programs of action. A "continuing" office of the conference was established in New York City following the meeting in Chicago, but proper funding, broad church support, and imaginative leadership failed to materialize and the office closed within a year.[76] Thus the leaders of the Conference on Religion and Race failed in an ambitious effort to become major ecumenical spokesmen on matters of race. But the gathering in Chicago and subsequent efforts to maintain the enthusiasms generated there pointed to growing sentiments among church people that more should be done nationally to help African American citizens secure long-denied basic rights.

The National Council of Churches through the Department of Racial and Cultural Relations was an official sponsor and financial supporter of the Conference on Religion and Race, but its top leadership never endorsed enthusiastically the idea of the continuing office of the conference.

It created another layer of bureaucracy and increased the babble of voices striving to offer some form of national religious leadership on racial matters. There was too much of a tinge of established policies and procedures there. J. Oscar Lee and his followers were the voice of the National Council in this instance, in the eyes of some following tradition too much and possessing too limited a vision.[77]

In any case, the aftermath of the Conference on Religion and Race did not clarify leadership problems in the mainline churches about racial issues. Indeed, individual denominations under the National Council's umbrella seemed readier than the ecumenical organization to adopt an activist stance. On May 20, 1963, the General Assembly of the United Presbyterian Church, U.S.A., established a Commission on Religion and Race to address racial problems in the denomination and in the country at large. The Presbyterians also voted to fund their commission with a hefty budget of $150,000 for the remaining six months of 1963.[78]

The Conference on Religion and Race also highlighted the increasingly significant impact that Martin Luther King, Jr., was making on the predominantly white churches. He was a member of the steering committee that planned the conference, and he delivered one of the major speeches there.[79] In the 1950s religious leaders from the black community other than King had frequently addressed groups in the mainline churches. Two of them were Howard Thurman, dean of the chapel at Boston University during and after the time King was a student there, and Benjamin Mays, president of Morehouse College and a close friend of the King family.[80] Both men were urbane, sophisticated speakers and preachers.

King, however, represented a younger generation of black clergy whose direct action tactics were transforming the civil rights struggle. In the late fifties and early sixties he also engaged in a busy schedule of speech making throughout the country, much of it before white church groups. He made a major speech to the triennial General Assembly of the National Council of Churches in 1957 and wrote the sermon for Race Relations Sunday that same year. King's willingness to engage in direct action and to preach powerfully to white congregations about the consequences was immensely compelling. Clearly by 1963 he was the leading African American interpreter of the black freedom struggle, in all its moral urgency, to white church people nationwide.[81]

On April 3, 1963, two and a half months after the close of the conference in Chicago, King launched his now-famous campaign to desegregate the tough, deep-south city of Birmingham, Alabama. The intense white opposition there to mass marches and demonstrations eventually caught the attention of the nation and the world and landed King in jail. From that jail in Birmingham the young black minister penned his famous *Letter,* addressed to the white clergy of the city (and of the nation). It was King's most powerful indictment of the white churches for their lack of involvement in the black struggle for freedom. It was also very widely read in the white religious community, being published first in its entirety in *The Christian Century,* probably the best-known ecumenical weekly in Protestantism. From behind bars King wrote:

> In the midst of a mighty struggle to rid our nation of racial and economic injustice I have heard many ministers say, "Those are social issues with which the gospel has no real concern," and I have watched many churches commit themselves to a completely otherworldly religion which makes a strange, unbiblical distinction between body and soul, between the sacred and the secular. . . . But the judgment of God is upon the church as never before. If today's church does not recapture the sacrificial spirit of the early church it will lose its authenticity, forfeit the loyalty of millions, and be dismissed as an irrelevant social club with no meaning for the 20th century.

Passages like these, coupled with his activism, made King a personal model for many younger clergy. In a Birmingham jail he offered not only a powerful rebuke to the continuing inactivism of most white religious leaders, but also words that could help create, finally, the *kairos.*[82]

An unusual set of events in late May 1963 helped to focus matters in final form for the churches. A group of African American intellectual and cultural leaders in New York, fearful that racial violence might occur throughout the nation following the recent demonstrations in Birmingham, arranged a private meeting in New York with Robert Kennedy to express their worries and to seek greater federal support for possible solutions to the racial crisis. Kennedy brushed aside their entreaties. In their search for help, some participants in the failed meeting with the attorney general then turned to friends in the National Council of Churches. The church people were simply "there" in New York City, they were sympathetic, and perhaps their contacts and resources could make a difference.[83]

The topmost leadership of the National Council was finally galvanized into action. On June 7, 1963, the General Board of the council announced the formation of the new Commission on Religion and Race, designed to allow America's premier ecumenical body to become fully and flexibly involved in the day-to-day struggle over racial issues. The new commission was to report directly to the General Board, bypassing entirely the Department of Racial and Cultural Relations and all other aspects of the council's bureaucracy. That arrangement gave the commission an unusual degree of freedom in decision making and planning. It also received substantial budgetary support—$175,000 for the rest of 1963, and $275,000 for 1964—more than ten times the annual operating budget of the Southern Project. The first meeting of the new commission was held on June 28, 1963, in New York.[84]

By July 15 the executive director of the group, Robert Spike, a young minister drawn from the national staff of the United Church of Christ, had been hired and begun his work. Spike, too, was almost an epitome of the new breed of national church leaders in the mainline churches. A native of Buffalo, New York, he had received his theological training in the late 1940s and early 1950s at Colgate-Rochester Divinity School and at Columbia University and Union Seminary in New York City. There was a direct line of influence extending back from several of his favorite teachers at Colgate-Rochester to Walter Rauschenbush, and the Niebuhrian tradition in Morningside Heights was at its peak when he studied there. Moreover, Spike had been the minister at Judson Memorial Church in Greenwich Village for several years in the late forties, reviving the social activism of a famous urban church that had waned during and immediately after World War II. Spike had come under the influence of Truman Douglass, by 1960 probably the leading spokesperson in the United Church of Christ for involving the churches directly in racial matters. Douglass, an influential member of the executive board of the National Council in 1963, served as a crucial advocate when Spike secured the position as executive director of the council's Commission on Religion and Race.[85]

The Commission on Religion and Race brought together tendencies and people who for some time had been thinking about, and hoping for, direct commitments nationally by the churches in racial matters. The quick response of the National Council to entreaties for help from the black community is explained in large part by that fact. Jon Regier and his staff, that of Home Missions, were the closest allies of the commission and were among the people within the council who drafted the enabling legislation on very short notice. Within the larger bureaucratic structure of the council, strategically placed people like Ed Espy (soon to become the general secretary), J. Irwin Miller (president of the council), and Eugene Carson Blake, Stated Clerk of the United Presbyterian Church, U.S.A., a key member of the General Board and eventual chairman of the board overseeing the commission, all enthusiastically supported the new venture.[86]

Although J. Oscar Lee became a member of the new commission, he was not made its chairman, or even a codirector, a clear signal that the top officials of the council were moving beyond the Department of Racial and Cultural Relations in shaping the new response to the racial crisis. Clearly, too, the Southern Project was to be supplemented, or even supplanted. Perhaps not coincidentally, Will Campbell resigned as director in July 1963, and less than a year later the program was terminated. The Department of Racial and Cultural Relations never recovered fully from the events in the late spring and summer of 1963.[87]

The quick creation of the Commission on Religion and Race was also possible because its proponents were part of a large network of church officials representing mainline Protestant denominations with their national headquarters, or key divisions of their denominational bureaucracies, in New York City. Like Regier and Espy, these church leaders were relatively young, ambitious, and activist oriented. Many of them were recent seminary graduates and thus were strongly influenced, like

Colin Williams, by the writings of Dietrich Bonhoeffer and American critics of the "suburban" church. It is easy to see why Williams was a friend of many of these people and worked closely with Regier, Spike, and the commission staff in the months immediately following its establishment.[88] In *Where in the World* and *What in the World* he was not only writing primers for study by lay people, but also articulating publicly in a very basic way the thoughts and convictions of his colleagues.[89]

The twelve-story Interchurch Center, now completed and fully occupied, also facilitated the interchange of ideas. The Presbyterians and the Methodists, especially, housed several important national divisions and boards in the building. There was a constant circulation of information, plans, and personal support among these groups. The Episcopalians and the United Church of Christ had their national offices elsewhere in the city, but it was not hard to join deliberations at the Interchurch Center or to share ideas by phone or informal get-togethers. For example, the National Board of Missions of the United Presbyterian Church, U.S.A., notably activist and liberal in the programs it advanced throughout the sixties, occupied offices at "475." Regier, a Presbyterian, received strong support from several of the staff of the National Board of Missions, including the director, Kenneth Neigh, and his two principle assistants, David Ramage and Bryant George. Ramage, Neigh, and Regier started their careers in the Midwest, they and George were contemporaries of one another, either as students or faculty, at McCormick Seminary in Chicago, and all had become experts in interracial ministries in inner city areas of the Windy City before coming to New York. Bryant George, one of the few African Americans on *any* national denominational staff, representing the small but not insignificant African American constituency of the United Presbyterian Church, had known Ramage since they were teenage leaders of national Presbyterian youth groups. These men were politically savvy, tough minded ("steely-eyed" one secular co-worker later dubbed them), and deeply committed to supporting change in national racial practices. Neigh was a member of the General Board of the National Council and was an influential spokesperson there. These men helped Regier draft the documents establishing the Commission on Religion and Race, supported also by people like Arthur Walmsley, an Episcopalian from downtown, and Truman Douglass, head of the Board of Homeland Ministries of the United Church of Christ and, as previously mentioned, mentor of Bob Spike. When the United Presbyterians established *their* commission on race in May 1963, that group, too, established its offices in "the Godbox" on Riverside Drive. Its director, Gayraud Wilmore, and his staff worked closely with Spike's people, and this added another yeasty ingredient to the mix at the Interchurch Center.[90]

Union Theological Seminary played a similar role to that of the Presbyterians in providing recruits who helped shape the activist programs at the Interchurch Center. The center and the seminary were on opposite sides of the same street corner, which symbolized their interconnections. Two recent graduates of Union, Bruce Hanson and John Pratt, joined the staff of the Commission on Religion and Race. Although Reinhold Niebuhr was ill and did not participate directly in any of these developments, his spirit seemed to hover over much of what was transpiring.[91] Younger members of the seminary faculty, like Roger Shinn, helped to plan programs instituted by the National Council, such as the Student Interracial Ministry (a series of summer interracial pulpit "exchanges" begun in 1960), and joined demonstrations in the South and elsewhere that often were the result of these activities.[92]

There was a sense of irony about all this. High-level church leaders, often thought of as plodding and unimaginative bureaucrats, had become program innovators, moving out ahead of a largely culture-bound church to try to lead American mainline Protestantism toward some broad realization of deeply rooted biblical concerns for the poor and dispossessed and for a society of near equals, especially regarding race. This was risky business, for these people at the Interchurch Center and in various denominational headquarters in New York City and elsewhere in the country were a distinct minority, a small elite within the churches. They possessed considerable decision-making power and had access, through denominational gift giving and endowments, to substantial financial resources. For a time at least, given the national focus on racial matters and the powerful pressures for change emanating from both religious and secular allies in the African American community, they might carry their vast local constituencies with them. But a constant though unspoken problem was that they might move too rapidly, or too far out ahead of their cautious lay constituencies, tethered so much to local parishes and often to parochial visions of life.[93] These bureaucrat-leaders were also very middle-class, too exclusively white, and almost entirely male—the epitome of the leadership throughout the mainline churches. By the end of the 1960s the bursting forth of feminism, the national furies unleashed by the Vietnam War, continuing racial antagonisms, and the emergence of a militant young black leadership within the churches as well as in the larger society challenged at many points all previous leadership groups in the National Council and the denominations. The council then struggled painfully to change, but it was not enough to avoid setbacks and reversals everywhere.

But that was all in the future. In 1963 opportunity beckoned to the "new breed" of church leader in the National Council of Churches and in the denominations served by the council.[94] These people sought to forge a new public stance for the mainstream churches regarding racial issues, to involve the churches directly in support of the demands of black Americans that the latter be given long-denied political and economic rights and be admitted fully into the mainstream of American life. *Kairos* seemed about to be made manifest. And in a sense these national church leaders also signaled a return to the Social Gospel of the early twentieth century, but to focus now much more directly on racial concerns, which was a less frequent interest of the earlier church activists.[95]

Certainly the work of these church people was a major realization of the attitudes embodied in Colin Williams's *Where in the World*. The publication of that little book coincided almost exactly with the creation of the National Council of Churches' Commission on Religion and Race. Excitedly Williams noted at the end of his essay "that a responsible Church body has officially broken free from its own internal machinery, in response to God's urgent call from the needs of the world" and has offered "to allow itself" to shape its servant-missionary role "around this worldly need." Such action, exclaimed Williams, "is a miracle of grace!"[96] In this flush of enthusiasm Williams perhaps overstated the theological and historical significance of what had transpired. But he was sufficiently clear-eyed to conclude with a troubling thought: "The big question now is, will the churches be free enough to support the necessary action when it lies outside their ordered forms?"[97] The remainder of this study will attempt to provide answers to that question.

Notes

1. *Christian Century,* October 29, 1958, pp. 1246–1248; *National Council Outlook,* November 1958, pp. 3–7; *New York Times,* October 13, 1958, p. 18. For worries about proper understanding and support by local churches of the work of the NCC, see *National Council Outlook,* December 1951, p. 15.

2. *National Council Outlook,* March 1951, pp. 1, 2, 15; December 1953, pp. 3–5, January 1958, p. 21; NCC news release, November 30, 1954, RG 2, box 1, folder 18; press copy of General Maxwell D. Taylor address, "The Price of Peace," to National Council of Churches General Assembly, St. Louis, December 6, 1957, RG 2, box 2, folder 8; NCC news release, September 5, 1957, RG 2, box 2, folder 7; items in NCC Archives; *New York Times,* December 11, p. 6; December 12, 1952, p. 1; December 3, 1957, p. 29; November 19, 1958, pp. 1, 6.

3. *National Council Outlook,* March 1951, p. 15; June 1959, pp. 17–18; "Resolution in Memory of John Foster Dulles, General Board Meeting, Seattle, Washington, June 3–4, 1959," RG 4, box 25, folder 6, NCC Archives; interview with Arthur Flemming, February 15, 1988.

4. *National Council Outlook,* November 1952, pp. 5–8, 20–21; Donald Haggerty and Alan Thomson, eds., "A Guide to the National Council of Churches in America Archives, 1950–1972," mimeographed, Presbyterian Historical Society, Philadelphia, p. 412.

5. *Inter-Church News,* September 1959, pp. 1, 4; November 1959, pp. 1, 4; *National Council Outlook,* February 1951, p. 20; January 1954, p. 11; September 1954, p. 12; September 1953, p. 14; September 1955, p. 8; September 1956, p. 13; September 1957, p. 13; September 1958, p. 6.

6. *National Council Outlook,* September 1954, pp. 12, 22; September 1956, pp. 13–14; November 1956, pp. 4–7, 24–25; September 1957, pp. 13–14.

7. Ibid., September 1954, p. 12.

8. Ibid., November 1956, pp. 24, 25. See also the comments of Senator Paul Douglas of Illinois on p. 6.

9. R. H. Edwin Espy, "Policy and Practice of the National Council of Churches in the Field of Race Relations," January 30, 1958, RG 5, box 12, folder 16, NCC Archives.

10. *Christian Century*, June 25, 1952, p. 744. The text of the Federal Council of Church's statement is in RG 4, box 5, folder 10, NCC Archives. The document published in 1952 repeated verbatim many sections of the earlier resolution.

11. A subtext to the 1952 statement entitled "The Facts About Segregation in the Churches" noted that "over 90 percent of the 6.5 million Protestant Negroes in the United States were in "separate [segregated] Negro denominations" and thus were "without association in work and worship with Christians of other races except in interdenominational organizations which involve a few of their leaders." The remaining 10 percent of black Protestants were members of pre-dominantly white denominations, but 95 percent of *these* were in segregated local congregations. Thus "only one-half of one percent of the Negro Protestant Christians of the United States worship regularly in churches with fellow Christians of another race," and even here, because of discriminatory housing and employment practices, there were "only on an average two or three Negro individuals in the white churches." "The Churches and Segregation: A Background Statement and Resolutions submitted by the Division of Christian Life and Work," p. 3, RG 4, box 5, folder 10, NCC Archives.

12. Ibid., pp. 2, 6, 7–8.

13. *New York Times,* March 22, p. 10; March 24, p. 27; March 25, 1952, p. 28; *Christian Century*, June 25, 1952, p. 744.

14. *Christian Century*, June 25, 1952, p. 740.

15. The *Christian Century* editorial cited in n. 14 suggested that in addition to the African American church groups, both the socially liberal United Council of Church Women and conservative lay businessmen who helped each year to raise the council's budget may have subtly tugged the council in opposite directions, but that ultimately "the church's conscience was aroused and had to speak." Ibid., pp. 739–740. Cavert's quoted remarks are in Samuel M. Cavert to Harold Fey, June 25, 1952, RG 4, box 5, folder 10, NCC Archives. See also Cavert to Members of the General Board of the National Council of Churches: Executives of State and Local Councils, March 26, 1952, and attached news release, March 24, 1952, RG 4, box 5, folder 10, NCC Archives; *New York Times,* March 22, 1952, p. 10.

16. Between the March and June 1952 meetings of the General Board of the National Council, clergy and lay persons lobbied behind the scenes, both in support of modifications of the Statement on Segregation, and urging the council not to back down from its original proposal, in the latter case also often criticizing the leaders for not voting in the affirmative in March. A sampling of these letters include Ernest J. Arnold to Samuel M. Cavert, March 13, 1952; Francis Sterrett to J. Oscar Lee, March 24, 1952; Philip H. Steinmentz to Cavert, April 24, 1952; Eliot White to Cavert, April 24, 1952; C. E. Dillard to Cavert, April 29, 1952; Betty Carr to "Sirs" [no date], Patrick D. Miller to Cavert, June 4, 1952; all of these items are in RG 4, box 5, folder 10, NCC Archives.

17. For relevant comments in this regard, see *Christian Century*, June 25, 1952, pp. 739, 740. When the final vote of approval took place in June 1952, the only dissenting vote (abstention) came from the Presbyterian Church, U.S., a predominantly southern denomination. *National Council Outlook*, September 1952, p. 9.

18. John H. Blacklidge to Samuel M. Cavert, April 27, 1952, RG 4, box 5, folder 10, NCC Archives.

19. R. H. Edwin Espy, "Policy and Practice of the National Council in the Field of Race Relations," January 30, 1958, RG 5, box 12, folder 16, ibid.

20. J. Oscar Lee to Dr. Samuel McCrea Cavert, February 28, 1949, RG 18, box 61, folder 15, ibid.

21. Samuel McCrea Cavert to Bishop Clare Purcell, December 19, 1949, Cavert to Charles H. Tuttle, March 3, March 25, June 15, 1949, folder 18, ibid.

22. J. Waties Waring to Samuel McCrea Cavert, January 6, 1950, ibid. As might be surmised, Judge Waring's views meant social ostracism for him and his family in white South Carolina. An excellent biography is Tinsley E. Yarbrough, *A Passion for Justice: J. Waties Waring and Civil Rights* (New York, Oxford University Press, 1987).

23. R. H. Edwin Espy, "Policy and Practice of the National Council in the Field of Race Relations," January 30, 1958, p. 7, RG 5, box 12, folder 16, NCC Archives.

24. On the department's response to aspects of the *Brown* decision, see "Suggestions for Action re *May 31, 1955 Decision of the U.S. Supreme Court on Segregation in the Public Schools,"* in folder "NCC—Dep't of Racial and Cultural Relations, 53, 54, 55," drawer 3, file cabinet 10, BHLA Archives. See also J. Oscar Lee to Samuel McCrea Cavert, February 28, 1949, RG 18, box 61, folder 15; Cavert to Bishop Clare Purcell, December 19, 1949, RG 18, box 61, folder 18; Francis Sterrett to J. Oscar Lee, March 24, 1952, Samuel M. Cavert to "Members of the General Board of the National Council of Churches; Executives of State and Local Councils," March 26, 1952, RG 4, box 5, folder 10; all items in NCC Archives.

25. On Haynes, see Wills, "An Enduring Distance" in Hutchison, *Between the Times,* pp. 172–179, 189 fn. 8; Haggerty and Thomson, "A Guide to the NCC Archives," p. 462.

26. Interview with J. Oscar Lee, March 22, 1990. Lee spent only one year in a local parish, devoting the rest of his career to positions in state or national church bureaucracies.

27. Four decades later Lee concluded that the National Council of Churches' interest in racial issues in the early fifties was "down the scale a bit" from that of the Federal Council. He argued this was primarily because the sheer size of the National Council meant that many more social concerns besides race were now a part of its agenda. Ibid.

28. *Sixth Annual Interdenominational Institutes on Racial and Cultural Relations; The Department of Racial and Cultural Relations: What It Does* (n.d.), pamphlets in personal possession of J. Oscar Lee, Gaithersburg, Maryland, copied by author; "Report of J. Oscar Lee . . . to the Administrative Committee of the Department . . . for the Period January Through March 1948," p. 2, RG 18, box 56, folder 2; *Interracial News Service,* July–August 1950, p. 1, RG 18, box 59, folder 10; "Minutes," Executive Committee, Department of Racial and Cultural Relations, March 17, 1952, September 13, 1956, May 9, 1957, RG 6, box 45, folder 4; items in NCC Archives.

29. Incomplete files of this publication are in RG 18, box 59, folders 9, 10, NCC Archives.

30. "Make Brotherhood Real: Report on the 28th Anniversary of Race Relations Sunday," February 12, 1950, RG 18, box 61, folder 11, ibid.; later in the

decade the demand for race relations materials declined somewhat, but in 1957 printed items (more than the official "Message") disbursed by Lee's agency still numbered approximately 90,000. "Minutes," Executive Committee, Department of Racial and Cultural Relations, March 28, 1957, RG 6, box 45, folder 4, ibid. For examples of the national "message" written by a major church leader each year, see *National Council Outlook,* January 1954, p. 13; January 1957, p. 21. Martin Luther King, Jr., was the author of the sermon in 1957.

31. Interview with J. Oscar Lee, March 22, 1990; "Fifth Annual Retreat for Denominational and Interdenominational Secretaries in Racial and Cultural Relations," May 20–21, 1952, RG 5, box 5, folder 18, NCC Archives; "Minutes," General Committee, Department of Racial and Cultural Relations, April 19, 1955, in folder "NCC—Dep't of Racial & Cultural Relations, 53, 54, 55," drawer 3, file cabinet 10, BHLA.

32. Interview with J. Oscar Lee, March 22, 1990.

33. "Minutes," Executive Committee, Department of Racial and Cultural Relations, April 20, 1956, RG 6, box 45, folder 4, NCC Archives.

34. A detailed recent analysis of the Emmett Till case is Stephen Whitfield, *A Death in the Delta: The Story of Emmett Till* (New York, Free Press, 1988).

35. Ralph Smeltzer to Arvild Olsen, March 20, 23, 1956, RG 6, box 45, folder 8, NCC Archives. On Smeltzer's work, focused on a somewhat later time period, see Stephen L. Longenecker, *Selma's Peacemaker: Ralph Smeltzer and Civil Rights Mediation* (Philadelphia, Temple University Press, 1987).

36. Smeltzer to Olsen, March 23, 1954, RG 6, box 45, folder 8, NCC Archives.

37. R. H. Edwin Espy to Jane Lee J. Eddy, December 18, 1959, RG 4, box 26, folder 36, ibid.

38. Minutes, Executive Committee, Department of Racial and Cultural Relations, April 20, September 13, 1956, folder 4; Edith I. Caster to J. Oscar Lee, July 5, 1956, Norman J. Baugher to Eugene Carson Blake, January 23, 1956, Bishop S. L. Greene to Blake, July 8, 1957, folder 20; both items in RG 6, box 45, ibid.

39. "Autobiographical statement of Will Davis Campbell" (n.d.), RG 6, box 47, folder 2, ibid.; oral history with Will Davis Campbell, vol. 157, Mississippi Oral History Program (University of Southern Mississippi, Hattiesburg, 1980), pp. 1–55; Will D. Campbell, *Brother to a Dragonfly* (New York, Seabury Press, 1977), especially pp. 3–124. Campbell's *Forty Acres and a Goat: A Memoir* (Atlanta, Peachtree Publishers, 1986) focuses especially on his work in and thoughts about the black freedom movement from the 1950s to the 1980s.

40. Will Campbell to Alfred Kramer, July 16, 1956, Kramer to Campbell, July 20, 1956, RG 6, box 47, folder 2, NCC Archives; Campbell interview, Mississippi Oral History Program, pp. 33–35.

41. Will D. Campbell to J. Oscar Lee, January 9, 1957, RG 4, box 19, folder 34; Campbell to Lee, March 24, 1958, "Field Report, Southern Project," March 23–26, 1959, Little Rock, Arkansas, RG 6, box 47, folder 5; both items in NCC Archives; Campbell to Harold Fleming, November 4, December 9, 1957, RG 75-01, box 46, folder 5, Southern Regional Council Papers, Atlanta University (hereafter cited as SRC Papers); Campbell interview, Mississippi Oral History Program, pp. 58–65.

42. George Barrett to C. A. Olsen, March 29, 1960; "Report of Southern Project to General Committee, Department of Racial and Cultural Relations, January 26, 1961"; W. D. Campbell to J. O. Lee, January 13, 1961; "Minutes of

meetings held on February 28 and March 1, 1961, in Nashville, Tenn., at the call of Rev. Will Campbell"; Will D. Campbell to J. Oscar Lee, February 27, 1962; all items in RG 6, box 47, folder 6, NCC Archives.

43. Campbell, *Forty Acres and a Goat,* p. 46.

44. J. Oscar Lee, "Department of Racial and Cultural Relations, the National Council of Churches, *Report re Events at Little Rock, Arkansas";* Claude D. Nelson, "Notes on a Visit to Arkansas, Oct. 10–13, 1957"; statement of the Council of Church Women of Little Rock, September 9, 1957; statement by the Greater Little Rock Ministerial Association, September 23, 1957; Will Campbell to "Oscar," September 26, 1957; Campbell to J. Oscar Lee, November 19, 1957; all items in RG 6, box 47, folder 12, NCC Archives.

45. Campbell to Lee, September 26, 1957, ibid.

46. Campbell to "All Human Relations Personnel in the South," August 20, 1957, folder 5, ibid., is an extended analysis of Nashville's efforts at school desegregation in late 1956 and early 1957. See also Campbell to J. Oscar Lee, January 9, 1957; Campbell to "Dear Friend," March 6, 1957 [concerning Koinonea Farm, Americus, Georgia]; both items in folder 5, ibid.

47. Campbell's schedule of meetings and workshops are reflected in Campbell to J. Oscar Lee, January 9, 1957, October 12, 1959; Campbell to "Dear Friend," March 27, 1957; both items in folder 5, ibid.; Campbell to Harry S. Jones, April 8, 1958; Campbell to Galen Weaver, January 16, 1961; Jim L. White to Campbell, January 11, 1963; items in RG 75–01, box 46, folder 5, SRC Papers. On "Consultations," see Campbell to Alfred Kramer, September 9, 1959; "Field Report, Southern Project," March 23–26, 1959; Campbell to J. Oscar Lee, March 24, 1958; W. Harold Row to Campbell, January 15, 21, 1959; all items in RG 6, box 47, folder 5, NCC Archives. On frequent advice giving about civil rights activists, both within and outside the church, see Campbell to Fred Routh, August 11, 1958, Campbell to Paul Anthony, October 24, 1959, RG 75–01, box 46, folder 5, SRC Papers.

48. All items in RG 75–01, box 45, folder 5, SRC Papers; Will Campbell to J. Oscar Lee, January 13, March 8, 1961, May 1, 1962; Campbell to Stanley Leibner, December 6, 1962; items in RG 6, box 47, folder 6, NCC Archives.

49. Minutes, Executive Committee, Department of Racial and Cultural Relations, April 20, 1956, RG 6, box 45, folder 4; R. H. Edwin Espy to Mrs. Jane Lee J. Eddy, December 18, 1959, and Eddy to Espy, December 30, 1959, January 26, 1960, RG 4, box 26, folder 30; all items in NCC Archives.

50. *"The Church in the Midst of Changing Racial Patterns:* A Report on the work of the Southern Project of the Department of Racial and Cultural Relations to the General Board, December 3, 1959," p. 3, RG 6, box 47, folder 5, ibid.

51. As was typical of most new or "experimental" programs of the National Council, the sources of support included not only the few large gifts from foundations noted earlier, but also a number of smaller gifts, ranging from a few hundred to several thousand dollars from individuals and the denominations within the National Council of Churches. By 1960 one-third of the council's member churches were contributing to the Southern Project. Documentation of foundation support is in fn. 44, the earliest gifts in fn. 38. For other sources of financial aid, see Minutes, Executive Committee, Department of Racial and Cultural Relations, September 13, 1956, RG 6, box 45, folder 4; Edwin T. Dahlberg to Dr. S. W. Shane, June 28, 1957, RG 4, box 19, folder 34; J. Oscar Lee to Mrs. Lucius R. Eastman, April 10, 1956, November 13, 1957, Edwin T. Dahlberg to

Dr. Reuben F. Nelson, December 12, 1958, Dahlberg to Oscar A. Benson, December 18, 1958, Dahlberg to Rev. C. D. Pettaway, June 8, 1960, RG 6, box 45, folder 20; "Financial Support for the Southern Project," May 18, 1961, RG 6, box 47, folder 1; all items in NCC Archives.

52. Campbell suggests his uneasiness about his role as a "liberal" among southern whites in a captivating passage of *Forty Acres and a Goat,* pp. 47–52.

53. For evidence of this aspect of Campbell's work, see Eugene Carson Blake to S. W. Shane, June 28, 1957, RG 4, box 19, folder 34; Fred T. Laughon to Alfred S. Kramer, December 22, 1956, Will D. Campbell to J. Oscar Lee, July 9, November 18, November 22, 1957, March 1, 1961, RG 6, box 47, folder 28; Campbell to Lee, October 12, 1959, RG 6, box 47, folder 5; all items in NCC Archives. The handholding phrase, not to be taken negatively, is in Alfred Kramer to J. Oscar Lee, January 23, 1963, RG 6, box 47, folder 6, NCC Archives. Early in 1960 after conferring with Campbell, Stephen Currier and his wife gave $21,000 in small gifts to forty-five pastors and churches throughout the South and $15,000 to fourteen state and local councils of churches in recognition of the efforts of all of these people to improve race relations in their communities. Often the gifts replaced funds lost from local contributors because of these activities. Campbell to J. Oscar Lee, January 28, 1960, RG 6, box 47, folder 5, NCC Archives.

54. In 1959 Campbell stated to his superiors in New York City that "any engagement to Montgomery or Atlanta would involve a visit to the Southern Christian Leadership Conference office, the Southwest Regional NAACP office, [and the] Southern Regional Council." Campbell to J. Oscar Lee, October 12, 1959, RG 5, box 47, folder 5, ibid.

55. The observations about Myles Horton are in Campbell to Alfred Kramer, September 9, 1959, RG 6, box 47, folder 5, ibid. In 1962 Campbell informally opposed a Kennedy administration plan to invite only CORE and SNCC people to a national conference on public accommodations in Washington, urging that the NAACP also be included. Campbell to Stanley Leibner, December 6, 1962, folder 6, ibid. On Campbell's reactions to northern clergy in Albany, Georgia, see his "Perhaps, and Maybe," *Christian Century,* September 19, 1962, p. 1133, and his interview, Mississippi Oral History Program, pp. 66–68.

56. Alfred S. Kramer to J. Oscar Lee, January 23, 1963, folder 1; Kramer to Will Campbell, March 6, 1963, folder 6; both items in RG 6, box 47, NCC Archives.

57. Campbell's resignation became effective August 31, 1963. See Campbell to Elbert B. Jean, September 23, 1963, folder 6, ibid. The Southern Project, staffed by Campbell's assistant, Elbert Jean, limped along into the early part of 1964. It was formally terminated on May 31, 1964, although essentially the project had ceased to function by the end of March. Elbert Jean to Alfred S. Kramer, January 22, 1964; Jean to James W. Patton, March 20, 1964; Albert W. Sweet, Jr., to Jean, June 3, 1964; B. Julian Smith to Jean, June 4, 1964; "Check List for Closing the Southern Office" May 26, 1964; all items in folder 25, ibid.

58. *"The Church in the Midst of Changing Racial Patterns,"* folder 5, ibid. This essay became the basis of somewhat more extended reflections by Campbell, published in 1962, on the dilemma of race relations and the church's role within that dilemma. Will D. Campbell, *Race and the Renewal of the Church* (Philadelphia, Westminster Press, 1962).

59. Leslie Dunbar to Harold Letts, April 3, 1963, RG 75–01, folder 22, box 45, SRC Papers.

60. *Forty Acres and a Goat,* p. 13.

61. Campbell, *"The Church in the Midst of Changing Racial Patterns,"* p. 6, RG 6, box 47, folder 5, NCC Archives.

62. For detailed documentation of the Air Force manual controversy and earlier attacks extending back to 1950, see RG 17, boxes 6 and 7, ibid.

63. *National Council Outlook,* January 1955, p. 16; June 1958, p. 19. On Espy's ecumenical outlook and its effect on his work with the National Council of Churches, see interview of J. Oscar McCloud with Gayraud Wilmore, December 23, 1981, tape 857, Oral History Collection, Presbyterian Historical Society, Philadelphia.

64. *National Council Outlook,* June 1958, p. 19; press release, "The Rev. Dr. Jon L. Regier" (n.d.), folder 125, box 115, SNCC Papers; Willard M. Wickizer, "The State of the Mission," December 3, 1960, RG 2, box 3, folder 4, NCC Archives.

65. Press release, "Biographical Sketch of J. Irwin Miller, President of the National Council of Churches," December 7, 1960, RG 3, box 3, folder 5, NCC Archives; *Interchurch News,* December 1960–January 1961, pp. 1, 5; interview with J. Irwin Miller, May 29, 1990.

66. "Address by J. Irwin Miller, President, National Council of Churches, February 22, 1961," RG 4, box 27, folder 12, NCC Archives. In the topmost margin of p. 1 is Miller's penciled notation: "Delivered to the General Board."

67. In a similar vein, see Jon Regier, "Churches for the Times," *Interchurch News,* October 1961, p. 7; Ed Espy's remarks in "Notes taken in luncheon meeting with Mr. Tucker re long-range planning, April 5, 1961," RG 4, box 27, folder 12, NCC Archives; "A New Approach to Nationwide Task [reorganizing the Division of Home Missions], *National Council Outlook,* January 1959, p. 9.

68. Interiew with Colin Williams, August 18, 1990.

69. There are sharply differing estimates of the number of copies of these books that the National Council distributed, from 100,000 to 300,000 copies for each essay. The lowest figure is probably most accurate, but even those numbers confirm the extremely wide readership generated for the books within the American churches. Interview with Colin Williams, August 18, 1990; Andrew Beech, in a telephone interview, October 29, 1990, provided estimates secured from William Walzer, director in the 1960s of Friendship Press, the publishing subsidiary of the National Council of Churches.

70. Williams, *Where in the World* (New York, Friendship Press, 1963), pp. 1–15.

71. Ibid., p. 59.

72. Williams attached a small bibliography to *Where in the World,* pp. 114–116, which suggested many of the studies that shaped the new view of mission. See, for example, Peter L. Berger, *The Noise of Solemn Assemblies* (Garden City, N.Y., Doubleday, 1961); Gibson Winter, *The Suburban Captivity of the Churches* (Garden City, N.Y., Doubleday, 1961), and *The New Creation as Metropolis* (New York, Macmillan, 1963; D. T. Niles, *Upon the Earth* (New York, McGraw-Hill, 1962); Martin E. Marty, *The New Shape of American Religion* (New York, Harper, 1959). See also Dietrich Bonhoeffer, *The Cost of Discipleship* (New York, Macmillan, 1959), and *Prisoner for God: Letters and Papers from Prison* (New York, Macmillan, 1960); John D. Godsey, *The Theology of Dietrich Bonhoeffer* (Philadelphia, West-

minster Press, 1960); and Marty's essay in *Christian Century*, "Bonhoeffer: Seminarians' Theologian," April 20, 1960, pp. 467–469.

73. *Where in the World*, pp. 102.

74. See especially Aldon D. Morris, *The Origins of the Civil Rights Movement: Black Communities Organizing for Change* (New York, Free Press, 1984).

75. David R. Goldfield, *Black, White, and Southern; Race Relations and Southern Culture, 1940 to the Present* (Baton Rouge, Louisiana State University Press, 1990), pp. 118–148, 294–297; Taylor Branch, *Parting the Waters: America in the King Years, 1954–1963* (New York, Simon and Schuster, 1988), chaps. 7, 11, 14. The best account of King's Albany campaign is in David Garrow, *Bearing the Cross: Martin Luther King, Jr., and the Southern Christian Leadership Conference* (New York, William Morrow and Company, 1986), pp. 173–231. See also *Christian Century*, September 5, p. 1057; September 19, p. 1133; September 26, 1962, p. 1155.

76. *Chicago Tribune*, January 15, pp. 1, 2; January 16, p. 7; January 17, p. 3, January 18, 1963, p. 3; *New York Times*, April 16, 1964, p. 25; folder entitled "Continuation Committee, 1963–64," box 1; folder entitled "Weaver (1963, 1964)," box 2; both items in series 7, National Catholic Conference for Interracial Justice Papers, Marquette University archives, Milwaukee, Wisconsin (hereafter cited as National Catholic Conference Papers).

77. On National Council endorsement of the conference, see "Program Committee Summary," May 16, 1962; Matthew Ahmann to Leslie Dunbar, May 24, 1962; NCC news release, "U.S. Religious Groups Call Conference on Religion and Race," June 21, 1961, all items in box 467, folder 3, SRC Papers. On NCC financial support, see "Financial Statement, ending April 30, 1963," folder entitled "Continuation Committee, 1963–64," box 1, series 7, National Catholic Conference Papers. The director of the continuing conference was Galen Weaver, a national staff person of the United Church of Christ, but closely related to J. Oscar Lee as a member of the executive board of the National Council's Department of Racial and Cultural Relations. "Newsletter," March 5, 1963, in folder entitled "Newsletter, March 1963–February 1964," box 2, series 7, National Catholic Conference Papers.

78. *New York Times*, May 21, 1963, p. 18. A detailed discussion of the historical background and eventual creation of the Presbyterian commission is in the essay "The United Presbyterian Church and Race Relations, 1936–1963," prepared by Gayraud Wilmore, the executive director of the commission, and attached to Minutes, Commission on Religion and Race, United Presbyterian Church, U.S.A. (UPCUSA), August 2, 1963, RG 61, box 1, folder 3, UPCUSA Commission on Religion and Race Papers, Presbyterian Historical Society, Philadelphia (hereafter cited as UPCUSA-CORAR Papers). See also statement of Marshal Scott, "United Presbyterian Commission on Religion and Race," July 17, 1963, folder 1; Minutes, UPCUSA Commission on Religion and Race, July 24, 1963, pp. 5–6, folder 3; both items in RG 61, box 1, UPCUSA-CORAR Papers.

79. Matthew Ahmann to Martin Luther King, Jr., May 3, 1962, J. Oscar Lee to King, June 22, 1962, folder 22; King to Lee, July 2, 1962, folder 29; Ahmann to King, January 24, 1963, folder 25; all items in box 17, Martin Luther King Papers, Martin Luther King Center, Atlanta (hereafter cited as King Papers, Atlanta).

80. "Speaking Engagements, 1962–63," Howard Thurman Papers, Boston

University Archives; Benjamin Mays, *Born to Rebel: An Autobiography* (New York, Charles Scribner's Sons, 1971), especially pp. 241–264.

81. Detailed evidence of King's exhausting schedule of talks and sermons is in boxes 36–47, Martin Luther King Papers, Boston University Archives; and Secondary Correspondence, boxes 37–60, King Papers, Atlanta. On his sermons for the National Council of Churches, see *National Council Outlook,* January 1957, p. 21; text of "The Christian Way of Life in Human Relations," December 4, 1957, RG 2, box 2, folder 7, NCC Archives.

82. Martin Luther King, Jr., "Letter from Birmingham Jail," *Christian Century,* June 12, 1963, pp. 768–73. The quotation is on p. 772. King had been an editor-at-large for the *Century* for several years prior to 1963. The editor, Harold Fey, wrote King that the letter was "the most memorable article to appear in The Christian Century during my editorship." Harold Fey to King, September 8, 1958, Fey to Maude Ballou, March 17, 1959, folder III-16, box 22, King Papers, Boston University Archives; Fey to King, July 6, 1962, May 22, 1963, undated postcard, folder 6, box 6, King Papers, Atlanta. On the creation of the letter, see Branch, *Parting the Waters,* pp. 737–45. On King as a model for white clergy, see, for example, Robert Spike to King, October 16, 1964, folder 34, box 17, King Papers, Atlanta.

83. On the black leaders' meeting with Robert Kennedy, see *New York Times,* May 25, p. 1, May 26, 1963, p. 59; Arthur M. Schlesinger, Jr., *Robert Kennedy and His Times* (Boston, Houghton Mifflin, 1978), pp. 356–360, and especially Branch, *Parting the Waters,* pp. 809–813. The connections with the churches are documented in interview with Jon Regier, February 8, 1987; and Robert Spike, *Civil Rights Involvement: Model for Mission* (Detroit, Detroit Industrial Mission, 1965), pp. 9–10, a pamphlet available at the Wisconsin, State Historical Society, Madison.

84. The enabling resolution of the General Board was reprinted in *Interchurch News,* June–July 1963, p. 6. See also *Interchurch News,* August–September 1963, p. 5; Minutes, Commission on Religion and Race, NCC, June 28, 1963; Victor Reuther to Eugene Carson Blake, telegram, June 20, 1963; both items in folder 2, box 15, Victor Reuther Papers, Archives of Labor History, Wayne State University; "Report of the Executive Director to the Commission on Religion and Race of the National Council of Churches," July 26, 1963, p. 4, RG 11, box 6, folder 20, NCC Archives. For precise budgetary estimates and income for the commission, see Minutes, Commission on Religion and Race, NCC, January 16, 1964, pp. 1–2, Exhibit A, folder 9, box 15, Victor Reuther Papers.

85. Remarks of Jerald C. Brauer, Memorial Service for Robert Spike, October 28, 1966, Robert Spike Collection, Joseph Regenstein Library, University of Chicago; telephone interview with Winthrop Hudson, March 9, 1991; interview with Dean Wright, November 12, 1990; interview with Robert Newman, November 20, 1990.

86. Telephone interview with Jon Regier, February 8, 1987; interview with J. Irwin Miller, May 29, 1990; R. Douglas Brackenridge, *Eugene Carson Blake: Prophet With Portfolio* (New York, Seabury Press, 1978), pp. 77–105. Blake, best known as an ecumenist in the 1950s, became increasingly involved in civil rights activities in the early sixties, culminating in his arrest, along with other nationally known clergy, demonstrating at a segregated amusement park in Baltimore on July 4, 1963. *New York Times,* July 5, 1963, pp. 1, 44; *Christian Century,* July 17, 1963, p. 902.

87. Minutes, Executive Committee, Department of Racial and Cultural Relations, May 15, 1963, July 12, 1963, July 19, 1963 (special meeting), May 15, 1964; "Report on Southern Project" (presented to Executive Committee, Department of Racial and Cultural Relations, May 15, 1964); all of these documents in RG 6, box 45, folder 3, NCC Archives.

88. Williams attended all of the meetings of the commission during 1963 and early 1964 as a "co-opted" staff member from the Department of Evangelism. Minutes, Commission on Religion and Race, NCC, June 28, 1963, p. 1, folder 2; Minutes, Commission on Religion and Race, NCC, January 16, 1964, pp. 1, 2–3, folder 9; both items in box 15, Victor Reuther Papers.

89. Interview with Colin Williams, August 18, 1990.

90. Telephone interviews with Jon Regier, August 29, 1989, June 20, 1990; interview with Kenneth Neigh, October 30, 1989; interview with David Ramage, October 9, 1989; interview with Bryant George, October 23, 1989; interview with Arthur Walmsley, March 24, 1987; interview, J. Oscar McCloud with Gayraud Wilmore, tape 857, Oral History Collection, Presbyterian Historical Society, Philadelphia. The "steely-eyed" comment came from interview with John Mudd, August 23, 1989.

91. Even though in poor health, late in 1963 Niebuhr penned a brief essay much in tune with the feelings being articulated by those who supported the new Commission on Religion and Race. "The Crisis in American Protestantism," *Christian Century*, December 4, 1963, pp. 1498–1501. See also Fox, *Reinhold Niebuhr*, chap. 12, especially pp. 281–283.

92. Interview with John Pratt, June 16, 1985; interview with Bruce Hanson, July 26, 1985; Robert Handy, *A History of Union Theological Seminary in New York* (New York, Columbia University Press, 1987), pp. 265–66; "Annual Report," Department of Racial and Cultural Relations, 1962, pp. 13–14, RG 6, box 45, folder 5, NCC Archives; Religious News Service bulletins, August 16, August 19, 1963, box 18, folder 20, UCC BHM Archives; "Student Interracial Ministry," item in folder "Dep't of Racial and Cultural Relations: Agendas, Minutes and Corres.," drawer 3, cabinet 10, BHLA Archives.

93. Hints of these problems are clearly evident in the extended remarks of Spike to the commission, entitled "Report to the Commission on Religion and Race," attached to Minutes, Commission on Religion and Race, meeting of February 21, 1964, folder 13, box 15, Victor Reuther Papers.

94. In 1967 the theologian Harvey Cox used this term to describe an emerging set of leaders in American Protestantism who paralleled closely the group described here. Harvey Cox, "The New Breed in American Churches: Sources of Social Activism in American Religion," *Daedalus*, XI (Winter 1967), pp. 135–149.

95. Scholars have disagreed about the importance of racial issues to adherents of the Social Gospel in the first two decades of the twentieth century. Compare David Reimers, *White Protestantism and the Negro* (New York, Oxford University Press, 1965), pp. 53–54, with Ronald C. White, Jr., *Liberty and Justice for All: Racial Reform and the Social Gospel* (San Francisco, Harper's, 1990). By far the most thorough treatment of the subject is in Luker, *The Social Gospel in Black and White*. Even more effectively than Ronald White, Luker demonstrates the many-sided racial views and concerns of supporters of the Social Gospel.

96. *Where in the World*, p. 102.

97. Ibid., p. 103.

2

The Churches and the
Civil Rights Act of 1964

From the beginning in June 1963, the Commission on Religion and Race assumed as one of its major responsibilities the coordination of all support from organized religion for civil rights legislation. Jewish and Roman Catholic leaders encouraged this approach. At its first meeting the commission heard a report that these two large religious groups "would welcome the stimulus which would be given by firm National Council of Churches action."[1] If these activities of the religious establishment were in part the result of the massive marches of African American citizens of Birmingham against police dogs and the blistering power of water hoses, those same demonstrations also helped to draw President Kennedy more fully into the fray. On June 11, 1963, Kennedy, struggling also with Governor George Wallace over the integration of the University of Alabama, went on national television to endorse the "moral issue" of equality for African Americans. Then a week later, on June 19, 1963, he introduced into Congress his first major piece of civil rights legislation.[2] These were the beginnings of what eventually became the Civil Rights Act of 1964.

And just prior to his initiatives with Congress, the president held a series of meetings with leaders of major interest groups in the nation to nourish their support for his pending civil rights program. Accordingly, on June 17 a large group of national church officials gathered at the White House. Kennedy invited J. Irwin Miller to chair the meeting and to oversee efforts at follow-up.[3] This little moment was another indication of the leadership role being thrust upon the National Council of Churches as it moved into direct political action. Although subsequent church lobbying was always couched in the broadest ecumenical terms, the National Council always was *primus inter pares*.

And with gathering momentum a concatenation of events was shaping a national political agenda of considerable significance for mainline church people. Massive demonstrations in southern cities, often orchestrated by black religious leaders; militant white resistance to the demonstrations; President Kennedy's televised appeal in early June urging Americans to accept racial change especially because of the deep moral issues involved, followed quickly by his proposed civil rights legislation, all helped to arouse churchgoers. And now the National Council of Churches possessed an organizational weapon, its Commission on Religion and Race, to transform informal leadership status into concrete plans of action. Events in the South, long-sought presidential action and church leadership were combining to create among church people a major commitment to national social activism.[4]

Successful lobbying has always relied on two key tactics, pressure applied directly on legislators in Washington and pressure applied somewhat at a distance by grass-roots' constituents. The National Council of Churches recognized that reality in appointments to the commission staff and in the commission's earliest plans for action. A key appointment was Dr. Anna Hedgeman, a shrewd, politically savvy African American who had worked in Democratic circles, both in Washington and in New York City, and had run for elective office several times. Her appointment also epitomized the important though not always adequately recognized role that women played in the National Council from its beginnings in late 1950.

Mrs. Hedgeman was a prominent member of United Church Women, one of the eight ecumenical agencies that came together in 1950 to form the administrative core of the council. Deeply rooted in grass-roots ecumenical groups of churchwomen that began during and after the Civil War, exhibiting a streak of independence because it *was* an independent church group from 1941 (the moment of its founding) to 1950, and possessing strong social activist leanings, United Church Women always seemed a bit of a burr under the saddle to the overwhelmingly male leadership of the National Council.[5]

Even before joining the National Council of Churches, United Church Women operated on the principle of racial inclusiveness. In 1945, meeting in Washington, D.C., national board members moved to private homes rather than stay in downtown hotels that refused to serve black members. In 1948 the women crafted one of the earliest public condemnations of school segregation, asserting that "discrimination and segregation are contrary to our Christian principles and inimical to the democratic pattern." Following the *Brown* decision in the mid-fifties, United Church Women tried for several years through dozens of "human relations workshops" to aid local churchwomen, especially in the South, to cope with the immediate difficulties of school desegregation.[6]

In 1961 this group launched its own special program entitled "Assignment: Race," apart from the official work of the National Council's Department of Racial and Cultural Relations, to seek to end formal discrimination within the mainstream churches and within its own membership. A daunting task that was never realized, the project disappeared shortly after the money funding the first three years was not renewed.[7] Nevertheless, United Church Women, both in national leaders like Dr. Hedgeman and in its rank and file membership, symbolized an important constituency within the churches, too often overlooked, that was to provide strong support for the new programs of the Commission on Religion and Race.[8]

One of the first tasks of the commission was to coordinate the churches' somewhat belated effort to participate in the March on Washington, planned for the late summer of 1963. Dr. Hedgeman directed that effort to a very successful conclusion—an estimated 40,000 church people swelled the ranks of those who marched to the Lincoln Memorial on August 28, 1963, in support of jobs and the vote for African Americans.[9]

Many of the church people who participated probably could share the powerful personal feelings that Robert Spike, the executive director of the Commission on Religion and Race, expressed shortly after the event ended:

> When the National Council of Churches delegation, over 100 strong, moved into the stream of marchers . . . one of the deepest longings of my ministry was for a moment fulfilled—the longing that the Church of Jesus Christ be in the *midst* of the human struggle, not on the sidelines. And we were there—in an act so full of symbolism that no one could escape it, and with the satisfaction that we were no longer token representatives. The power of Protestantism was marching with us, and we had a right to be there at long last, because we were bearing some of the far reaching burdens of the struggle.[10]

There were hints of the triumphalism of the 1950s echoing in these words, and perhaps the sense of the presence of *kairos*. Certainly Spike's thoughts were very different from the concerns of the church of the fifties—thoughts of social activism in support of the poor and the dispossessed, of a certain prophetic urgency, containing a touch of arrogance for some, but appropriate and "biblical" in its tone and content for many others.[11]

But there were other implications to be drawn from the churches' involvement in the March on Washington. In the broadest sense, it was a first test of the churches' ability to organize widespread grass-roots' support for specific aims and goals in the civil rights struggle. Although for church people participation was a powerful symbolic moral act, the political implications of going to Washington were also very clear. Church leaders were among those who met with President Kennedy immediately after the conclusion of the march and who lobbied congressmen before returning to their homes. Perhaps James Reston caught the sense of the moment best in words written just as the March on Washington came to an end.

> If there is no effective moral reaction out in the country, there will be no effective political reaction. . . . While the politicians here are not saying

much about the March, they are listening, and if such a mammoth demonstration, dramatizing the basic religious concept of equality, does not get an impressive response from the churches, Congress could easily conclude that the nation was indifferent or worse.[12]

Hedgeman and the commission set out to organize and coordinate efforts to make certain that local church people *did* respond to ensure passage of an effective civil rights bill.

By the second meeting of the commission in July 1963, its members were rapidly developing ideas for creating political pressures on Congress. Victor Reuther, Methodist layman and brother of Walter Reuther, chaired a small planning group that proposed guidelines for lobbying that the churches followed until Kennedy's proposed civil rights bill was enacted almost a year later. The most crucial of their early suggestions was to "concentrate our legislative efforts" on a limited number of "key States."[13] The commission quickly decided that meant paying special attention to the Midwest. In that region were large rural districts where labor unions and other traditional supporters of civil rights were weak and, except in the cities, where the black vote was neglible. Many congressmen from the area were uncommitted to civil rights legislation. In a region with deep religious roots, moral arguments pressed by church people might be especially effective. The targets were primarily Republicans, who possessed great strength in the Midwest and whose support was essential to passing a strong civil rights bill. The area ranged from Ohio on the east to Iowa, Minnesota, and the Dakotas on the west. This plan of action, eventually known as "the Midwest strategy," evolved naturally out of discussions among people backing the civil rights legislation, or as one participant remembered, "the way any good lobbying works."[14]

A second recommendation of the Reuther committee reflected the recognition that for many midwestern churchpeople the civil rights issue was not a burning concern even in 1963. One church leader at the time noted a "kind of irony" in the fact that the fate of the bill might rest with such people.[15] Thus Reuther's committee proposed that a nine-state "legislative conference" be held in the Midwest as soon as possible as a training session and educational device for church leaders throughout the region. The gathering was held in Lincoln, Nebraska, on September 4 and 5, 1963. The two hundred people attending heard theologians, congressmen from the Midwest, and the veteran lobbyist of the NAACP from Washington discuss "the necessity for a coalition of conscience" to secure enactment of the civil rights bill. Within weeks of the conference in Lincoln, similar "civil rights workshops" were held in churches in Columbus, Ohio, Denver, Indianapolis, and Minneapolis.[16]

In October the commission dispatched four-person teams, like circuit-riding Methodist evangelists, into Ohio, Illinois, Nebraska, and South Dakota, where critical congressional votes were located. The teams included a minister to interpret theologically why voting for civil rights was important, a young African American civil rights worker to speak personally about the effects of racial discrimination (like those giving "testimony" at an old-time revival?), a legislative expert to answer questions about the bill before Congress, and a contact person from the appropriate local council of churches. Speakers on this "breakfast and lunch circuit" urged listeners to initiate telephone, telegram, and letter-writing appeals to their congressmen and to join delegations being organized to visit their representatives in Washington.[17]

In July 1963 Victor Reuther's planning committee made another suggestion to the Commission on Religion and Race—to create "close working relationships with the Leadership Conference on Civil Rights." Implementing the recommendation firmly established the churches' presence in Washington as well as in the hinterlands. The Leadership Conference on Civil Rights (LCCR) had been established in 1949 in New York City, chiefly by people seeking congressional enactment of a federal Fair Employment Practices Committee. By 1960 the conference had become the principal lobbyist for civil rights legislation, coordinating the efforts of over sixty church groups, labor unions, and minority-group agencies. In July 1963 the LCCR moved its office from New York to Washington. One could draw several implications from this development—that the legislation pending before Congress was very important, that it had a good chance of enactment into law, and that the Leadership Conference could play a major role both in shaping and assuring passage of the bill.[18]

Protestant, Catholic, and Jewish groups, including the National Council of Churches, had worked with the Leadership Conference from time to time at least since the mid-1950s. Most of the connections were "passive," consisting of "consultative conferences" and informal discussions, without active lobbying on Capitol Hill.[19] The early informal contacts were possible in part because the churches were establishing offices in Washington to protect institutional interests there. The National Council of Churches, for example, opened a part-time Washington office in 1953, principally to insure the continuation of tax exemptions for clergy. Earlier, beginning in 1945, the Federal Council of Churches also had a small office in the capitol city, but only to report on political activities to member churches.[20]

The Protestant churches' long commitment to a ministry to migrant laborers first caused National Council officials to begin thinking about lobbying overtly in Washington. Church study groups had underscored the central importance of economic issues in migrant workers' lives, and they had concluded that only federal legislation was likely to improve the migrants' wages, working conditions, and even the literacy of their children. By 1960 the National Council's Washington office had begun to work openly in support of such legislation. When the moment came, it was but a short additional step to begin supporting civil rights legislation as well.[21]

A key participant in all of these developments was James Hamilton, who became the associate director of the National Council's Washington office in November 1958. Hamilton had been in the capitol city for several years, principally as a law student at George Washington University. To finance his studies, Hamilton had served as one of the door-keepers in the House of Representatives, thus observing national politics at very close range and beginning a long self-education in the intricacies of representing the churches' interests on Capitol Hill. In June 1963 Jim Hamilton became one of the first staff members of the National Council's Commission on Religion and Race. His work in Washington paralleled and was of equal importance to that of Anna Hedgeman in New York in coordinating the churches' support for the Civil Rights Act.[22]

Hamilton (and thus the commission) became directly involved in the activities of the Leadership Conference on Civil Rights as soon as the latter group established its central office in Washington in July 1963. One of the first steps taken by Hamilton and the Leadership Conference was to arrange for testimony by leaders of the three major faith communities in congressional hearings convened prior to the formal consideration of Kennedy's civil rights bill. The churches also sent representatives to LCCR briefings on the civil rights legislation held at the capitol just before the March on Washington.[23] As debate on Kennedy's program began in the House of Representatives in September 1963, the Leadership Conference convened weekly strategy sessions open to all the organizations under its umbrella and held almost daily meetings with crucial Democrats supporting the bill. Hamilton attended most of those meetings and soon became one of the central figures within the Leadership Conference.[24]

Because of the complexity and protractedness of the debate in the House of Representatives, it was crucial that the Leadership Conference maintain a precise accounting of the voting of congressmen known, or even suspected, of supporting their political position. Soon the conference created an elaborate watchdog system, made up largely of volunteers, who sat in the House galleries, kept track of the votes of House members, and alerted their leaders when parliamentary emergencies arose. Conference lobbyists could then meet quickly with the floor managers of the bill to contain or minimize the difficulties. Hamilton was one of the five LCCR people present regularly throughout the debates to supervise the proper functioning of this system. The churches provided many of the "gallery watchers" ("vultures" one frustrated critic called them) who made up the human tabulating machine that appeared in the House gallery each day.[25]

Hamilton also developed close links with church people outside Washington, chiefly through existing ecumenical state and local councils of churches, and with the widely dispersed network of denominational officials that supported the National Council's activities. To 5,000 of these people Hamilton's office mailed regular information sheets on the legislation as it moved through the House and then on to the Senate. Occasional "immediate action memos" were sent to a more select list of Protestant leaders when critical votes in the House were pending. Thus in a relatively short time, Hamilton, Hedgeman, and the Commission on Religion and Race had fashioned out of the existing ecumenical church structure an effective system of grass-roots supporters able to respond quickly and specifically to the people in Washington who were monitoring day-to-day developments in Congress.[26]

When the House approved a strong civil rights bill on February 10, 1964, there was only one *no* vote among the fifty-five representatives from Illinois, Indiana, and Ohio. Eight of the twelve congressmen from Iowa, Nebraska, and South Dakota, all Republicans, voted in favor. The exact relationship between those votes and church pressures cannot be measured precisely, but the results suggest that the religious groups had begun to make their political presence felt.[27]

As the couriers delivered the House-approved legislation to the Senate for further scrutiny and a final decision, the churches and their allies refocused their political energies on the upper chamber. Soon the senatorial opponents of the civil rights bill launched a filibuster, hoping to wear out the pro–civil rights forces by talking the measure to death. It was a classic southern maneuver on race-related issues. Cloture (a vote to end a filibuster) had *never* been invoked in the Senate in an instance of civil rights legislation. It was difficult to achieve in any case since it required a two-thirds vote of the Senate. These developments demanded from proponents stamina and an increasing volume of support as public pressure grew, especially in April and May 1964, to resolve the issue one way or another.[28]

In responding to these challenges, the churches made use of tactics first learned while working for passage of the bill in the House. Hamilton and other commission staff members once again moved about the Midwest, particularly in Nebraska, Iowa, and Minnesota, holding workshops on the bill and on how local churches and individuals could exert pressure on their leaders in Washington to support a strong civil rights act.[29] The mainline churches, usually middle-class and possessing many members who were well educated, well connected, and politically aware, were in an excellent position to transform the entreaties of national church leaders into specific political pressures.

There are many indications that they did so. B'nai B'rith, a Jewish fraternal organization, gathered all the lawyers in Iowa who were members and as a group descended on Bourke Hickenlooper, a very hesitant Iowa senator, to urge that he vote for the bill. One of the lobbyists was a former law partner of Hickenlooper's. Quaker professors from Earlham College in Indiana came to Washington and lobbied the senators from that state. A leading Quaker layman, president of a large national corporation with facilities in Kentucky, spent considerable time talking with the two senators from the Bluegrass State, John Sherman Cooper and Thruston Morton. Hamilton later recalled contacting a businessman in Omaha, a Methodist, who in turn prevailed upon his minister to go to the president of the largest bank in the state, also a parishioner, to buttonhole a reluctant Republican senator from Nebraska to vote for the Civil Rights Act. The list of such informal contacts and subtle pressures could go on and on. They were a normal part of the political process, but not necessarily tactics used regularly by church people involved *as church people* in public life. Hamilton summed it up for a reporter in 1964: "[This] wasn't the church operating as a church, it was the church operating in lay fields, involving the business community, reaching into the power structure." These words demonstrate clearly how quickly representatives of the mainline churches learned the ways of applying sophisticated political pressures, of "reaching into the power structure." It is easy to see why the more experienced lobbyists of the Leadership Conference on Civil Rights from the labor unions and the National Association for the Advancement of Colored People (NAACP) welcomed them as full partners in the task of securing comprehensive civil rights legislation.[30]

Beginning in April 1964, the Leadership Conference orchestrated, state by state, the continual arrival in Washington of large delegations of citizens who crowded into congressional offices to press again and again for support for the civil rights bill. Religious groups were prominent in nearly all the delegations.[31] But as the battle in the Senate neared final resolution, the churches also operated as an independent force. By late March all the major faith communities were sending large groups to Washington to lobby. The most dramatic example occurred on April 28, 1964, on the Georgetown University campus where an interfaith rally drew 6,500 people, a "religious expression of unprecedented scope on behalf of specific legislation." Archbishop Patrick O'Boyle, head of the Catholic Archdiocese of Washington, noted people had come from as far away as California to speak of "our deep religious convictions about the dignity of man and the rights of all men." The next day almost two hundred ministers, priests, and rabbis met with President Johnson at the White House to dramatize the religious groups' presence in Washington.[32]

On April 29, at the Lutheran Church of the Reformation just a block from the Capitol, the National Council of Churches initiated daily worship services that would not end until "a strong and just civil rights bill was passed." For six weeks the services continued, presided over by 125 Protestant and Orthodox church leaders invited to Washington to lead these daily "demonstrations." Surely the most imaginative effort of this sort was a round-the-clock vigil initiated on April 19 by Catholic, Protestant, and Jewish seminary students from all over the country. Held near the Lincoln Memorial and visible to thousands of motorists and pedestrians entering and leaving the city each day, the vigil continued uninterruptedly until Congress passed the Civil Rights Act in mid-June.[33]

As the long struggle in Congress neared its climax in the late spring of 1964, the churches had exerted their influence at almost every level of the political process. Upon analysis, however, all the entreaties for racial change from religious groups could not have succeeded if politicians perceived little support for the proposed law in the churches in their districts at home. The National Council's Commission on Religion and Race and many of the national leaders of the liberal churches had worked hard to educate and to energize people at the grass roots. Did they succeed?

Letters church people wrote to the directors of the Leadership Conference offer hints of an answer. As the Senate debate over the bill reached a climax in April and May 1964, church members flooded the conference office with requests for information, personal offers of help, or detailed descriptions of what had been done to organize local support or to prod congressmen.[34] Like church representatives at the national level, some local church leaders became expert political tacticians. Ernest A. Rueter, a campus minister at Purdue University in Indiana, wrote to Leadership Conference officials offering a steady stream of suggestions from December 1963 until the bill passed seven months later. Purdue was in the congressional district of Charles Halleck, the Republican minority leader of the House; Rueter organized people statewide to pressure Halleck to support the civil rights legislation.[35] The young cleric also headed the delegation from Indiana that came to Washington in May 1964 under Leadership Conference auspices. By that time Rueter was also providing advice and information about local networks of civil rights' supporters in Iowa, Nebraska, and other midwestern states. Thus in April 1964 the executive director of the Leadership Conference felt compelled to write Rueter's denominational superiors about the minister's work, stating that of the many people involved in the battle, "few have such a noteworthy record of accomplishments."[36]

Equally revealing of grass-roots activity are the archives of members of Congress at the time, containing constituent mail on the civil rights question written while the legislation was being considered. Even a limited survey of such materials reveals how widely and actively church people urged support for the pending act.[37] Hubert Humphrey, for example, almost literally overwhelmed by the volume of mail flowing into his office, in a few days in early April 1964 received letters from 67 individuals and petitions with 410 names attached favoring the legislation. Forty-two percent of the letter writers and 40 percent of the petitioners, all of them identified clearly by letterhead or text, were church people. And we can assume that many others who did not identify their church connection were motivated by religious concerns. Roughly comparable figures emerged from an examination of the files of Senators Everett Dirksen of Illinois and Bourke Hickenlooper of Iowa, and Congressmen James Bromwell of Iowa and Charles Halleck of Indiana. (See Table 2-1.)[38]

The data take on added significance when one examines constituent letter writing to the midwestern legislators on comparable issues of moral import, both before and after the great legislative struggle over civil rights. The Voting Rights Act of 1965, nuclear testing in 1961 to 1962, the Test Ban Treaty with the Soviet Union in 1963, the passage of Medicare in 1965, all produced voter response, but from much smaller numbers, both among church people and the general public.[39] The Supreme Court decision in 1963 abolishing prayers in the public schools provoked many church people to strong demands for a legislative reversal of that decision. It was the only other issue that seemed to stir the midwestern faithful in numbers and in passion comparable to the civil rights legislation of 1963 through 1964. But even the school prayer issue awakened intense response only in limited areas and seemed to represent church constituencies both politically and theologically more conservative than those activated by the racial crisis.[40]

What kind of church people took the time to write about racial matters in 1963 and 1964? About half were ministers, priests, or nuns (very few rabbis). Lay people wrote, too, and signed petitions in very large numbers. Although Protestants were overwhelmingly in the majority, a significant number of Catholics also appeared, 15 percent or more.[41] These facts underscore once again the broad ecumenical nature of the churches' political effort. From the first systematic planning of national strategy by the Commission on Religion and Race in New York City in June 1963, through the extended efforts at lobbying in Washington by the commis-

TABLE 2–1 Church-Related Mail About the
Civil Rights Bill Received by Selected Legislators

Legislator	Dates	Church Letters		All Letters	
		no.	*%*	*no.*	*%*
J. Bromwell	7/2–10/31/63, 1/1–2/25/64	312	37	854	100
E. Dirksen	1/1–6/30/64[a]	52	39	132	100
C. Halleck	8/20–10/1/63, 1/25–1/10/64	78	44	177	100

Sources: Boxes 3, 4, James Bromwell Papers, University of Iowa Library, Iowa City; boxes 1–3, 11, 23, 28, Alpha File, 1964, Everett Dirksen Papers, Dirksen Congressional Center, Pekin, Ill.; boxes 73, 74, 76, Charles Halleck Papers, Lilly Library, Indiana University, Bloomington.

[a]Constituent mail to Dirksen about civil rights is arranged with all other constituent correspondence alphabetically by years. Data in the table is based on a sample, drawn from the full constituent mail file, January through June 1964, under "A," "Groat-Hahne," "Rinaldo-Robson," and "Voakes-Walker."

sion and its allies and the rapid creation of grass-roots support, especially in the Midwest, the work had always been consciously cast in ecumenical terms, even though Protestants usually predominated.

These events were part of a wider surge of ecumenism that was affecting the American religious community and even worldwide Christendom in the early sixties. Pope John XXIII's irenic tendencies and the Second Vatican Council, which convened in 1962, were indicators of the new ecumenical thrust. Another sign was the decision of the National Council of Churches in 1963 to admit for the first time Roman Catholic and Jewish representatives as regular participants into their policymaking bodies.[42] The political efforts of the churches in 1963 and 1964 both reflected these historical developments and gave added impetus to them.

Women were very evident among the letter writers. Catholic nuns who were school teachers and hospital administrators, Protestant and Jewish housewives by the dozens, and women who were national church leaders—all wrote their congressmen, signed petitions, or offered advice and support to the Leadership Conference in Washington. Anna Hedgeman did important organizing work through the Commission on Religion and Race, and women helped organize and staff the watchdog system in the galleries of the House late in 1963. Women have always played a prominent role in American religious communities, and as noted earlier, from the beginning were very much a part of the National Council of Churches. Thus it was not surprising that they joined in large numbers the public contest over racial issues. There were links between these events and the beginnings of the contemporary women's rights movement; Title VII of the Civil Rights Act of 1964 was a historic breakthrough in affirmative action for women. And surely when women participated so fully in the great national movement toward social justice for African Americans, their experiences began to empower *them* to assert their own claims to equality.[43]

Letter writers from the churches, having taken the time to compose lengthy personal notes, often provided thoughtful rationales in support of the pending civil rights legislation. In many ways, of course, their arguments resembled those made by civil rights supporters who were not church members. But there was one emphasis in the letters of church people that, while not unique to them, was sounded more insistently than any other. As one minister somewhat inelegantly expressed it, "I am supremely interested in a Civil Rights bill from the moral angle."[44] Perhaps because they *were* church people, these writers were often able to perceive that dimension of the debate, to discuss it openly, and to use it as a powerful justification for support of the Civil Rights Act.

The arguments took a variety of forms. Some thought as a moral issue the pending bill should transcend party lines. It was legislation that both Democrats and Republicans should support because it went "to the heart of every Christian and democratic principle we hold dear." Most supporters in Congress accepted this principle. A few of the writers pressed their line of reasoning even further and asserted that the moral demands upon "anyone who professes to be a Christian" meant they "had no other choice" than to support "the cause of civil rights." In a letter to James Bromwell, an executive in the Lutheran Church-Missouri Synod put the arguments almost as strongly, but perhaps more persuasively:

> Please work with all courage towards corrective civil rights legislation . . . [for] civil rights *are* a moral issue. The God of the Gospel is also the God of justice, and holds society and government reponsible for equality under the law. If there are risks in granting these rights across the board, they are not as great as in not doing so. Furthermore, as I am sure you agree, when a thing is right we must take the risks of right action. Law and order, and the good common sense of men, will take care of the rest—if we deserve it!"[45]

Most lay people, however, eschewed the more formal ethical arguments and spoke out of direct experience and a "practical theology" grounded in that experience. Thus a woman in Cedar Rapids, Iowa, made her appeal to her congressman very concrete:

> I have a feeling of sickness inside of me that comes from a realization of the suffering of Negroes and the guilt of whites. I share in the suffering and in the guilt. I write you, as my representative . . . to help me rid myself and my country of this suffering and this guilt. I feel that passage of the civil rights legislation . . . will make it possible for healing to begin.

Another person spoke with a powerful moral sense about Jim Crow practices and how they might be altered, in part by the new law:

> [Jim Crowism] says that I cannot freely choose my own friends regardless of their color without suffering great damage to my reputation and job opportun[ities]. . . . Civil rights legislation, long overdue, will assist all of us to move more freely among all kinds of people that we may develop [better] our own wits and character. . . . I would like to be treated "equal before the law" without this preferential treatment over those of another color. What I desire for myself I must desire for all to maintain my own sense of decency.[46]

Some saw, read, or heard about dramatic events that stirred them. On September 11, 1963, a Methodist minister in the Midwest responded this way:

> Life magazine carried a very dramatic story and pictures of the great Freedom March in Washington. . . . It was no doubt a long day for these people who came for many miles to join in the historic occasion. But it has also been a long day for the people present who represented the many generations of people who have been oppressed in America. Is it not about time for that day to end?[47]

Still others wrote out of deeply felt and long-remembered personal experiences. A man's direct relationships with African Americans in

World War II—one "easily the best instructor" in an air force electronics school, another "an illiterate older teenager employed as a kitchen worker" in Louisiana who "liked to talk to me"—caused him to see that "Negroes vary in education, ability, and personality, but only as we white people do." The writer went on: "I feel guilty that I, like so many whites, have known about racial discrimination all my adult life and have never tried to do anything about it." Thus he concluded that "especially in the light of recent events, the time has come for all of us, you . . . and constituents back in Iowa like me to listen to our consciences on this greatest moral issue of our time" and support passage "of Civil Rights Bill H.R. 7152."[48]

Clearly church people in many areas of the Midwest were deeply moved both by calls from their religious leaders to support the civil rights legislation vigorously and by the onrush of events. Evidence of this can be seen not only in the massive outpouring of letters to congressmen, but also in the unprecedented political activity that stirred the churches locally.[49] These activities began almost as soon as the House of Representatives began to consider the bill and continued until final passage took place ten months later. On Sunday mornings some ministers preached directly on the issue of race and then left time during or immediately after the service for people to write to Washington. In a wide variety of other local settings—in public forums, women's society gatherings, interchurch and interfaith meetings, even in a staff meeting at a small Catholic hospital, and eventually in public marches and demonstrations—people had the issues presented to them and then discussed. Action often followed, usually in the form of powerfully worded resolutions or petitions urging passage of the civil rights legislation. As early as July 1963, for example, nearly nine hundred members of Disciples of Christ churches in West Lafayette, Indiana, proclaimed that "segregation is an intolerable travesty upon the dignity of man" and urged their congressman (Halleck) to "promote legislation" to end the practice. In September 1963 Presbyterian ministers and elders meeting in Marshfield, Indiana, expressed to Charles Halleck their "deep concern with the unequal and often unjust treatment of our Negro brothers in our free society" and pressed Halleck to help pass "a strong civil rights bill" that "will help the Negro . . . to make his full contribution to our American democracy." Similar statements appear over and over again in congressional files.[50]

A certain spontaneity suggested how unusual the efforts were for the people involved. A large gathering organized by local clergy in Delaware County, Iowa, in early September 1963, was described by a local politician as "quite unique" because none of the organizers "had even been involved in a rally on a public issue so they were not quite sure how to conduct it, but they went ahead anyway." Because no African Americans lived in the area, they asked a black doctor from outside to be on the program. And at least in eastern Iowa a hint of the intensity of interest created can be gathered from the geographical origins of the hundreds of church petitioners—small towns like Clinton, Epworth, Postville, and Waukon, as well as larger cities like Cedar Rapids and Iowa City. Clearly some sort of political alchemy was at work within the churches at the grass roots.[51]

Latent yet deeply held personal beliefs surfaced, pushing people into the political arena. Belief in equality before the law, awareness of the great gap between ideal and current racial practices, and a sense of moral urgency to correct these injustices, were central concerns of midwestern church people as they wrote to their political leaders in Washington. Religious persons were especially sensitive to the clear ethical issues posed by the pending legislation. They (and others not so religiously inclined) were ready to support fundamental change in the law because they had come to realize it was simply the right thing to do. The fact that substantial numbers of Americans still were denied the right to vote and to have access to public accommodations because of their skin color was a moral contradiction that overcame, at least for the moment, any other hesitancies or prejudices about race these churchgoers possessed. Nudged by individual conscience and belief, many were ready to write their congressmen and in some instances to go directly to Washington or to demonstrate at home in order to secure passage of the Civil Rights Act. A nun writing from Dubuque, Iowa, summed up much of this attitude: "Injustice unremedied only breeds greater trouble. This generation can make a noble beginning—or it can, by negligence, hand a bigger and graver problem to a future generation. We hope you [her congressman] will urge coming to grips with the problem now."[52]

Intimately linked to these grass-roots feelings and attitudes was the considerable effect of the national lobbying effort. The National Council of Churches through its Commission on Religion and Race had created a network that exerted pressure on Congress not only in Washington and on Capitol Hill, but also from parishes a thousand miles westward in small places like Rochester, Indiana; Farley, Iowa; and Waseca, Minnesota. It is impossible to explicate the exact role church leaders in New York City and the nation's capitol played in stirring people to political action in the Midwest and elsewhere. But surely the local campaigns would have been far less focused and effective without the early workshops and forums organized by Anna Hedgeman, without the tens of thousands of "action memos" mailed by Jim Hamilton to churches in the Midwest, or without the careful coordination and dispatching of delegations of church people from throughout the Mississippi Valley to Washington to press Congress to support the civil rights bill.

After extended debate throughout the spring of 1964, the Senate finally voted cloture with four votes to spare on June 10. On July 2, 1964, President Johnson signed the Civil Rights Act into law. It was a much stronger bill than the one proposed by Kennedy over a year earlier. It expanded African Americans' right to vote, guaranteed access to public accommodations (hotels, restaurants, and the like) throughout the nation, and established federally mandated guidelines for companies and labor unions for "equal employment opportunity"—that is, affirmative action.

Senators Frank Lausche (Ohio), Everett Dirksen (Illinois), Bourke Hickenlooper and Jack Miller (Iowa), Carl Curtis and Roman Hruska (Nebraska), all considered doubtful supporters early in the battle, voted for cloture. All were of special concern to church groups. Of this group, only Hickenlooper voted against the bill at final passage, standing alone among the twenty-four midwestern senators of both parties in the final vote.[53] These results, like those in the House of Representatives, suggest that the "Midwest strategy," whether generated from the bottom up or the top down, or, most likely, through a combination of such forces, had definitely influenced the outcome.

Six days after the triumphant signing session at the White House, Hubert Humphrey wrote to Jim Hamilton of the National Council of Churches to express "deep appreciation for your splendid efforts during the civil rights debate in the Senate" and to assert that, without the "unremitting support" of Hamilton and the Leadership Conference, "this bill could never have become law."[54] Humphrey was correct in a sense, but his words oversimplified historical reality. To the senator the clearest evidence of the churches' presence was in the manifold forms of direct lobbying on Capitol Hill. The equally significant grass-roots support of the churches in his home state of Minnesota and throughout the Midwest (and elsewhere in the nation) was perhaps harder to recognize.

Moreover, the religious groups were only part of a broad coalition supporting the Civil Rights Act. The churches probably made their greatest contributions in the Midwest and to a somewhat lesser degree in Washington. But the African American community, organized labor, the Leadership Conference, and the politicians who fashioned the congressional strategies that eventually succeeded were also essential participants. Clarence Mitchell, the shrewd NAACP lobbyist in Washington, later offered the following assessment of what happened:

> I don't agree with those who make it appear that the church was the decisive factor. I think we needed everybody we had. . . . For example, when you get right down to the question of approaching individual congressmen, the labor groups have a great deal of know-how in this area. A man like Andrew Biemiller [the AFL-CIO lobbyist] . . . is just indispensable. If we had, let's say, a leading archbishop or the head of the National Council of Churches but had not Andy Biemiller, I don't think we could have won. By the same token, I think if we had Andy without them, we couldn't have won. So they were all important in my judgment.[55]

Mitchell was being gracious and diplomatic, but he was also historically accurate, and his words suggest the need to modify Humphrey's judgments a bit.

Many Protestants, usually those more evangelical and more conservative theologically than most members of the mainline churches, viewed the political activities of the mid-sixties with considerable doubt. They felt that the churches should focus their energies on purely spiritual tasks and "saving souls" and should let the secular world solve its own problems. This attitude reflected long-standing differences between the conservative and liberal wings of American Protestantism on the issue of direct church involvement in politics. Thus at the time the mainline groups paid relatively little attention to such arguments.[56]

More intriguing, perhaps, were the reactions of the many conservative church people who did not summarily reject the idea of church involvement in the political process, but who were inactive because they did not share the dominant national attitudes on racial issues. A few were ministers in mainstream churches, unable to say much publicly about their conservative feelings. But they revealed themselves in letters to their Republican political leaders. One, who feared "federal control which is riding with the Civil Rights Bill," in June 1964 admonished Bourke Hickenlooper to "go to the [Republican national] convention and fight, fight that we might have a clear-cut choice at the next presidential election! (I don't need to mention names, do I?)" Supporters of Barry Goldwater for president feared that individual prerogatives of *whites* (especially small businessmen) might be circumscribed as the government moved to protect the rights of blacks. They expressed no overt racism, but they tended toward a moral insensitivity that ignored or lost sight of the deep-seated inequities and humiliations African Americans had suffered for so long.[57]

Such people were not in the majority politically in 1964, and within the mainstream Protestant churches, they had no organization or advocates to represent their views on national politics. In part their interests in public affairs were just arising or yet to develop nationally. However, even as racial issues dominated public discussion, as noted earlier there was intense concern in some midwestern church circles that the Supreme Court had declared prayers in the public schools unconstitutional. That issue seemed to disquiet especially the independent, evangelical churches, not the more liberal, mainline religious groups. The not so shadowy outlines of the religious politics of the late seventies and eighties were taking on shape and substance more than a decade earlier.[58]

Moreover, the mainline churches' deep involvement in racial issues in 1963 and 1964 provided conservative church people with a model showing how direct political intervention could achieve a specific legislative agenda. The tactics of the liberal churches were a double-edged sword, which could be used to advance conservative as well as liberal ends. It was not long before exactly that happened. Perhaps ironically, then, the political successes of the mainline churches in the 1960s served as a precondition for the emergence of Jerry Falwell, Pat Robertson, and the Moral Majority in the 1980s.[59]

As we gain distance from and perspective on the sixties, the limits of the political achievements of the mainline churches in that era become more visible. The political power of the liberal religious community was never again mobilized so fully and effectively as it was in 1963 and 1964. As we noted earlier, church people directly supported the Voting Rights Act in 1965 and other civil rights legislation. Briefly once again the Commission on Religion and Race orchestrated a national effort that drew ministers by the hundreds to Selma, Alabama, to join Martin Luther King, Jr., in the last and most massive march there in support of voting rights for African Americans. And there was even one more brief gathering of church people in Washington in the second week of March 1965, several thousand strong, to worship and pray at the now-familiar Lutheran Church of the Reformation on Capitol Hill, and then to lobby nearby for the pending Voting Rights Act. But this was only a brief revival of the spirits and feelings that swept the churches in 1964.[60] And even though James Hamilton's Washington office continued to work closely with the Leadership Conference, never again was there an attempt to organize grass-roots church support for a piece of legislation comparable to that mounted in 1963 and 1964.[61]

Perhaps a massive effort like that of 1963 through 1964 was not needed again because such a turning point is one of a kind. Subsequent civil rights legislation required less effort precisely because the first victory was so decisive. But there are other explanations for the loss of momentum in the churches, related to deeper and more encompassing factors. The mainstream churches succeeded in their political activities in 1964 in part because the issues were so clear and unambiguous. The moral dimensions of the debate, especially, were very compelling. As the racial revolution deepened, however, the issues became much more complex. The debates concerned jobs, housing, and the reallocation of national resources, fundamental economic and social questions that directly affected wider and wider segments of American society. Church people, like the rest of the nation, could no longer agree among themselves as to proper courses of action.[62]

The documents suggest that even as the churches' political involvement blossomed, mass commitments in support of the African American community could not be pressed too far. For some supporters of the civil rights bill, especially those in small towns in the Midwest, it was all a bit of an abstraction since they lived in communities without any blacks. The social and political changes associated with the Civil Rights Act in many cases did not affect middle-class mainline church members in really drastic ways. Ending discrimination in public accommodations was not too much of a personal sacrifice. And scarcely concealed fears of possible public disorders aroused even by the March on Washington in 1963 appeared in some letters from church supporters of the new racial legislation. The law-and-order issue also subtly intertwined itself with the many expressions of racial good will in 1963 and 1964, lurking underneath the surface of things, waiting to burst into full public view a little later, when large-scale racial disturbances and unrest occurred.[63]

Moreover, by 1969 the churches were stung as deeply as the secular white community by the whiplash of the black power movement and specific demands from highly self-conscious blacks. In May of that year James Forman's "Black Manifesto," addressed to all of the mainline churches and demanding from them $500 million in "reparations," met with widespread rebuff. The contrast between the mainline churches' enthusiastic embrace of Martin Luther King, Jr., in the early sixties and their rejection of the more militant Forman in 1969 could not have been clearer. Indeed, King himself developed more radical social and economic views by the time of his death, a fact mainstream church people largely ignored.[64] Moreover, by 1969 most of the mainline Protestant denominations were facing stiff internal challenges from militant black clergy and laity seeking greater autonomy within the churches. Those challenges, too, deeply eroded the earlier sense of consensus on racial questions.[65] We will return again to these themes later and comment more fully upon them, particularly as they relate to the National Council of Churches.

But in June 1964, those unhappy developments were scarcely more than a small dark cloud just above the horizon. The initial attempts of the National Council of Churches' Commission on Religion and Race and its allies at direct involvement in the political process in support of the black freedom movement had met with considerable success. And even as cloture was achieved in the Senate and the Civil Rights Act became law, the commission and certain other mainstream church groups were moving onto new battlegrounds, especially in Mississippi, to try and "share the burden" (Robert Spike's words at the March on Washington). They sought to expand yet more widely the churches' new role in the ongoing national racial struggle and to press more deeply into the *kairos* of the sixties.

Notes

1. Minutes, NCC Commission on Religion and Race, June 28, 1963, p. 3, folder 2, box 15, Victor Reuther Papers.

2. *New York Times,* June 12, 1963, pp. 1, 20; June 20, 1963, pp. 1, 17. Overviews of the political struggle in the Kennedy years are in Mark Stern, *Calculating Visions: Kennedy, Johnson, and Civil Rights* (New Brunswick, N.J., Rutgers University Press, 1991), pp. 9–112; and Robert Weisbrot, *Freedom Bound: A History of America's Civil Rights Movement* (New York, Penquin Books, 1991), chap. 3.

3. "Meeting of the President with Religious Leaders, June 17, 1963," verbatim transcript, pp. 15–21, folder entitled "Civil Rights Meeting with Religious Leaders," box 97, Presidential Office Files, Subjects, John F. Kennedy Library, Boston, Massachusetts. The promised follow-up to this meeting by Kennedy's staff never occurred. See Louis F. Oberdorfer to J. Irwin Miller, June 20, 1963, Miller to Oberdorfer, June 21, 1963, box 23, Lee C. White Papers, White House Staff Files, Kennedy Library.

4. Since the twenties and the fight over Prohibition, the churches had tended to avoid large political agendas. Although liberal Protestant leaders like Reinhold Niebuhr expressed vigorous views on public issues, official church bodies, affected by the widespread uncertainties associated with the Great Depression and World War II, and by the conformity of the cold war in the fifties, were reluctant to get directly involved in politics. The deep commitment of the mainline churches to the racial struggle in 1963 ended all this. As noted earlier, there is no systematic treatment of the churches in American life from the 1930s to the 1960s to document these developments, but see p. 8, n. 7.

5. An early instance of gender conflict over the membership qualifications of a small group of Unitarian women who prior to 1950 had been members of United Church Women made clear that males controlled the National Council of Churches and that the women were, in an apt phrase of a recent writer, "subordinated insiders." "Report of the Executive Committee of the General Department of United Church Women re Membership on the Board of Managers, October 10, 1951," in folder entitled "UCW—1951"; Minutes, Board of Managers, UCW, May 14–15, 1952, pp. 9–10, in folder, "UCW—1952"; Appendix E; all items in box 2, Church Women United Papers, Methodist Archives, Drew University (cited hereafter as CWU Papers). See also Virginia L. Brereton's superb "United and Slighted: Women as Subordinated Insiders," in Hutchison, *Between the Times,* pp. 143–167. For the history of United Church Women prior to 1950, see Gladys Gilkey Calkins, *Follow Those Women: Church Women in the Ecumenical Movement* (New York, National Council of Churches, 1961), pp. 5–88, and Margaret Shannon, *Just Because* (Corte Madera, Calif., Omega Books, 1977), pp. 1–53. An important denominational study of gender issues is Catherine M. Prelinger, ed., *Episcopal Women: Gender, Spirituality, and Committment in an American Mainline Denomination* (New York, Oxford University Press, 1992).

6. Calkins, *Follow Those Women,* pp. 94–97. The quotation is on p. 95.

7. Appendix H attached to "Minutes," Board of Managers, May 1–3, 1962, in folder "UCW—1962"; Appendix C attached to "Minutes," Board of Managers, UCW, April 30–May 2, 1963, in folder "UCW—1963"; "Minutes," National Finance Committee, UCW, March 17–18, 1964, p. 1, in folder "UCW—1964"; "Minutes," Christian Social Relations Unit, Program Committee of United Church Women, January 20–22, 1965, p. 3, in folder, "UCW—1965"; all items in box 2, CWU Papers; Shannon, *Just Because,* pp. 113–118.

8. On United Church Women's support of the March on Washington and the National Council's lobbying for the 1964 Civil Rights Act, see "Minutes," Board of Managers, UCW, April 28–30, 1964, p. 1, in folder "UCW—1964"; "Minutes," Executive Committee, UCW, October 8–10, 1963, p. 5, in folder "UCW—1963"; both items in box 2, CWU Papers; Shannon, *Just Because,* pp. 117, 124–125.

9. For biographical information about Hedgeman, see her *The Gift of Chaos: Decades of American Dissent* (New York, Oxford University Press, 1977), pp. 3–90. On the NCC Commission on Religion and Race involvement in the March on Washington, see especially RG 11, folder 20, box 6, NCC Archives. In less than six weeks Hedgeman and the commission gathered 40,000 church people for the march. A broader sense of the churches' involvement in these events appears in folders entitled "March on Washington, 1963: General Correspondence, August 13–15," "March on Washington, 1963: General Correspondence, August

16–19," and "Inter-office Memos, 1963," Bayard Rustin Papers, A. Phillip Randolph Institute, New York; Ray Gibbons to The Committee for Racial Justice Now, October 16, 1963, pp. 2–3, box 18, folder 17, UCCBHM Archives; Brewster Kneen, "The Fellowship of Reconciliation and the March on Washington," July 31, 1963; Grover C. Bagby to Robert W. Spike, August 21, 1963; "For Immediate Release" [no date], General News Service, UMC; folder 1341-5-3:23, files of General Board of Church and Society, United Methodist Church (UMC), Methodist Archives, Drew University.

10. "Report of the Executive Director," Commission on Religion and Race, September 5, 1963, RG 11, box 6, folder 20, NCC Archives.

11. Spike, in ibid., cites several vivid examples of reactions of both churchly and nonreligious individuals at the march to underscore his understanding of the important new role the churches were beginning to play in the black freedom struggle. See also Ray Gibbons to The Committee for Racial Justice Now, October 16, 1963, p. 3, box 18, folder 17, UCCBHM Archives.

12. *New York Times,* August 30, 1963, p. 20. The Commission on Religion and Race widely distributed Reston's column in church circles immediately after the March on Washington. Hedgeman, *Gift of Chaos,* p. 89. See also *Interchurch News,* October 1963, p. 1; *New York Times,* August 29, 1963, p. 17. Politicians and other secular leaders also sensed the importance of the churches' involvement and the potential political benefits. G. Mennon Williams to Walter Reuther, August 29, 1963, Ralph McGill to Reuther, August 30, 1963, in folder 10, box 494, Walter Reuther Papers, Walter Reuther Labor Archives, Wayne State University.

13. Minutes, Commission on Religion and Race, June 28, 1963, p. 7; Minutes, Commission on Religion and Race, July 26, 1963, pp. 3–4; both items in folder 2, box 15, Victor Reuther Papers.

14. *National Observer,* July 13, 1964, p. 1; interviews with James Hamilton, March 15, 1985, January 9, 1986; interview with Arnold Aronson and Marvin Caplan, January 9, 1986. Similar ideas, independently conceived, about a possible political strategy for the churches are in Harry Ashmore to Robert Spike, August 21, 1963, RG 95, folder 16, box 15, Eugene Carson Blake Papers, Presbyterian Historical Society. See also Minutes, Commission on Religion and Race, June 26, 1963, p. 4; Report of the Legislative Committee, attached to "Agenda," Commission on Religion and Race, July 26, 1963; both items in folder 2, box 15, Victor Reuther Papers; Stephen Horn, "Periodic Log Maintained during the Discussions concerning the Passage of the Civil Rights Act of 1964," p. 53, box 125, Miscellaneous Manuscript Collections, Manuscript Division, Library of Congress. Horn was a legislative assistant to Senator Thomas Kuchel of California, the Republican co-floor manager of the civil rights bill in the upper house.

15. Spike, *Civil Rights Involvement,* p. 14. Following an extensive trip through the Midwest in September–October 1963, James Hamilton reported to the commission in New York City that "the naivete and the lack of understanding and involvement [concerning the civil rights legislation] in the midwest are shocking." Minutes, Commission on Religion and Race, October 22, 1963, folder 8, box 15, Victor Reuther Papers.

16. Minutes, Commission on Religion and Race, July 26, 1963, folder 4, Robert Spike to "dear Friends," August 14, 1962, folder 6; both items in box 15, Victor Reuther Papers; James Hamilton to Anna Hedgeman, October 31, 1963, in

folder entitled "Correspondence, NCC-CORR," Washington office, NCC. The schedule of workshops can be followed in Hamilton, "Expense Statement," September 26, 1963, Washington office, NCC.

17. The young African American speakers, recruited from the staff of the Southern Christian Leadership Conference or the Student Nonviolent Coordinating Committee, were heavily involved in civil rights activities in the Deep South. For a detailed analysis of the meetings in the Midwest, see report of Anna Hedgeman in minutes, Commission on Religion and Race, October 22, 1963, pp. 1–3, RG 11, box 6, folder 20, NCC Archives.

18. Minutes, Commission on Religion and Race, meeting of July 26, 1963, p. 3, folder 4, box 15, Victor Reuther Papers; interview with Arnold Aronson and Marvin Caplan, January 9, 1986. See also the newsletter of the Leadership Conference on Civil Rights, *Memo,* July 25, 1963; Marvin Caplan to Fielding Simmons, December 24, 1963; "Memorandum on the Principal Activities of the Leadership Conference on Civil Rights from 1963 to July 1966," in folder entitled "Civil Rights Act of 1964, Background Material"; all items in box 1, Leadership Conference on Civil Rights Papers, Manuscript Division, Library of Congress (hereafter cited as LCCR Papers).

19. Interview with Arnold Aronson and Marvin Caplan, January 9, 1986; Lewis J. Maddocks to NAACP, Washington Bureau, July 18, 1961, folder entitled "LCCR—1961," list of participating organizations, Leadership Conference on Civil Rights [1961], LCCR—1961 folder; "Program," plenary session, Consultative Conference on Desegregation, September 16–17, 1957, in folder entitled "LCCR, 1957"; list of participants in meeting at Willard Hotel, September 18, 1956, LCCR, 1957 folder; Arnold Aronson to "Participants in meeting at Willard Hotel," September 25, October 11, 1956, LCCR, 1957 folder; Roy Wilkins to "All Cooperating Organizations," December 5, 1956, LCCR, 1957 folder; items in box 104, Washington Bureau, NAACP Papers, Manuscript Division, Library of Congress.

20. Samuel A. Cavert, *The American Churches and the Ecumenical Movement: 1900–1968* (New York, Association Press, 1968), p. 194.

21. Interview with James Hamilton, January 9, 1986.

22. Interview with Hamilton, January 9, 1986; Minutes, Commission on Religion and Race, meeting of June 28, 1963, p. 1; Commission on Religion and Race, agenda sheet, July 26, 1963; both items in folder 4, box 15, Victor Reuther Papers; Hamilton personal appointments book, 1963, Washington office, NCC.

23. Eugene Carson Blake of the National Council of Churches, Father John Cronin of the National Catholic Welfare Conference, and Rabbi Irwin Blank of the Synagogue Council of America testified before a subcommittee of the House Judiciary Committee on July 24, 1963. This action of Blake, Cronin, and Blank was a significant new expression of ecumenicity on a major public issue. For a verbatim text of the testimony, see folder 3, box 15, Victor Reuther Papers. For the Leadership Conference's activities, see "Report of the Legislative Committee," attached to "Agenda," July 26, 1963, Commission on Religion and Race; Minutes, Commission on Religion and Race, meeting of July 26, 1963; both items in folder 4, box 15, Victor Reuther Papers. Hamilton personal appointments book, 1963, Washington office, NCC.

24. A close ally of Hamilton and the LCCR was the Friends Committee for National Legislation. In 1963 this Quaker group brought to Washington Richard Taylor, a political scientist then teaching at Coe College in Cedar Rapids, Iowa,

to lobby on "human rights" issues. Although the Friends Committee never officially joined the Leadership Conference, Taylor was involved in many of the latter's strategy sessions. The Friends Committee for National Legislation played a quiet, important, and still largely unknown role in the lobbying effort on civil rights in Washington in the sixties. Interview with Richard Taylor, June 18, 1985; Richard Taylor to Arnold Aronson, July 18, August 15, September 23, October 7, 1963, April 15, 1964; Taylor to Marvin Caplan and Hamilton, January 21, 1964, box 2; special citation of LCCR to Taylor, June 11, 1964, box 1; all items in LCCR Papers.

25. Congressional Quarterly, *Revolution in Civil Rights, 1945–68* (Washington, U.S. Government, 1968), pp. 54–55. See also Charles and Barbara Whalen, *The Longest Debate: A Legislative History of the 1964 Civil Rights Act* (Washington, D.C., Seven Locks Press, 1984), p. 109; Hamilton to Grover Bagby, March 31, 1964, in folder entitled "Correspondence, NCC-CORR," Washington office, NCC. For the precise accounting of votes through the "vulture" system, see Aronson to Jean Graham, February 24, 1964, box 1, LCCR Papers. On the weekly strategy sessions of the Leadership Conference, see *Memo,* July 25, 1963, January 13, February 3, 1964; and "Important! Read at Once!" n.d., in folder entitled "Correspondence"; all items in box 1, LCCR Papers. For the "vulture" reference, see *Memo,* February 11, 1964, box 1, LCCR Papers.

26. Minutes, Commission on Religion and Race, meeting of June 28, 1963, p. 4, folder 2, box 15, Victor Reuther Papers; Hamilton to Carol Anderson, April 10, 1964, in folder entitled "Correspondence, NCC-CORR"; Hamilton to Spike, May 1, 1964; "Digest of Civil Rights Act of 1963," n.d.; Hamilton to "Selected Denominational Officials," July 4, October 10, 1963, in folder entitled "Immediate Action Memos, Selected Denominational Officials"; *Memo,* July 1, December 15, 1963, February 1, 15, April 1, 15, 1964, in folder entitled "Memo"; items in Washington office, NCC.

27. For the votes, see *Congressional Quarterly Almanac,* 20 (1964), pp. 82–83.

28. Whalen and Whalen, *The Longest Debate,* pp. 124–148; *Memo,* April 1, 1964, pp. 1–2, Washington office, NCC.

29. Hamilton to Jay Moore, May 1, 1964, in folder entitled "Correspondence, NCC-CORR"; both items in Washington office, NCC. Hamilton, "Expense Statement," June 23, 1964; Hamilton and his associates also taped talks on civil rights issues by nationally known religious leaders and circulated them widely in the Midwest.

30. For Hamilton's statement, see *National Observer,* July 13, 1964, p. 18. See also interview with Richard Taylor, June 18, 1985; interview with John Pratt, June 16, 1985; interview with Hamilton, March 15, 1985; Herman Edelsberg to Nicholas D. Katzenbach, May 11, 1964, with attachments, box 28, Burke Marshall Papers, Kennedy Library; Richard Taylor, "Congress Makes a Law: The Civil Rights Act of 1964," in R. J. Tresolini and Richard Frost, eds., *Cases in American National Government and Politics* (Englewood Cliffs, New Jersey, Prentice-Hall, 1966), p. 97.

31. Horn, "Periodic Log during Passage of Civil Rights Act," p. 26A; *Memo,* May 4, May 11, May 18, 1964, box 1, LCCR Papers. Many of the coordinators of the state delegations, usually volunteers, were ministers. See especially *Memo,* April 20, May 18, 1964, box 1, LCCR Papers.

32. *Memo,* May 15, 1964, in folder entitled "General Correspondence on Civil Rights"; "Civil Rights Act of 1964: A Report on the Activity of the Council for

Christian Social Action," September 1, 1964, in folder entitled "United Church of Christ"; *Bipartisan Civil Rights Newsletter,* March 17, 1964, in folder entitled "General Correspondence on Civil Rights"; all items in Washington Office, NCC.

33. Spike, *Civil Rights Involvement,* p. 14; *Memo,* May 4, June 19, 1964, box 1, LCCR Papers; Horn, "Periodic Log during Passage of Civil Rights Act," p. 199; *New York Times,* April 29, 1964, pp. 1, 29.

34. See, for example, Ruth Harrison to Arnold Aronson, January 29, 1964; Caplan to Edgar Metzler, March 27, 1964; Andrew Juvinall to Grover Bagby, March 28, 1964; Father James Stewart to Aronson, April 11, 1964; Aronson to Rev. Mario Shaw, O.S.B., April 23, 1964; Sister Mary Luke to Aronson, May 15, 1964; Dan Asher to Aronson, May 21, 1964; all items in box 1, LCCR Papers.

35. Between September 1963 and mid-February 1964 (H.R. 7152 passed the House of Representatives on February 10), Rueter wrote Charles Halleck at least seven times, more than any other constituent interested in civil rights. Halleck responded regularly, even asking Rueter to interpret his actions on the civil rights bill to one clerical constituent. Ernest A. Rueter to Charles A. Halleck, September 24, 1963, box 74, Reuter to Halleck, December 3, 1963, box 75; Halleck to Rueter, January 28, February 4, 1964, Rueter to Halleck, January 30, February 1, 4, 10, 1964, telegram, Rueter to Halleck, February 7, 1964, box 76; all items in Charles Halleck Papers, Lilly Library, Indiana University, Bloomington, Indiana.

36. The quotation is in Arnold Aronson to Gary Oniki, April 9, 1964, in folder entitled "Correspondence," box 2, LCCR Papers. See also Marvin Caplan to Martin Luther King, Jr., December 6, 1963, Caplan to Rueter, January 10, 23, March 3, 5, 1964, Aronson to Lawrence McVoy, February 26, 1964, all in Correspondence folder; "Re: Rep. Charles Halleck," memo, December 6, 1963, Rueter to "Dear Fellow Citizen," February 28, 1964, both items in folder entitled "Civil Rights Act of 1964: Discharge Petition"; all items in LCCR Papers. Work similar to Rueter's done by a church layman can be seen in Harry Reynolds to Leadership Conference on Civil Rights, May 12, 1964, Caplan to Reynolds, May 19, June 17, 1964, in Correspondence folder, LCCR Papers.

37. Statements in the text are based on a survey of the archival records of five midwestern legislators: Senators Everett Dirksen of Illinois, Bourke Hickenlooper of Iowa, Hubert Humphrey of Minnesota, and Representatives James Bromwell of Iowa and Charles Halleck of Indiana. Humphrey, the only Democrat, played an extremely significant part as co–floor manager of the civil rights bill in the Senate. Dirksen's support, and that of other northern conservatives influenced by him, assured achievement of cloture and the final passage of the act. Hickenlooper represented a constituency in Iowa that epitomized the conservative, small-town and rural, overwhelmingly white and Protestant communities that political strategists had pinpointed for special attention by religious groups. Halleck was the minority leader of the House. Bromwell, a moderate Republican, was a member of the House Judiciary Committee, which played an important role in the deliberations over the bill.

38. The Humphrey data covers the week of April 6–13, 1964. Untitled envelope, box 23K.10.7B, Hubert Humphrey Papers, Minnesota Historical Society, Minneapolis. See also box 23K.10.8F, Humphrey Papers. A sampling of Humphrey's correspondence from comparable time periods up to the first week of June 1964 suggests the days in April were representative. See box 23K.10.9B, and

box 23K.10.10F, Humphrey Papers. The archival collections of Dirksen, Hickenlooper, Halleck, and Bromwell contain almost all the constituent mail addressed to them concerning the Civil Rights Act. Hickenlooper's mail from Iowa constituents (270 letters) was almost entirely from church people. See boxes 9, 9B, Legislative File, General, Bourke Hickenlooper Papers, Herbert Hoover Library, West Branch, Iowa. Because of the volume of mail and the means used in some congressional offices to organize the materials, the sampling methods did not produce exact equivalents, but the numerical results are suggestive.

39. The Voting Rights Act of 1965 serves as an especially useful comparison. It has been viewed as equal in historical significance to the Civil Rights Act of 1964, and given its closeness in time, it might have provoked the same elements of the electorate to vigorous public support. But debate and passage of the law created little stir among midwestern letter writers. Constituent mail on the topic addressed to Halleck, Dirksen, and Hickenlooper (Bromwell had been defeated and Humphrey elevated to the vice-presidency in November 1964) was far smaller in volume and included far fewer letters from church people than the mail on the bill in 1964. See box 84, Halleck Papers; folder entitled "Civil Rights, 1965, Constituent Correspondence," box 10, Legislative File, General, Hickenlooper Papers; boxes 3, 39, 80, Alpha File, 1965, Everett Dirksen Papers. Comments about constituents and nuclear testing, the Test Ban Treaty, and Medicare are based on material in folder entitled "Nuclear Testing, 1961–62," box 10, and folder entitled "Test Ban Treaty, 1963," box 15; both items in Bromwell Papers; boxes 76, 84, Halleck Papers; and box 39, Alpha File, 1965, Dirksen Papers.

40. People in Halleck's district were especially active in this regard. Winona Lake, Indiana, a national center for evangelical church groups, was in Halleck's jurisdiction and may help to explain this fact. Between January 1 and February 10, 1964, more of his churchgoing constituents expressed themselves on this subject than on the racial issue, at the moment when the debate in the House of Representatives over the civil rights bill reached its peak. Voters in Bromwell's district in Iowa were far less vocal. Seee box 76, Halleck Papers; folder entitled "Prayer, 1962–64," box 12, Bromwell Papers.

41. The absence of Jewish correspondents was not surprising in the heavily Protestant, small-town sections of the Midwest. Jews from urban areas did write occasionally to the congressmen. See Rabbi Jordon Taxon to Everett Dirksen, telegram, April 7, 1964, Alpha File, Dirksen Papers; Halleck to Ernest Rueter, January 28, 1964; Rueter to Halleck, January 30, 1964; both letters in box 76, Halleck Papers; Charles G. Workman to James Bromwell, September 23, 1963, box 3, Bromwell Papers. The correspondence of the Leadership Conference included a much larger proportion of letters from Jewish groups and individuals than did the papers of the midwestern legislators. See especially box 1, LCCR Papers. See also folders entitled "Correspondence, NCC-CORR," and "General Correspondence on Civil Rights," Washington office, NCC. Catholic constituents often were connected to religious orders and Catholic colleges and seminaries. See Nano Byrnes to James Bromwell, July 11, 1963, and Marilyn Beales to James Bromwell, July 19, 1963, box 3; Sister Mary Marcellus to Bromwell, December 14, 1963, box 4; both items in Bromwell Papers; Sister M. Ignatia Manhart to Bourke Hickenlooper, March 2, 1964; Sister Mary Redempta to Hickenlooper, May 22, 1964; both letters in box 9, Hickenlooper Papers; petition from the faculty, St. Joseph's College, Rensselaer, Indiana, September 19, 1963, box 74; Rev. George C. Muresan to Halleck, January 28, 1964, Interracial Com-

mittee, Blessed Sacrament Parish, Lafayette, Indiana, to Halleck, telegram, February 5, 1964, box 76; both items in Halleck Papers.

42. *New York Times,* December 1, p. 69; December 2, 1963, p. 16. See also ibid., June 4, p. 35, July 25, p. 24, and July 28, 1965, p. 72.

43. Mrs. Paul Ford to Humphrey, April 7, 1964; Gloria Smith to Hubert Humphrey, April 9, 1964; Sister M. Monique to Humphrey, April 11, 1964; all in box 23.K.10.8F, Humphrey Papers; Mrs. Paul Jones to Bromwell, July 26, 1963; Mrs. Milton Randolph to Bromwell, August 16, 1963; Sister Mary Eugene to Bromwell, n.d.; petition from Women's Presbyterial Society, Northeast Iowa Presbytery, October 15, 1963; all items in box 3, Bromwell Papers; "Minutes," Administrative Committee, United Church Women, April 26, 1964, p. 3, in folder "UCW—1964," Box 2, CWU Papers. On women's role in the watchdog system in the House galleries, see James Hamilton to Grover Bagby, March 31, 1964, in folder entitled "Correspondence, NCC-CORR," Washington office, NCC. On development of an interest in women's equality among young women who participated in movement activities in the South, see Sara Evans, *Personal Politics: The Roots of Women's Liberation in the Civil Rights Movement and the New Left* (New York, Oxford University Press, 1980).

44. J. Richard Wagner to Bromwell, July 15, 1963, box 3, Bromwell Papers.

45. Robert Bernhard to Bromwell, July 25, 1963; John W. Briggs to Bromwell, July 28, 1963; Arnold W. Bringewatt to Bromwell, August 23, 1963; all letters in box 3, Bromwell Papers. See also Ray E. Mills to Halleck, September 12, 1963, box 74, Halleck Papers.

46. Mrs. Myra Ervin to Bromwell, August 28, 1963, box 3, Bromwell Papers; Oliver C. Hotz to Halleck, September 8, 1963, box 73, Halleck Papers.

47. Milton R. Vogel to Bromwell, September 11, 1963, box 3, Bromwell Papers. See also Mr. and Mrs. Murl McDonald to Bromwell, September 1, 1963; Mrs. Robert Sedlack to Bromwell, September 22, 1963; Bert Davison to Bromwell, September 22, 1963; Charles G. Workman to Bromwell, September 23, 1963; Sister Mary Eugene to Bromwell, n.d., all letters in box 3, Bromwell Papers.

48. Burton G. Fox to Bromwell, November 24, 1963, box 4, ibid. See also Richard W. Wilmer to Bromwell, August 13, 1963, box 1, ibid. The Humphrey Papers contain similar letters. One man recalled how in 1914, as a student band member at the University of Nebraska, a black bandsman bunked with him on an overnight train to a football game. The young African American "never touched me all night. [To do that] he [must] have balanced over the edge of the bed." The African American eventually became a lawyer. The letter writer concluded: "I think all this adds up to: Let us all be good neighbors to each other." Howard A. Savage to Humphrey, April 11, 1964, box 23.K.10.8F, Humphrey Papers. See also Mrs. Paul Ford to Humphrey, April 7, 1964; Diane Schmitz to Humphrey, April 9, 1964; George Savage, Jr., to Humphrey, April 11, 1964; all in box 23.K.10.8F, Humphrey Papers; Roland A. Duerkson to Halleck, September 18, 1963, box 74, Halleck Papers.

49. Letters, petitions, and postcards in the Humphrey Papers from a wide array of people nationally indicate that the churches were very active outside the Midwest, especially in New England and the Middle Atlantic states, and even in border areas like Missouri, Kentucky, and Maryland. Contrariwise, in Charles Halleck's district in northwestern Indiana, civil rights seemed far less of a concern

even while the congressional debate was going on. Worries over the Supreme Court decision banning prayers in the public schools and a proposed national park in the "dunes" area of Lake Michigan were equal to concern over the racial crisis. Humphrey's role as co–floor manager of the civil rights bill in the Senate and his greater prominence as a national political figure probably help to explain the heavier volume of his mail and its wider geographical distribution. For documentation of these observations, see boxes 23.K.10.7B, 23.K.10.8F, 23.K.10.9B, and 23.K.10.10F, Humphrey Papers, and folders covering September 1963 to February 1964 in boxes 74 and 76, Halleck Papers.

50. For quotations, see John J. Masterson to Halleck, July 25, 1963, and attached petition; and "The Ministers and Elders of the Crawfordsville Presbytery . . . [a] resolution," September 16, 1963; all items in box 72, Halleck Papers. See also Jack L. Zervas, October 8, 1963, and attached petition; Clinton, Iowa, Interfaith Group petition, December 5, 1963; petition from Women's Society, Northern Iowa Presbytery, October 15, 1963; Sister Mary Marcellus to Bromwell, December 14, 1963, and attached signatures; all items in box 4, Bromwell Papers. Perhaps the most unusual petition among dozens in the Humphrey Papers was a statement signed by 350 missionaries in Japan, representing six mainline Protestant denominations, urging passage of the civil rights bill. Maurice E. Troyer to Humphrey, April 10, 1964, and attached petition, box 23.K.10.8F, Humphrey Papers.

51. Petition from interfaith group, Clinton, Iowa, December 5, 1963; petition from Bethlehem United Presbyterian Church, Postville, Iowa, December 7, 1963; petition from First Presbyterian Church, Waukon, Iowa, December 8, 1963; petition from First Presbyterian Church, Iowa City, Iowa, October 8, 1963; Warren J. Connor to Bromwell, February 17, 1964; all items in box 4, Bromwell Papers. There are many similar items in boxes 23.K.10.7B and 23.K.10.8F, Humphrey Papers.

52. Sister Mary Marcellus to Bromwell, December 14, 1963, box 4, Bromwell Papers.

53. Concerning the contents of the Civil Rights Act of 1964 and the final votes on it, see *Congressional Quarterly Almanac*, 20 (1964), pp. 86, 338. On maneuverings in the Senate and by President Johnson before passage of the bill, see Whalen and Whalen, *The Longest Debate*, pp. 194–229. A superb discussion of the evolution of federal affirmative action policy, beginning with the Civil Rights Act of 1964, is in Hugh Davis Graham, *The Civil Rights Era: Origins and Development of National Policy, 1960–1972* (New York, Oxford University Press, 1990).

54. Humphrey to Hamilton, July 8, 1964, in folder entitled "General Correspondence on Civil Rights," Washington office, NCC. For similar assessments, see Whalen and Whalen, *The Longest Debate*, p. 233; Caplan to Robert Eschenbach, February 23, 1966, folder entitled "The Civil Rights Act of 1964: Background Material," LCCR Papers.

55. Clarence Mitchell interview by John Stewart, February 9, 1967, transcript, p. 34, John F. Kennedy Oral History Program, Kennedy Library. For a similar assessment by a key staff member of the Leadership Conference, see Marvin Caplan to Robert Eschenbach, February 23, 1966, in folder entitled "The Civil Rights Act of 1964: Background Material," LCCR Papers. See also Denton L. Watson, *Lion in the Lobby: Clarence Mitchell, Jr.'s Struggle for the Passage of Civil Rights Laws* (New York, William Morrow, 1990), pp. 541–625.

56. For hints of such attitudes, see Martin Hoyer to Hickenlooper, May 25, 1964; C. D. Loehr to Hickenlooper, May 11, 1964; James D. Bruton to Hickenlooper, May 25, 1964; all items in box 9, Hickenlooper Papers.

57. Rev. Burton G. Murray to Hickenlooper, June 24, 1964, ibid. See also W. LaRoy Anerson to Hickenlooper, February 18, 1964; Frank E. Jacobs to Hickenlooper, April 18, 1964; Ralph Draper to Hickenlooper, June 12, 1964; all items in ibid.; Mrs. Richard C. Bross to Halleck, box 74; Calvin K. Smith to Halleck, September 18, 1963, box 76; Austin Drewry to Halleck, February 3, 1964, box 75; all letters in Halleck Papers.

58. For concern about outlawing school prayers, see, for example, Karl E. Johnson to Halleck, January 4, 1964; R. I. Humberd, to Halleck, January 15, 1964; both letters in box 76, Halleck Papers. Recently there has been renewed interest in church-state relations among political scientists and other scholars, probably in part because of the development in the 1970s of conservative church involvement in national politics. Most of these studies ignore or pass quickly over the political activities of the mainline churches in the sixties and the possible connections between those activities and church-state issues in the Reagan era. See A. James Reichley, *Religion in American Public Life* (Washington, D.C., Brookings Institution, 1985); Allen D. Hertzke, *Representing God in Washington: The Role of Religious Lobbies in the American Polity* (Knoxville, University of Tennessee Press, 1988); Richard P. McBrien, *Caesar's Coin: Religion and Politics in America* (New York, Macmillan, 1987). For earlier treatments, see Luke Ebersole, *Church Lobbying in the Nation's Capitol* (New York, Macmillan, 1951), and James L. Adams, *The Growing Church Lobby in Washington* (Grand Rapids, Mich., Eerdmans, 1970).

59. On the reorientation in political concerns of the churches reflecting a broader shift in the last twenty-five years in cultural roles and institutional power between the "established," mainline churches and more conservative, evangelical religious groups, see Roof and McKinney, *American Mainline Religion,* and especially Wuthnow, *The Restructuring of American Religion.*

60. See note 34 and especially throughout from the Bromwell and Hickenlooper Papers. See also "Report of the Executive Director," Commission on Religion and Race, April 1, 1965, p. 2, RG 6, box 47, folder 29, NCC Archives; NCC *Memo,* January–June 1965, Washington office, NCC; Eugene Carson Blake for NCC Commission on Religion and Race, teletypes, April 1, 1965; Hamilton to W. Garner Werntz, August 16, 1965; Hamilton to Mrs. Donald Frey, August 16, 1965; items in folder entitled "General Correspondence on Civil Rights," Washington office, NCC.

61. Hamilton was the first chairperson of the "Compliance" committee of the Leadership Conference, established to assure follow-up to the Civil Rights Act of 1964. The National Council of Churches' financial contributions to the conference, substantial in the mid-sixties, declined to a mere trickle and even disappeared briefly later in the decade. Hamilton to Ann K. Davis, April 15, 1974, folder entitled, "LCCR, 1974, Correspondence," Washington office, NCC.

62. Public opinion polls have suggested that in the sixties and later there was a gap in attitudes on political and social issues between lay people in the pews and clerical leaders, especially the leaders at the national level. But much of that data was gathered after the mid-sixties and reflects the divisiveness that began in the late sixties. At least in responding to the civil rights struggle in 1963 and 1964, the clergy and laity of the mainline churches often seemed closely attuned to one

another. On the polls and the issues their results raise, see Reichley, *Religion in American Public Life,* pp. 269–281. The data presented in this chapter contradict the assertion that as advocates for the Civil Rights Act "church lobbyists and ministers . . . largely neglected to bring the laity along in their political witness" in Hertzke, *Representing God in Washington,* p. 31.

63. Duerksen to Halleck, September 18, 1963, box 74; Donald B. Orander to Halleck, September 18, 1963, box 76; both letters in Halleck Papers; C. P. Hunter, Jr., to Bromwell, July 8, 1963; Arnold W. Bringewatt to Bromwell, August 23, 1963; Mr. and Mrs. Murl McDonald to Bromwell, September 1, 1963; Norma T. Speer to Bromwell, September 20, 1963; John M. Ely to Bromwell, September 8, 1963; items in box 3, Bromwell Papers; Richard P. Walters to Hickenlooper, April 21, 1964; Marvin Hoyer to Hickenlooper, May 25, 1964; George L. Gallaher to Hickenlooper, June 29, 1964; items in box 9, Hickenlooper Papers.

64. *New York Times,* May 2, p. 46, May 3, pp. 1, 14, May 5, p. 1, May 6, pp. 1, 37, 42, May 10, pp. 1, 15, 32, September 4, 1969, p. 1. Numerous responses of mainline church people to Forman's proposals, both individual and denominational statements are in RG 3, box 4, folder 12, and especially RG 5, box 13, folder 16, NCC Archives. On Martin Luther King's explicitly stated radicalism, increasingly evident after 1965, see Garrow, *Bearing the Cross,* 536–537, 563–564, 567, 581–582, 585, 595–596; and Adam Fairclough, "Was Martin Luther King a Marxist?" in C. Eric Lincoln, ed., *Martin Luther King, Jr.: A Profile* (New York, Harper's, 1984), pp. 228–242.

65. Partial documentation of the tensions in the late sixties within Protestant groups and institutions normally at the forefront of the struggle for racial change is in interview with Charles Cobb, Sr., November 22, 1988; *Newsletter,* December 1966–November 1969, box 36, folders 6–9; Minutes, Board of Directors, Episcopal Society for Cultural and Racial Unity, January 1966–November 1969, box 7, folders 10–13; box 15, folder 7, box 75, folder 14; all items in Episcopal Society for Racial and Cultural Unity Papers, Martin Luther King Center; Handy, *History of Union Theological Seminary in New York,* pp. 159–314.

3

"Visitors in Hell":
Church Involvement in the
Movement in Mississippi

Like raw recruits entering battle for the first time, the Commission on Religion and Race seemed intent on tasting and testing every facet of the civil rights struggle in the first months of its existence. As we have noted, activist white church leaders wanted to move quickly in part to "catch up," and thus perhaps to assuage pangs of guilt for not having moved much at all previously. Edler Hawkins, widely respected black activist and Presbyterian minister, drove this point home at the first meeting of the commission when he noted that the church had been "silent too frequently, and even when it has spoken, it has not used its own distinctive language to stress . . . the moral dimension of this issue." A bit later another person on the commission spoke of being "chagrined by the remembrance of our hesitancy and expediency in the years just past."[1]

Or perhaps people wanted to embrace the entire spectrum of possibilities as protection against feelings of inadequacy, of lack of experience and understanding. Better than most, Robert Spike was able to voice those misgivings in the summer and fall of 1963. Sometimes, he said, he felt an "overwhelming feeling of . . . dipping the ocean with a bucket that surrounds so much of what we do," or, "it seems a bit [like] Don Quixote." This was, Spike went on, because the struggle for racial justice, as blacks already knew, was

> a vast network of problems and issues that invades every area of American life. It is political. It is economic. It is psychological. It is theological. . . . What once seemed to most [white] people to be "an" issue in a whole catalogue of perplexing social problems now blends endlessly into a configuration of radical social change, like a gigantic storm system coming up from the horizon and filling the sky.[2]

As Edler Hawkins had urged, Spike also thought biblically in trying to explain to his fellow workers what confronted the churches, and those images, too, were often troubling. At a commission meeting in New

76

York in October 1963, Spike had this to say about segregation and racial prejudice:

> Segregation by race, discrimination in whatever subtle form it presents itself, is Old Adam, Pride unbridled, sickening in its insinuation, sinuous in its comfortable position of power. Such power yields not at all to education. Persuasion reels abashed. The armor of racial pride, like any of our prides, is a tough one. It is perhaps tougher than the variety of our small prides, in our intelligence, [in] our super manhood, [in] our competencies. This one is thickened by the coating of fear that began in the cradle . . . the coziness of the family bed as contrasted with the terrors that lie outside the window.[3]

A "vast network of problems" that "invaded every area of American life," a society riven by racial discrimination, "sinuous in its comfortable position of power"—these were not comforting ideas and words, and they tempered somewhat the enthusiasm and excitement that agitated the mainline church leaders as they swung into battle in mid-1963. But Spike went on to assert further biblical understandings, to urge his fellow church people to pray "for all those who fear their fellows of a different color or station. What a waste of power, what a foolishness of mind! Release them from this bondage, O God, that they may be free. . . . Let all the nasty dreams be seen for the frauds they really are. Turn the ogres into clowns. Let thy Kingdom come." And so came hope in the midst of doubt and hesitation, and the willingness to fly "headlong into the eye of the storm, sometimes foolishly, but I am proud to feel, gallantly."[4]

A perhaps foolish but gallant move "into the eye of the storm" aptly characterized the endeavors of the commission in its first months. Quick and effective involvement in the March on Washington in August 1963 and the long but ultimately successful participation in the struggle to legislate into existence the Civil Rights Act of 1964 were examples of that furious early activity. But the commission did not stop there. They sought to extend, ironically, Will Campbell's practice of providing outside "good offices" to southern communities engulfed in racial discord. In the summer and early fall of 1963 attempts at mediation took place in Savannah, Georgia; Danville, Virginia; Clarksdale, Mississippi; and Wilmington, North Carolina, and some involvement also occurred in two northern cities, Chatham, New Jersey, and Dayton, Ohio.[5]

None of these efforts achieved very much. In the southern cities, especially, there was open rebuff. Since the great Birmingham demonstrations in the spring of 1963, tensions were clearly escalating throughout the South. Those in power were resisting change more openly and forcefully.[6] Thus northerners like the commission members, even though national church leaders, were viewed with considerable suspicion. They lacked Will Campbell's cachet, initially at least, as a southerner, and they were much more ignorant than he about local conditions. Commission members also seemed more willing than Campbell to identify with local

African Americans and the national civil rights organizations like SNCC, CORE, and SCLC that were helping them. Whether such attitudes hindered or helped is hard to determine; probably the greatest gain was the large dose of realism and hard-nosed education commission members received from immediate contact with the daily racial struggle in the South.[7] Partly because the requests for help overtaxed the limited resources of the commission, and partly because questions were raised at the time about the general effectiveness of these efforts, the mediation—or "community action"—program was quietly ended by mid-1964.[8]

The commission also attempted to work on the desegregation of the mainline churches themselves. Colin Williams, head of the Department of Evangelism of the National Council and eager to help, was assigned this task at the first meeting of the commission. It was a daunting responsibility and although Williams organized "consultations" of ecumenical groups in several northern cities to attack this problem, the program never really got off the ground. It, too, disappeared in less than a year. This was a testimony to the powerful presence in northern communities of the same racism that manifested itself more openly and forcefully in the South. And it was the first hint of the difficulties the National Council and the commission would encounter later when they attempted to work directly on racial problems in the North beginning in 1964.[9]

Gradually, however, during the summer and fall of 1963, the commission staff seemed to focus its attention increasingly on events taking place in Mississippi. This state was the center of the deepest and most intense opposition to the sweeping changes the civil rights revolution was projecting across the South and the nation. For example, Citizen's Councils, made up of white, middle-class extreme segregationists were first formed in Greenwood, Mississippi, shortly after the *Brown* decision. Well into the 1960s these councils strongly shaped public attitudes in states like Georgia, Alabama, and Louisiana and dominated most of public life in Mississippi. One might also recall the violent assaults on Freedom Riders in Jackson, the capital city of the state, in May 1961 and the riots that occurred at the University of Mississippi in the fall of 1962 because of the admission of the first African American, James Meredith. These events were instrumental in bringing about significant federal intervention in Mississippi, but that fact did not diminish in any important way the opposition of the white power structure of the state to *any* alterations in race relations. Indeed, the first efforts, beginning in 1961, by young SNCC workers to effect change locally in such towns as McComb and Greenwood, failed when met with the violence of white night riders and daily police harassment. But the SNCC workers and their local allies in the black community did not give up and by 1963 were mounting further challenges to the status quo.[10]

On the night of June 11, 1963, one week after the commission on Religion and Race was created by the General Board of the National Council of Churches, Medgar Evers, the state director of the NAACP in

Mississippi, was shot and killed from ambush in front of his home in Jackson. The commission and the National Council sent a delegation of church leaders to attend Evers's funeral. This constituted a symbolic act of considerable importance and was the first offical act of the commission and the first step in what became a steadily expanding involvement of the mainline churches in Mississippi affairs.[11]

At Evers's funeral, Aaron Henry, state president of the NAACP, a Methodist layman, and a resident of Clarksdale, approached the national churchmen and asked them to come to his hometown to support local blacks in forthcoming demonstrations. A shrewd move to focus outside attention on the little town in northern Mississippi and to pressure local officials, this was also another very early contact between Spike, his staff, and local African Americans in Mississippi. The venture in Clarksdale fared poorly. Understandably viewed by local whites as interlopers from the north, the National Council people were rejected at every point. People in a "sympathy" worship service supporting the black demonstrators were served injunctions; a meeting in Memphis with Clarksdale businessmen changed nothing.[12] Failure in Clarksdale revealed the naivete of the northern church people and the rock-hard racial intransigence of white Mississippians. Later Spike recalled that "we came out of that experience . . . feeling that this was the wrong way to do it," to enter a situation suddenly and to retreat just as suddenly when rebuffed, leaving both sides "to face the consequences" of such a "disruption." Yet also unwilling to back off completely, commission people searched for additional ways to stay involved in Mississippi.[13]

In early August 1963, the commission began to offer legal aid to embattled civil rights workers and their local supporters in Mississippi. The church people present in Clarksdale discovered that many local African Americans had been arrested for participating in demonstrations in nearby towns and had been detained in local jails for more than six weeks simply because they lacked the money to pay the bail needed for release. It was, of course, an effective method of intimidation by local law officials. In addition, seventeen young civil rights workers had been arrested for their activities and sent to the Mississippi state penitentiary at Parchman, known for its brutal treatment of prisoners, especially blacks. By this time the commission had on its staff a full-time lawyer who was also a recent graduate of Union Theological Seminary. Because in 1963 there were literally no local lawyers in Mississippi willing to take civil rights-related cases, Jack Pratt was sent there by the commission to help.[14]

On August 16, 1963, Pratt, armed with $10,000 in bail bond money provided by the Board of Homeland Ministries of the United Church of Christ, secured the release of the seventeen young men and women in the Parchman penitentiary, and the forty people still in the county prison at Greenwood, Mississippi. This activity set in motion in the months that followed a bail bond program sponsored by the commission, administered by Pratt, and funded by member denominations of the National

Council. It was used in Georgia and Alabama as well as in Mississippi. By early 1964 over $35,000 had been expended for such purposes.[15]

Pratt reported later on the events in Mississippi to church groups in the north. His words revealed how some of the "captives" interpreted their release when freed from their long ordeal:

> Two old ladies, one 76 and the other 79, [imprisoned for fifty-six days] . . . came down the rickety flight of stairs from the women's cell block [in the Leflore County jail]. One carried a little shoe box and the other a brown paper bag in which were the few possessions they had been allowed to take to the jail with them. . . . Even though the sheriff evidenced displeasure, I mounted the stairs and helped them to ground level. The older of the two searched my face and then said to me, "Do I know you?" I replied, "I am from the National Council of Churches." She turned to her companion and said, "Hear that? Praise God, the church has come and set us free!"

Pratt concluded: "In that one line this old, simple, courageous soul stated, for me at least, the mission of the church."[16] A certain patronizing tone lurked in these words, but they also struck an unmistakable note of biblically grounded social concern that perhaps also can be admired.

By mid-1963 the most important civil rights group in Mississippi was the Student Nonviolent Coordinating Committee (SNCC). The Commission on Religion and Race quickly established relations with this group, as well as with the more traditional and well-established NAACP and Martin Luther King, Jr.'s (and Andrew Young's) better-known Southern Christian Leadership Conference (SCLC). A representative of SNCC became a member and attended early meetings of the commission's governing board, One also recalls that in 1963 Anna Hedgeman utilized SNCC field-workers from Mississippi (Charles Cobb) and Alabama (Thomas L. Brown) as speakers before midwestern church groups when developing grass-roots support for passage of the Civil Rights Act. In its early efforts at mediation in southern communities, too, the commission encountered the young SNCC organizers—in Savannah, Georgia, and Danville, Virginia, as well as in Mississippi. And it was SNCC's executive director, James Forman, who came to the National Council in the late summer of 1963 seeking bail bond assistance for the long-imprisoned black citizens of Greenwood and Itta Bena, Mississippi, among whom SNCC staff had been working for some time.[17]

There were mutually reinforcing reasons for the growing contacts between the national church people and SNCC. By mid-1963, under the leadership of Robert Moses, a veteran worker in Mississippi, SNCC was developing new tactics to replace earlier protests that had been all but destroyed by powerful white opposition. Increasingly the SNCC staff stressed efforts at voter registration, especially in the Delta region of the state. In late 1963 they also sought to recruit as temporary workers white, upper middle-class students from elite universities like Yale and Stanford, who by their mere presence might focus greater attention of the media, the federal government, and the general public on the racial intransigence of the Magnolia State. Aided by this sort of outside attention, Moses and his co-workers believed, the difficult effort to bring about racial change in Mississippi might take a more favorable turn.[18]

The National Council of Churches, with its broad public recognition and prestige throughout the country, its many connections within the national social and political establishment, and its own considerable financial and human resources, fit well into the evolving strategy of the civil rights organizations in Mississippi. The early actions of the Commission on Religion and Race also indicated clearly that the churches were ready to aid substantially the activities in Mississippi. Finally, Bob Spike and the members of the commission especially admired the SNCC workers in Mississippi. Spike described them as "the most militant, most capable, most competent of the young Negro leadership in the civil rights movement." Thus to "stay particularly close to the movement in Mississippi" was the surest way to insure that the mainline churches were on the cutting edge of the racial revolution.[19]

The rapidly expanding activities in 1963 of these northern churchmen in the Deep South call up reminders of parallel developments that were a part of the "first" Reconstruction almost exactly one hundred years earlier. In the late 1860s northern church people flocked south to try and help the new African American citizens create some sort of permanent means to maintain their recently achieved personal freedom. The churches focused chiefly on education and the development of common schools, secondary academies, and nascent colleges. Christian social consciences were certainly at work then, but so also was a frequent heavy paternalism toward former slaves and a cultural imperialism that inevitably accompanied northern victory on the battlefield.[20]

The aid of the churches in support of African Americans in the "second" Reconstruction was important, but in Mississippi and elsewhere it was a different phenomenon from that of a century earlier. In the 1960s a much smaller group of church people actually worked in the Deep South, and for different purposes and programs. But the most significant difference in the sixties was that local African American communities and people were setting the pace, defining the terms of the struggle, providing the most powerful and influential leaders, both locally and nationally. Northern church people could help, but they could not tell African Americans how to do it. This was largely the reverse of circumstances in the 1860s. In most instances the religious leaders in New York understood and accepted that fact.

Again Robert Spike articulated well the feelings of the most sensitive church leaders. In mid-July 1963, in a tense gathering in Savannah, Georgia, he personally became acutely conscious of the shift in roles between white and black when asked by Andrew Young to say a few words to dozens of blacks suffering harassment from local police and marauding bands of armed whites women with their dresses and persons burned by tear gas, young men bandaged and battered, and all in a near state of hysteria, as a result of the pressures they had been subjected to the preceding days, . . . singing the songs of freedom without pause, in a growing crescendo of desperation— "Before I'll be a slave, I'll be buried in my grave, and go home to my Lord and be free." "We shall overcome."

For him a white man and an outsider, to speak at that moment seemed inappropriate. "Words seem to come very cheap when you are only a visiter in hell."[21] He had come to provide some reassurance from the nation's churches and left deeply moved by the courage and tenacity of Savannah's black people taking charge of their lives with little or no help from the outside. Shortly afterward Spike restated his views more broadly, but the import of his thoughts was much the same as it was that night in Savannah. "What we [the National Council of Churches] have tried to do is to let the world set the agenda for our work—to take the world of the civil rights struggle seriously, and to develop a ministry in response to that."[22] It seemed almost an exact reprise of the point of view urged upon the churches by Colin Williams in *Where in the World* in 1963. In any case this was the credo, not always fully realized, that those committed to racial justice in the mainline churches attempted to follow throughout much of the rest of the 1960s.

By September 1963, the staff of the Commission on Religion and Race had begun to discuss in some detail the idea of a comprehensive program of community development in the Delta area of Mississippi, the flat, largely rural, yet immensely productive cotton land adjoining the Mississippi River, which occupied much of the northwest and west central portions of the state.[23] A year later a rudimentary version of this ambitious plan of social, political, and economic development appeared with the founding of the Delta Ministry. We will analyze that ministry—its origins and implementation—in detail in the next two chapters. Suffice it to say here that "consultations" (a churchly bureaucratic substitute for "meeting") held late in 1963 in Mississippi and in nearby Memphis to discuss how to implement the idea of the Delta Ministry were also opportunities to stay in close contact with the "movement" people working in the state. And not surprisingly the churches soon participated directly in a major SNCC-sponsored voter registration campaign in Hattiesburg, an important city in south-central Mississippi. Encouraged by Robert Moses and other SNCC leaders, from mid-January to early June 1964 over one hundred ministers came to Hattiesburg from other parts of the country, where they joined the demonstrations at the Forrest County Court House and served as canvassers for potential registrants in the black community.[24]

The events in Hattiesburg signaled the decisive alignment of the National Council of Churches with SNCC (although technically the demonstrations there were guided by COFO, an umbrella organization representing all the major civil rights organizations in Mississippi). This meant, for example, direct involvement in SNCC's efforts to nurture grass-roots, community-based programs and leadership within the local African American community and also direct support of SNCC's voter education and voter registration campaigns. It was also the first attempt at cooperation between two potentially competing church agencies, the National Council's Commission on Religion and Race and the United Presbyterians' recently established commission of the same name. After some initial tugging and hauling it developed acceptably that although there was joint sponsorship the Presbyterians recruited most of the minister-participants. Jack Pratt of the National Council Commission staff was also present at the outset to provide legal assistance in case there were arrests of picketers. The participation of the ministers was scheduled to last only six weeks, but the response was so positive that the plans were extended until the end of April, with half a dozen or more ministers involved each week. Similar "actions" were carried out on a more limited basis during the same period in Canton and Greenwood, Mississippi.[25]

The involvement of the churches in movement activities in Hattiesburg highlighted both the strengths and weaknesses of such a step. As Robert Moses and Larry Guyot, the key SNCC leaders, had hoped, the churches were an important resource being committed to the struggle in Mississippi. They provided a new group of highly enthusiastic supporters who brought with them an extensive network of contacts outside the South, which potentially was an important source of financing and political lobbying. But the ministers were also only temporarily committed. Eventually they would leave and once again local black people would have to face unprotected the hostility of local whites, compounded by the brief addition to picket lines in Hattiesburg of white "outside agitators."[26] In part to counteract this difficulty, the churches made a more permanent ecumenical commitment in Hattiesburg beginning in May 1964. For the next three years this "presence" was embodied largely in the person of Robert Beech, a young Presbyterian minister who moved with his family from Illinois to Hattiesburg in order to participate continuously in movement activities there. Beech also became one of the first staff members of the Delta Ministry when it began in September 1964.[27]

The Hattiesburg experience also forced the churches to solve jurisdictional disputes, which inevitably appeared in any ecumenical effort. In part the project could be mobilized and organized rapidly because many of the planners worked together in New York City, chiefly at the Interchurch Center. As noted earlier, the Presbyterian Commission on Religion and Race had its offices there and was in almost daily personal contact with Spike and his staff. The Presbyterians, too, had developed their own connections with the SNCC people. Eugene Carson Blake, a seasoned veteran of ecumenical ventures, served on the governing boards of both commissions and was an important advisor who helped to establish guidelines to be followed. In Hattiesburg the National Council of Churches ultimately served officially as sponsor, even though individual denominations, especially the Presbyterians, but also some Episcopalians and Jewish rabbis, made substantial contributions. This was the pattern that would be followed in the summer of 1964 and in the establishment of the Delta Ministry later that same year.[28]

As far back as November 1963, at the time of a successful mock election held in Mississippi in which 80,000 blacks "voted," the SNCC people had begun to talk about a major effort to promote voter registration the following summer. And the idea to recruit workers for the summer project in 1964 from northern colleges, once again in part to attract widespread public and media attention to the terrible racial situation in Mississippi, was at the center of those discussions. In the earliest planning sessions for the Delta Ministry held late in 1963 and early in 1964, as well as during the voter registration drives in Hattiesburg, Canton, and Greenwood, there was ample opportunity for church people to hear about the plans for the summer of 1964 and to offer support. Here was another opportunity to be drawn further into movement activities in Mississippi.[29]

At the meeting of the National Council's commission in January 1964, Spike first broached the subject of SNCC's plans, predicting that "this summer will be an extremely active one." He went on to state that there were "inklings" that "thousands [a considerable overestimate] of students will be going into the south this summer" and that "one of the major emphases is going to be voter registration." Clearly Spike had been talking with Robert Moses and others from Mississippi. Moreover, he had some precise thoughts already about how the churches might help. To prepare the students properly so that they were "effectively used," the commission could "concretely help at the point of an orientation program which might be offered in June at several locations and which would be open to all students."[30] Since this suggestion was an almost exact description of what occurred six months later, it appears that Spike was rather far along in making an arrangement with the SNCC people before discussing it fully with his own organization. Probably he knew the commission would quickly endorse such a proposal, which it did, but this incident suggests how eager Spike and the commission were to commit the churches yet more deeply to the struggle in Mississippi. (It was also only five days before fifty ministers from the mainline churches joined the picket lines in Hattiesburg).

By the time of the next meeting of the commission in February 1964, a new member, Bruce Hanson, had been added to the commission staff with explicit responsibility to "set up and coordinate the orientation-training program for students going into the south this summer." A month later a location for the orientation sessions had been secured at Berea College in Kentucky.[31] This was an especially pointed symbolic choice. Berea had been founded by abolitionist church people in the 1850s in a slaveholding area normally inhospitable to such actions. Even so, the college maintained a liberal interracial policy of student admissions until

1904, when a nationwide deterioration in race relations provided the opportunity for the Kentucky legislature to pass a law that ended integration at the school. The National Council's action in the spring of 1964 highlighted that nineteenth-century tradition and perhaps was meant in part to put pressure on the current Berea administration to restore fully the earlier policies.[32]

Hosting the orientation sessions was too great a risk for Berea. Questions were raised by an influential alumnus; in late April the president of the college, Francis Hutchins, with the concurrence of the executive committee of the Board of Trustees, rescinded the arrangements with the National Council. Spike strongly objected, but his entreaties were brushed aside.[33] Utilizing their far-flung church contacts, Spike and the commission quickly secured a substitute meeting place at Western College for Women in Oxford, Ohio, which had Presbyterian connections. It was a small, intimate campus in a college town in southwestern Ohio, centrally located geographically in the country, with ample dormitory facilities and classrooms to accommodate a conference of 400 or more students. Here, June 12 to 27, 1964, the now-famous orientation sessions were held for the students going to Mississippi during "Freedom Summer."[34] The role of the Commission on Religion and Race in the events of the summer of 1964 in Ohio and in Mississippi was different from that which it had played previously. The churches were important public actors in the drama of the March on Washington in 1963 and the campaign to secure passage of the 1964 Civil Rights Act. They were direct contributors, for example, to the daily decisions to support the Civil Rights Act, both in Washington and in the Midwest. But in the midst of the activities focused on the South in the summer of 1964, the Commission on Religion and Race operated more quietly and inconspicuously. They were neophytes regarding Mississippi, and they were white. They lacked first-hand experience and thus basic understanding of that complex and dangerous situation. In this instance Spike and his staff did what they knew they could do well—to serve as facilitators and enablers, especially to the SNCC people and black native Mississippians who were attempting to prepare properly the 800 college students going to the Magnolia State for the summer.

Several preliminary planning meetings were held at the Interchurch Center in New York City beginning in late February 1964. Everyone agreed at the outset that the principal aim of the orientation sessions in June in Ohio was to educate two large groups of students about the extremely dangerous situation they were entering in Mississippi and how to function effectively in such a situation. By the end of March, Bruce Hanson could report specifically to the commission that the planners had determined that the students needed to "become knowledgeable of the local situations" in Mississippi, to develop skills related to "voter registration and education, literacy training, and community development," to study the "culture and history of the Negro . . . in the U.S." and to learn "the art of non-violence and interpersoanl relations." Roughly, these words represented the content of the two weeks of orientation carried out at Western College for Women.[35]

In order to achieve these ends the National Council of Churches brought together two sets of people to do the planning: First, SNCC field-workers from Mississippi, supplemented by representatives of SCLC and CORE, and second, a small group from Columbia University—social psychologists, sociologists, and psychologists, and a few of their graduate students—who were interested in group dynamics and community change and were members of a network of social scientists known as the National Training Laboratory (NTS). The people from the NTS offered advice about structuring small-group discussions and facilitating the intense training of northern white, middle-class students by the SNCC staff. A separate two-day meeting was held in late March to plan the curriculum for the Freedom Schools in Mississippi, a gathering that also included people from other organizations.[36]

Given the class, racial, and educational disparities between these two groups, one might expect tensions to develop almost immediately. It was not the case. The educational specialists and the young African Americans each had special expertise to offer that for the most part did not overlap. Certainly, though, the less academic SNCC workers had the most to offer—extensive experience in Mississippi and the ability to reflect and act upon that experience. The entire orientation program and the summer's efforts beyond that rested on their ability to convey how difficult it was to survive as civil rights workers in Mississippi. Most significantly, perhaps, the SNCC people were unfazed by the situation in which they found themselves in the planning sessions. The sheer power of their personalities occasioned immediate attention and respect.[37] Relationships like these continued on into the orientation sessions in Ohio and throughout the rest of the summer.

It seems unnecessary to recapitulate in detail what transpired at Oxford. The National Council people served largely in supervisory and administrative capacities and did not play a central role in implementing the daily program. That was chiefly the task of SNCC and CORE workers from Mississippi and certain special speakers, like Vincent Harding, who lectured on African American history, and John Doar, who tried to explain to an unenthusiastic audience the position of the Justice Department regarding Mississippi.[38]

At certain points, however, the church people did assert themselves and those actions cast a revealing light on the political forces that swirled about at Oxford and later in Mississippi seeking to shape the direction of events in both places. Some of the National Council's staff present at Oxford took steps privately and made statements publicly that were designed to assure that the gathering in Ohio, especially, remained in "moderate" ideological channels. In one of the general sessions of the Oxford meetings, Jack Pratt, the legal counsel for the Commission on

Religion and Race, stated his public opposition to the National Lawyers' Guild, a left-of-center group of lawyers that, along with at least three other legal organizations, had been invited by SNCC and CORE to provide assistance in Mississippi during the summer. National Council people also prevented the official appearance at Oxford of Anne and Carl Braden, representatives of the Southern Conference Educational Fund (SCEF), a small, non-Communist left-of-center organization working to end segregation in the South.[39]

Both people from the National Lawyers' Guild and the Bradens had been subjected to congressional investigations in the 1950s concerning alleged "subversive activity." Even though these charges were never proved, in the public mind the "Communist" label was quickly attached to both. Some of the people on the Commission on Religion and Race possessed similar cold war mindsets,[40] although their liberal attitudes on certain domestic issues, especially race, at times enabled them to seek common cause with groups more radical politically than themselves. This helps to explain their strong support of SNCC's work in Mississippi. Moreover, Robert Moses and the young SNCC and CORE staff were uninterestd in continuing old ideological battles. They were too young to be caught up in McCarthy era anticommunism; they pragmatically tried to work with all who were willing to join the effort to end segregation in Mississippi—the moderate National Council of Churches *and* the more radical Bradens and the Lawyers' Guild.[41] Thus the "red-baiting" by National Council people at Oxford revealed a cold war mentality that continued to exert a powerful influence in the early 1960s. Visible student opposition at Oxford to Jack Pratt's views of the National Lawyers' Guild also suggested such attitudes had a much less significant impact on younger people.[42]

Another incident that occurred during the summer was perhaps the most disturbing indication of cold war attitudes at work. Responding to a request by William Sullivan, one of J. Edgar Hoover's principal assistants, on July 16, 1964, Edwin Espy, the general secretary of the National Council of Churches, turned over to Sullivan a list of all the participants in the orientation sessions at Oxford, which had been prepared by the Commission on Religion and Race for internal use within the mainline churches. The list included not only the names and addresses of students, but also of SNCC and CORE staff, of local black citizens of Mississippi who came to Ohio to assist in the orientation, and the names of other adults—academics, National Council people, and others—who were participants.[43]

At least as early as 1962 before he became the general secretary of the National Council, and then again beginning in mid-April 1964, Espy had been trying to cultivate a private, personal connection with Sullivan. In 1964 the general secretary was especially interested in securing, through Sullivan's intercession, a "statement from J. Edgar Hoover on the National Council."[44] This elliptical phrase pointed to the steady, and now increasing (because of the churches' growing involvement in the racial crisis), criticism of the National Council from right-wing groups both within and outside the churches as a "proto-Communist" or extreme left-wing organization. Espy believed a public statement by Hoover asserting that the National Council had never been investigated for subversive activities would help immensely in counteracting the accusations made against the council.[45]

There is no evidence to indicate Hoover ever made such a statement,[46] but it is clear that Sullivan very effectively exploited the opening that Espy provided him. Requesting, and receiving, the list of those at the orientation sessions in Ohio meant an immense boost to a program begun by FBI field agents in early June 1964 to keep thereafter under surveillance that very group of students. As Kenneth O'Reilly has observed, "few twenty-year olds possessed old-left pedigrees," and thus "such trolling was not very useful." Perhaps more importantly, the list identified key SNCC and CORE field-workers in Mississippi and also local black Mississippians who were supporting the COFO people. Information of this sort was a valuable supplement to the data regularly gathered in Mississippi by local police and the Mississippi Sovereignty Commission and used to attack and discredit publicly the civil rights forces.[47]

Sullivan also used his contacts with Espy to hint at Martin Luther King, Jr.'s now well-established extramarital sexual activity, a shrewd attempt to push Hoover's great urge to discredit King in religious circles that included some of the latter's strongest supporters.[48] To conclude, Espy's efforts to secure public support from the FBI to help neutralize constant attacks from the right upon his organization inevitably required a quid pro quo of some sort. In the end he gave to Sullivan and his boss, both concretely and intangibly, much more than he received. He also revealed the moderate, "establishment" nature of the National Council, at least in the central offices in New York, and demonstrated how powerfully cold war attitudes still affected most liberals, religious and otherwise, in 1964.

In spite of the disagreements just discussed, however, close cooperation between the National Council of Churches and the movement people in Mississippi continued uninterruptedly throughout the summer of 1964. A constant worry in the minds of the Commission on Religion and Race, and certainly all of the SNCC workers, was the possibility that violence might break out at any time and that black and white workers would be seriously hurt or killed. That fear became a reality during the second week of the orientation in Ohio with the disappearance of James Chaney, Andrew Goodman, and Mickey Schwerner near Philadelphia, Mississippi, and the discovery of their bodies two months later beneath an earthern dam in the same area. Some of those involved in the planning sessions during the spring came to feel that the churches might help to lessen the possibilities of violence if they were able to provide throughout the summer "minister-counsellors" in as many of the freedom centers as possible. The mere presence of ministers, so the reasoning went, might serve at least as a partial restraint on the violence that lurked so near the surface throughout Mississippi.[49]

In late April the commission issued the first call for "ministers and laymen in Mississippi, Summer of 1964," to serve "as counselors to the workers in a given summer project." The mimeographed bulletin suggested that the presence of such a counselor might be both "necessary and helpful," especially when "incidents of anger or violence . . . can be avoided sometimes by a person who earns the trust of the group and has the capacity to 'spread oil on troubled waters.'" The counselor's principal responsibility would be "simply and profoundly in being available."[50] Critics might envision such a plan quickly producing instances of *in loco parentis* or heavy-handed adult intervention in the daily functioning of the freedom centers. The available evidence suggests that for the most part the people from the mainline churches who came to assist in the Summer Project understood and carefully adhered to instructions given them at the outset to follow the leadership of the COFO (SNCC) workers and to remain as unobtrusive as possible. Moreover, in addition to the ministers, other professionals came to Mississippi that summer—lawyers, doctors, nurses, social workers.[51] With the possible exception of certain small sets of lawyers, these groups did not work as constantly in the Summer Project as did the minister-counselors. But together all of the professionals—including the ministers—established a context of older helpers and observers that was accepted, indeed welcomed. Finally, the powerful role that ministers had historically played in the black community probably served to influence local acceptance of these *white* ministers, so visibly, surprisingly, present and working with the young people pressing for racial change.

By late June 1964 the minister-counselor program was blossoming rapidly. So many volunteers were planning to come to Mississippi that the commission chose Warren McKenna, a white, Episcopal pirest then serving a predominantly black parish in Roxbury in Boston, to be in Jackson as the full-time director of orientation for these people. McKenna came to the orientation sessions in Ohio to prepare properly for his duties, then went immediately to Mississippi. The National Council of Churches secured an office on Farish Street on the edge of Jackson's African American community and only a few blocks from the state capitol. This became the "reporting place for churchmen [and women] recruited by the Commission" and "in-state headquarters" for the summer of 1964.[52]

Eventually approximately 275 ministers and lay people from all over the country, including other southern states, spent time in Mississippi as "counselors."[53] Most came for ten days to two weeks, some stayed a month or more, a few stayed for only a few days. Then they were replaced by others. (Twenty years later some still expressed feelings of guilt about not having stayed longer.) By the end of August 1964, nearly all had left. They represented all of the major mainline denominations and included a sizable contingent of rabbis and a scattering of Catholic priests.[54] Almost 20 percent were lay people, male and female. Twenty percent were women—some former missionaries, some the wives of ministers also attending, many staff members in national denominational offices. (One woman stated, only half facetiously, that part of her motivation for coming to Mississippi was "pure selfishness in the desire for an experience 'in the world,' after such a long period of working for the Kingdom behind a desk.")[55]

Why *did* these church people come to Mississippi? Testimonies offered over two decades later suggest that many had been prepared by earlier experiences, some reaching back to childhood. "I was reared in a Christian home where racial equality was taken for granted." "Perhaps having a summer playmate when I was 7 to 10 who was black was a memory that urged me into the 'long trip' into the South." For others the first stirrings were in college or soon after. One noted that "as a student at the University of Missouri" a number of years earlier "I took home at Christmas time a German Catholic, a Jew, and a Chinese student who had no place to go at that time of year. . . . The social aspects of the Gospel have always called me into action." For another his first moments of concern were much less focused: "I graduated from Vanderbilt in 1958 and wondered why college life seemed so dull to me. The 1959 beginnings of the civil rights movement came as an answer to me. I became fully involved during seminary in Austin, Texas, and continued as [an] Episcopal clergyman in West Texas."[56]

Like this Episcopalian, before 1964 a number of the ministers already had become involved in civil rights demonstrations, both locally and in national events like the March on Washington in 1963 and the Freedom Rides in 1961.[57] Others had been caught up in interracial ministries, worked overseas in non-Western cultures, or had close contact with native Americans in the United States. These experiences caused them to develop a special sensitivity toward the powerlessness of nonwhite peoples. One minister noted that "at the time [1964] we were living in Horton, Kansas, in the midst of Indian reservations, and there was a strong prejudice against the Native American, which was expressed in a 'nigger' mentality. The appeal [to go to Mississippi] spoke to me, as I saw a relationship between the local Indian prejudice and the suppression of blacks."[58]

But from the perspective of two decades later the most frequently sounded note was that some sort of moral demand had been placed upon them. "The church had an obligation to be involved in the voters' rights struggle. I felt it was 'the right thing to do.'" Another minister put it much more compellingly: "I went to Mississippi in the summer of 1964 because I felt 'called' to do so. By this I mean it was an act required by my profession of faith. The injustice inflicted on blacks I felt was so appalling that I could not in conscience do other than to respond."[59]

A day-long orientation session, conducted by Warren McKenna and others at the National Council offices in Jackson, quickly opened the eyes of new arrivals to the realities of being a movement person in Mississippi. It was a one-day capsule of the programs run in Ohio for the student volunteers. Especially effective was the demonstration of nonviolent techniques rendered by two SNCC workers—how to curl up in the fetal position on the ground when being attacked, when to cover the bodies of others unable to protect themselves. One of the young SNCC staff people at the close of one of those sessions tensely reminded those who watched, "You are in Mississippi, USA, but you're no longer the white middle-class that you were before you came. The rednecks call all the white volunteers 'low class niggers.'" Then the minister volunteers left Jackson, to scatter about the state "still not quite believing, not quite absorbing all that we had been told." It was too late to pull back, though. Now "we were no longer audience; we were on stage."[60]

Arthur Cotton, the SNCC worker was right—these idealistic, well-meaning, middle-class church people entered a tangled world of hate and oppression most knew little or nothing about. Suddenly their worlds turned upside down and they became a part of the underclass, an outcast group. They were going to be harassed and attacked physically and mentally if they "got out of line"—the exact reason they had come to Mississippi! A common emotion nearly all shared and remembered starkly twenty years later was fear. Law officials were not, as thought previously, dispensers of a sort of evenhanded justice. In Mississippi they were often the instigators of a system of injustice. One woman reported that she was "amazed" after leaving the state "at how long it took me to get over having my heart turn over at the sight of a police car. And I had only one week like that. Think of what it would be for persons who always fear authorities!"[61]

The ministers and lay people joined pickets at court houses, searched out potential registrants, taught, and served as librarians in Freedom Schools and Centers. As a result they, like local African Americans, the COFO staff, and the students, were physically and emotionally intimidated, a few were arrested and jailed, one or two were beaten.[62] One minister assigned to Greenwood, an especially tough town, took people to register each day. Much later he recalled that

> there was the inevitable line-up of whites yelling at us, spitting at us. One guy even urinated in my direction once. I caught a bit of it on my pants. The hardest thing for me was not to respond in some physical manner. I had fought in the Golden Gloves in high school and I usually had a very aggressive manner in my lifestyle. I can remember thinking: "You dirty S-O-B. I could take you out with one punch." Not exactly the acceptable thoughts of a clergymen, but my rage was right under the surface and I had to keep remembering the mandates of our instructor—"Don't lose your cool."[63]

Another minister recalled a moment in Canton when he and a companion, walking down a road in the African American community to a restaurant for lunch, heard someone yell, "jump! jump!" Tumbling into a ditch, a truck roared by, "coming down into the ditch and missing us by six inches." Later this same person hid for two hours in a back bedroom of a black person's home while the deputy sheriff's car circled the neighborhood looking for him. When he left Mississippi, he said, "I felt that I had been in Hell for three weeks. I came home with double pneumonia and total exhaustion."[64]

In these times of fear and rage occurred bonding of the deepest sort with local African Americans. There was the irony once again of a reversal of roles—whites feeling safe only in the black community; an immediate sense of deep uneasiness and fear when in the white sections of town. An Episcopalian laywoman put it this way: "Walking down the streets of Canton's Negro section, we were obviously of the Movement. From every person, from every yard, came greetings. 'Hi, y'all.' To my northern accented 'Hi,' came the cheery report, 'Fine!'" At night there were long conversations between black hosts and white visitors on unlighted front porches, kept that way for security purposes. The wife of a northern clergyman noted in a letter home that "we were told that Negroes sitting on benches along the street weren't just sitting—they were watching to see that our office [the NCC headquarters in Hattiesburg] and the COFO office across the street were safe."[65]

Bolstered by this daily support, the church people struggled to develop a place for themselves in the movement community. It was a touchy situation. Turnover was frequent, probably too often in many cases. A "generation gap" sometimes was there, especially when the ministers were middle-aged. Many of the students either were in rebellion against earlier church allegiances, or were openly secularist. As one clergyman noted, "most of these kids think the Church is a bunch of crap and that most ministers are finks, simply because we talk so much about love and brotherhood but seldom do anything about it." Yet this minister also suggested that simply being there in Mississippi, sharing the dangers, seemed to nurture some feelings of altered views toward clergy.[66]

In a variety of ways the church people worked toward acceptance. Because the National Council people nearly always had a rented car, or owned one themselves, they were quickly pressed into service as chauffeurs, and that in turn provided many opportunities for extended conversations with their young transportees. And after careful observation the first day or so at a Freedom House, the ministers usually could find other tasks beyond car driving to occupy their time (and to prove their worth). Adept as a carpenter (a word possessing a bit of a biblical ring), one minister with the tool kit he had brought along "made 5 bookcases, two shelves, [and] fixed doors for the freedom school." This same person also had the job of finding "free sleeping space for 35 workers, as they needed it," a task that required "many home visits to prospective hostesses who had no phones." And so it went.[67]

As time passed the ministers sensed a growing degree of acceptance.

Students came to talk (at length), and "never seemed to hesitate to bum cigarets from us or pan off K.P. on us." One of the clergy reported that local young people from the Freedom School held a farewell meal for him "in one of the homes," and then "all the staff and some of the kids gathered at the Freedom House to talk until about midnight." The writer concluded: "I felt I was serving some real purpose as a minister—no, not really as a minister, but as a Christian." Another "M–C" perceptively suggested that the students "wanted to know if a minister could really be a person." And so, "this became my task, to be a person, . . . to need them, to respond to them, to care for them, as they did for me."

He then went on to describe a relationship he developed with "Jimmy," a young African American from Los Angeles who, although "warm and sensitive" also "delighted in antagonizing white students, by telling them of his own hostilities towards white people." The minister came to see that while Jimmy was conveying to his white peers "bitterness," he was also "radiating warmth." Jimmy, the minister concluded, wanted the others' "love, but he wanted it to be sincere, based on recognition of real feelings." Eventually communicating this understanding to Jimmy, "we established a real fellowship," because, as the young African American explained it eventually to another student, "John [the minister] . . . has the audacity to believe me." The minister concluded: "It would have been even more true if Jimmy had said that I believed *in* him."[68]

And there were moments of crisis when these church people performed other aspects of a "pastoral" role. A young African American on the staff at Holly Springs was killed in a head-on collision while driving people to nearby Memphis. The minister in the Freedom Center there helped to secure lawyers at the hospital immediately after the accident to provide legal release for the dead man's companion, who had been automatically arrested even though injured himself; the minister was then asked to help in preparing a memorial service, which helped "the community and the staff" to continue their work "with a deepened resolve as a tribute to their friend and co-worker." In Canton, when a black church used as a Freedom School was burned to the ground, a large group of young people vowed to torch a nearby white church in retaliation. The minister-counselor recalled later that "after about five hours of talking and pleading," he and others "finally convinced the group that to do that in response would ignite the police and sheriff departments and there would be bloodshed and great trouble." He was able to conclude: "Dr. King's non-violence program was followed."[69] Actions such as these were yet another way the ministers were drawn deeply into the inner context of the movement. And in all of the moments cited above they also seemed to fulfill the intentions of National Council of Churches officials when the latter created "minister-counselors"—to help avoid "incidents of anger or violence" and "simply and profoundly . . . [to] be available" to those working for change in strife-torn Mississippi.

Another of the aims of the ministers was to reach out to the local white community, especially the clergy and the churches, probing for hints of openness and the chance to talk about the changes white Mississippians were having to face.[70] These efforts, frequently undertaken, met with little success and sometimes with vehement rebuffs. Neatly summing up much of this experience, one visiting Episcopalian contacted the rector in Cleveland, Mississippi, who met him at his door with the words: "Come in—but your not welcome."[71] One of the ministers who sought to attend a Sunday service at the Disciples of Christ church while in McComb, was recognized as a civil rights worker and "thrown bodily out of the building." Another young cleric who remained in Mississippi for a year tried to join a local church of his denomination in Gulfport-Biloxi. He was informed by the minister of the church he would never be welcome in the latter's home, nor would he ever be visited by the local clergy. Meetings of churchwomen were held in private homes and announced privately by phone to prevent the wife of this "outsider" minister from attending. Eventually the outsiders joined a black Missionary Baptist Church.[72]

Rejection by white Mississippi church people simply intensified the feelings of respect and admiration the ministers developed toward the black people they had come to support. Despite a community scarred by poverty ("Homes ranged from a few small, neat and attractive places to huts, shacks, and hovels held together by odd pieces of wood, metal and building block. Health and sanitation conditions were appalling. As a result, we found a staggering number of sick and invalid people with little hope of regaining their health"), remembrances of the ministers twenty years later were still vivid and nearly all positive. They remembered food and other essentials willingly shared, "the buckets of fried chicken brought to the Freedom House by neighbors," and "the elderly people who let me live in their house even though it put their lives in jeopardy." One minister summed it up this way: "Our hosts were so accepting of our cultural foibles, and gracious to allow us to play some role in THEIR struggle."[73]

The ministers also remembered the courage and determination of the young civil rights workers, that

> the real heroes are the Negro 'Snick' personnel, who faced the worst dangers and took more than their share of the violence. Always they were intent on helping anyone threatened. Always they took hardship as a matter of course. These were the real leaders and that is as it should be. It was a privilege to work with them.

And they remembered "the spiritual power of the [movement] meetings," especially the singing with its passion and feeling rooted in the black church.[74]

Above all else these church people remembered spirited individuals, unbroken by threats, arrests, or loss of jobs, powerfully supportive of the push of the African American community toward "freedom." The following characterization of the hostess for several of the women visitors probably could have been repeated numerous times with only slight variations:

> There was neither gratitude nor fawning in our relationship with our hostess, but rather fierce pride. She reigned over her house, and the six women volunteers billeted with her, like an African matriarch. At six in the morning she did the daily shopping before the heat set in, yet she spent the hottest part of the day over a wood stove producing Southern fried chicken, rice, cornbread. A widow four times, but unsubdued, she answered the door concealing a long knife behind her skirts.[75]

In the years that followed some of the ministers returned to Mississippi to visit their African American friends; some still correspond regularly with their hosts. These small acts are suggestive of the powerful ties that were established back in 1964.[76]

How could a strong sense of connectedness between previous strangers of different races, sharply differentiated social classes, and even different ages, develop so quickly? Perhaps part of the answer rested in what the ministers represented to African Americans in Mississippi. As one minister who stayed permanently in the state explained it much later, until the sixties white Mississippians often dubbed the few African Americans who agitated for their civil rights "crazy niggers," and that perception was seldom challenged. The isolation of such people was often very great. In the sixties, however, new sources of authority, beginning with young blacks in their own communities and then extending to groups of whites outside the state in alliance with these young blacks, suggested the "crazy niggers" were not so crazy.[77] And in the summer of 1964 a most unlikely outside source, the predominantly white mainline churches, sent *ministers* to stand (too briefly) with the "crazy niggers," to affirm to the world the soundness of what they were doing. That was an important symbolic act, understood as such both by the ministers and the African American people of the communities in Mississippi in which they served.[78]

The effects on the minister-counselors of their involvement in Mississippi paralleled in some ways the experiences of the white student volunteers with whom the church people worked so closely in 1964.[79] All of the minister-counselors were older than the students, some considerably so. They were already established in careers, often had families, and had received advanced theological training that shaped much of their thinking and their daily approach to life. Perhaps most important, they were in Mississippi for much shorter periods of time than were the students. Thus they were not quite as ready, or able, to be shaped by their experiences in Mississippi as were the student volunteers. Most of them remained more moderate politically than the students, less critical of establishment institutions (because they were a part of the establishment). But they did share with the students an intense indealism, even though the source of that idealism was not always the same. The two groups also shared a sense of excitement in seeing that idealism "come alive" in the interracial, communal sharing in staff meetings in the Freedom Centers, MFDP rallies, and voter registration canvasses. Many of the church people were also exhilarated by the fact that the institutional church was visibly "taking a stand" on a major social issue with powerful moral implications. Moreover, *they* were a key part of that visible representation.[80]

Combined with daily threats of physical danger and overt white community hostility and harassment, it is easy to understand that the lives of the minister-counselors were deeply affected, even after only two or three weeks of exposure to such an environment. In a very short time many of the illusions these church people held about American racial prejudice and the deep class differences and barriers predicated on that prejudice were stripped away. Later some of the ministers were able to recognize more fully what had happened to them. As one of them expressed it, "that was the first time I ever risked my life for anything I believed in," and as a result it "changed my life, from an armchair moralist to Christian activist." Yet another spoke in greater biographical detail: "I grew up on a farm in Southeastern South Dakota, and despite college and seminary, was still abysmally ignorant concerning the realities of racial injustice. My involvement in this project transformed my theological understanding and shaped my ministry from that time to this day." Another participant, in recent years a college teacher, added: "My suspicion is that the most permanent change was not in the South as such, but in the minds and hearts of us northerners, who received a mighty 'education in reality.' All of my teching and writing about our society since those years has been deeply shaped and formed by my experience amongst the black poor and oppressed [in Mississippi and other parts] of the South."[81]

While perhaps in a small way the ministers contributed to the overall success of the summer of 1964 and thus the permanent alteration of race relations in Mississippi, the long-term consequences of their involvement were most fully revealed in their own lives. Some of the ministers remained in Mississippi to continue to work in the black freedom movement on a semipermanent basis. Almost all the first full-time staff of the Delta Ministry, the civil rights group sponsored by the National Council of Churches that began work in the Delta and elsewhere in the state in late 1964, were ministers who were in the Summer Project. At least three of those people are still living in the Magnolia State, still engaged in race-related causes. Recently one of them wrote: "It [the summer of 1964] changed my life. I'm still here."[82]

The rest left Mississippi, but many remained deeply involved in race-related activities. Several of the ministers entered interracial ministries, both locally and at the national level, the latter usually as staff persons in denominational social action agencies.[83] A Presbyterian who was a campus chaplain at the University of Texas in 1964 moved to Alabama a year later where he and his wife worked at Stillman College, a predominantly black school. Even those who eventually left the parish ministry often continued to work at jobs connected somehow to 1964. A former minister-counselor living in California two decades later observed: "Isn't it interesting that even though I am no longer doing parish ministry, that I am still heavily involved: this time as an elementary teacher in a racially mixed urban school [in Berkeley, California]." Others provided similar stories.[84]

We should not blink away the fact, however, that there were difficulties the minister-counselors encountered, or created themselves, within the Freedom Centers. They had been warned by Warren McKenna at the outset that "you can't just arrive and say to the Project, 'bring us your problems.' . . . You *must* be a part of the program," and to do that, "yours will at best be just one more voice." The ministers themselves acknowledged they were not always able to implement these suggestions. And they observed and reported disorganization and poor leadership among the young people, both black, and white.[85]

Perhaps most intriguingly, there were hints of racial animosity, between the COFO staff and the students. This, too, was anticipated by McKenna at the ministers' orientation:

> The staff is mostly Negro. . . . They've been beaten and ostracized for a number of years. This has made both Snick and Core into tight-knit groups. Now hundreds of affluent white kids come. There is bound to be conflict. . . . [And] it is only when the whites come that publicity and protection come too. They can't help but be a bit resentful.

McKenna's suggestion as to how to respond was implicit in a final recollection: "At one meeting a Negro minister told me, 'I will hate you this summer, but forgive me.'" Within this context one of the ministers forthrightly noted Stokely Carmichael's views expressed in a speech in Shaw, Mississippi. The young SNCC leader spoke "with sharp humor, power, and almost bitterness," and evidenced "a tendency for polarization of black against white (not without reason, of course)." The clergyman concluded that Carmichael's words only made "for all the more urgency in stirring up apathetic whites at home if we want to end up with a free, open, 'race-less' society."[86]

The tensions of the summer and especially the frequent violent attacks of whites upon people and property in the black community also meant that at times the latter people armed themselves as a method of self-protection. The church people were strongly opposed to such actions, but they had to face reality. One incoming counselor confronted the subject at the orientation sessions on her first day in Mississippi. She noted that one of three African American ministers in her group "was himself from Mississippi originally," and he had come back "to his own hometown to preach non-violence." Later he confided that he was "appalled at the state of siege he found. Everyone had arsenals; his own father drove with a pistol strapped to the car seat." He was so frightened "at the spector of an explosion" that "he contrived to stay much longer than he intended." In Canton, where the violence of whites on blacks and resulting tensions were especially severe, one of the counselors there noted that "when you look into the faces of some of the young CORE leaders, you know it would take nothing to start a full scale bloodbath." Even the local black hostess of this counselor voiced "feelings of frustration and futility over and over again. She said, 'You can say anything to me, call me anything, but don't hit me.'" The counselor concluded that "if there was ever a place where the church is needed, Mississippi is it."[87]

One minister stationed in Laurel in early August recalled later sensing that while he was there the mood shifted "from non-violence to self-defense," perhaps especially after the bodies of Chaney, Goodman, and Schwerner were found. He remembered that he "drove a group to a Sears Roebuck store in Laurel, and when they came out they carried a .22 rifle." He went on that "I very much protested . . . but I was not in a position to [win the] protest." He, too, thought that "it could have been a very bloody war, but somehow that was averted." Perhaps in a small way the minister-counselors' steady espousal of nonviolence had some effect, but other factors probably explained the avoidance of communal bloodbaths. Perhaps the lack of such terrible events were the result, as one observer speculated, of "the strain or forgiveness in Christianity that has kept retaliation out of the goals of the Negro." Yet more realistic and persuasive was the argument used at one point by another counselor and his friends that retaliatory violence might provoke even more horrendous and thoroughgoing return attacks—a spiral of human and physical destruction in which both sides would lose greatly.[88]

There were also clear indications that numerous "apathetic whites at home" existed who possessed no sense of urgency about the race problem. There was, for example, open opposition in home parishes to the involvement of their ministers in Mississippi. Some of the clergy paid their own way and used vacation time as a method of reducing criticism. One Episcopal priest and a group of civil rights workers were admitted to a Sunday worship service in a parish in Hattiesburg without incident. But immediately afterward the leaders of that parish contacted vestry members of the priest's church in Texas and "requested relief from my agitating activity." The young man lost his job.[89]

The push toward polarization in the words of Stokely Carmichael, the threat of open, large-scale interracial violence, and persistent hesitation by white church people outside Mississippi to support their own ministers' work in the black freedom movement seemed a muted concern on both sides of the racial line for most of the summer of 1964. We know now, however, that these attitudes were harbingers of the changed views that would sweep over both the national black and white communities in the late sixties and after. As we shall see, the churches would be affected by these developments just as profoundly as the rest of the nation. And at the end of the summer the defeat of the MFDP challenge to the seating of an all-white Mississippi delegation at the Democratic National Convention confirmed in the minds of many SNCC-COFO people that national liberal white leaders could not be trusted. A steady move toward an exclusively black make-up to SNCC and the rapid collapse of COFO in Mississippi in 1965 only confirmed these developments.[90]

Still, throughout nearly all of the summer of 1964 the predominant feelings in the Freedom Houses in Hattiesburg, Clarksdale, Canton, and McComb remained an emphasis upon interracial cooperation, open communication, and shared daily risk taking of black COFO staff people, white student volunteers, and adult legal, medical, and religious supporters. In retrospect the summer of 1964 in Mississippi was one of the last moments when the model of the nonviolent, "beloved community" of Martin Luther King still prevailed nationally and bound black and white together.

And now we can also see more fully the limitations of the efforts of the people from the National Council of Churches who went to Mississippi to help in the life-and-death battle there. From the outset some among the leaders carried too much of the intellectual and emotional baggage of the cold war with them and severely compromised their credibility publicly and, even more sadly, privately. Ministers and lay people who went to Mississippi were too few in number, hardly even a "saving remnant." They stayed for a very short time and then returned northward and westward to the safety of their homes. As comfortable, middle-class Americans, almost unfairly (naively?) they were thrust into a cultural context for which they were largely unprepared. An African American minister in Los Angeles, musing with Robert Spike in early 1964 about both the dangers and the opportunities of the involvement of white church people in the tough, scary world of black oppression in this country, put it very succinctly. For these people the game had been switched. They thought "they had been playing hop-scotch, and suddenly it's facing a cross."[91]

Yet in spite of imperfections and mistakes committed, the involvement of the National Council of Churches occurred and deserves recognition today for its contributions to the movement for black freedom in Mississippi and elsewhere. And we must not forget how profoundly experiences and events in Mississippi in the summer of 1964 spoke to sensitive people from the churches and gave *them* a new sense of themselves and of possibilities for change in the world. The power of what happened during that long, hot summer in the Deep South still reverberates across the years. Much later one of the participants recalled:

> It was the most intense moment of my life, and I felt that I was where history was, that my role as a young clergyman was much in keeping with the Old Testament prophets. . . . There was no other moment in my life when I

had such a certainty that this was where I ought to be, that this is where the church ought to be, and as a clergyman my presence was the presence of the church.

There is a note of pride about all this that many people in Mississippi and elsewhere would claim to be the arrogance of an "outsider" from the North. This was recognized by the writer as he put his thoughts to paper; his reply was simply, "if you must know what I felt, that is the truth."[92]

Is it possible that words like these suggest that a certain spirit of the Old Testament prophets was at work amongst these church people who went to Mississippi? Perhaps so; perhaps not. But we can no longer ignore what they said and did in the summer of 1964. And there was more to come. In the fall of that year the National Council of Churches initiated the Delta Ministry, a long-term program of community development for the poor in Mississippi. In part this program was intended to demonstrate that the churches were committed over the long haul to the betterment of those most deeply affected by racial prejudice and the poverty so closely intertwined. Now we must turn and examine that project in detail.

Notes

1. Minutes, Commission on Religion and Race, NCC, June 28, 1963, p. 2, folder 2; "Report of the Executive Director of the Commission on Religion and Race of the National Council of Churches," July 26, 1963, p. 4, folder 4; both items in box 15, Victor Reuther Papers.

2. "Report of the Executive Director," Commission on Religion and Race, NCC, September 5, 1963, p. 11; "Some Guidelines for the Future of the Commission on Religion and Race of the National Council of Churches," September 23, 1963; both items in RG 11, box 6, folder 20, NCC Archives.

3. Robert Spike, "Devotions," Exhibit A attached to Minutes, Commission on Religion and Race, October 22, 1963, RG 11, box 6, folder 20, NCC Archives.

4. Ibid., p. 2; "Some Guidelines for the Future of the Commission on Religion and Race of the National Council of Churches," September 23, 1963, p. 1, ibid.

5. "Report of the Executive Director to the Commission on Religion and Race of the National Council of Churches," July 26, 1963, pp. 1–4, folder 4; Minutes, Commission on Religion and Race, NCC, October 22, 1963, pp. 3–5, folder 8; both items in box 15, Victor Reuther Papers.

6. In July 1963, Spike visited Savannah himself, guided through the maze of the conflict there by his good friend Andrew Young. It was an eye-opening and bone-chilling experience for Spike. For the first time he became directly involved in the deeply threatening atmosphere of violence and intimidation that southern blacks faced regularly, now intensified by demonstrations, mass arrests, and the use of tear gas by the police. In his report on the experience to the commission two weeks later, he said it felt like being "in the catacombs of Rome in the first century, or in the Warsaw ghetto twenty-five years ago, or in Sharpsville, South Africa, not so very long ago." But, instead "it was really happening in my own, own land, not more than two miles from the home of white friends where I have spent many pleasant and serene times. [The latter] seemed a million miles away."

He was, he said, "a visitor in Hell." "Report of the Executive Director to the Commission on Religion and Race of the National Council of Churches," July 26, 1963, pp. 1–2, folder 4, box 15, ibid.

7. These comments are based on the citation of material in folder 8 in note 5.

8. "Community Action," Exhibit B, attached to Minutes, Commission on Religion and Race, NCC, October 22, 1963; "Report of the Executive Director," Commission on Religion and Race, NCC, September 5, 1963, p. 4; both items in RG 11, box 6, folder 20, NCC Archives.

9. Minutes, Commission on Religion and Race, NCC, June 28, 1963, pp. 4–5, folder 2; "Report of the Executive Director to the Commission on Religion and Race of the National Council of Churches," July 26, 1963, p. 5, folder 4; Minutes, Commission on Religion and Race, NCC, October 22, 1963, pp. 7–8, folder 8; Minutes, Commission on Religion and Race, NCC, January 16, 1964, p. 3, folder 9; Minutes, Commission on Religion and Race, NCC, February 21, 1964, pp. 4–5, folder 12; all items in box 15, Victor Reuther Papers.

10. Concerning the Citizen's Councils, see Neil McMillen, *The Citizens' Council: Organized Resistance to the Second Reconstruction, 1954–64* (Urbana, University of Illinois Press, 1971). Detailed analysis of events in Mississippi in the early sixties is in Taylor Branch, *Parting the Waters: America in the King Years, 1954–1963* (New York, Simon and Schuster, 1988), chaps. 12, 13, 17, 19; Carson, *In Struggle,* chaps., 3, 4, 6; and in Neil McMillen's excellent "Black Enfranchisement in Mississippi: Federal Enforcement and Black Protest in the 1960s," *The Journal of Southern History,* XLIII (August 1977), pp. 351–372.

11. Spike, *Civil Rights Involvement,* p. 10.

12. Ibid.

13. Ibid., p. 10, "Report of the Executive Director to the Commission on Religion and Race of the National Council of Churches," July 26, 1963, pp. 7–8, folder 4, box 15; Minutes, Commission on Religion and Race, NCC, October 22, 1963, p. 5, folder 8, box 15; ibid., both items in Victor Reuther Papers; "Summary Report on Visit to Clarksdale, Mississippi by the Special Delegation Appointed by the Commission on Religion and Race, National Council of Churches," July 6–9, 1963; "Chronological Report by Robert Dobbs . . ."; Ray Gibbons, "Commitment in Clarksdale," August 14, 1963, W. S. Kincade to A. Dudley Ward, July 8, 1963; items in folder entitled "Clarksdale," John M. (Jack) Pratt Papers, in possession of author.

14. "Report of the Executive Director, National Council of Churches, Commission on Religion and Race," September 5, 1963, pp. 2–3, RG 11, box 6, folder 20, NCC Archives.

15. John M. Pratt, "Report on the Release of 57 Prisoners in Mississippi," August 23, 1963; Pratt to "Representatives of Denominational Religion and Race Staffs," October 21, 1963; both items in folder entitled "Prisoner Release," Pratt Papers; minutes, Commission on Religion and Race, NCC, October 22, 1963, pp. 6–7, folder 8, box 15, Victor Reuther Papers. Later Pratt and the commission intervened directly in court cases on behalf of black Mississippians arrested unfairly for civil rights activities, and in general remained very active in the Mississippi courts at least until mid-1964, when secular national legal organizations took over and expanded the legal services provided by the churches. Pratt, "Report on Legal Procedures and Bail," February 20, 1964, attached to "Agenda," Commission on Religion and Race, meeting of February 21, 1964, folder 9, box 15, Victor Reuther Papers.

16. Pratt, "Statement to General Assembly of the Council of Churches of Southern California-Nevada," January 26, 1966, pp. 4–5, in folder entitled "Writings," Pratt Papers.

17. Robert Spike to William Mahoney, July 17, 1963, folder 25, box 115, SNCC Papers; Minutes, Commission on Religion and Race, NCC, October 22, 1963, pp. 1–2, 3–4, folder 8, box 15, Victor Reuther Papers; Carson, *In Struggle,* p. 90; "Report of the Executive Director," Commission on Religion and Race, September 5, 1963, p. 3, RG 11, box 6, folder 20, NCC Archives; John M. Pratt, "Report on the Release of 57 Prisoners in Mississippi," August 23, 1963, p. 1, in folder entitled "Prisoner Release," Pratt Papers.

18. Carson, *In Struggle,* pp. 77–82, 96–101; Doug McAdam, *Freedom Summer* (New York, Oxford University Press, 1988), pp. 36–38, 40.

19. Spike, *Civil Rights Involvement,* p. 13.

20. Leon Litwack, *Been in the Storm So Long: The Aftermath of Slavery* (New York, Vintage, 1980), chap. 9; James McPherson, *The Abolitionist Legacy: From Reconstruction to the NAACP* (Princeton, Princeton University Press, 1975), chaps. 9–12; Jacqueline Jones, *Soldiers of Light and Love: Northern Teachers and Georgia Blacks, 1865–1873* (Chapel Hill, University of North Carolina Press, 1980).

21. "Report of the Executive Director to the Commission on Religion and Race of the National Council of Churches," July 26, 1963, folder 4, box 15, Victor Reuther Papers.

22. Spike, *Civil Rights Involvement,* p. 16.

23. "Report of the Executive Director," Commission on Religion and Race, NCC, September 5, 1963, p. 9, RG 11, box 6, folder 20, NCC Archives.

24. *Hattiesburg American,* January 20, p. 1; January 22, pp. 1, 2; January 23, pp. 1, 6; January 25, p. 2; February 4, pp. 1, 2, 3; February 13, p. 8; February 22, p. 2, February 24, 1964, p. 10; Robert Stone, "Interim Report: Clergy Participation with Council of Federated Organizations, Hattiesburg, Mississippi," February 29, 1963; Frank Heinz, press release, "Freedom Day in Hattiesburg, Mississippi" (n.d.); both items in RG 61, box 1, folder 11, UPCUSA-CORAR Papers; Minutes, Commission on Religion and Race, NCC, February 21, 1964, p. 6, folder 12, box 15, Victor Reuther Papers; telephone interview with Robert Moses, January 27, 1989; typescript of interview with Moses, p. 20, folder 2, box 2, Anne C. Romaine Papers, Martin Luther King Center; "Ministers in Hattiesburg, Mississippi, January–May, 1964," folder 30, box 2; "Ministers' Project Orientation," undated memo, folder 2, box 21; both items in Delta Ministry Papers, Atlanta.

25. Interview with Robert Stone, January 22, 1989; interview with Lawrence Guyot, June 13, 1988; Gayraud Wilmore to Eugene Carson Blake, May 4, 1964, RG 95, folder 18, box 15, Blake Papers; Robert Stone, "A Brief Review of Recent Developments in the Commission on Religion and Race's Mississippi Program," April 22, 1964, folder 11; Minutes, Executive Committee, Commission on Religion and Race, UPCUSA, March 2, 1964, folder 4; both items in RG 61, box 1, UPCUSA-CORAR Papers. Spike, "Report to the Commission on Religion and Race," February 21, 1964, pp. 3–4, Arthur C. Thomas, "Report to the Commission on Canton, Mississippi" (n.d.), attached to "Report"; both items in folder 9, box 15, Victor Reuther Papers; "Participants in Canton, Mississippi Voter Registration Project, February–May, 1964, folder 30, box 2; "Participants in Greenwood, Mississippi Freedom Days," folder 18, box 15; both items in Delta Minis-

try Papers, Atlanta; Wilmore, "Black Presbyterians and Their Allies," in Coalter, Mulder, and Weeks, *The Presbyterian Predicament,* p. 124.

26. Concern about ministerial abandonment of vulnerable local citizens in Hattiesburg was voiced explicitly in unsigned memo, "To Whom It May Concern," postscript dated March 12, 1964, RG 95, folder 17, box 18, Blake Papers.

27. Robert Beech to Jon [Regier], March 14, 1969, and attached "Resume," dated February 1969, folder 21, box 21, Delta Ministry Papers, Atlanta; interview with Robert Beech, October 13, 1989.

28. On cooperation between the UPCUSA commission and NCC commission, see Minutes, Commission on Religion and Race, UPCUSA, August 2, 1963, RG 61, box 1, folder 3, UPCUSA-CORAR Papers; Gayraud Wilmore to Robert Spike, March 5, 1964, RG 95, folder 17, box 18, Blake Papers; Minutes, Commission on Religion and Race, NCC, February 21, 1964, p. 6, folder 12, box 15, Victor Reuther Papers. On early Presbyterian connections with SNCC, see Gayraud Wilmore to James Forman, October 29, 1963; Forman to Wilmore, November 19, 1963, folder 373, box 22, SNCC Papers; Minutes, Commission on Religion and Race, UPCUSA, December 18, 1963, folder 3; January 8–9, 1964, folder 4; both items in RG 61, box 1, UPCUSA-CORAR Papers. On Blake's influence, see pp. 6, 9, Minutes, January 8–9, 1964, folder 4; "Communication from Executive Secretary," February 25, 1964, folder 17; both items in RG 61, box 1, UPCUSA-CORAR Papers; interview with Lawrence Guyot, June 13, 1988.

29. Carson, *In Struggle,* chap. 8; McAdam, *Freedom Summer,* pp. 28–34; Howard Zinn, *SNCC: The New Abolitionists* (Boston, Beacon Press, 1964), pp. 186–189; Henry McCanna to David Hunter [memo on "Mississippi Contacts"], November 20, 1964, RG 5, box 16, folder 9, NCC Archives.

30. Minutes, Commission on Religion and Race, NCC, January 16, 1964, p. 6, folder 9, box 15, Victor Reuther Papers.

31. Minutes, Commission on Religion and Race, NCC, February 21, 1964, p. 10, folder 12, ibid.; "Objectives of the Commission on Religion and Race of the National Council of Churches," p. 3, attached to Robert Spike to Commission on Religion and Race, NCC, March 23, 1964, folder 10, ibid.; Minutes, Commission on Religion and Race, NCC, March 26, 1964, p. 3, ibid.

32. Press release, NCC, April 1, 1964, folder 125, box 115, SNCC Papers; Elizabeth S. Peck and Emily Ann Smith, *Berea's First 125 Years* (Lexington, University Press of Kentucky, 1982), especially chaps. 1–3.

33. Minutes, Board of Trustees, Berea College, April 24, 1964, pp. 13–14; "Report of the President," p. 3, attached to April 24, 1964, minutes; both items in Special Collections, Hutchins Library, Berea College; telegram, Spike to T. J. Wood [chair of Berea's Board of Trustees], April 24, 1964, in folder entitled "Correspondence, NCC-CORR," Washington office, NCC; Minutes, Commission on Religion and Race, NCC, May 12, 1964, p. 4, folder 11, box 15, Victor Reuther Papers.

34. From its beginnings in the mid-nineteenth century, Western College for Women was closely associated with the Presbyterians, although not officially connected to any single Presbyterian denomination. Herrick Young, for example, the president of the college in 1964, had been a Presbyterian teacher-missionary for many years in Iran and executive secretary of the Presbyterian Church, USA's Board of Foreign Missions. Narka Nelson, *Western College for Women* (Oxford, Ohio, Western College, 1967), pp. 236–241, 279. The arrange-

ments made with the National Council of Churches are documented in Herrick Young to author, May 25, 1985; telephone interview with Margaret Flory, May 11, 1987.

35. Minutes, Commission on Religion and Race, NCC, March 26, 1964, p. 4, folder 10, box 15, Victor Reuther Papers; "A Statement on the Mississippi Summer Program of the Commission on Religion and Race, National Council of Churches," folder 125, box 115, SNCC Papers.

36. Interviews with Bruce Hanson, July 26, 1985, November 23, 1990; interview with Matthew Miles, October 9, 1990; telephone interview with David Johnson, October 15, 1990; John O'Neal and Lois Chaffee to Myles Horton, March 9, 1964; "Participants . . . COFO Curriculum Conference," attached to O'Neal and Chaffee to Horton, March 14, 1964; both items in folder 6, box 41, Highlander Center Papers, Wisconsin State Historical Society, Madison; Bruce Hanson to CORR Staff, Henry McKenna, John [*sic*] Regier, April 20, 1964, RG 6, box 48, folder 2, NCC Archives.

37. During conversations twenty-five years later, the powerful impact of the SNCC people still loomed large in the minds of the Columbia academics who had worked with them. Interview with Matthew Miles, October 9, 1990; telephone interview with David Johnson, October 15, 1990.

38. An important description and analysis of the summer of 1964, both in Ohio and in Mississippi, is in McAdam, *Freedom Summer*. But see also Carson, *In Struggle*, chaps. 8, 9; Seth Cagin and Philip Dray, *We Are Not Afraid: the Story of Goodman, Schwerner, and Chaney and the Civil Rights Campaign for Mississippi* (New York, Macmillan, 1988); Sally Belfrage, *Freedom Summer* (Charlottesville, University Press of Virginia, 1990); Elizabeth Sutherland, ed., *Letters from Mississippi* (New York, McGraw-Hill, 1965); and Daniel Perlstein, "Teaching Freedom: SNCC and the Creation of the Mississippi Freedom Schools," *History of Education Quarterly* (Fall 1990), pp. 297–324.

39. Len Holt, "The Making of a Mississippi Rights Volunteer," clipping from the *National Guardian*, June 21, 1964, in folder entitled "COFO—Council of Federated Organizations," box 1, Charles Horwitz Papers, Tougaloo College Archives, Jackson, Mississippi; Anne Braden, "Those Who Were Not There: The Cold War Against the Civil Rights Movement," *Fellowship*, June 1990, pp. 9–11. On the work of the Southern Conference Educational Fund, see Linda Reed, *Simple Decency and Common Sense: The Southern Conference Movement, 1938–1963* (Bloomington, Ind., Indiana University Press, 1991), chap. 8.

40. There were important differences among the staff of the Commission on Religion and Race regarding radical groups like the National Lawyer's Guild. Jack Pratt was consistently the most outspoken in public condemnation of the guild. Robert Spike, more influential than Pratt, also harbored considerable suspicions of the guild, but was more circumspect publicly and perhaps more pragmatic in regard to Mississippi. For example, at a commission meeting in June 1964, Spike described the guild as a group with "far left connections" and stated that the commission staff had "taken a position that it would not work with the Lawyer's Guild" in Mississippi. In the same breath, however, Spike acknowledged that the commission "has worked with individual members of the Guild." Arthur Thomas, the commission's staff person in Mississippi throughout the summer of 1964, seemed much closer in his attitudes to the pragmatic position maintained by the SNCC people. Minutes, Commission on Religion and Race, NCC, June 29, 1964, p. 8, RG 6, box 47, folder 30, NCC Archives; "Rough

Minutes of a Meeting Called by the National Council of Churches to Discuss the Mississippi Project," September 18, 1964, folder 125, box 115, SNCC Papers.

41. Braden, "Those Who Were Not There," pp. 9–10; Zinn, *SNCC,* pp. 236–238; Emily Stoper, *The Student Nonviolent Coordinating Committee: The Growth of Radicalism in a Civil Rights Organization* (Brooklyn, Carlson Publishing Company, 1989), pp. 56–58.

42. National leaders of the NAACP and CORE as well as the mainline churches were bothered by the willingness of SNCC to allow the National Lawyers' Guild to participate in the summer program in Mississippi. Kenneth O'Reilly, *"Racial Matters:" The FBI's Secret File on Black America, 1960–1972* (New York, Free Press, 1989), pp. 181–182. For the students' response to Pratt at Oxford, see Holt, "The Making of a Mississippi Rights Volunteer," p. 2. Much later Pratt concluded that his opposition to the National Lawyer's Guild at the orientation sessions and elsewhere, urging "blacks and his own people not to use Lawyers' Guild lawyers," was a "moral decision" he now "regretted." Interview with Pratt, June 16, 1985.

43. R. H. Edwin Espy, to William C. Sullivan, July 16, 1964, and attached list of "Participants in Orientation Project," with covering memo, Robert Spike to "Denominational Commissions on Religion and Race," July 9, 1964, RG 4, box 31, folder 23, NCC Archives. It is likely Espy checked with Spike, and perhaps other NCC officials, before giving Sullivan the list since Spike had designated the document "Confidential" before releasing it within church circles. There is no evidence that the staff people of the Commission on Religion and Race working closest with COFO in Mississippi ever knew about Espy's actions. For similar actions by CORE officials with the FBI, see O'Reilly, *"Racial Matters,"* p. 182.

44. R. H. Edwin Espy to William Sullivan, January 31, 1962, February 15, February 23, August 6, 1962; Sullivan to Espy, February 6, February 19, July 24, 1962; items in RG 4, box 28, folder 29; Espy to Sullivan, April 16, 1964, RG 4, box 32, folder 8; all of the above in NCC Archives.

45. Espy to Sullivan, December 16, 1964, ibid.

46. Throughout the 1960s Hoover received a steady stream of inquiries from church people—individuals and local church officials—asking about the ideological purity, or lack thereof, of the National Council of Churches. In his replies, Hoover almost always stated that there was no evidence that the council had ever engaged in subversive activities. But a statement to *individuals* was a far cry from the public endorsement Espy sought in 1964. The preceding comments are based on the 2,658 pages of documents in FBI files regarding the National Council of Churches, covering the years 1962–69, which were released to me as a result of FOIA request #265,732.

47. O'Reilly, *"Racial Matters,"* p. 178. On sharing of information between national and local officials, see Arthur Thomas FBI file, #52–84534, FOIA request #272,969, especially memo, Jackson (52-NEW) to Director, January 31, 1966; Director, FBI to SAC, Jackson, February 3, 1966; and Jackson (52-NEW) to Director, February 1, 1966 (teletype). Sovereignty Commission surveillance of racially related activities in Mississippi between 1963 and 1967 is amply documented in two boxes of folders under the title, "Mississippi Sovereignty Commission," Paul Johnson Papers, University of Southern Mississippi, Hattiesburg. Evidence of sharing of information about the summer workers between the Justice Department and the Sovereignty Commission is in Burke Marshall to Dan H. Shell, July 16, and attachment entitled "Mississippi Summer Project: Workers

in State as of June 29, 1964," in folder entitled "Sovereignty Commission: July, 1964," Paul Johnson Papers.

48. William Sullivan to R. H. Edwin Espy, November 20, 1964, and attached newspaper clipping, RG 4, box 32, folder 8, NCC Archives. The fullest account of J. Edgar Hoover's vendetta against Martin Luther King, Jr., is in David Garrow, *The FBI and Martin Luther King: From "SOLO" to Memphis* (New York, Norton, 1981).

49. Telephone interview with Bruce Hanson, November 23, 1990.

50. "Exhibit D" [memo, Bruce Hanson, Arthur Thomas to National Staff for Campus Christian Life], April 1964, attached to Minutes, Commission on Religion and Race, NCC, May 12, 1964, folder 11, box 15, Victor Reuther Papers.

51. Information bulletin entitled "The Medical Committee for Human Rights" and attached "Medical Committee for Human Rights: Cash Analysis from: July 1, 1964 to Dec. 31, 1964," folder 5, box 12, Delta Ministry Papers, Atlanta: "History of SNCC and Summer of '64 Program," mimeographed booklet, folder 61, box 112, SNCC Papers.

The Medical Committee for Human Rights began in July 1964 as a volunteer organization of doctors, nurses, dentists, psychologists, and social workers who came to Mississippi to provide emergency medical aid for student workers who were physically attacked, to arrange for local medical care for sick or injured summer volunteers, and to help the local black community meet major unfilled health needs. In 1964 the mainline churches paid for about 5 percent of the Medical Committee's budget.

52. Rev. Arthur C. Thomas, "Report of the Associate Director of Community Action," p. 2, attached to "Agenda," Meeting of the Commission on Religion and Race, NCC, June 29, 1964, folder 13, box 15, SNCC Papers.

53. A nearly complete list of those who went to Mississippi, arranged by denominations, is in "Ministers, Adult Laymen Recruited by National Council of Churches for Work in Mississippi Summer Project, June 15 to Sept. 1, 1964," attached to Arthur C. Thomas to Denominational Representatives (n.d.), in miscellaneous materials, box 3, Arthur C. Thomas Papers, Martin Luther King Center. There are two principal sources for the reconstruction of the activities of the minister-counselors in Mississippi. First, the commission staff asked each participant to submit a written evaluation of their experience to Warren McKenna shortly after returning home. The papers of Robert Beech, now living in Bovey, Minnesota, contain over thirty of these evaluations. Rev. Beech graciously allowed me to use these materials. Second, utilizing current yearbooks and other sources of the five denominations providing the largest number of minister-volunteers for the project (Episcopal; United Church of Christ; United Presbyterian Church, U.S.A.; Disciples of Christ; United Methodist), I matched current addresses with the names of 123 of the participants. I then wrote those people, provided a brief questionnaire to jog their memories, and asked them to reply. Eighty of them did, often with detailed and thought-provoking reflections. A summary of their comments is in James Findlay, "In Keeping With the Prophets: The Mississippi Summer of 1964," *Christian Century*, June 8–15, 1988, pp. 574–576.

54. Recruitment of Roman Catholics was severely hampered by the public opposition to the project of the Catholic bishop of Mississippi. Irene Tinker Walker, "Letter from Canton, Mississippi," p. 2, in folder entitled "Mississippi, 1964," Paul Moore Papers, Cathedral of St. John the Divine, New York City.

55. List of "Ministers, Adult Laymen Recruited by National Council of Churches . . . ," miscellaneous materials, box 3, Thomas Papers; Mary Lou Pettit to Warren McKenna, August 11, 1964, in folder entitled "Delta Ministry Reports, 1964," box 3, Robert Beech Papers, Bovey, Minnesota. At least two of the husband-wife teams came as parents to join their children, who were already there as student volunteers. Walker, "Letter From Canton, Mississippi," p. 2, Moore Papers.

56. Phillip M. Kelsey to James Findlay (nd.); John C. Raines to Findlay, July 28, 1986; Kring Allen to Findlay, August 5, 1986; Eugene Bogen to Findlay, July 30, 1986. See also John Baumgartner to Findlay, July 25, 1986.

57. Rims Barber to Findlay (n.d.); John Baumgartner to Findlay, July 25, 1986; Henry Bird to Findlay (n.d.); Burke E. Dorworth to Findlay, July 18, 1986; John Else to Findlay, September 3, 1986; Charles Harper to Findlay, August 21, 1986; Howard McClintock to Findlay (n.d.); John Raines to Findlay, July 28, 1986.

58. Harvey Beach to Findlay (n.d.). See also Kring Allen to Findlay, August 5, 1986; Russell Bennett to Findlay, July 30, 1986; Burke A. Dorworth to Findlay, July 18, 1986; John D. Fischer to Findlay (n.d.); Donald R. Fletcher to Findlay, September 19, 1986; G. F. Gilmore to Findlay, August 2, 1986; Henry Little to Findlay, August 1, 1986. One minister vividly recalled an earlier moment as a farmworker of "not having any control over my own destiny" if "any protest of working conditions were made." That produced "a longstanding bias against discrimination of any kind," a key motivation for going to Mississippi. Donald Paton to Findlay, July 31, 1986.

59. John Baumgartner to Findlay, July 25, 1986; Russell Bennett to Findlay, July 30, 1986. Another participant noted that if one believed, as he did, that "the civil rights movement was one in which God was clearly at work," then "the analogy with the Exodus was very powerful." George McClain to Findlay (n.d.). See also Carl Cooper to Findlay, July 23, 1986; Burke E. Dorworth to Findlay, July 18, 1986; Elliott F. Gauffreau to Findlay, July 28, 1986; David C. Hall to Findlay, October 13, 1986; Charles Harper to Findlay, August 21, 1986; Everett McNair to Findlay, July 25, 1986; Edward N. McNulty to Findlay, July 21, 1986; Eugene Monick to Findlay, January 30, 1987; Walter H. Rice to Findlay, September 27, 1986.

60. Walker, "Letter from Canton, Mississippi," p. 5, Moore Papers.

61. Mabel Metze to Findlay, September 19, 1986. Another participant remembered that when the call came a year later for people to march at Selma, "I very reluctantly declined to go. I could not face the danger and the fear again. My experience left me feeling like I had been in a war zone." Arden Clute to Findlay, July 27, 1986. See also Henry Bird to Findlay (n.d.); Russell Bennett to Findlay, July 30, 1986; John Baumgartner to Findlay, July 25, 1986; Elliott Gauffreau to Findlay, July 28, 1986; Robert C. Gregg to Findlay, July 27, 1986; George Phelps to Findlay, August 10, 1986; James F. Quimby to Findlay, August 6, 1986; Donald Paton to Findlay, July 31, 1986.

62. Timothy Shaw, "Greenwood-Atlanta Report," July 18, 1964, anonymous report on work at Holly Springs, Mississippi, both items in folder entitled "Reports and Reactions"; Barbara Woodard, "Mission to Mississippi," "Rabbi Rav A. Soloff Arrested in Mississippi," both in folder entitled "Delta Ministry Reports, 1964"; all items in box 3, Beech Papers.

63. Edward Setchko to Findlay, August 2, 1986.

64. Kring Allen to Findlay, August 5, 1986.

65. Walker, "Letter from Canton, Mississippi," p. 10, Moore Papers; Kathleen Henderson, "Mississippi, August 2–10, 1964," in folder entitled "Reports and Reactions," box 3, Beech Papers.

66. Donald G. Gall to Warren McKenna, August 22, 1964, in folder entitled "Delta Ministry Reports, 1964," box 3, Beech Papers.

67. Everett W. MacNair, Mrs. MacNair to Warren McKenna, August 19, 1964, folder 1, box 15, Delta Ministry Papers, Atlanta. See also anonymous [report from Holly Springs], in folder entitled "Reports and Rections," box 3, Beech Papers; John R. Warner, Jr., to Warren McKenna, August 18, 1964; William Brison to McKenna, August 18, 1964; Robert F. Klepper to McKenna, September 2, 1964; Barbara Woodard, "Mission to Mississippi," August 11, 1964; all in folder entitled "Delta Ministry Reports, 1964," box 3, Beech Papers.

68. Donald A. Gall to Warren McKenna, August 22, 1964; John R. Warner, Jr., to McKenna, August 18, 1964; both items in folder entitled "Delta Ministry Reports, 1964," box 3, Beech Papers.

69. Anonymous [report of minister-counselor from Holly Springs], in folder entitled "Reports and Reactions," ibid.; Kring Allen to James Findlay, August 5, 1986. See also Henry Bird, "Minister-Counselor Report to NCC Office . . . July 21–31, Shaw-Cleveland-Mound Bayou Projects," folder entitled "Delta Ministry Reports, 1964," box 3, Beech Papers; David Hall to Findlay, October 13, 1986. One of the few African American minister-counselors got caught with others in the COFO headquarters in Philadelphia, Mississippi, in August 1964 when it was under siege by a mob shortly after the bodies of Chaney, Goodman, and Schwerner were discovered nearby. At the urging of his companions, the Episcopalian offered thoughts on the resurrection to calm those (including a young Jewish rabbi and the openly skeptical COFO leader) evidently facing imminent death. Interview with Robert Hood, April 7, 1990.

70. The original plan was to circulate the ministers in the white community much more fully than finally happened. In April 1964, the Commission on Religion and Race envisioned "white community teams" that were to be groups equal in importance to the "minister-counsellors." These people were to live "openly in selected white communities" in Mississippi and were to serve as "agents of reconciliation, and to attempt to understand and speak to the pain which comes . . . to segments of the white communities . . . [in] a time of dislocation and all-too-rapid change." Southern ministers "committed to the cause of equal justice to all" were especially to be sought out for this work. Clearly this proposal misjudged the public temper in Mississippi and had to be scaled back. NCC, Commission on Religion and Race to Presidents, Deans and Religious Advisors of Colleges, Universities and Seminaries, April 16, 1964, attached as "Exhibit E" to Minutes, Commission on Religion and Race, NCC, May 12, 1964, folder 11, box 15, Victor Reuther Papers.

71. Henry Bird, "Minister-Counselor Report to NCC Office, Jackson—for period July 21–31," in folder entitled "Delta Ministry Reports, 1964," box 3, Beech Papers. See also Arden Clute to Warren McKenna, September 10, 1964; "Report to Warren McKenna from George H. Phelps," July 23, 1964, p. 2; Carroll Lemon to Warren McKenna, August 14, 1964; Bill Brison to Warren McKenna, August 18, 1964; Lloyd B. Stauffer to Mr. Schoeder, September 1, 1964; Dick Williams, "Mississippi Minister's Project—Evaluation, August 3–17"; all items in Delta Ministry Reports, 1964 folder, box 3, Beech Papers.

72. Donald McCord to James Findlay, July 25, 1986; John F. Else to Findlay, September 3, 1986.

73. Walker, "Letter from Canton, Mississippi," Moore Papers; David Hall to Findlay, October 13, 1986; Rims Barber to Findlay (n.d.).

74. The quotation is in Everett W. MacNair, Mrs. MacNair to Warren McKenna, August 19, 1964, folder 1, box 15, Delta Ministry Papers, Atlanta. One cleric stated that "my memory [of Mississippi] is doused in music." William M. Weber to Findlay, August 22, 1986. See also James H. Corson to Findlay (n.d.); William M. Moreman to Findlay, October 10, 1986.

75. Walker, "Letter from Canton, Mississippi," p. 11, Moore Papers; for another description of the same woman, see Mabel Metze to Findlay, September 19, 1986. Another clergyman-visitor caught well what he admired about people like this southern black woman: "a combination of inner toughness and outer gentleness." Elliott Gauffreau to Findlay, July 28, 1986.

76. James F. Quimby to Findlay, August 6, 1986; Donald Paton to Findlay, July 31, 1986; Anthony C. Thurston to Findlay, August 1, 1986.

77. Interview with Rims Barber, July 21, 1986.

78. One of the participants mused later that "practically speaking we accomplished little beyond a ministry of presence, both with the students and as a visible testimony to Hattiesburg folks. But that was our greatest strength." Jack W. Wilson to Findlay (n.d.). See also Arden Clute to McKenna, September 10, 1964; "Grace" to "Dear Henry" (n.d.), attached to Henry L. Bird, "Minister-Counselor Report to NCC Office . . . July 21–31"; Irene Tinker Walker to McKenna, "Memo on the Role of Ministers in Mississippi," all items in folder entitled "Delta Ministry Reports, 1964," box 3, Beech Papers; Everett MacNair to McKenna, August 19, 1964, folder 1, box 15, Delta Ministry Papers, Atlanta; John Baumgartner to Findlay, July 25, 1986; Russell Bennett to Findlay, July 30, 1986; Donald R. Fletcher to Findlay, September 19, 1986.

79. For a detailed discussion of the long-term effects of the experience in Mississippi on the student volunteers, see McAdam, *Freedom Summer,* chaps. 4, 5, 6.

80. Arden Clute to Warren McKenna, September 10, 1964; George Robbins to Henry [Bird] (n.d.), attached to Bird, "Minister-Counselor Report to NCC Office . . . July 21–31"; Irene Tinker Walker to Warren McKenna, "Memo on the Role of Ministers in Mississippi"; all items in folder entitled "Delta Ministry Reports, 1964," box 3, Beech Papers; John Baumgartner to Findlay, July 25, 1986.

81. George McClain to Findlay (n.d.); Donald Gall to Findlay, July 30, 1986; John Raines to Findlay, July 28, 1986.

82. Rims Barber to Findlay (n.d.). See also Roger Smith to Findlay, September 19, 1986.

83. On interracial ministries, see Kring Allen to Findlay, August 5, 1986; Henry Bird to Findlay (n.d.); G. F. Gilmore to Findlay, August 2, 1986; Mabel Metze to Findlay, September 19, 1986; William M. Moreman to Findlay (n.d.); William M. Weber to Findlay, August 22, 1986; David B. Weden to Findlay, August 4, 1986; Henry K. Yardon to Findlay, August 11, 1986. On denominational staff persons, see Burke E. Dorworth to Findlay, July 18, 1986; John D. Fischer to Findlay (n.d.); Charles H. Harper to Findlay, August 21, 1986; George McClain to Findlay (n.d.); George E. Owen to Findlay, July 26, 1986; Anthony Thurston to Findlay, August 1, 1986.

84. Donald R. Fletcher to Findlay, September 19, 1986; Arden Clute to Findlay, July 27, 1986; John F. Else to Findlay, September 3, 1986; Robert Gregg to Findlay, July 27, 1986; David C. Hall to Findlay, October 13, 1986; Everett MacNair to Findlay, July 25, 1986; Charles Millar to Findlay (n.d.); John C. Raines to Findlay, July 28, 1986; Edward Setcko to Findlay, August 2, 1986; John R. Warner, Jr. to Findlay, July 30, 1986. Some were affected personally. The daughter of one minister, also in Mississippi as a volunteer, married a Howard University graduate and integrated her immediate family. Another adopted two mixed-race children, in addition to three natural offspring. Kathleen Henderson to Findlay (n.d.); Henry Bird to Findlay (n.d.).

85. Walker, "Letter from Canton, Mississippi," p. 3, Moore Papers; Donald Gall to McKenna, August 22, 1964; George H. Phelps, "Report to Warren McKenna . . . ,' July 23, 1964, p. 2; Arthur D. Wilmost to McKenna, August 23, 1964; John R. Warner, Jr., to McKenna, August 18, 1964; Caroll Lemon to McKenna, August 14, 1986; Henry Bird, "Minister-Counselor Report to NCC Office, Jackson . . . July 21–31," p. 1; Frazer A. Thomason to McKenna, August 26, 1964; items in folder entitled "Delta Ministry Reports, 1964," box 3, Beech Papers.

86. Walker, "Letter from Canton, Mississippi," p. 5, Moore Papers; Henry L. Bird, "Minister-Counselor Report to NCC Office . . . July 21–31," in folder entitled "Delta Ministry Reports, 1964," box 3, Beech Papers.

87. Walker, "Letter from Canton, Mississippi," p. 2, Moore Papers; Barbara Woodard, "Mission to Mississippi," p. 2, in folder entitled "Delta Ministry Reports, 1964," box 3, Beech Papers.

88. John R. Warner, Jr., to Findlay, July 30, 1986; Walker, "Letter from Canton, Mississippi," p. 12, Moore Papers; Kring Allen to Findlay, August 5, 1986.

89. The Texas incident is recounted in Eugene Bogen to Findlay (n.d.). See also Bill Brison to McKenna, August 18, 1964; Lloyd B. Stauffer to Mr. Schoeder, September 1, 1964; both items in folder entitled "Delta Ministry Reports, 1964," box 3, Beech Papers. See also John R. Warner, Jr., to Findlay, July 30, 1986; Phillip M. Kelsey to Findlay (n.d.); Walter Hanson Rice to Findlay, September 27, 1986; Carl L. Cooper to Findlay, July 23, 1986. Cooper concealed his going "from my parents who lived in North Carolina where I had grown up. I knew they would have serious misgivings about my participation."

90. Carson, *In Struggle,* pp. 123–129, chaps. 10–14; August Meier and Elliott Rudwick, *CORE: A Study in the Civil Rights Movement* (New York, Oxford University Press, 1973), describe and analyze these developments in detail.

91. Spike, "Report of the Executive Director," p. 5, attached as "Exhibit A" to Minutes, Commission on Religion and Race, NCC, February 21, 1964, folder 12, box 15, Victor Reuther Papers.

92. John R. Warner, Jr., to Findlay, July 30, 1986. See also David C. Hall to Findlay, October 13, 1986. Richard F. King's important book, *Civil Rights and the Idea of Freedom* (New York, Oxford University Press, 1992), chaps. 2 and 3, describes similar personal experiences among the long-term participants in the movement, out of which emerged powerful communitarian and philosophical expressions of the idea of "freedom." See also Vincent Harding, "Community as a Liberating Theme in Civil Rights, History," pp. 17–29, in Armstead and Sullivan, *New Directions in Civil Rights Studies.*

4

"Servanthood" in Mississippi: The Delta Ministry, 1964–1966

On September 1, 1964, a small group of church people known as the Delta Ministry opened an office on the main street of Greenville, Mississippi. They had chosen Greenville as their headquarters in part because of its widespread reputation as the most open town in Mississippi regarding race relations. One of their first acts was to hire as staff secretary a local African American, Thelma Barnes. Passersby glimpsed Mrs. Barnes working at her new job. Soon the ministry received a "suggestion" either to move their new staff person to a back room or fire her. A prompt refusal resulted in an eviction notice. The Delta Ministry relocated its headquarters in the black section of Greenville, where it remained for almost a decade.[1] This incident announced in an ugly and rather grim manner the beginnings of an important, yet little-recognized civil rights organization of the sixties, revealed a bit about powerful and surprising mainline church commitments to racial change and equality, and suggested once again how all-pervasive racial prejudice was in Mississippi in the sixties, even in the most "liberal" community in the state.

As we have already seen, the Commission on Religion and Race of the National Council of Churches began to involve itself in the racial struggle in Mississippi almost from the time it came into existence on June 7, 1963. Beginning with the national church leaders who attended the funeral of Medgar Evers in Jackson in mid-June 1963, the commission steadily expanded its and the mainline churches' commitments to the difficult struggle to end segregation in Mississippi. The commission supported local African American demonstrators in Clarksdale and later in Hattiesburg, provided legal assistance and bail money to dozens of arrested demonstrators and civil rights workers, involved itself in the planning and implementation of the orientation sessions for the students going to Mississippi in the summer of 1964, and then provided a presence within the movement throughout that summer by means of "minister-counselors."

All of these activities required close cooperation with the civil rights groups in Mississippi—with Aaron Henry and the Mississippi chapter of the NAACP in Clarksdale and especially with the leaders of SNCC and CORE, as well as other civil rights people, who had joned together in the umbrella organization known as COFO to implement the programs that drew the northern churches directly into the black freedom struggle in the Deep South. In all of these activities the National Council people were distinctly junior partners, understanding quite properly that their role was to assist local people and COFO where it was deemed their expertise, their money, and their connections outside Mississippi could enhance efforts at voter registration and other programs already underway.

Within a few weeks after the formation of the commission, however, the staff began to think about and plan for a more permanent, long-range commitment of the churches in Mississippi. The brief, unhappy experience in Clarksdale in July and August of 1963, when the commission's efforts to mediate in an extremely tense situation were met with total rebuff, led to the first thoughts about some sort of long-term involvement. Later on Robert Spike pinpointed this intertwining of events and ideas. He recalled that "we came out of that experience [in Clarksdale] . . . feeling that this was the wrong way to do it," to enter a situation suddenly and to retreat just as suddenly, leaving both sides "to face the consequences of such disruption" from the outside. "As a result [of Clarksdale]," Spike noted, "we determined to establish as soon as possible a long-term Mississippi-based ministry that would work at the basic roots of the problem—focusing particularly in the Delta." Here was "the beginning of what we have come to call the Delta Ministry."[2]

In the months that followed these first thoughts about potential involvement on a long-term basis in Mississippi were sharpened, eventually to assume concrete form. In September 1963, the Commission on Religion and Race began to discuss more specifically their idea of a comprehensive program of community development "on the advice of people in the civil rights front" [probably COFO staff from Mississippi]. They mused in a rather grandiose and not always entirely realistic way about new "economic and social structures [that] have to be developed," of the need to "think through involvement with the federal government," and of the need to work at "manpower retraining" and "encouraging . . . industrialists to bring in the right kind of industry."[3] But at the same time the commission people had also begun to be a bit more understanding about the prospects of such a project in the Deep South and were realizing how difficult such a task would be. As usual, Bob Spike voiced the mood. The struggle in Mississippi and elsewhere would be

a fight to [the] finish—a showdown with some of the most deeply established hypocrisies of our common life. And since human beings are involved, there will be both resistance and hatred, weakness and treachery, on both sides. . . . There will be contending and struggle. There must also be thought and careful planning. . . . And the long, painful process of changing institutions and their habits (sometimes garbed as traditions) must be worked at with great skill and political ingenuity."[4]

Spike's words seemed almost to prefigure the subsequent history of the Delta Ministry and of the churches' involvement in Mississippi that we began to trace in the last chapter.

Certain people outside of Mississippi and even earlier national church commitments in the Magnolia State nudged the National Council toward its long-term involvement there. Until the middle of 1964 Andrew Young was director of the Southern Christian Leadership Conference's Citizenship Education Program, an effort to train African Americans all over the South in the rudiments of political participation as a prelude to voter registration. Young, an ordained minister of the United Church of Christ and a graduate of Hartford Seminary in Connecticut, had worked at the Interchurch Center in New York City on the staff of the Department of Youth Work of the National Council of Churches before returning south in 1961 to join the SCLC. Young's concern for voter education dovetailed closely with the voter registration efforts being mounted in Mississippi in 1964. For that reason and because he was a personal friend of most of the church leaders in New York, Young's ideas were listened to carefully. He had become very familiar with conditions in Mississippi and soon after the Commission on Religion and Race was established began to press his friends in New York about creating a "program of leadership training and area development for the Delta area."[5]

Ghosts from the recent past added their bit to whet the interests of the National Council. For over twenty years an experimental cooperative agricultural and interracial enterprise, known as Providence Farm, had flourished in Holmes County in the Delta area. Founded in the 1930s by friends of Reinhold Niebuhr and Sherwood Eddy, the rising racial tensions of the mid-1950s had resulted in powerful local white pressures for the "socialistic" experiment to end. Facing daily harassment by local law agents and many white citizens, and a strangling economic boycott, the farm was closed in 1956 and its assets sold. One of the founders and leaders of the experimental community, A. E. Cox, was then hired and remained thereafter in the employ of the National Council of Churches. These events were well known throughout national church circles and in 1963 and 1964 still served as a reminder of earlier efforts by visionary church people to grapple with the severe racial problems afflicting the Delta area of Mississippi.[6]

In the 1950s the National Council of Churches, through its Department of Town and Country, also maintained extensive contacts with African American pastors throughout the rural South. Beginning in 1945 the Federal Council of Churches and then after 1950 the National Council provided annually an extensive program of four- to six-day "institutes" for rural black ministers designed to upgrade their formal pastoral training. A number of these institutes were held in Mississippi, mostly at predominantly black colleges and academies. While not intimately connected to the later civil rights activities of the sixties, these earlier tentative attempts at interracial gatherings and national church involvement with local African American communities in the Deep South provided contacts and experiences in Mississippi that were a part of the historical "background" out of which the Delta Ministry ultimately emerged.[7]

By the end of 1963 National Council officials (including, significantly, the head of the Department of Town and Country as well as members of the Commission on Religion and Race) had held at least two "consultations" with appropriate people to consider in detail the idea that became the Delta Ministry. These meetings took place at Tougaloo College near Jackson, Mississippi, and at LeMoyne College in Memphis and included experts on southern rural life, representatives of COFO, and local citizens, mostly black but a few white, from the Delta area. Out of these discussions emerged sufficient agreement on goals and methods that on February 26, 1964, the General Board approved a detailed proposal, presented by the Division of Home Missions and the Commission on Religion and Race, concerning the project in Mississippi. This approval by the General Board constituted the formal authorization of the Delta Ministry.[8]

The National Council of Churches was drawn to Mississippi in part because of dramatic events and the influence of young civil rights activists. But the Magnolia State and the Delta area in particular were also a region possessing profound economic and social problems, perhaps worse than any other place in the nation, complicated by pervasive and unyielding racial prejudice. The people on the Commission on Religion and Race and their close associates were eager to help in trying to change that situation. Certain traditional missionary impulses of the churches seemed to be evident in these concerns, but in important ways the Delta Ministry offered an alternative model of the church's mission in the world. We shall return later to this last point.

The Delta, comprising the northwest and west-central portions of Mississippi and part of the vast floodplain formed over the centuries by the Mississippi River, stretched almost two hundred miles south from Memphis, Tennessee, to Vicksburg and was over sixty miles wide at its center. Blessed with fertile alluvial soil, the Delta had become the center of cotton production in the state after the Civil War. A source of great wealth for white landowners, it was also a place of appalling poverty for the blacks who tilled the land. Matters were worsening in the 1960s. Technological change, accelerating noticeably after 1950, was rendering the black laborers who "chopped" and then picked cotton on the plantations an economic anachronism. By 1960 the meagre livelihoods of hundreds of thousands of blacks were being eliminated by machinery in the fields, especially the mechanical cotton picker and "crop-dusters" that all but eliminated weed chopping and cotton harvesting by hand. The state of Mississippi was essentially uninterested in providing either job retraining or minimal welfare assistance for these people, fueled in part by fierce and deep-seated racial prejudice. One result was a large, continuing exodus of the youngest and most ambitious members of the African American community northward, a trend informally encouraged by the state. A more direct and immediate result was to allow unbelievable levels of poverty to exist in a land of unusual agricultural riches.[9]

Data compiled by the National Council of Churches in 1964 revealed something of the dire human needs throughout the Delta and made clear that racial prejudice deeply affected every aspect of the problems there. In all but two of the counties of the Delta, the death rate for whites was "higher than the state average" and with one exception, "higher still for non-whites." There were only fourteen accredited school systems in the Delta, "all of them white." The median income per person for nonwhites in the area was $456 annually. "An average 5% of the farms" controlled "50% of all farmland." By November 1964 special reports from the Mennonites, the Disciples of Christ, the Lutherans, and the Church of the Brethren substantiated these findings and more.[10]

The deep involvement of the mainline churches in Freedom Summer in Mississippi helps to explain why the Delta Ministry actually did not begin until September 1964, even though full authorization had been secured the preceding February.[11] Events at the end of the summer also made clear once again that Spike and his cohorts were not always in agreement with the COFO people and their supporters in Mississippi. In August 1964 the members of the commission were in Atlantic City at the Democratic National Convention attempting to work with the Mississippi Freedom Democratic party (the political arm of the movement in Mississippi) to unseat the all-white Mississippi delegation to the convention. Although the National Council people played a rather minor role (Spike was hospitalized just before the convention began after tripping over an obstacle on an Atlantic City street and injuring himself severely), eventually they supported the majority compromise, an arrangement hotly rejected by SNCC and the MFDP. Perhaps because the church people were only bit players in the overall drama and much of the time tried to mediate between the disputants, the anger of the defeated movement people toward President Johnson and his supporters was never focused to the same degree on Spike and his staff.[12] Nevertheless, the developments in Atlantic City unhappily reinforced whatever distrust had arisen out of the differences between the National Council and COFO that were revealed publicly at Oxford, Ohio, in the preceding June.

Quite apart from these frictions, movement people might well view the creation of the Delta Ministry as an invasion of their "turf" by a group from the white establishment, another good reason to be suspicious of, or even to oppose, the project. Such attitudes did exist, in several forms. Robert Moses recalled later that shortly after the Democratic convention, he, Spike, and others met in Atlanta to discuss how the National Council of Churches should proceed toward long-term involvement in Mississippi. Moses tried then to make it clear that SNCC and COFO were not trying to act as a controlling force regarding "who had access to the people." At the same time, never did the church group come directly to COFO gatherings and ask for advice. There was an element of insensitivity in all that, and it bothered Moses. The SNCC leader also recalled that James Forman, the national executive director, was more unfriendly to the National Council and its plans than he, especially after Atlantic City, when disillusionment and cynicism regarding the "establishment," including the church, grew very rapidly within movement circles. Moses also felt that COFO could have served as an "umbrella organization" under which the Delta Ministry operated. The churches wanted greater independence and thus chose not to follow this idea.[13] To Moses this was regrettable, but he did not try to block the churches, and soon the Delta Ministry began.

At this moment the movement was entering a very difficult time in its existence. The defeat of the MFDP at Atlantic City meant for many of their delegates and their supporters at home severe disillusionment with the national liberal political establishment and with whites generally. Calls for the ending of all alliances with whites and even total separation from the white community became stronger and more insistent within SNCC. Moreover, the cooperation between all civil rights groups in Mississippi that had existed for at least a year prior to Atlantic City began to disintegrate. Especially the old antagonisms that had existed between SNCC and the NAACP reasserted themselves. In part these were class frictions—between middle-class African American doctors, school-teachers, and small business people and the mass-based, poor, predominantly rural farm workers and inhabitants of small Delta communities who were the heart of SNCC's support. The NAACP strongly supported the compromise at Atlantic City and urged the MFDP to accept it. Following the convention, the state NAACP joined with young moderate Mississippi whites in the Democratic party on a number of issues to undermine the possibility of an independent black political movement that SNCC, CORE, and the MFDP had worked so hard to create. Thus with the support of the national Democratic party and powerful local white moderates, throughout the rest of the sixties the NAACP continued to flourish in Mississippi, while COFO quickly collapsed, SNCC soon after began to disintegrate both in the state and nationally, and the MFDP in the late sixties either disappeared or was absorbed into the Democratic party.[14]

Into this very fluid political situation the fledgling Delta Ministry entered. Although the ministry's relations with SNCC were never perfect, over time the church group remained more in sympathy with the aims of SNCC and the movement than with the more moderate NAACP and its white allies. The National Council of Churches' "servant-ministry" was with the poor—thus sympathy with movement purposes was natural and fairly consistent. And when the ministry began independently, not under SNCC's tutelege as Robert Moses had hoped, the personal restraint of Moses at the outset also helped. Another constructive move at the beginning was the final selection of Arthur Thomas as director. An ordained Methodist minister, with an additional graduate degree in economics from Duke, in 1960 Thomas had organized a small interracial church in Durham, North Carolina, the first in that city in the twentieth century. He had been interested in the labor movement in the fifties, then moved on to civil rights, a pattern followed by many liberal young people. Thus early on he participated in civil rights demonstrations in Durham and elsewhere in North Carolina.[15] Given these activities, Thomas eventually caught the eye of Robert Spike and his friends in New York City, and by October 1963, he had joined the staff of the Commission on Religion and Race as its field representative in the South.[16]

As the churches became ever more deeply involved in Mississippi, Thomas went frequently to that state—to Hattiesburg to support the ministers demonstrating there in the spring of 1964 and to Canton as early as February 1964, where a smaller group of outsiders supported a voter registration campaign by local blacks, which provoked white violence and, in return, an effective boycott of white merchants that made Canton a tinderbox of racial turmoil. Thomas learned quickly how to work effectively behind the scenes and developed many contacts among movement people. He was also very sympathetic with the aims of SNCC and CORE (Canton was in the one area of Mississippi where CORE workers were the principal representatives of the movement). During the summer of 1964 Thomas was the chief agent of the commission in Mississippi, traveling widely throughout the state, deepening his understanding of conditions there and making certain the minister-counselor program functioned properly. It is easy to see, therefore, both why he became the first director of the Delta Ministry and why people like Bob Moses had respect for him and knew they could work with him when the ministry came into existence in September 1964.[17]

The summer of 1964 in Mississippi also became the principal training ground for most of the early Delta Ministry staff. We have already noted that Warren McKenna, who became the assistant director of the ministry and second in command to Thomas, throughout the summer ran the one-day orientation sessions for minister-counselors in Jackson. McKenna first joined with Thomas at Oxford, Ohio, in June, went to Mississippi immediately thereafter, and did not leave the state for over two years.[18]

The summer activities provided Thomas and McKenna with an unusual opportunity—to select the staff for the ministry after almost every potential candidate had been in Mississippi for a brief period and experienced directly the difficulties and anxieties associated with life in the African American communities there. Those who responded most sensitively and successfully to the intense experiences of the summer were prime candidates for being asked to serve on the ministry staff. One, Robert Beech, had been in Hattiesburg since March 1964, first as a minister-picketer, then as the semi-permanent head of an office funded by the National Council of Churches. Two other early staff members, Harry Bowie and Rims Barber, participated in the summer program and worked in McComb and Canton, where severe unrest fully tested their mettle. Even the first chairperson of the executive board overseeing the ministry, Paul Moore, Episcopal Suffragan Bishop of Washington, D.C., spent considerable time during the summer in Mississippi, chiefly in Hattiesburg and McComb.[19] As the ministry began in September 1964, movement people knew that everyone in the little church group already had lived in the African American community, shared the fears and overt harassment constantly inflicted on its citizens, worked at voter registration and teaching projects, and been directed by SNCC and CORE workers in those projects. Thus in most instances the ministry staff did not have to "prove" themselves; that had already been done. That fact in turn created a rough sort of acceptance that was immensely important in facilitating the ministry's work at the outset.

Comparing the Delta Ministry's full-time program staff with the SNCC and CORE workers, one notes both similarities and differences. Ministry people were a bit older, mostly in their late twenties or early thirties, they were somewhat better educated (all with college or seminary degrees), but not necessarily better prepared to deal with the profound challenges in Mississippi. Time and experience in the Deep South had to be added. These people were near-perfect representatives of ecumenical, mainline Protestantism—Presbyterians, Methodists, Episcopalians, Baptists, Disciples of Christ, United Church of Christ—and eventually included even a Jewish layperson. Charles Horwitz worked first for COFO and SNCC and thus was able to note some important distinctions; the ministry always possessed more material resources (regular salaries, a small fleet of cars) and ultimately was easier to work for because it was never beset with deep internal tensions, as was SNCC. About half of the ministry staff were married, a higher percentage than in COFO, but only two or three of the outsiders brought their families with them. Unlike the SNCC workers, they were nearly all male. Women were hired, but only for secretarial jobs originally. Thelma Barnes's capabilities, though, were recognized quickly and she became a staff member. Women from outside Mississippi, both black and white, did participate, but primarily as volunteers or short-term workers.[20]

The wives who accompanied their minister husbands had a difficult time in Mississippi. Occupying the traditional female role of mother and minister's wife to an extremely busy husband, ignored, indeed harassed, by a normally sympathetic local white population, these women were thrown largely on their own resources, leading lonely and at times personally threatened lives. Virginia Hilton, the spouse of the public relations director of the ministry, Bruce Hilton, recalled later that at first she was also largely ignored by the mostly male ministry staff. She vividly remembered being "terribly isolated." Virginia survived at first by developing her creative talents as an artist in order to vent her fears, anger, and frustration. She was also a registered nurse. Encouraged by one of the ministry staff, she developed in cooperation with a volunteer woman doctor from California a small, informal public health clinic and "freedom school" in Winstonville, an all-black "plantation hamlet" a few miles outside Greenville. It was an immensely satisfying experience and fit well into the intentions of the ministry's overall program. Eventually Mrs. Hilton became the staff nurse for a later ministry project, Freedom City.[21] Because of appropriate professional training, individual toughness, and creativity at a time of great personal stress, Virginia Hilton survived. But her experience was another cautionary note regarding the sexism that permeated the Delta Ministry just as it did the rest of American society (and the church) in the mid-1960s. And since many of the nearly all-male full-time staff were ministers, that fact was also a commentary on the traditional gender orientation of that most basic institution, even in the most liberal denominations of mainstream Protestantism.

The ministry was always a small group, usually no more than fifteen full-time persons. Alongside the permanent staff there also existed a sizable though shifting number of volunteers and part-timers, both blacks and whites. Most of the long-term people came from outside of Mississippi, although in time local people were included. Many of these latter persons began as volunteers from the communities being served, then moved on to jobs of increasing responsibility. People like Jake Ayers, Clarence Hall, Solomon Gort, Joe Harris, all black citizens of the Delta, and especially Curtis Hayes (one of the earliest members of SNCC in McComb) and the young people in the Freedom Corps he directed, became mainstays of the local programs the Delta Ministry so effectively mounted in its early years. Several of the "outsiders" had served as ministers of interracial parishes. All had been involved in some sort of civil rights activity prior to 1964. Their deep commitment to the ministry and its work was reflected in the fact that nearly all of them stayed in Mississippi for at least two years, some considerably longer. Five people at the core of the organization for almost a decade—Thelma Barnes (native of Greenville), Rims Barber, Owen Brooks, Harry Bowie, and Roger Smith—still live in Mississippi, all of them actively engaged in race-related work both within and outside the church.[22]

The ministry did not devote itself exclusively to concerns in the Delta. It had representatives in towns both east and south of that area, a legacy of church involvement in movement activities prior to the ministry's founding. As noted, Bob Beech arrived in Hattiesburg in the spring of 1964 and remained there, eventually to become one of the first three staff people of the ministry. As a result of the summer of 1964, similar arrangements to those in Hattiesburg developed in McComb in the southwestern part of the state, where Harry Bowie, a black Episcopal priest, worked, and in Canton further to the north and east, where Rims Barber, a white Presbyterian from Iowa, stayed until 1966. These arrangements suggested a flexibility and informality in daily operations, not entirely unlike the practices of SNCC. It also meant that the ministry functioned in areas where civil rights activities were well rooted, enabling them to add further to what SNCC, CORE, and the MFDP had begun. In effect the ministry had a double focus: on statewide issues developing out of the common concerns of staff and African Americans throughout the state, yet also on issues rooted in local communities, in the Delta and elsewhere.[23] This, too, was similar to SNCC's approach.

By February 1965 the National Council of Churches had also leased Mt. Beulah, a small college-academy with a twenty-three acre campus located in Edwards, Mississippi, twenty miles due west of Jackson. Mt. Beulah had been established during the "first" Reconstruction by the Disciples of Christ as a part of the effort by the churches then to provide new educational opportunities throughout the South for recently freed African Americans. In 1953 Mt. Beulah, also known as "Southern Christian Institute," had merged with Tougaloo College, just north of Jackson; the campus in Edwards had not been used for almost ten years. Prior to 1965 Tougaloo served as a major staging point for civil rights activities in the state. Faculty and students actively participated, and the president of the college supported them. This activist role at Tougaloo slackened considerably with the sudden termination of the presidency of A. D. Beittel in September 1964. Because of its strategic location in the center of the state, Bob Moses and his friends earlier had sought to rent Mt. Beulah from the Disciples, but had been turned down (another point of friction between SNCC and the mainline churches). When asked by the National Council of Churches, however, Disciples' denominational leaders agreed to lease Mt. Beulah to the Delta Ministry, despite opposition from local Disciples' churches.[24]

So Mt. Beulah, in addition to Tougaloo, became a key conference center, headquarters, and place of rest for black freedom movement people. It also became the hub of much of the Delta Ministry's daily activity. The ministry maintained its financial office there, and Art Thomas had an office and lived on the campus, as did several other members of the staff.[25] The involvement at Mt. Beulah also suggested that although its principal interests were always in the Delta, the ministry soon became, not entirely in a consciously planned way, something of a statewide civil rights organization. This was especially important from 1965 onward. Almost by default the little church group filled part of the vacuum created in the public life of Mississippi as COFO collapsed early in 1965 and SNCC and CORE gradually withdrew from the state after 1964.[26]

As a model for missionary work in the world outside the church, the Delta Ministry clearly broke with tradition. Heavy-handed missionary paternalism (or even that with a light touch) and the desire to preach to and convert those being helped was never a part of the ministry's work. Instead, taking their cue from movement people, these church persons lived with and learned about the aspirations of poor African Americans in the Delta and elsewhere, and then put together programs. The world, not the church, set the agenda for action. One of the staff, a Presbyterian minister, stated that in Mississippi, much more than anytime previously, he was "living the Word in community." He learned, he said, "how to be a listener as well as a preacher." The first lesson the Mississippi African Americans taught us, he went on, was "to be a servant. . . . We really learned how to work *with* people rather than *for* people."[27]

This "servant" concept of mission, fundamentally biblical in its origins, was at the heart of the Delta Ministry's daily actions. Perhaps it also suggested a revised understanding of how God entered and acted in the world; moving largely outside the church in the secular realm, rather than first in the church, then through efforts at conversion and example responding to those outside. As Colin Williams had suggested in 1963, the paradigm would be God-World-Church, rather than the traditional God-Church-World. A recent commentator has noted that this new paradigm also possessed powerful New Testament connotations, since even the doctrine of the Incarnation suggests "the holy within the profane, . . . God came *into* this world, and that is where we belong as well."[28]

The idea of the servant church was widely discussed and emphasized among many of the church officials who created the Delta Ministry or who were heavily involved in civil rights activity generally.[29] The connections with Colin Williams and his little study booklets have already been noted. *Where in the World* and *What in the World* specifically viewed the black freedom movement as a model example of God working within and through the secular realm. The writings and new insights about mission by scholars representing the World Council of Churches, which Williams's brief essays summarized, specifically mentioned the Delta Ministry as a promising missionary endeavor within that context. Given Williams's presence in New York as director of the Department of Evangelism of the National Council, his work with the World Council of Churches' study group on church mission, and his direct involvement with Robert Spike and the Commission on Religion and Race, it is easy to see how the ideas about a "servant" church circulated rapidly and effectively.[30]

There was a larger theological backdrop to these attitudes, embodied especially in the life and writings of Dietrich Bonhoeffer. Probably the peak of the influence in America of that German theologian martyred at the end of World War II occurred in the early sixties. Many of Bonhoeffer's most important essays in a rather limited overall corpus of writings had been translated into English by that time. His little book, *The Cost of Discipleship*, which suggested a "servant" model of the church in the world, became a best-seller of sorts in mainline church circles. Seminarians (who became the young ministers who went to Mississippi), especially, were deeply attracted to his ideas about the church in a religionless world "come-of-age," of the church simply "being there for others," taking its part "in the social life of the world, not lording it over men [and women], but helping and serving the world."[31] Art Thomas, for one, was influenced by Bonhoeffer and clearly incorporated the latter's ideas and actions into his own belief system. And there seemed to be traces of Bonhoeffer's influence in the words of Robert Spike when in 1963 he reflected on the black freedom "revolution" and asserted that

> despite the prospect of increased racial tension and the complexity of being forced to reorder our society, there is the feeling that God is to be praised for the very existence of the struggle. . . . A society in conflict over justice is a most familiar place for a Christian man to find himself. . . . [Within such a society] for the Christian, his basic calling is always to give his life away for others.

These words reflected well the "servant" motif that underlay the work of the Delta Ministry.[32]

Finally and inescapably for the full-time staff and the volunteers within the ministry, their understanding of a "servant" church was always shaped in cooperation with, and in large part by, the people they came to serve. This is what Rims Barber meant when he said that during the years of the ministry he "lived the Word in community." Not with the Gospel always on one's sleeve, but unobtrusively, even silently. Spike put it well once in a commission meeting when a bishop asked him the old missionary question "of how the hearts of a people could be changed" in the midst of civil rights' activity. In reply Spike "shared his belief that a commitment that results in suffering is really what changes hearts."[33] Using the parlance of a slightly later day, what developed in Mississippi seemed to be what is now called *praxis,* the experience of local people fused with the support of a suffering, servant church. The essential initial ingredient out of which the liberation theologies of the 1970s emerged seemed at work in Mt. Beulah, Hattiesburg, McComb, and Greenville where the Delta Ministry carried out its daily duties.[34]

All this did not mean that the ministry began its work without some sense of direction. Church people both in New York and in Mississippi suggested some of the initial guidelines. First, the ministry was to be a program of "direct relief" to ease human suffering in the African American community. Second, this new church group hoped to become "a ministry of reconciliation" between the white and black communities of Mississippi. Third and most important, the ministry wanted to help initiate a process of "community development," which would include "aiding people to identify their common problems, needs, concerns," helping people draw "potential leadership from their midst," and finally, mobilizing "technical skills" and "economic resources" in order to create "an adequate base for livelihood" among the poorest people in Mississippi.[35]

For thousands of African American farm workers losing their jobs and in many instances their homes because of mechanization, needs were immediate and elemental. Direct relief was a necessary first step in a long, complicated process of community building. As soon as it came into existence, the Delta Ministry began asking urgently for help. Churches outside Mississippi soon created a massive flow of food and clothing, which continued without interruption throughout the mid-1960s. Initial relief efforts centered in Greenville and adjoining rural areas, but eventually the ministry expanded the program to eight counties of the Delta—and never filled the stomachs nor clothed fully the bodies of those in want.[36]

The ministry also pressured the federal government to expand its surplus commodity distribution program and, later in the sixties, food stamp allotments to the poorest segments of the rural Mississippi population. In 1965, cooperating with the National Student Association, which provided the financing, the ministry informed the U.S. Department of Agriculture that even though a private group they were ready to distribute surplus commodities in counties where state officials provided none. Embarrassed by this proposal, less than a year later nearly all counties in the state were offering commodities directly, and over 100,000 needy persons, mostly black, not previously served were receiving essential food. The ministry also fought persistently to lower eligibility requirements for Food Stamps (poor people had to pay for stamps, even if without regular income), a restriction not ended until the late 1970s. And in 1971 the ministry was a direct participant in a lawsuit that gave access to medical support previously denied under Medicaid to 50,000 welfare mothers in Mississippi.[37]

The most lasting impact of the ministry was in more long-term community building efforts. The earliest work focused on tactics and issues associated with the welter of civil rights activities occurring in Mississippi during and after the summer of 1964. Thus the church people placed great stress, first, on joining with the groups that sought full political participation for black Mississippians, and second, on helping to extend long-denied educational opportunities to those same people.

From the outset the ministry aligned itself with the Mississippi Freedom Democratic Party (MFDP), the grass roots political organization that sprang up, in concert with COFO and SNCC, in 1963 and 1964. Throughout the sixties, the MFDP remained the only indigenous political organization totally committed to the mass of black voters, actual and potential. Where that party was well established, Delta Ministry people worked under its direction. If organizing was poor, the ministry launched out on its own. For example, Owen Brooks, a Bostonian who joined the ministry early in 1965, settled in the small Delta town of Cleveland, Mississippi, and lived there for over four years. With guidance from Amzie Moore, an almost legendary local movement leader, Brooks soon became an expert political organizer and came to know the hamlets of rural Bolivar County "like the back of my hand."[38] Other Delta Ministry staff were helping to build grass-roots political networks in the African American communities in Hattiesburg and McComb and in Sunflower, Washington, and other counties in the Delta.[39]

The impact of the Voting Rights Act of 1965 and the cumulative effects of registration drives from 1963 to 1966 led many observers to believe that in 1967 for the first time African Americans could win local offices in the Delta and elsewhere in Mississippi.[40] In late 1965 and especially in 1966 the ministry, with financial support from the Presbyterians and the assistance of Myles Horton and his staff at the famous Highlander School in Tennessee, began to work concretely toward those ends. They initiated "Citizenship Education" Workshops—modeled after Highlander programs and similar to Andrew Young's work in the early sixties—in key counties in the Delta to train black voters in the intricacies of local politics.[41]

Along with other movement-oriented organizations the ministry also helped to establish in late 1965 a Freedom Information Service, a news bureau of sorts, designed to coordinate the gathering and dissemination of information about political activities throughout the state and to provide a centralized communication system on political matters for the black community. A member of the Delta Ministry staff, Charles Horwitz, a former *Newsweek* reporter in Chicago, helped to direct this program for several years.[42] And as a permanent African American electorate became a reality, the earlier, narrower emphasis on voter registration was replaced by more comprehensive efforts at political education, including the just-mentioned leadership training workshops and sophisticated lobbying and legal strategies at the statehouse in Jackson in concert with the other civil rights groups and Robert Clark, the sole black legislator. The Delta Ministry pursued these broader policies throughout the rest of the 1960s.[43]

Community building also stressed the importance of effective and meaningful education, something that had been largely denied the black population in Mississippi. SNCC and COFO had recognized this crippling fact when in the summer of 1964 they created the informal system of "Freedom Schools." These schools were intimately linked with voter registration, for the movement people believed that knowledge, like the vote, translated eventually into power. The Delta Ministry fully endorsed this point of view.[44]

Another moment to translate broad educational ideas into a specific program (and in a sense to keep the spirit of the movement alive) came early in 1965. The just-enacted Economic Opportunity Act included appropriations for an innovative program for disadvantaged preschool children called Head Start. Tom Levin, a New York psychiatrist who had been in Mississippi during the summer of 1964, staff persons from the Office of Economic Opportunity, and individuals in Mississippi envisioned a series of Head Start programs to be held in the summer of 1965, especially in the Delta and other rural areas, where the educational deficiencies of the heavily black population were especially severe. The parents of the children to be served were to play a major role both in planning and then implementing this program. For the first time poor people were being offered a realistic stake in the educational process, and they responded enthusiastically. The summer program, incorporated as the Child Development Group of Mississippi (CDGM), was a tremendous success, evoking the same community allegiance and deep commitments that SNCC and COFO had generated in the summer of 1964 and before.[45]

Those very commitments quickly aroused local white opposition, including familiar threats and acts of physical harassment. The parents vigorously responded. When one center burned to the ground on a Sunday evening, the school missed only one day; by Tuesday attendance was again 100 percent, in makeshift quarters. At another spot parents voluntarily posted twenty-four-hour armed guards around their training centers for the entire summer. In yet another location the African American community built a new building for the Head Start school, donating from their meagre resources all the materials, since government regulations did not allow investment of public monies in capital equipment.[46]

The participatory democracy that was a hallmark of the movement's approach to its work in Mississippi was central to the earliest programs of CDGM. The parents of the children enrolled were hired as teacher's aides and were directly involved in the planning of daily activities. The effect of these intimate connections between parent and child in the kindergarten-type Head Start centers revealed itself in public reports written by the teacher's aides, now preserved in the archives. These reports provided evidence of the highly deficient education the teacher-aides themselves had received; but that was no barrier to their ability to create a system of caring and discipline that coaxed the children, ages three to five, into a larger world of possibilities beyond their immediate, poverty-stricken lives. Near McComb, for example, five-year-old Lee was observed not eating "when he first came." The parent-trainee thus gave him "a lot of spical attention by feeding him and sitting with him at Milk brake and seeing to him drinking his milk. Now he eat and drink like he is in a contiest." The parent concluded with an encouraging flourish that "with the right training [Lee] will begome a great artist." Another child, Gladys, had "a great problem of being shy when it came to aldults." Relaxed and open with her friends, with older people she "shut up like a clam." But "with my help" and that of "the other trainees," she "will now talk to us with no problum." Moreover, Gladys had "also learned to color with in the lines, draw, and [use] soissor." Even more basic were the efforts to get three-year-old Samuel "to use the bathroom." At first "he did not know what it was made for," but after a while was "getting use to it and like to flush it."[47]

These same public reports contained brief but illuminating observations from the parent "resource teachers" about the impact of CDGM on *themselves* and their families. The widening horizons and deepening personal sensitivity of one mother were revealed as she wrote that

> C.D.G.M. have taught me how to teach my kids at home and at Headstart, which I really didn't know. . . . It also have enable me to meet new friends at workshop and get together and share our ideas together. It also give me a experience of how differce children react and how to solve their problem, . . . [and has] enable me to love kids more and more.

Even more powerful and elemental were the comments of a woman in Holmes County as she reflected on her CDGM experience:

> We are a race of people that never had anything for our children except standing around at the end of the cotton fields while we work hard all day. We have never made enough money to feed our kids. So for some children it [CDGM] gives them a good hot meal to eat. If it wasn't for this program they would probably not get anything to eat. It give the teachers and workers a chance to learn while they work with the children. Some people don't understand that its very hard for our children to get along in Miss. This program give them a great opportunity to be free of fear and that's something that most of us have including our children. They are poor and this program give them food and great learning and new ideals and opportunity that they never had.[48]

Even the dry statistics in one of the earliest funding proposals offered a hint what was happening in this program:

> The original CDGM grant proposal [in May 1965] requested a Head Start grant to cover 3,239 children. Before the grant was awarded enthusiastic community support required an amended application to provide service to 4,167 children. . . . [Later] it was necessary to submit a supplementary request to provide service to an additional 642 children. . . . [Finally demand] for even further service increased the population of the Child Development Centers by another 1,692 children until the final enrollment . . . totalled 6,500 children. This last addition was undertaken by the communities without further Head Start funds.[49]

One participant–observer concluded appropriately: "Clearly these people [African Americans in rural Mississippi] perceived the program as theirs, not something imposed on them" and were ready to defend it, fiercely and enthusiastically.[50] And it is also easy to see why a group like the Delta Ministry, committed to "the least of these, our brethren," unwaveringly supported CDGM.

The ministry participated in a variety of ways, especially at the outset. Art Thomas, the director, was a key figure in the earliest meetings in New York City in March 1965, where CDGM began to emerge out of intense discussions among a small group of people, mentioned earlier. The ministry supported with staff and facilities the earliest planning for CDGM, before any federal monies were available. Thomas was one of the first advisors and a member of the board of directors of CDGM, as were local Mississippians involved in other aspects of the ministry's program. Mt. Beulah became the state headquarters of CDGM and also the site of one of the largest Head Start centers. Perhaps most important, the refusal of the state government to endorse the CDGM proposal, normally a necessity for OEO grants, was circumvented by securing sponsorship from an institution of higher education in Mississippi, Mary Holmes College, a small, predominantly black, Presbyterian two-year junior college at West Point, in the northeast portion of the state. Delta Ministry staff, along with National Council of Churches and Presbyterian officials in New York City, worked out these arrangements with the president of Mary Holmes College.[51] Typically, once the Head Start program was clearly established on its own the ministry people slipped into the background, but their overt support was always quietly available.

In a number of ways the new educational venture threatened the white power structure. Most obvious was that CDGM was integrated (especially at the staff level). New jobs and substantial amounts of money also were being pumped into the black community (an estimated 10 percent of all new jobs generated in Mississippi in 1966), particularly among people who never before had received such largesse. And in the process of creating Head Start centers, people learned how to run organizations and even how to apply for further government grants. Soon African American school administrators and teachers also began to oppose CDGM because it ran programs *they* wished to control. That people who had been active in the civil rights movement and in the MFDP also were leaders of CDGM was another cause for concern. In summary, CDGM's potential as a source of community organization and power for the poor, within the black community and the state, was very real and threatening.[52]

Scarcely four weeks into the summer program in 1965, after a brief but intense investigation, Senator John Stennis and other Mississippi politicians launched a barrage of criticism that disrupted operations and eventually forced the removal of CDGM headquarters from Mt. Beulah to Mary Holmes College. In spite of these difficulties, in August 1965, CDGM, still with active Delta Ministry involvement, applied for another Head Start grant, this time for a year-long program in 121 centers, at a cost of $5.6 million. The political implications of such a program further fueled the opposition from state politicians and Mississippi Democrats in Washington. After a delay of almost six months, during which time 50 of the original 84 Head Start centers, serving over 3,000 children, remained in operation through volunteer efforts, CDGM was refunded in February 1966, but for the last time as the exclusive state agency for Head Start.

In September 1966, as CDGM prepared its third grant application, hastily constructed local "paper" agencies incorporated as Mississippi Action for Progress (MAP) and designed to be more reponsive to moderate, middle-class white and black (NAACP) interests were designated by

OEO to receive all the Head Start money in Mississippi. Alerted in part by the Delta Ministry, angry and vehement spokespersons for the National Council of Churches, the United Church of Christ, and especially the National Board of Missions of the United Presbyterian Church, USA, joined a national coalition of labor, legal, educational, and civil rights groups (*not* including the NAACP) to exert intense pressure on the Johnson administration to reverse itself and refund CDGM. Eventually CDGM received partial funding yet was placed under very restrictive guidelines that greatly reduced the nonprofessional dimensions of the program, previously one of its greatest strengths. It was never quite the same program again, although it did continue to exist for several years thereafter.[53]

CDGM's experience also revealed clearly a fundamental tension affecting efforts in the 1960s to build community among oppressed people in the Deep South and elsewhere. Change in Mississippi for African Americans was in part made possible with the support of the federal government. The War on Poverty provided opportunities, through participation in the programs of the Child Development Group, for African American parents as well as their children, to acheive a new sense of self-worth. But one result of that developing sense of self was a change in relationships, *in power*, between classes and races. Those in control politically in Mississippi were unable to tolerate such changes. They made their opposition clear to OEO officials (and probably Lyndon Johnson) and used their considerable influence (John Stennis particularly, as a key member of the Senate Appropriations Committee, which controlled the flow of funds to Vietnam) to destroy CDGM in Mississippi, at least partially. Thus a Head Start program Sargeant Shriver, the director of OEO, had praised in 1965 as a national model, was driven into the ground in 1966 with that same person's full acquiescence! Democracy enhanced ended in democracy undermined. Such painful historical ironies revealed fully the difficulties and ambiguities embedded in the work of the Delta Ministry.[54]

The history of CDGM also highlighted once again certain key characteristics of the ministry. It revealed their special method of involvement in local affairs, as mediators or in coalition-building roles on boards and in programs. Nearly always they were to be found working behind the scenes supporting projects often initiated by others, but projects always meant to enhance the lives of the poorest and most deprived in society. Here again quiet servanthood was the model.

The director of the ministry, Art Thomas, made large contributions to the shaping of these approaches. In interviews with former members of the ministry two decades later, nearly all acknowledged the strength of his leadership and that at the outset he did much to create the ministry's special character. A person who knew Thomas well stated much later that Art was "definitely charismatic in a low-key manner." He was quiet but forceful, a person who led by the power of logical argument and careful planning rather than through dramatic public acts of leadership or speech making. As a small testimony to his personal sensitivity, one staff person remembered that Art was the only one of his colleagues whom he ever saw cry, not a thing that white males then were known to do often in the presence of others.

One also recalls that early on Thomas recognized Thelma Barnes's many talents and moved her out of a secretarial position onto the program staff, where over the years she amply repaid the confidence he placed in her. Thomas seemed more prepared than most males in or outside the church to end some of the sexist constraints that still weighed on women. He cared deeply about people as people, on a fully equal, democratic basis. Thus there were no "stars" in the ministry. That, too, was exactly as Thomas wanted it. And because he was a key person in making the earliest personnel decisions, it seems no accident that nearly all of the staff people were also quiet, unassuming, but highly competent and committed people. All this seems very much in tune with the biblical "servant" concept. The parallels in leadership style between Thomas and certain of the SNCC leaders, especially Robert Moses, are also noticeable. This may help to explain why the Delta Ministry people "fit in" in Mississippi as well as they did in late 1964 and after.[55]

Community building usually meant that the ministry worked cooperatively with parallel secular organizations. But one effort begun in 1966 differed significantly. This was "Freedom City" (suggestive of its utopian aspects—it was never more than a small village). This project was the outgrowth of an incident that occurred in late January 1966 at the semiabandoned federal air base just outside of Greenville. A large group of dispossessed black farm workers and their families, people fired and then evicted unceremoniously from their homes in mid-1965 for daring to strike in the Delta cotton fields to protest bad working conditions and unconscionably low wages, had gathered temporarily at Mt. Beulah. With literally no place to live, after lengthy discussion they finally decided to go to Greenville, enter the military installation, and assert "squatters' rights" to some of the barracks there. Penniless and homeless, they entered federal property illegally if only to proclaim publicly the desperateness of their plight. They were quickly and forcibly evicted, but not until they had attracted national media attention, to the embarrassment of government officials all the way to the White House. And it was probably not a mere coincidence that immediately after the air base incident the funds for the second CDGM contract were suddenly released by OEO and long-sought surplus commodities were made available by the Agriculture Department for use among the poor in Mississippi.[56]

Despite much criticism, Delta ministry staff were with the African American demonstrators throughout the "sit-in," and afterward the ministry struggled to create with these people a permanent solution to their ills.[57] By mid-1966 a plan had evolved to create on land near Greenville, recently sold to the ministry, a model village. This "Freedom City," or

"New City," would demonstrate publicly that the poorest, most dependent persons, with proper support, could become self-sufficient and independent, and could create a community *they* helped to define. It would
also serve as an alternative to the plantation system that had held them in
thrall so long. Throughout the spring of 1966, the staff of the ministry
debated at length and with great intensity the ideas and then the plans that
became a nascent Freedom City.[58]

For some the creation of the model village became a touchstone of
success for the ministry's entire program. For Thomas and Warren
McKenna, associate director of the ministry, Freedom City was an especially significant undertaking. McKenna drafted the documents that
shaped the first steps toward Freedom City; Thomas believed the project
so important that he required all of the full-time staff to spend part of
their time working on it. In 1971, five years after he had left Mississippi
and at a time of deep retrenchment in the entire program of the ministry,
Thomas urged NCC officials in New York to retain Freedom City as a
key part of the ministry's program.[59]

There are several possible explanations for the strong commitments to
this project. Perhaps it was felt that because the ministry initially encouraged the black workers' rebellion in the fields, it was only proper that the
ministry assist in the extended search for long-term solutions to the
problems of these people. Perhaps it was the heady, experimental atmosphere of the times that encouraged this attempt to create a small test case
in social reordering.[60] Certainly there were concrete, immediate problems of housing, feeding, and clothing properly over a hundred destitute
people, and the ministry seemed the only agency, public or private,
willing to step forward and attempt to develop humane solutions to these
problems. That in itself was an interesting commentary on the condition
of public affairs in Mississippi.

Freedom City was also an example of the utopian or experimental
communities religious people have established in America since the "City
on a Hill" in Massachusetts in the early seventeenth century. And like
many of those experiments, this one, too, ended in failure. Fifty destitute
African American families were to build their own homes on an eighty-
acre plot near Greenville, simultaneously learning trade skills and reducing construction costs. A health clinic eventually was completed and
staffed, and a literacy program for adults and children initiated. But
massive sums of money from both private and public sources were
required—gifts from individuals like Irving Fain, a Jewish philanthropist
from Providence, Rhode Island; church organizations like Church
Women United and the World Council of Churches; hundreds of thousands of dollars from the Ford Foundation to help build the homes, a
community center, and a sewer system; and finally the commitment of
large sums through OEO and the Department of Commerce.[61]

Over time the project gradually faltered. Only thirty of the projected
fifty houses were ever completed, and large amounts of time and energy

were required to educate and train adults and children. The two strongest advocates, Thomas and McKenna, had left the Delta Ministry by the end of 1966, and some of those who remained were less certain that the idea was really feasible. In the late sixties, when choices had to be made between Freedom City and programs that affected larger numbers of people or wider geographic areas, the experimental community some-times was the loser. And ultimately sources of funding dried up as con-cern for poverty went out of style in the Nixon years. Thus Freedom City, while certainly not abandoned, gradually lost its position of pri-macy in the hearts, and budgets, of ministry people.[62]

Notes

1. Bruce Hilton, *The Delta Ministry* (New York, Macmillan, 1969), pp. 39–40, 44–45; interview with Thelma Barnes, July 14, 1985; Warren McKenna to author, October 9, 1985; J. M. Wilzin to National Council of Churches, November 10, 1964, folder 37, box 2, Delta Ministry Papers, Atlanta.

2. Spike, *Civil Rights Involvement*, p. 10.

3. "Report of the Executive Director," Commission on Religion and Race, NCC, September 5, 1963, p. 9, RG 11, box 6, folder 20, NCC Archives; Min-utes, Commission on Religion and Race, NCC, October 22, 1963, pp. 8–9, folder 8, box 15, Victor Reuther Papers.

4. Spike, "Some Guidelines for the Future of the Commission on Religion and Race of the National Council of Churches," September 23, 1963, RG 11, box 6, folder 20, NCC Archives.

5. Interview with Jon Regier, August 7, 1986; Andrew Young to Robert Spike, April 25, 1961; Myles Horton to Young, May 8, 1961; items in folder 5, box 30, Highlander Center Papers; "The Second Year of Citizenship Schools: A Progress Report to the Field Foundation," folder 29, box 136, Southern Chris-tian Leadership Conference Papers, Martin Luther King Center, Atlanta (hereaf-ter cited as SCLC Papers). The quotation of Andrew Young is in Young to Truman Douglass and Wesley Hotchkiss, June 10, 1964, folder 14, box 136, SCLC Papers. James Bevel, a colleague of Young's in the SCLC and a resident in the Mississippi Delta in the early sixties, also contributed to the education of NCC people about the area. See James Bevel to Robert Spike, July 24, 1964, with attached proposal, "A School for Basic Education in the Mississippi Delta," and Spike to Bevel, July 28, 1964, all in folder entitled "Mississippi Delta," box 3, Thomas Papers.

6. Sam H. Franklin, Jr., "Early Years of the Delta Cooperative Farm and the Providence Cooperative Farm," unpublished typescript, pp. 82–92, in A. E. Cox Collection, Mitchell Memorial Library, Mississippi State University; Fox, *Rein-hold Niebuhr*, pp. 176, 282.

7. Harry V. Richardson, "Report on a Program for the Training of the Negro Rural Ministry for the Year Ending May 31, 1946," RG 26, box 18, folder 6; "Summary of Institutes—1947," RG 26, box 18, folder 6; "A Summary Report on a Program for the Training of the Negro Rural Ministry, 1945–1950," RG 26, box 18, folder 12; "Activity Sheet [Rural Ministers' Institutes], October, 1955," RG 7, box 5, folder 28; Minutes, Extension Unit, Department of Town and Country Church, NCC, June 21, 1955, RG 7, box 5, folder 18; Minutes, Exten-

sion Unit, Department of Town and Country Church, NCC, April 30, 1956, RG 7, box 5, folder 33; all items in NCC Archives.

8. An especially detailed outline of the consultations conducted by the National Council from September 1963 to May 1964 is in Henry McCanna to David Hunter, memo on "Mississippi Contacts," November 20, 1964, in RG 5, box 16, folder 9, NCC Archives. On the full evolution of the proposals leading to the formation of the Delta Ministry, see also Minutes, Commission on Religion and Race, NCC, October 22, 1963, January 16, 1964, RG 11, box 6, folder 20; Anna Hedgeman, "Summary Report," October 22, 1963, to January 9, 1964, RG 11, box 6, folder 20; "Report of the Executive Director," Commission on Religion and Race, NCC, January 16, 1964, RG 5, box 6, folder 33; all items in NCC Archives. The official approval of the Delta Ministry by the General Board is in "General Board Action Concerning *A Ministry Among the Residents of the Delta Area of the State of Mississippi*," February 26, 1964, folder 27, box 1, Delta Ministry Papers, Atlanta.

9. A superb history of the Mississippi Delta is James C. Cobb's *The Most Southern Place in the World: The Mississippi Delta and the Roots of Regional Identity* (New York, Oxford University Press, 1992). On the technological revolution in cotton production after World War II and its effects on southerners, both black and white, see Gilbert Fite, *Cotton Fields No More: Southern Agriculture, 1865–1980* (Lexington, University of Kentucky Press, 1984), chap. 9; and Gavin Wright, *Old South, New South: Revolutions in the Southern Economy Since the Civil War* (New York, Basic Books, 1986), chap. 8. On the migration of black Mississippians to Chicago, see Nicholas Lemann, *The Promised Land: The Great Black Migration and How It Changed America* (New York, Knopf, 1991), especially chaps. 1, 2; and for the 1930s, James R. Grossman, *Land of Hope: Chicago, Black Southerners, and the Great Migration* (Chicago, University of Chicago Press, 1989). For an excellent general treatment, see Joe William Trotter, ed., *The Great Migration: New Dimensions of Race, Class, and Gender* (Bloomington, Indiana University Press, 1991).

10. "Proposal for a Ministry Among the Residents of the Delta Area of the State of Mississippi"; Henry McCanna to David Hunter, memo on "Mississippi Contacts," November 20, 1964; both items in RG 5, box 16, folder 9, NCC Archives. Attachments to Frank Smith to Jack Pratt, September 26, 1963, in folder entitled "Writings," Pratt Papers, provide further confirmation of the dire economic straits of young African Americans, male and female, in the small rural communities of the Delta, complicated by the legal and economic reprisals exacted because of participation in civil rights activities.

11. Andrew Young also helped to delay the implementation of the ministry. In June 1964 he was invited to become the first director. After considerable hesitation, he decided late in the summer to remain with the Southern Christian Leadership Conference, especially since Martin Luther King, Jr., offered him the job of executive director of his organization. Correspondingly, Young may have used the possibility of joining the ministry as a method of "staying close to King" (Robert Moses's phrase) in the SCLC. Andrew Young to Truman Douglass and Wesley Hotchkiss, June 10, 1964; Hotchkiss to Young, August 31, 1964; items in folder 14, box 163, SCLC Papers; Jon Regier to R. H. Edwin Espy, September 1, 1964, RG 5, box 16, folder 9, NCC Archives; telephone interview with Robert Moses, January 27, 1989.

12. O'Reilly, *"Racial Matters,"* p. 187; Paul Spike, *Photographs of My Father* (New York, A. A. Knopf, 1973), pp. 85–96. Garrow, *Bearing the Cross,* pp. 345–

351, provides an excellent brief overview of the struggle at the Democratic convention. There were differences in point of view among the commission staff members—Spike was more friendly to SNCC than was Jack Pratt. Pratt went to the key meeting where the MFDP decided not to accept Johnson's compromise and spoke forcefully in support of the compromise. Spike, still hospitalized, was not present. One wonders if the differences between SNCC and the churches would have been stated as starkly as they were if Spike had spoken. Interview with Jack Pratt, June 16, 1985; telephone interview with Robert Moses, January 27, 1989. For a slightly different interpretation, see James Forman, *The Making of Black Revolutionaries* (Washington, D.C., Open Hand Press, 1985), pp. 390–396. Michael Thelwell, a SNCC staff person in Washington, recalled later the vilification of the MFDP and SNCC after Atlantic City and that almost alone Spike tried to reach out to the people in the SNCC Washington office, hoping to reestablish broken ties. Interview with Michael Thelwell, May 22, 1990. For further evidence of Spike's efforts to mediate between disagreeing civil rights groups, see "Rough Minutes of a Meeting Called by the National Council of Churches to Discuss the Mississippi Project," September 18, 1964, folder entitled "National Council of Churches, July 9–September 18, 1964," box 115, SNCC Papers.

13. Telephone interview with Robert Moses, January 27, 1989. See also interview with Ralph Luker, January 4, 1989; Tom Dent interview with Owen Brooks, August 18, 1978, Tom Dent Oral History Collection, Tougaloo College Archives, Jackson, Mississippi, and more generalized but applicable remarks in Stoper, *SNCC: Growth of Radicalism,* pp. 97–102.

14. This paragraph is based on comments in John Dittmer, "The Politics of the Mississippi Movement, 1954–1964," in Charles W. Eagles, ed., *The Civil Rights Movement in America* (Jackson, University Press of Mississippi, 1986), pp. 86–92; and Dittmer, "The Transformation of the Mississippi Movement, 1964–1968: The Rise and Fall of the Freedom Democratic Party," unpublished Walter Prescott Webb Lecture, 1991, pp. 14–35, cited by permission of the author.

15. Interview with Ralph Luker, January 4, 1989; Series I, II, and III, Thomas Papers.

16. Minutes, Commission on Religion and Race, National Council of Churches, October 22, 1963, p. 3, folder 8, box 15, Victor Reuther Papers.

17. Arthur E. Thomas, "Report to the Commission on Canton, Mississippi," Exhibit C, attached to Minutes, Commission on Religion and Race, NCC, February 21, 1964, folder 12, ibid.; Minutes, Commission on Religion and Race, NCC, February 21, 1964, pp. 3–4, folder 12, ibid.; Thomas, "Report of the Associate Director of Community Action," June 29, 1964, attached to "Agenda," meeting of the Commission on Religion and Race, NCC, June 29, 1964, folder 13, ibid.; "Participants in Orientation Project, Oxford, Ohio," July 9, 1964, RG 4, box 31, folder 23, NCC Archives; telephone interview with Robert Moses, January 27, 1989.

18. Interview with Warren McKenna, May 23, 1986; "Participants in Orientation Projects, Oxford, Ohio," July 9, 1964, p. 15, RG 4, box 31, folder 23, NCC Archives.

19. Interview with Warren McKenna, May 23, 1986; interview with Robert Beech, October 12, 1989; interview with Harry Bowie, July 15, 1986; Tom Dent interview with Harry Bowie, May 28, 1979, Tom Dent Oral History Collection; interviews with Rims Barber, July 21, 1986, June 24, 1989; interview with Paul Moore, Jr., October 28, 1986; undated notes in spiral green notebook; Sunday

bulletin, Church of the Mediator, McComb, Mississippi, July 26, 1964, mimeographed documents, "Ministers Project Orientation," and "Security Handbook"; items in folder entitled "Mississippi, 1964," Moore Papers.

20. Interview with Charles Horwitz, July 27, 1989. Bruce Hilton, a member of the Church of the Brethern who became the public relations officer in 1965, and Robert Beech in Hattiesburg brought their families with them. Interview with Roberta Miller, June 30, 1989; telephone interviews with Bruce and Virginia Hilton, July 16, 17, 1989; Robert Beech, "Resume," February 1969, p. 4, folder 21, box 21, Delta Ministry Papers, Atlanta. Owen Brooks and Warren McKenna left their families in Boston. Telephone interview with Owen Brooks, July 6, 1989; interview with Warren McKenna, May 23, 1986.

21. Interview with Virginia Hilton, May 31, 1991. Further evidence of sexism manifested within the staff of the Delta Ministry is in interview with Thelma Barnes, July 14, 1986; interview with Sarah Johnson, July 17, 1986; interview with Jean Phillips, July 17, 1986.

22. "Delta Ministry Staff (as of February 1, 1967)," in "Delta Ministry" file, reel 158, NAACP Legal Defense Fund, Inc., Papers, Collection on Legal Change, Wesleyan University (hereafter NAACP Legal Defense Fund Papers); interviews with Rims Barber, July 21, 1986, June 24, 1989; interview with Harry Bowie, June 29, 1989; interview with Owen Brooks, July 14, 1986; interview with Charles Horwitz, July 27, 1989; interview with Fred Lowry, November 22, 1988; interview with Roger Smith, June 29, 1989; interview with Curtis Hayes, January 14, 1991; boxes 1 and 2, Thomas Papers.

23. Interview with Rims Barber, June 24, 1989; interview with Harry Bowie, June 29, 1989. From September 1964 to January 1965, ministers came to McComb, where they supported a voter registration drive in a manner reminiscent of the work earlier in Hattiesburg and Canton. "McComb Report"; "List of Ministers in McComb from Sept. 1 to Jan. 5, 1965"; both items in folder 10, box 1, Harry Bowie Papers, Wisconsin State Historical Society. John Dittmer, "The Movement in McComb, 1961–1964," unpublished paper in possession of Findlay, places the actions in McComb in proper historical perspective. There was also an informal connection between the ministry and John Else, a Disciples of Christ minister, who was in the Gulfport-Biloxi area in the summer of 1964 and stayed on for a year after. John F. Else to Findlay, September 3, 1986; "Minutes," October 14, 1964, Coordination Committee on Moral and Civil Rights (Disciples of Christ), folder 10, box 15, Delta Ministry Papers, Atlanta.

24. First thoughts at the Interchurch Center in New York about Mt. Beulah, and eventual implementation of these ideas in Mississippi, can be traced in "A Proposal for the Delta Ministry Academy to be located at Mt. Beulah, Edwards, Mississippi," RG 5, box 16, folder 10, NCC Archives; Minutes, Commission on Religion and Race, NCC, March 26, 1964, p. 3, folder 10, box 15, Victor Reuther Papers; folder entitled "Agreement, NCC-UCMS," RG 4, United Christian Missionary Society Papers, box DHM 8, Disciples of Christ Historical Society, Nashville; "Main Points in Lease Agreement," February 1, 1965, in folder entitled "Mt. Beulah ad hoc committee," box 3, Horwitz Papers. On Tougaloo's role in the racial struggle, and SNCC's interest in Mt. Beulah, see Clarice T. Campbell and Oscar A. Rodgers, Jr., *Mississippi: The View From Tougaloo* (Jackson, University Press of Mississippi, 1979), pp. 182–183, 196–217; and especially John Dittmer, "From the Mississippi Movement to *Mississippi Burning,*" unpublished

paper presented to the Organization of American Historians, April 1990, pp. 8–10; telephone interview with Robert Moses, January 27, 1989.

25. On the daily activities of the ministry's staff at Mt. Beulah, see interview with Robert Beech, October 13, 1989; interview with Fred Lowry, November 22, 1988; interview with Roger Smith, June 29, 1989.

26. Carson, *In Struggle,* chaps. 10–13; Meier and Rudwick, *CORE,* chaps. 11–12; "Delta Ministry Work in Cities," April 8, 1966, p. 1, in folder entitled "Delta Ministry Program," box 3, Beech Papers.

27. Interview with Rims Barber, June 24, 1989.

28. Harvey Cox, "The Secular City 25 Years Later," *Christian Century,* November 7, 1990, p. 1025.

29. See especially the entire issue of *Social Action* [United Church of Christ], xxx (November 1954), which included brief essays by Spike, Art Thomas, and two officials of the United Church; Spike, *Civil Rights Involvement: Model for Mission,* p. 16; Paul Moore to Jon Regier, December 4, 1964, folder entitled "Delta Commission Membership," box 6, Thomas Papers; Leon Howell, "The Delta Ministry," *Christianity and Crisis,* August 8, 1966, p. 190.

30. Thomas Wieser, ed., *Planning for Mission: Working Papers on the Quest for Missionary Communities* (London, Epworth Press, 1965), pp. 8–9, 11, 164–167; *The Church for Others and the Church for the World: A Quest for Structures for Missionary Congregations* (Geneva, World Council of Churches, 1967), pp. 69, 116–20. The formulation of "God-World-Church," which so neatly summarizes this point of view, first appeared in Wieser, *Planning for Mission,* pp. 7–9. Spike, in *Civil Rights Involvement: Model for Mission,* pp. 5–8, adopts the same paradigm, with a few modifications. See also his theological "Presentation" at an American Baptist "Metropolitan Conference" in New York City, November 12, 1964, RG 6, box 47, folder 31, NCC Archives. Colin Williams, in *Where in the World,* chap. 2, specifically speaks about "The Servant Method" of mission (p. 24) and "The Servant Form of the Church" (pp. 31–34) as the key missionary goal of the contemporary church.

31. Quoted in Williams, *Where in the World,* p. 100. See also Marty, "Bonhoeffer: Seminarians' Theologian," pp. 467–469; Geoffrey B. Kelly and F. Burton Nelson, eds., *A Testament to Freedom: The Essential Writings of Dietrich Bonhoeffer* (San Francisco, Harper Collins, 1990), pp. 1–46.

32. On Bonhoeffer's influence on Thomas, see interview with Ralph Luker, January 4, 1989; folder 12, box 2, Thomas Papers. Spike's comments are in his essay, "The Negro Rights Revolution: Questions in Midstream," November 29, 1963, p. 4, RG 11, box 6, folder 20, NCC Archives.

33. Minutes, Commission on Religion and Race, NCC, January 16, 1964, p. 7, folder 7, box 15, Victor Reuther Papers.

34. For a recent claim that a popular theological treatise of the sixties was another American anticipation of *praxis* and liberation theology, see Cox, "The Secular City 25 Years Later," pp. 1025–1027.

35. "Proposal for a Ministry Among the Residents of the Delta Area of the State of Mississippi" [February 1964], RG 5, box 16, folder 9, NCC Archives.

36. Four months after the ministry began, it had received 50,000 pounds of "unsolicited clothing." Hundreds of individuals and local churches outside of Mississippi participated. In early 1965 the ministry opened in Greenville a well-stocked food co-op where hungry people could come for free supplies. Interview

with Thelma Barnes, July 18, 1986; "Delta Ministry Fact Sheet," January 1965, p. 2, RG 5, box 16, folder 9, NCC Archives; Thelma Barnes to Margaret Teague, November 23, 1967; Barnes to Kathleen Vallenga, December 7, 1967, both items in box 24, folder 25, Delta Ministry Papers, Mississippi State University. The ministry also entered into agreements with the Mennonite Church and the Church of the Brethren, both widely known for their direct relief programs, for regular shipments of food and clothing to Mississippi. Memo of W. Ray Kyle, October 26, 1964, folder entitled "Greenville Mills"; Kyle to Jon Regier, July 28, 1965; both items in box 2, Thomas Papers.

37. Interviews with Rims Barber, July 21, 1986, June 24, 1989; Steven McNichols and Arthur Thomas, "Mississippi: A Crisis in Hunger," August 6, 1965, in folder entitled "USDA/NSA Commodity Proposal," box 2, Thomas Papers; Stephen Arons to Thomas, October 5, 1965, folder entitled "National Student Association," box 1, Thomas Papers; Rims Barber to author, July 9, 1988. For contemporary critiques of the surplus commodity and food stamp systems used in the Delta, see "Hunger in the Mississippi Delta," box 6, folder 99; and "Facts About the Food Stamp Program in Mississippi," box 5, folder 80; both items in Delta Ministry Papers, Mississippi State University. An excellent general assessment is in James C. Cobb, "'Somebody Done Nailed Us on the Cross': Federal Farm and Welfare Policy and the Civil Rights Movement in the Mississippi Delta," *Journal of American History* (December 1990), pp. 922–932.

38. Interview with Owen Brooks, July 14, 1986; Tom Dent interview with Owen Brooks, August 18, 1978, Tom Dent Oral History Collection. Brooks's review of his first six months' work for the ministry in Bolivar County is in "Greenville Project Report, Sept. 15, 1964–Sept. 15, 1965," folder 6, box 2, Delta Ministry Papers, Atlanta.

39. Greenville Project Report; "Report and Evaluation—Hattiesburg"; "Mc-Comb Report"; "Bolivar County Report"; all items in folder 6, box 2, Delta Ministry Papers, Atlanta. The ministry participated in political organizing drives in ten counties in the Delta in 1965. On connections between the Delta Ministry and the MFDP in McComb, see "McComb Report," folder 10, box 1; and folders 2 and 3, box 2, Bowie Papers.

40. The hopes of the African American community were only partially fulfilled. In local elections in August and November 1967, twenty-two blacks were elected to public office in the state, including the first representative to the state legislature since Reconstruction. *Delta Ministry Reports* (newsletter), November 1967, box 4, folder 37, Delta Ministry Papers, Mississippi State University. Frank R. Parker, *Black Votes Count: Political Empowerment in Mississippi After 1965* (Chapel Hill, University of North Carolina Press, 1990), examines Mississippi politics after the passage of the Voting Rights Act and demonstrates how new methods of racial discrimination blocked the full achievement of African Americans' political rights.

41. See especially folder 2, box 81, Highlander Center Papers.

42. "Proposal for the Freedom Information Service" [from the Delta Ministry], November 15, 1965, folder 6, box 81, ibid.; interview with Charles Horwitz, July 27, 1989.

43. By 1969 the number of black elected officials in Mississippi had risen to 91. Most were in local communities and affected peoples' lives directly—justices of the peace, constables, county supervisors, coroners. Despite the continued oppo-

sition of the white power structure, blacks were securing a degree of control over aspects of their public life. Parker, *Black Votes Count,* chaps. 2–6, discusses the methods used by whites to prevent black accession to power after 1965 and the tactics devised by the latter to defeat the whites' efforts. On Delta Ministry participation in these counterresponses, see Rims Barber to author, July 9, 1988; *Delta Ministry Reports,* November 1967 and November–December 1969; "A Delta Ministry Proposal for the Foundation of the 1969 Municipal Elections," folder 5, box 14, Delta Ministry Papers, Atlanta; "The Delta Ministry Report, 1969," RG 2, box 5, folder 1, NCC Archives.

44. For a detailed analysis of the Freedom Schools, see Perlstein, "Teaching Freedom," pp. 297–324.

45. There is no recent, scholarly history of CDGM; it is badly needed. However, see Polly Greenberg, *The Devil Has Slippery Shoes: A Biased Biography of the Child Development Group of Mississippi* (New York, Macmillan, 1969). As an OEO official, Greenberg helped in the earliest planning, then resigned and went to Mississippi to assist in the early efforts at implementation.

46. James Monsonis, "Parties, Politics, and Poverty: Some Aspects of Conflict in a Mississippi Poverty Program," pp. 16–17, in folder entitled "Reports: CDGM by Dunbar, Monsonis, Robinson," box 1, Thomas Levin Papers, Martin Luther King Center.

47. Mrs. Dorothy Jean Tucker, "Case History of all the Children at the table of France," Sweet Home Center, McComb, Mississippi, reel 12, Child Development Group of Mississippi Papers, Wisconsin State Historical Society (hereafter cited as CDGM Papers).

48. Virgie Safford, Old Pilgrim Rest Head Start Center, Durant, Mississippi; unidentified author, Second Pilgrim Rest Center, Durant, Mississippi; both items in reel 12, CDGM Papers.

49. "Proposal for a Full Year Head Start Program of the Child Development Group of Mississippi," p. 1, in folder entitled "CDGM Proposal #2" box 1, Thomas Papers.

50. Monsonis, "Parties, Politics, and Poverty," p. 17, in "Reports: CDGM by Dunbar, Monsonis, Robinson folder, box 1, Levin Papers.

51. "Oral History Memoir of Dr. Tom Levin," pp. 9–13, folder entitled "History, oral—July, 1965, Interviewee Tom Levin," box 3, Levin Papers; "Statement to the Evaluation Committee," miscellaneous documents, box 5; "Confidential Report to the Executive Committee, Commission on the Delta Ministry," October 1, 1965, p. 1, miscellaneous documents, box 1; Bryant George to President, CDGM, March 2, 1966, attached to Minutes, Board of Directors, CDGM, March 6, 1966, miscellaneous documents, box 4; items in Thomas Papers; Arthur C. Thomas to Members of the Board, CDGM, April 20, 1965; Thomas to D. I. Horn, May 7, 1965; both items in folder 27, box 12, Delta Ministry Papers, Atlanta; Tom Levin to Moe Foner, April 20, 1965; Levin to S. A. Ianni, August 28, 1965; both items in folder entitled "Correspondence, January–August, 1965," box 1, Levin Papers; interview with Jon Regier, August 7, 1986.

52. Monsonis, "Parties, Politics, and Poverty," pp. 7–8; Leslie Dunbar, "An Essay in Self-Reliance," pp. 3–6; both items in folder entitled "Reports re: CDGM by Dunbar, Monsonis, Robinson," box 6, Levin Papers. For a clear sense of how CDGM provided jobs and money for the African American Community

of Mississippi, see "Revised Budget for Central Administration for CDGM, March 8, 1966," in RG 301.7, box 44, folder 2, National Board of Missions Papers, UPCUSA, Presbyterian Historical Society.

53. These two paragraphs provide only the barest outline of a complex but fascinating story, which casts much light on Mississippi history in the sixties and on the ambiguities and tensions embedded in Johnson's War on Poverty. The best brief summary-analysis is Pat Watters, "Mississippi: Children and Politics," undated essay, reel 13, CDGM Papers. See also White House Task Force, *OEO During the Administration of President Lyndon B. Johnson, November 1963–January 1969,* vol. I, pp. 43–59; "War Within a War: the Story of CDGM," in folder entitled "Mary Holmes Junior College—1966: Correspondence," box 4, Kenneth Neigh Papers, Princeton Theological Seminary; "Proposal for a Full-Year Head Start Program [1967] of the Child Development Group of Mississippi, pp. 6–13, in folder entitled "CDGM" drawer 3, file cabinet #5, Commission for Racial Justice, United Church of Christ, Cleveland, Ohio; RG 301.7, box 44, folders 2, 3, 3a, 4; RG 301.7, box 45, folders 19, 20, all items in National Board of Missions Papers, UPCUSA; unpaginated clippings, *Washington Post, New York Times,* and *New Republic,* October 1966, RG 16, box 16, folder 34, NCC Archives; "The Refunding of CDGM," *Christianity and Crisis,* January 23, 1967, pp. 314–315.

54. Shriver's deeply ambiguous official reactions to the CDGM crisis in 1966 and a national church leader's powerful response are in Sargeant Shriver to the Editor, October 19, 1966, *New York Times;* Hyman Bookbinder to Friend, October 20, 1966; Joseph W. Merchant to the Editor, October 22, 1966, *New York Times;* all items in folder entitled "CDGM-OEO-CCAP, Fall, 1966," box 5, Thomas Papers. See also the devastating criticisms of OEO's actions toward CDGM in September and October of 1966 in Citizen's Crusade Against Poverty, "Final Report on the Child Development Group of Mississippi," October 10, 1966, reel 13, CDGM Papers.

55. Comments in these paragraphs are based on interview with Ralph Luker, January 4, 1989; interview with Fred Lowry, November 22, 1988; interview with Robert Beech, October 12, 1989; interview with Charles Horwitz, July 27, 1989; interview with Bruce and Virginia Hilton, July 17, 1989; interview with Virginia Hilton, May 31, 1991; Leon Howell, "The Delta Ministry," *Christianity and Crisis,* August 8, 1966, pp. 190–191. Bruce Hilton offered an intriguing comment—that the Delta Ministry might have become a much different organization if Andrew Young had accepted the first offer to be director since he and Thomas were very different persons.

56. *Delta Democrat Times* (Greenville, Miss.), January 31, p. 1, February 1, 1966, pp. 1, 2, 3, 12. The best description of the air base incident from the ministry's perspective is in Hilton, *The Delta Ministry,* chaps. 6–8. The editorial of the *Delta Democrat Times* on the affair, February 2, 1966, p. 3, presents a sharply contrasting point of view, representative of moderate "establishment" white opinion in Greenville.

57. The fullest account of events from the evictions at the air base until mid-1966 is in Hilton, *The Delta Ministry,* chaps. 8, 9. See also Leon Howell, *Freedom City: The Substance of Things Hoped For* (Richmond, Va., John Knox Press, 1967), chaps. 1, 2.

58. Warren McKenna, "New City," handwritten and typewritten copies of draft proposals, in possession of author. Some of the staff were not as enamored

of the idea of Freedom City as were Thomas and McKenna. Harry Bowie left the Delta Ministry for a short time, partly because of disagreements with Thomas over this project. Interview with Harry Bowie, July 15, 1986; interview with Robert Beech, October 12, 1989.

59. Thomas, "A Report on the Delta Ministry," February 1, 1971, in folder entitled "Mississippi Delta Ministry, January—1971," box 4, Thomas Papers.

60. In his recollections two decades later, Warren McKenna attested to the ferment concerning social and economic cooperative experiments then bubbling among movement people in Mississippi on which he drew for the shaping of his proposals regarding Freedom City. McKenna to Findlay, July 1, 1988. In 1965 the Ministry also actively considered the viability of small farm cooperatives in Mississippi, seeking to build on successful models in Israel. "Proposal for 5 Acres of Land," in folder entitled "Agricultural Coop Village"; David DeRienzis, "'Moshav' or Co-op Farm Plan in Mississippi"; J. Oscar Lee to Jon Regier, June 18, 1965; all items in box 2, Thomas Papers.

61. Interview with Thelma Barnes, July 18, 1986; Warren McKenna to Irving Fain, March 16, 1966; Fain to William Carhart, April 2, 1966; Carhart to Jane Hinchcliffe Mavity, July 23, 1968; items in miscellaneous documents, box 4, Thomas Papers; "A Progress Report: DOC," March 16, 1969, folder 3, box 13, MFDP Papers, Martin Luther King Center; Howard Dressner to R. H. Edwin Espy, October 28, 1970, RG 6, box 8, folder 25, NCC Archives.

62. For indications of the shifting priorities of the ministry, see "Memorandum," Owen Brooks to John F. Anderson, folder 45, box 13, Delta Ministry Papers, Atlanta; interview with Harry Bowie, July 15, 1986; interview with Rims Barber, July 21, 1986; interview with Sarah Johnson, July 17, 1986; and especially interview with Thelma Barnes, July 14, 1986; "Report of the Delta Ministry, February 17–18, 1967," p. 7, RG 2, box 5, folder 1, NCC Archives. An excellent recent analysis of the air base incident and its long-term economic effects on impoverished African Americans in the Delta is in Cobb, "Somebody Done Nailed Us on the Cross," pp. 918–931.

5

Reconciliation and "The Justice Place": The Delta Ministry, 1966–1974

In the first half of 1966, the Delta Ministry experienced a special challenge resulting from a thorough internal evaluation by officials of the National Council of Churches. In part arising naturally out of the desire of the people in New York to assess the results of the project after a period of time had passed, the review also reflected other, more complex, forces at work. The ministry and its activities were exposing some of the deep ambiguities that existed within mainline Protestantism, especially in the churches in Mississippi. The rank and file who occupied the pews and funded the mainline churches were primarily middle-class whites. The Delta Ministry came to Mississippi officially representing these people, yet was fundamentally motivated by biblical injunctions to serve the poor and the dispossessed. Their program and daily actions were based on powerful biblical precepts that implicitly, if not directly, urged Christians to work to create a society more nearly of equals and certainly to end racial discrimination. But in Mississippi, the local mainline churches were a central element in a social structure that daily lived by and wielded much of its power through racial discrimination and the belief that black people were fundamentally inferior to whites. Moreover, the ministry represented "outside forces," national ecumenical and denominational agencies with headquarters in the North, who by their very location were objects of great suspicion, fear, and scorn. Tensions and disagreements thus were bound to emerge between the ministry and middle-class whites both in and out of the mainstream churches inside Mississippi in particular and among the Mississippians' allies in religious circles outside the state.

We have already seen how quickly white opposition to the ministry's presence surfaced, even in "liberal" Greenville, especially as it began to support many of the programs of COFO, SNCC, and the MFDP. The fact that it was a church group, in a state where deep religious commitments (to Protestant traditions especially) were widely in evidence, did not matter. The label "outside agitator" largely overrode church identification. Thus everyone in the ministry experienced threats and harassment like those that were a part of daily life for black Mississippians. As noted earlier, a few of the staff came with their families; these people found it difficult to secure housing when potential rentors were threatened by diehard segregationists. Phone lines were tapped; there were frequent threatening anonymous calls late into the night. Mt. Beulah experienced surveillance by local and state police who parked patrol cars at the entrance to the academy grounds to "observe" activities there. Such incidents were very threatening and put people constantly on edge.[1]

Sometimes the attacks were more serious. Bob Beech had his home in Hattiesburg fired into, while he and his family were there. At least once at Mt. Beulah pistol shots were fired at buildings filled with people. Rims Barber recalled an incident in Canton at a voter registration rally where a local white drove up and emptied a revolver at him at a distance of about twenty feet. Miraculously, he was not hit. Another member of the staff learned sometime after the fact that residents of the little Delta town where he was working on voter registration in 1965 threatened to kill him, but that the local Methodist minister finally dissuaded them. Perhaps most grisly and tragic was the moment early in 1965 when an auto crash occurred in front of Delta Ministry headquarters in Greenville. A grievously injured person, refused service by local ambulances because he was black, died on the scene in the arms of a member of the ministry. Perhaps this might account, one person involved noted later, "for some of the seeming D[elta] M[inistry] indifference to the white community."[2]

This "seeming indifference" of the ministry was a criticism raised often by Mississippi churches from the mainstream denominations. This was an especially provoking comment since the General Board of the National Council had asserted at the beginning, in February 1964, that one of the primary purposes of the ministry was to initiate "a ministry of reconciliation," especially "by assisting in the establishing of communication between the white and Negro communities."[3] According to white Mississippi church persons, the Delta Ministry was failing noticeably in this regard, making little or no effort to maintain positive relations with people from the same church groups as those the ministry staff represented. But since the late 1950s the mainline churches in Mississippi had been one of the principal institutions out of which extreme segregationists exerted their control over the Magnolia State. For example, after the riots at Oxford late in 1962 over the admission of James Meredith to the University of Mississippi, a group of twenty-eight young Methodist clergy in the state publicly condemned those actions. Within a year all but seven of the ministers had left Mississippi.[4] Such a response even to mild clerical criticism offered a hint of the hostility the Delta Ministry faced as it began its work.

Extensive evidence makes clear that from the beginning the ministry staff made repeated efforts to reach out to the white community in general and the white churches in particular and received little response.

Wilmina "Billie" Rowland, a Presbyterian staff person from the national offices in Philadelphia, spent four months in Greenville in mid-1965 and devoted much of her time attempting to establish personal contacts with local church people. She was almost totally rebuffed. Al Winham, a middle-aged minister on the ministry staff who lived in Jackson for six months in late 1965 and early 1966, reported that

> one pitch I *always* use with white clergy is that Marge [Winham's wife] and I are "lonesome" and would welcome social contact. Invariably I am promised they will "look me up"; to date, without exception, this has not occurred. Several have said they would like me to speak to lay groups and I have eagerly accepted. No date has been set. Have visited several local white churches and always fill out the visitor's card; no follow-up contact has been made.

In Edwards, the small town very near Mt. Beulah, Winham reported attending "by invitation" the week after the Selma march in 1965 a Sunday service of the local Methodist church. In the middle of his sermon the minister indicated "he was departing from [his] prepared text, whereupon there followed a 20 min. denunciation." Winham also noted grimly that the "lady who invited us was not present." He felt he had been "set up," in order for a pointed attack to be made publicly on the ministry by a fellow churchman. A Presbyterian minister in Greenville upon whom one of the ministry staff made a lengthy call, six months later told the ministry's public information officer that "nobody from Delta Ministry had ever cared enough to even drop by my office." Another staff person who had lived and worked at Mt. Beulah for almost a year remarked angrily in March 1966 that

> since last July I know of no reporter for the Jackson papers who has been on this campus, yet there is an unceasing barrage of vituperation appearing regularly in those papers against Mount Beulah and the DM program. . . . There is no outlet, except through personal discussion and experience, to tell the truth.

The writer sadly, almost poignantly, concluded:

> Although we long for a mutual relationship with the white churches, and although we have stood prayerfully interested and available for many months, we have thus far met with only rejection because of the explicit DM involvement with an integrated society and with the poor.[5]

National and especially statewide leaders of the churches, whom one might expect to exercise some restraint, were not much different than the rank and file in their response to the ministry. Prominent leaders in the mainline churches, including the Methodist and Episcopal bishops in Mississippi, began to raise questions with NCC officials almost as soon as plans for the ministry were announced. They felt the preliminary preparations had been inadequate, they feared the "divisiveness" of working primarily among poor blacks. They also introduced the now familiar claim of the need for "reconciliation" between white and black and the failure of the ministry to achieve such. Along with the cry "let us take care of our problems ourselves," throughout the sixties these were key recurring points of criticism raised among local religious groups.

During the spring and summer of 1964 the Episcopal bishop in Mississippi, John Allin, carried on a thinly veiled campaign of opposition to the yet-to-be implemented mission work. Shortly after the Delta Ministry officially began, Allin asked top officials of the National Council to postpone the program, to give "the churches in Mississippi an opportunity to initiate their own approach to the situation in the Delta." His suggestion was rejected; the bishop continued as a frequent critic thereafter. Edward J. Pendergrass, the Methodist bishop, sometimes more blatant in his criticism than Allin, sometimes working indirectly, was no less persistent. His active opposition was an important factor in the failure of the Methodist Church to provide any support for the ministry until the fall of 1966, even though they had promised over $100,000 to the budget both in 1965 and in 1966.[6]

As noted earlier, state officials of the Disciples of Christ strongly opposed the leasing of Mt. Beulah to the National Council of Churches. When the decision to do so was finalized, local Disciples followed a "scorched earth" policy at the little academy, removing everything which might be of help to the new tenants, including step ladders, all of the kitchen equipment, and even the light bulbs from their sockets in the buildings. This steady opposition, coupled with lower-than-expected contributions to the Delta Ministry's budget by other mainline churches in addition to the Methodists, helped to precipitate the reevaluation of the Ministry in 1966.[7]

The constant opposition to the Delta Ministry from Mississippi church people in 1965 and 1966 can be linked to other developments statewide around civil rights issues which occurred during the same time period. One quickly recalls the ministry-supported Head Start program of CDGM, enthusiastically supported by poor blacks and their children, which began in the summer of 1965 and which provoked vehement white opposition, ending in the refusal in Washington to refund CDGM in September 1966, and the creation of a new group of Head Start programs more responsive to local white control, known as Mississippi Action for Progress, or MAP. Some of the Delta Ministry's earliest white friends, including Hodding Carter III, actively backed these new groups and openly opposed the ministry from 1966 onward.

The Voting Rights Act, passed in August 1965, also established powerful national guidelines that finally assured large-scale voting of African Americans in Mississippi. However, beginning in late 1965 white Mississippi politicians set out to erect new and more subtle barriers that would frustrate and delay black political power. Delta Ministry participation, often in cooperation with the MFDP, in efforts to increase black voter registration and to prepare black leaders for their new political responsibilities clearly placed the ministry in opposition to continuing all-white political dominance. The Delta Ministry supported those who had been all but powerless, but who now were gaining, or threatening to gain, new elements of power for themselves. It is not hard to see, therefore, why mainline church leaders in Mississippi—clergy and lay people alike—supported the review of the work of the Ministry which occurred in the spring of 1966. Many of these white church people were also those involved in the efforts to limit the political and social gains of newly enfranchised blacks. Thus negative conclusions reached in New York about the ministry might well mean the end of this church group, which worked for "an integrated society and with the poor" and which seemed to threaten the positions of power and control held by white church people in Mississippi society.[8]

Finally, national race relations were also changing. During James Meredith's personal march through Mississippi, begun early in June 1966, Stokely Carmichael dramatized for the first time the slogan, "Black Power!" Coupled with large and widespread disturbances in northern urban black communities in the summers of 1965 and 1966, these events suggested a new militancy among African Americans, even in Mississippi, that could challenge the integrationist approach of groups like the Delta Ministry and the old-line civil rights organizations. SNCC's disintegration and withdrawal from Mississippi by the end of 1966, in part because of internal disagreements over black separatism, was one of the clearest indications of these new national trends.[9] Inevitably affected by all of these local and national events, it is not surprising that the Delta Ministry, too, underwent a crisis of considerable importance in the first half of 1966.

The evaluation committee for the Delta Ministry, appointed by the president of the National Council of Churches, began its work in January 1966 and did not submit its final report to the General Board of the National Council until four months later, in mid-May 1966. Splitting into subcommittees to study every aspect of the ministry's work, the group spent considerable time in Mississippi and listened to a large number of witnesses.[10]

The evidence shows clearly that the committee did not intend to prepare a "whitewash." Indeed, National Council officials may have even bent too far toward the ministry's opponents in their efforts to be fair. No Mississippi African Americans, especially those whom the ministry served, were on the review panel (several critics were included) and most opponents who cared to were given lengthy opportunities to speak directly to the evaluation committee in Mississippi.[11]

Eventually the evaluation committee strongly endorsed the ministry's work, making clear that it was going to be continued, and that the National Council of Churches (and by implication the national leadership of the many Mississippi churches that were critics) would continue to provide strong backing.[12] The final report also summarized well the broad nature of the ministry's achievements: it had "kept pressure on for social change and social justice in the closed, traditional Mississippi society," it had "ministered to a group (the very poor) with whom no one else has had a ministry," it had "brought into being important projects" such as CDGM, and it had "been a sign of sacrificial Christian ministry."[13]

But the committee also set forth many of the arguments of those who disapproved of church activism in Mississippi. The report spoke of "poor communication and interpretation," of the reluctance of the ministry to build bridges to local white churches, even after the little group had become "better known . . . and respected in the Mississippi community," and of fears that the ministry's "total emphasis on the Negro poor" had "accentuated the cleavage" between middle-class blacks and whites and poor blacks.[14] Yet, interestingly, the committee also provided what amounted to a final rebuttal to these charges by including with its report a forceful response to the entire document prepared by Paul Moore, Jr., then Suffragan Bishop of the Episcopal Diocese of Washington and chair of the governing board of the Delta Ministry.

Moore confronted the long-debated reconciliation issue directly. *Did the ministry accentuate differences between the races and even between classes in the African American community?* The bishop bluntly concluded that it was truer to assert that "we have 'revealed' the cleavage already there. You might say there is more real communication now than ever before, but the established community does not like what it is hearing." Moore then moved to the heart of his statement—a biblically rooted explanation of his and the ministry's understanding of "reconciliation," seemingly so ardently desired by white church people. "We feel true reconciliation between unequal and alienated groups is not possible without justice." At an earlier moment Moore elaborated more fully on this theme, in a statement made verbally to the evaluation committee:

> We [the Delta Ministry] engage in a ministry of reconciliation by helping the poor to gain enough self-confidence, articulateness, and power to negotiate on a basis of equality of person with the powers that be. We feel that true reconciliation between unequal and alienated groups is not possible without justice (crying peace, peace, when there is no peace). Despite heavy criticism that we are agitators . . . we continue to feel that the above understanding of reconciliation is truly biblical.[15]

Interestingly, following a series of discussions in March 1966 with members of the governing board that oversaw the ministry, the evaluation committee defined the "basic objective" or the ministry almost exactly as Moore did—"to enable persons and groups in communities to come together in equality and with justice."[16] And probably the evaluation committee shared with Moore the belief in the fundamentally biblical nature of such an approach to human relations.

Perhaps it was no accident, then, that during its first year of operation the Delta Ministry's headquarters in Greenville came to be known to some local black citizens as "the Justice Place." Eventually people also applied the term to Mt. Beulah and even when there was more general talk about the little church group.[17] It was a considerable compliment, yet also a telling phrase. In retrospect the term seemed to catch the essence of a key motivating force underlying the ministry's work, running parallel to and mutually reinforcing the strong sense of "servanthood" that also shaped how the ministry functioned. Moreover, trying to bring together persons and groups "in equality and with justice," explained much about what caused the deep differences between the ministry and the white churches in Mississippi when all of them talked about, and tried to work at, "reconciliation." In rare instances perhaps people in Mississippi *could* get a glimpse of what biblical "reconciliation," as it applied to race relations, was really all about. Consider this series of events Bob Beech reported to the central office of the ministry:

In January [1965], one afternoon, three white women came to see me at our office on Mobile Street [in Hattiesburg]. We were in the process of unloading a semi-trailor of clothes and food into our warehouse and I was busy. . . . By the time I got to them, they were beginning to be uncomfortable, I guess at seeing so many Negroes and so few whites. It turned out that they were poor white people from Purvis, Mississippi, in Lamar County next door to the west. They had been referred to us . . . in their quest for food and clothing. . . . An OK was given for the food, boxes filled and placed in their dilapidated truck, and an invitation given them to come to one of the five clothing centers on a subsequent day. . . . They did come back . . . stood in line with the Negroes, were waited on, and left. They came back again and again, each time bringing a few new faces with them. . . . They became less reserved and finally very cordial and open. We began to talk about the similarity between their troubles and those of the Negroes, and about segregation and prejudice itself. It turned out that they felt almost no hostility toward Negroes and that they explained their attitude with Bible teachings, quite simply, but very accurately. "God made us all of one blood," "There's just one heaven—and one hell," "A Negro's prayer is as good as a white man's." Finally the invitation came to visit their church and worship with them. We did—my mother and brother who were visiting me and myself. I have never before shared in a holiness service and that in itself was quite an experience. But to do so with men who had been pointed out to me previously as members of the Klan added yet another mixed feeling! I was asked to preach first. I took as my text the last half of Matthew 25 and indicated that this was what our organization was working in Mississippi to carry out. Each one who preached subsequently made allusion to what I had said and indicated that Negroes were people too—and equal in the sight of God. We were warmly received after the service . . . (those who had previously been pointed out as Klan oriented spoke to us but were much more reserved) and we were invited back.[18]

Brought together by common economic and religious concerns, a Delta Ministry staff person and seemingly bigoted poor whites were able to bridge great differences in race, class, and even church distinctions to "reconcile" one with another. Interestingly, all of this occurred outside of the mainstream churches in Mississippi, which had been complaining so loudly about the lack of "reconciliation" between themselves and the ministry. The healing force came from surprising, unexpected sources; that, too, had a strong biblical flavor to it. And finally these events illuminated once again how well the Delta Ministry carried out its "servant" mission to the dispossessed of Mississippi.

Although the Delta Ministry's difficulties in 1966 were in part the result of actions by people outside the organization, inside there also were troubles, especially a very shaky financial operation. This fact provided further ammunition to the ministry's critics and was a major concern throughout the evaluation committee's deliberations. In 1965, the first full year of operation, the budget deficit of the ministry was a startling $161,000. Partly this disparity resulted when over $25,000 had to be spent unexpectedly on capital repairs at Mt. Beulah in order to make it usable (the Mississippi Disciples' "scorched earth" policy added to these woes). Dependent largely upon sums donated by the separate denominations under the NCC's ecumenical umbrella rather than from the National Council's own general budget, opposition to the ministry caused funding commitments not to be honored. In 1965 American churches designated $113,000 for the ministry, barely a quarter of the amount projected as "realistic" by its supporters. As Bishop Moore put it charitably, "the mandate was too big for the budget."[19] Gifts from churches in Europe and Africa,[20] large infusions from the basic financial reserves of the NCC, and even fund-raising attempts by the ministry staff closed some of the gap in 1965, but the negative trends continued. In the first quarter of 1966 the ministry spent $15,000 *per month* above its approved budget. In that one quarter of the fiscal year it spent 42 percent of its annual budget allocation. Throughout this same period, people in New York struggled to develop with the ministry staff realistic budgeting and accounting procedures, but not until April 1966 did NCC officials, with the cooperation of Art Thomas, begin to impose the severe budgetary controls that would eventually achieve solvency.[21]

The net effect of the struggle to balance the budget was to leave the Delta Ministry conducting essentially a "holding action" throughout the late spring and summer of 1966. Several full-time staff were terminated or agreed to work without pay, and key programs were eliminated or severely curtailed. As might be expected, all of these activities produced a considerable lowering of morale of the remaining staff.[22] Inevitably the financial disarray also provoked strong criticism of Art Thomas, the director, and to a lesser extent of Paul Moore, chair of the Ministry's governing board, because of their key policymaking positions as the crisis developed.[23] In the middle of the summer of 1966, Thomas and Moore resigned; in mid-August Warren McKenna, the associate director, was asked to leave, ostensibly to help ease the financial situation.

There may have been additional reasons for McKenna's departure. A personal trip to Communist China in the 1950s and his very liberal political views had always made him suspect to right-wing critics of the ministry. Although officials of the National Council strongly denied there was any connection, contributions by certain mainline churches, especially the Methodists, increased noticeably soon after McKenna left. Perhaps it would be most accurate to say that the increase in contributions picked up after *all* the top leadership of the ministry had departed by the end of the summer of 1966.[24] In any case, the financial crisis played a central role in the departure of important leaders who had shaped much of the early vision of the Delta Ministry. But that fact did not mean the end of the organization, as some of its critics hoped.

In the midst of the fiscal crunch, the National Council of Churches once again provided a clear signal that it was not going to abandon its venture in Mississippi. The evaluation committee had proposed closing down all operations at Mt. Beulah as a major money-saving maneuver. In response, Bishop Moore delivered a ringing defense of the need for the little school before the General Board of the National Council in early June 1966: "The heart of this ministry, both programmatically and symbolically, is Mt. Beulah. It is a sanctuary, a training center, and a warm community of spiritual power. It is an outward and visible sign of our presence. It has been essential from the very start." Without Beulah, Moore went on, there would have been no "integrated conferences" in a land of almost total segregation, no place for the ministry staff and their friends to "rest, think, and confer," no haven for "refugees" of various kinds—"people who have been put off plantations, people who are afraid, people whose houses have been burned down, etc." The bishop then offered this very pointed conclusion:

> Our opponents realize the importance of Beulah. Therefore, it is Beulah that they have most consistently attacked. If we give up Beulah as a center for the Delta Ministry, it will be considered a resounding victory for the forces of reaction in Mississippi, no matter what we say. This will invite a stepping-up of antagonistic behavior on the part of those who are against our work, and will result in a sense of betrayal amongst the poor people with whom we have been working.

Evidently his remarks had an effect since the recommendation of the evaluation committee to eliminate Mt. Beulah was not implemented.[25]

Moreover, in the fall of 1966 the ministry began to revive. Utilizing evidence of the new budgetary controls placed on the ministry, in late September 1966 two key groups in the Methodist Episcopal Church's powerful Board of Missions, the Women's Division and the National Division, overrode strong opposition from Bishop Pendergrass and his supporters in Mississippi and voted to provide the ministry $130,000 for the following year. The long-awaited support of the Methodists had finally materialized, and at least for a time the financial base of the minis-

Civil Rights March on Washington, D.C., August 28, 1963. Members of the
Protestant Episcopal Church of St. Stephen and the Incarnation in the nation's
capital joined with other churchmen from around the nation on the March on
Washington for Jobs and Freedom. (*Courtesy Religious News Service*)

Summer volunteers with a young local resident, probably in Harmony, Mississippi, in the summer of 1964. (*Courtesy collection of Kenneth Thompson, Board of Global Ministries, United Methodist Church*)

Rev. Paul Moore, then Suffragan Bishop of the Episcopal Diocese of Washington, D.C. (left), and Ralph Featherstone, a SNCC worker, in Mc-Comb, Mississippi, in the summer of 1964. Moore was the first chair of the governing board of the Delta Ministry. (*Courtesy collection of Donald McCord*)

Delta Ministry staff, black and white, singing "We Shall Overcome" at a civil rights meeting in Greenville, Mississippi. The man in the middle with a bow tie is Warren McKenna, Assistant Director of the Ministry. (*Courtesy collection of Ken Thompson*)

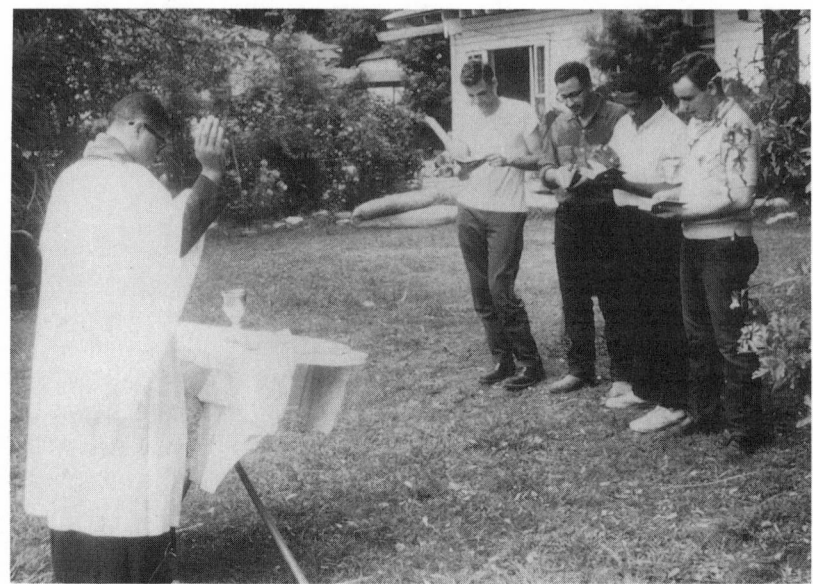

Rev. Harry Bowie (Episcopal), soon to be Delta Ministry staff member, conducts communion on the front lawn of Freedom House, McComb, Mississippi, in the summer of 1964. Note damaged cornice and window of the Freedom House, which had been bombed several days before. The communion table is an ironing board. (*Courtesy collection of Donald McCord*)

The COFO (umbrella organization of all civil rights groups in Mississippi in the summer of 1964) "office" in Biloxi, Mississippi. (*Courtesy collection of Donald McCord*)

Robert Stone, Presbyterian minister, and Freedom School students, McComb, Mississippi, in the summer of 1964. (*Courtesy collection of Donald McCord*)

Thelma Barnes, Delta Ministry staff, 1964. (*Courtesy Thelma Barnes*)

Two views from 1986 of the campus of Mt. Beulah, in Edwards, Mississippi, center of Delta Ministry and civil rights activity in the 1960s. (*Courtesy James Findlay*)

Remains of a six-foot cross set on fire by four men—believed to be Klan members—in front of the National Council of Churches' Delta Ministry administration building, Mt. Beulah, Mississippi, in 1967. (*Courtesy National Council of Churches*)

Porterville, Mississippi, Head Start Center graduation exercises, August 1967. (*Courtesy Presbyterian Historical Society*)

A used tire becomes a sandbox, Mt. Pisgah, Mississippi Head Start (CDGM, Child Development Group of Mississippi), August 1967. (*Courtesy Presbyterian Historical Society*)

Robert Spike, Anna Hedgeman, and Eugene Carson Blake. Three church leaders active in the lobbying for the 1964 Civil Rights Act. (*Courtesy collection of Ken Thompson*)

Robert Spike. (*Courtesy collection of Ken Thompson*)

NCC Commission on Religion and Race, in 1965 or 1966, in Robert Spike's office. (*Courtesy collection of Ken Thompson*)

Benjamin Payton (right), R. H. Edwin Espy (center), executive director of the National Council of Churches, and Eugene Carson Blake (left), at a press conference in late 1965 introducing Payton as the successor of Robert Spike as chairperson of the NCC's Commission on Religion and Race. (*Courtesy collection of Ken Thompson*)

Gayraud S. Wilmore, a Presbyterian theologian who was executive director of the United Presbyterian Church (USA) Commission on Religion and Race and a major black power spokesman within church circles in the late 1960s. (*Courtesy Presbyterian Historical Society*)

Jonathan's Wake, a group of church critics, conduct a mock funeral of the National Council of Churches at the NCC General Assembly, Detroit, Michigan, in late 1969. Note flower clenched in teeth of Malcolm Boyd (at rear of casket). (*Courtesy National Council of Churches*)

James Forman presenting his Black Manifesto demands to the NCC, November 1969. (*Courtesy National Council of Churches*)

Changing attitudes on race are reflected on a temporary construction wall in Denver, 1969. (*Courtesy Religious News Service*)

try was secure.[26] New people also began to take on the mantle of leadership of the ministry, drawn from the experienced, full-time staff. Owen Brooks, an Episcopal lay person originally from Boston, became acting director, assisted especially by Harry Bowie, an Episcopal priest who had run the ministry office in McComb since late 1964. Both were African Americans. The shift from white to black at key posts in the ministry was a necessary, overdue move, reflecting changed realities in race relations nationally and the pressing need in Mississippi to keep pace with the rapidly developing self-consciousness of the African American community there.[27]

The double focus on local programs in the Delta and broader-based statewide concerns remained, but these interests seemed a little less freewheeling and open-ended than previously. In part this reflected increasing involvement in bureaucratic federal programs that were either entirely new (like CDGM and other Great Society programs), or available but not utilized fully in Mississippi until pressured by the ministry and community groups (like surplus commodities and food stamps).

The ministry continued its most fundamental commitments, especially in politics and in education. As noted earlier, as the black electorate rapidly expanded after the passage of the Voting Rights Act in 1965, the ministry responded by redoubling its efforts at voter registration and in offering daylong workshops for many of the black candidates for office prior to local elections in November of that year. They did the same in 1967 and 1969, ofttimes expanding the workshops to several days. In November 1967, Robert Clark was the first African American since Reconstruction elected to the Mississippi state legislature. When he arrived in Jackson the following January lacking staff, ministry people immediately provided assistance. They helped Clark build a legislative agenda and then a lobbying effort closely tied to issues of race and poverty, the first of its kind in the state. The ministry also joined with key leaders of the MFDP to help negotiate black representation on the "Loyalist" delegation to the Democratic National Convention in Chicago in August 1968. Although in the deepest sense this action meant the final failure of the MFDP, representing the poorer segments of the African American community, to become a powerful independent political force in Mississippi, it also signaled the emergence of the entire African American community to a position of permanent importance in the Mississippi Democratic party and was another indication of their steadily expanding political power in the state.[28]

Sensitized by direct experience in Freedom Village with school-age children burdened with severe educational deficiencies, in 1966 and after the ministry broadened its educational concerns beyond CDGM. For several years they worked especially with lawyers of the NAACP Legal Defense Fund to secure proper representation of blacks on local school boards and as school teachers on integrated staffs and to require an appropriate curriculum and adequate school supplies for African American children in the Mississippi public schools forced to desegregate by Federal Court orders beginning in 1967 and 1968.[29]

There was something increasingly rooted about all of these activities. In Mississippi at least *kairos* was taking on a semipermanent status. As one staff member noted much later, the ministry was responding to a need for "institutionness" that would help to shape and direct the way in which poor, black Mississippians moved into the mainstream of public life in their state. At least part of the time in the late sixties some of the ministry staff took on "specialist" roles—Rims Barber in education, Owen Brooks in political organizing, Harry Bowie in economic development, Charles Horwitz in public information. Staff people also became adept at generating statistical data that was used in legal battles over food stamp qualifications and school redistricting. In part they were becoming *technicians,* providers of special services to those they served. Their long-established talents in coalition building were continued and accentuated as they devised programs in cooperation with other community organizations for poor people that were proliferating throughout the state. But their fundamental purpose throughout these years remained constant—to help the African American community, especially the poorest, to achieve human dignity and the power to speak for themselves as they struggled to move more toward the center of Mississippi life.[30]

In late December 1967, Owen Brooks, who had replaced Art Thomas as director, stated that "newly placed" among the ministry's "top priorities" would be economic development. This was a programmatic emphasis of growing significance for the rest of the sixties, focusing attention on a theme often mentioned but infrequently acted upon earlier. One of the three original purposes of the ministry enunciated by the General Board of the National Council in early 1964 was for a program of "community development which will mobilize technical skills, scientific knowledge [and] economic resources . . . to the end of developing an adequate base for livelihood" for the poor people of the Delta. The detailed evaluation of the ministry in 1966 caused the early goals to be reformulated, and economic development emerged even more explicitly as a primary concern of the ministry.[31]

By 1968 the Delta Ministry staff had concluded, based on considerable experience, that long-term economic assistance for the African American community in Mississippi should rest on two "clear and simple, though difficult to obtain" necessities; first, to "get industry to move into areas of high unemployment," and second, to develop black-owned small business to "consolidate the economic base" [of African Americans].[32] The focus now was on industrial development, even in predominantly rural areas, where cotton had always reigned supreme. Freedom Village had demonstrated painfully both how important this subject was and how hard it was to secure solid economic gains for impoverished African Americans in the Delta. From the little community's inception, the ministry had scoured the nation for light industry that might be drawn to

Greenville and nearby to provide jobs for the people of the model village. But lack of industrial job skills, low educational levels, and the corroding effects on personality of deep-seated racial prejudice all stood in the way of "New City" providing an effective labor force.[33]

Gradually ministry people came to see that if economic development was to be truly effective it would require huge sums of money—investment capital—sustained over an extended time period from both public and private sources. It would also require technical and managerial expertise the ministry did not possess. Experience in Freedom Village again served as a precedent for the broader economic concerns that developed after 1966. In late 1965 the ministry helped to found the Delta Opportunities Corporation (DOC), a nonprofit organization designed to generate capital for community projects like Freedom Village. This corporation became the principal agency that secured the funds to build Freedom Village.[34] Yet despite the large sums of money raised by the DOC, it was focused on very small numbers of people, and there was no guarantee that the programs of job retraining, literacy, health education, and home building it funded would succeed in permanently changing the lives of the people in the village.

In 1966 the ministry launched at Mt. Beulah its first formal economic venture, a small woodworking cooperative named Freedomcrafts. It provided toys and furniture for the Head Start centers of Mississippi and employment and new skills to a score or more dispossessed plantation workers. Cooperative economic ventures, egalitarian in nature and relatively easy to establish, strongly appealed to many who had been associated with the freedom movement. At least at Mt. Beulah, however, the cooperative could not be sustained permanently. Inadequate start-up capital, insufficient "entrepreneurial skills" among the workers, and especially a significant market loss when CDGM's role in the state was curtailed, all led to its eventual demise. From these beginnings the ministry's vision of new economic opportunities for unskilled blacks in the Delta grew and changed. In 1967, in addition to supporting the start of the Delta Opportunities Corporation's work with Freedom Village, the ministry got deeply involved in efforts to create a private funding organization in Mound Bayou, Mississippi, designed to attract small industries to that small, all-black Delta town north of Greenville. From there it seemed only a short step to the creation in 1969 of the areawide Delta Foundation.[35]

By 1969 there were a number of small organizations like the Delta Ministry involved in community development in Mississippi who could see the value of pooling outside contacts, capital resources, and professional expertise to launch a more substantive attack on the economic and social ills of the black community than was possible when each group operated independently. After a ministry-sponsored statewide conference on development pinpointed the need for cooperative efforts, on March 20, 1969, the Delta Ministry joined with fourteen other community organizations to create the Delta Foundation. This foundation sought to secure sufficient capital from "churches and foundations that have historically been involved in the support of Mississippi projects" to establish black-owned and managed *industries,* primarily in the Delta, on a scale that "would succeed and affect the total economy of the state."[36]

The Delta Foundation did several things. It served as a sort of clearing house for the receipt of grants, loans, and gifts from churches, local commercial banks, private foundations, and the state and federal governments—capital that was then invested in the creation of new light industry or the purchase of existing small manufacturing concerns that could be relocated profitably in the Delta. The foundation also served as the mother-corporation for all of the businesses created, overseeing generally the management of these companies, and serving as the recipient of whatever profits accrued annually from the businesses it had fostered. The bulk of the profits were to be reinvested. In essence the foundation was a "development corporation" designed to create jobs, whose profits were to be used "to create more jobs." But a portion of the income was also to be invested each year in "social overhead capital"—in housing, educational ventures, health facilities, or noncommercial but business-related projects that enhanced the African American community, especially in the Delta.[37]

This was a much more complex economic venture than the early cooperative enterprises, involving large amounts of capital, professional management, and the creation of a small industrial workforce. After careful study and planning, late in 1970 the first child of the Delta Foundation, a company known as Fine Vines, Inc., was established. Employing almost ninety workers, mostly women, nearly 60 percent of whom had never before held jobs outside their homes, Fine Vines mass-produced blue jeans on contract for Sears, Roebuck in unused buildings at the Greenville air base where, ironically, destitute black people had been evicted for trespassing four years earlier. By 1980 the portfolio of the foundation had grown to eight companies manufacturing bicycle wheels, blue jeans, attic stairs, house fans, railroad spikes, and electrical mechanical switches. These manufacturing concerns employed over 500 people, most of them African American residents of the Delta. The national economic downturn of the early 1980s, which hit Mississippi especially severely, forced the foundation into a reorganization, which meant some decentralization of its operations and the closing of several of the companies it had initiated. Nevertheless, the foundation weathered these economic difficulties and continues to operate today, supporting a scaled-back Fine Vines jeans manufactory, its railroad spike works, and a successful effort in the electronic industry.[38] While the foundation did not solve the problems of poor people in the Mississippi Delta, it was a creative model of economic self-help, which has demonstrated long-term staying power as well as strong commitments to the broad social and economic concerns of the community providing its work force.

Ministry involvement in the foundation was substantial from the beginning. Both Owen Brooks and Harry Bowie were on the original governing board. But Bowie, working closely with two other African Americans, Ed Brown and Charles Bannerman of Mississippi Action for Community Education (MACE), a statewide community development organization, played one of the most important roles in getting the foundation started. Bowie was on the board of managers of the foundation for over a decade, became the executive director of the foundation in 1985, and remains in that capacity today. His work and that of Owen Brooks epitomized the Delta Ministry technique of working cooperatively with similar groups in and outside the African American community.[39]

The ministry's wide contacts among religious groups also helped in the early days to link the Delta Foundation to crucial outside support. Especially significant were the contacts made with the Cummins Engine Company, then the largest manufacturer of diesel engines in the world. Cummins was directed by J. Irwin Miller, who the reader might recall was the president of the National Council of Churches in 1963, and who was then and later a strong supporter of the newly developed activism of the mainline churches on racial issues. An earlier statement bears repeating, that Miller integrated the work force at the Cummins plants in Indiana in the 1930s and was a pioneer in drawing young black engineers onto his managerial staff in the immediate postwar era. Miller provided the funding in 1969 for the initial planning of the Delta Foundation. He also urged two African Americans in Cummins's management to go to Mississippi, on paid leaves, to serve as consultants to the foundation in selecting businesses to be developed and managerial procedures to be set up. One of these original consultants remains today on the staff of the Delta Foundation.[40] Once again in their quiet way Delta Ministry people had helped to create insitutions that were to have a lasting impact on the African American community of Mississippi and to underscore in a somewhat different, yet still unmistakable manner, their commitment to the poor and a servant ministry to the dispossessed.

In spite of all these constructive developments, however, looking back we can see now that the late sixties and early seventies were also a time of increasing difficulty for the Delta Ministry. A shift in national attitudes, both within and outside the churches, was partly responsible. The great ghetto disturbances of the late sixties and the rise of the black power movement caused severe white backlash. People in local churches, part of that backlash, were increasingly unsympathetic to programs like that of the Delta Ministry. By 1968 the Vietnam War had become very divisive and siphoned off public funds and diverted public attention that otherwise might have been focused on poverty and related domestic issues. And the Nixon administration began to weaken or to dismantle the key agencies in the war on poverty. Beginning in May 1969, the controversies within the mainstream churches generated by the Black Manifesto further alienated potential supporters. The budgets of both the national church bureaucracies and the federal poverty programs began to shrink almost simultaneously. Heavily dependent on these two sources of income and support, the Delta Ministry was bound to suffer.

Mt. Beulah continued to be a constant drain on the ministry's resources. The problems at Beulah eased a bit in 1968 when the Presbyterian Church, U.S.A., assumed the lease from the National Council of Churches. The latter, already affected by declining revenues, had to reduce expenses in Mississippi.[41] But a Presbyterian plan to create at Beulah a statewide adult education "university" for poor people never received the necessary federal funding. And even the relatively well-heeled Presbyterians could not continue indefinitely to finance a campus where major capital improvements, unmet for over a decade, were still a pressing need.[42]

By 1970, as the termination date of Mt. Beulah's lease between the Disciples of Christ and the NCC-UPCUSA neared, it became clear that none of the parties involved wanted to extend the agreement. Tight budgets in the three church groups directly related to Beulah—the National Council of Churches, the Presbyterians, and the Disciples—were the determining factor. When the lease expired the owners, the Disciples of Christ, were going to sell the site. Delta Ministry people and their supporters tried desperately to dissuade the Disciples, but sufficient money was not available to provide a solution. On March 31, 1971, the lease expired, all ministry activities at Mt. Beulah soon ceased, and the African Methodist Episcopal Church bought the physical facilities in June 1971 for $50,000.[43] It seemed ironic that three major mainline Protestant groups could not sustain Mt. Beulah as a center for interracial activities, while a far less prosperous African American denomination had the money to buy the property. In any case, Mt. Beulah never again played the role in Mississippi it had in the 1960s. Paul Moore's words describing Mt. Beulah in 1966—a sanctuary, a training center, a warm community of spiritual power—were probably less accurate in 1971, but only slightly less so.[44] The fierceness with which Delta Ministry staff fought the closing and their extended effort to help in the search for a sympathetic buyer suggest that the sale of Mt. Beulah in 1971 was a considerable blow to them, both programmatically and psychologically.

Simultaneously with the disheartening struggle over Mt. Beulah, the ministry had to confront difficult internal problems. The budget stringencies of the National Council in New York that helped to create the Mt. Beulah situation also affected the ministry more directly. Promised pay increases for the staff were rescinded in March 1970, and direct staff reductions seemed just ahead. Then in 1971 the ministry's operating budget was slashed, from $310,000 to $125,000. Pressures generated in part by these crushing economic difficulties caused long-standing personal and group tensions finally to burst into public view. In early March 1971, some of the staff requested Owen Brooks's removal as director, in part because of Brooks's alleged black separatist tendencies. There were disagreements between "outsiders" (like Brooks) and native Mississippians, who now were a sizeable percentage of the staff. Perhaps these were also differences based on subtle class distinctions. Claims raised by women staff persons that sexist biases (confirmed in a hearing conducted by an official from the National Council of Churches office in New York) had affected job evaluations added to the turmoil. The cause of the basic rift is probably best explained by the need for an agonizing choice, based on the new budgetary realities, between two groups within the staff, each of which sought to continue long-established ministry programs—those who wanted to do detailed community organizing in only two or three local areas, and those who wanted to continue to provide assistance to existing statewide community groups for a broader effect. The second option was implemented; staff involved in local affairs were released. In any case, by the end of 1971 only four full-time people remained.[45]

The internal tensions that surfaced in 1971 were not entirely unexpected. Key members of the ministry had been working together for more than half a decade in the most trying conditions. Differences were bound to occur. Indeed, it is surprising how few disputes there were, given the strong personalities involved and the lengthy period they were together. Unlike SNCC and CORE, however, the Delta Ministry never was torn asunder by debates over black power or black separatism, or over the use of violence as a political weapon. Because of its religious grounding it consistently remained strongly committed to interracialism and nonviolence. But the ministry also recognized the powerful shifts in black consciousness that were developing nationally by 1966. Owen Brooks had been a major participant in the famous James Meredith March through Mississippi that year where it was noted earlier that "black power" was first insistently raised by Stokely Carmichael and others. Not accidentally (and also noted earlier), in late 1966 Brooks became the director, and along with Harry Bowie and Thelma Barnes, all African Americans, the three became the principal administrators of ministry programs. Early in 1968 Andrew Young also assumed the chairmanship of the ministry's executive board.[46]

But these changes never involved total exclusion of whites from the staff; moreover, those whites who continued were enthusiastic supporters, as they always had been, of black empowerment in Mississippi. They would sympathize fully with the following words of the National Committee of Black Churchmen, published in October 1969 and representing the views of many black leaders within the mainline churches on the vexing issue of black power:

> [We are] not involved in *Separatism* (in the sense of absolute disjunction), *Reverse Racism, Anti-Whiteism* or *American Apartheid*. [We do] stand for religious and cultural pluralism as one of the requirements of pride and empowerment. It is neither a cult of Black superiority [n]or Black domination.

[We believe] that oppression—whatever its color—will yield only to the solidarity and militant resistance of the oppressed and that power is necessary for any people to participate fully in determining the shape of the future for themselves and for all people.[47]

This meant belief in black *power*, but not in black separatism, a crucial distinction most whites, including many people from the mainstream churches, failed to make. Because the ministry *did* make the distinction and supported the concept as outlined above, it continued its work throughout the late sixties and early seventies largely unaffected by the great tumult engulfing white and black America over this issue. That in itself was a signal achievement.

The unhappy events of 1971 did seem, however, to point ot an underlying weakness of the ministry, that existed almost from the beginning and that may have added to the difficulties toward the end. This was the absence of a consciously shared common life based on mutually accepted religious practices, centered around corporate worship or group discussion of theological and biblical texts. It is clear that a real sense of community did exist within the staff,[48] but often there seemed to be nothing distinctively religious or Christian about it, nothing to distinguish ministry people from *all* participants in the movement in Mississippi. Perhaps this fact pointed to the success of the "servant mission" of the ministry. Once again it should be stated that the task was not to stand apart but to identify as fully as possible with those being served. But that left each person in the ministry to survive largely on whatever internal spiritual and personal resources they as individuals possessed.

Just prior to the establishment of the Delta Ministry, Art Thomas put into writing his thoughts about the necessity of "A Common Discipline of the Delta Ministry Staff." Apparently it was the only time anyone on the staff stopped and thought carefully about such issues, and then recorded those thoughts. Thomas wrote:

"The expectation is that the . . . staff will come together on a regular basis for worship and study. These sessions will be distinct from regular staff business meetings. As local field staffs develop, . . . they also will meet in continuing seminars designed to nurture their life together."[49]

Thomas anticipated a common "discipline" emerging, to help "equip the staff for the job to be done as servants of the Lord" and to enable the little group to be "sharers in a ministry which is common to all people of faith in the Delta." The last phrase was particularly telling, for it pointed—naively, we now know—to the hope that the ministry could work effectively with many people from local white churches, as well as dispossessed blacks. When cooperation with white churchgoers never materialized, an ecumenical worship-and-study discipline that could "be presented to local people in which they might participate" also became difficult to achieve.[50]

There are other possible explanations for the failure of the Delta Ministry to create a common religious life. The ecumenical movement in America, and especially the National Council of Churches, lacked a common communal history because they were recent developments. Liberal Protestantism was primarily an intellectual, not a devotional, movement. Even the "free Church" heritage of many mainstream churches, perhaps because it was rooted in the individualist heritage of nineteenth-century evangelicalism, often lacked powerful liturgical traditions. (This was not true of Lutherans and Episcopalians.)[51] Thus the ministry would have to experiment, to combine from a variety of worship forms connected chiefly to denominational sources. This would take time and energy a hard-pressed staff was unable or unwilling to provide.

Equally interesting, and surely not unrelated, was the fact that only in rare instances did the group, including all the ordained ministers, stop to think theologically about what they were doing. Perhaps, as some claimed later, they didn't seem to have time to engage in such activity, or possibly theologizing was such a distinctive enterprise that the staff were reluctant once again to stand apart from movement people.[52] If not the ministry, then perhaps professional theologians who had close connections with the experiment in Mississippi—seminary faculty, national church officers, and the like—might be expected to spend time reflecting and writing about the "Justice Place." Paul Moore, for instance, in his efforts to defend the ministry spoke and wrote with considerable biblical and theological sensitivity. But unfortunately he never built on that capability to discuss systematically and for a larger public the issues raised by the work in Mississippi. Harvey Cox, a well-known young theologian in 1964, was an early member of the commission that oversaw the ministry. He incorporated themes from the black freedom struggle into his writings, but failed to maintain for very long his specific interest in the ministry.[53] In the next chapter we shall have more to say about Robert Spike's great potential as a major national church spokesman on racial matters, never realized because of his tragic and untimely death in late 1966.

On May 14 to 15, 1965, three theologians, including Harvey Cox, met with the staff of the Delta Ministry in Greenville to conduct a "wide-ranging discussion of issues which such a ministry faced." The theologians were members of the North American Working Group, the American component of the World Council of Church's task force studying worldwide new missionary forms of the church, which had played such a seminal role in the work of Colin Williams, and even Robert Spike, discussed earlier in this book. The Delta Ministry had been selected as one of several models to be examined of new missionary endeavors already existing in the American church. The conversations in Mississippi focused on such issues as the church's mission in the world of the sixties, the nature of Christian community, the balance between freedom and order, the concept of ministry. One of the theologians later recalled the intensity of the discussions, describing the meeting as "tempestuous" and that "at certain points tempers seemed very frayed." But the fruitfulness of the exchange prompted another participant to suggest that the meetings be continued, even if only "periodically." Apparently no further meetings were ever held. Here perhaps was the greatest opportunity for the work of the ministry to influence the wider church through new theological understandings gained from careful yet impassioned discussions between professional theologians and the ministry staff. It seems a sad commentary on the state of theological discourse in the mainline churches that, when at a key intersection of church and world, among church professionals best able to reflect meaningfully and lastingly upon such matters, so little was done to take advantage of that moment.[54]

The Delta Ministry survived as a community as well as it did in part because the African American community in Mississippi functioned within a Protestant churchly tradition, which constantly succored the ministry as well as its own people.[55] Already widely recognized are the many connections between the African American churches and the civil rights movement. These churches provided some of the leadership and much of the mass support, but most important served as a great spiritual reservoir of comfort and inspiration through its songs, prayers, and the steady preaching of a biblical message of suffering, sacrifice, and ultimate hope. It is not surprising that individual members of the Delta Ministry turned to the African American churches when their own local religious groups rejected them. Still, a person on the staff once lamented, "the one group to which D[elta] M[inistry] seems unable to minister is itself."[56] That seems a bit of an exaggeration, but there is enough truth in the words to make one wonder what the effect on programs and personalities might have been if the ministry had tried more often to utilize fully the rich biblical, theological, and liturgical resources of Western christendom, which were everywhere at hand, to build group supports and to nourish their individual hearts and minds. And perhaps we have inklings here of why *kairos* could not be sustained for too long a time in the Deep South.

In June 1974, the Delta Ministry held a "ten year celebration" at the Cathedral of St. John the Divine in New York City. A combined fundraising event and time to celebrate the past with friends in the North, it was a formal affair filled with speeches and "honorees" (some only remotely related to the ministry) and even the recreation of an off-Broadway production of "Don't Bother Me, I Can't Cope."[57] It was a night filled with ironies. It was a rather fancy event held in the great northern urban center where the ministry was conceived, but very far removed from the fear, anguish, and deep challenges of the soul that were the inner essence of the ministry's life in Mississippi. It also seemed a tinseled public celebration quite unlike the quiet, unassuming role the ministry usually occupied. And in retrospect this hour of huzzahs might best be viewed as an end point for the little church group. The ministry was almost over, rather than on the verge of being renewed.

In many ways the creation, successful implementation, and eventual decline of the Delta Ministry between 1964 and 1974 reflected well the national approach to race in those years—a brief commitment to racial equality in the mid-sixties, then a growing white backlash coupled with a consuming war in Southeast Asia that eventually snuffed out hopes raised and social change begun. But these observations largely ignore the real and lasting achievements of the ministry, along with its secular allies, in Mississippi. The intense efforts at community building among a long-dispossessed portion of society did succeed, at least in part. One pauses to remember the founding of the Child Development Group of Missis-sippi—an experiment in education that stirred the black community deeply—or the slow, painstaking efforts at voter registration and political education that went on for years. In each instance the Delta Ministry was deeply involved. Surely it was no accident that in 1986 the first African American to be elected to Congress in Mississippi since Reconstruction was from the congressional district in the Delta where the ministry's workers (and earlier SNCC, CORE, and COFO) were most active.[58] Nor was it accidental that Owen Brooks, the last director of the Delta ministry, became a member of Congressman Mike Espy's staff. Or that over five hundred blacks are now in elected offices in Mississippi, the end result of that moment in 1967 when the Delta Ministry's "citizenship workshops" helped to prepare the first twenty-one blacks—and then many others—elected in the sixties to local offices in Mississippi. One should also recall the ministry's never-ending efforts to alleviate hunger and other symptoms of deep economic distress in the Delta, one result being the rapid expansion of federal support like surplus commodities and food stamps to thousands of people in great need, another being the establishment of the Delta Foundation to create new industries that today provide industrial jobs for former black sharecroppers and plantation workers.

Until now, in the media and to a degree in the scholarly literature, the major figures and leading civil rights organizations have received most of the attention when people think about the racial revolution of the sixties. Now we are beginning to explore the work of lesser-known individuals and organizations, like the Delta Ministry, that also made crucial contri-butions to the history of the black freedom movement. Such a perspec-tive reminds us that events and programs at the local level were often unique, had their own rhythms of historical development, and were not always as intimately tied to national civil rights agendas as the current historiography has often maintained.[59] In addition, the history of the ministry enables us to see the surprising role played by national church bureaucracies as sources of innovation and change against the deep-seated resistance of local groups, both within their own churches and outside in secular Mississippi. It is also an unusual tale of direct intervention of the church in the daily affairs of the world in ways not normally seen in our modern, secularized society. And by its actions the ministry raised fundamental questions regarding the church's mission in the world, which even yet are not fully defined, understood, and accepted.[60]

In June 1968, Andrew Young—at the time almost personifying the Delta Ministry: African American, ordained minister of a mainline Protestant denomination, former staff member of the National Council of Churches, and chairperson of the ministry's governing board—in informal comments at a board meeting reflected on the meaning of the ministry's work to that point. His thoughts also embodied, perhaps, how *kairos* had been achieved for a time in Mississippi. Young's words, laced with biblical metaphors, went like this:

> This is really where the church ought to be. Something active with the least of these, God's children. Something dealing with the political, economic and social realities of the time. Something that is not afraid to face death for something they believe in. . . . This is, in fact, . . . a lifetime struggle. . . . We [must] begin to think about [our] work in these terms, and know that the Kingdom isn't going to come in a day, but that it will come and that it does come each day for some people in some place. That food for a hungry mother in the backwoods of Holmes County represents the coming of the Kingdom, that even the right to vote in Belzoni [a small town in the Delta] and the very fact that you dare to run a candidate in there, does represent some progress. Not the coming of the Kingdom, but certainly the promise of it growing in our midst.[61]

The ministry served as one of the Protestant churches' (and the larger society's) best critics and worked with poor Mississippians to achieve unusual things in the face of extreme difficulties. And the struggle for justice they were a part of had to continue, for more than a lifetime. Young's words seemed an appropriate final comment on the religious meaning and historical significance of the Delta Ministry.

Notes

1. Interview with Roberta Miller, June 30, 1989; interviews with Virginia and Bruce Hilton, July 16, 17, 1989; interview with Robert Beech, October 12, 1989; interview with Jean Phillips, July 17, 1986; interview with Charles Horwitz, July 27, 1989, interview with Roger Smith, June 29, 1989.

2. Hilton, *The Delta Ministry*, p. 149; interview with Jean Phillips, July 17, 1986; interview with Rims Barber, July 21, 1986; interview with Roger Smith, June 29, 1989; Rims Barber to Findlay, July 9, 1988. Soon after Mt. Beulah was opened in the spring of 1965, a representative of the Mississippi Sovereignty Commission went there and inquired in detail about the acitivities planned on the campus. Investigative Report of Tom Scarbrough, April 16, 1965, folder entitled "Sovereignty Commission: April, 1965," Paul Johnson Papers, University of Southern Mississippi. Hilton, *The Delta Ministry*, pp. 150–158, adds further examples of harassment and points to the mental and psychological effects of such

pressures on the Delta Ministry staff. See also "What About the Charge that DM Has Made No Effort Toward Reconciliation?" in "Delta Ministry" file, reel 156, NAACP Legal Defense Fund Papers.

3. Office of Information, National Council of Churches, undated memo entitled "The Delta Ministry," RG 6, box 48, folder 1, NCC Archives.

4. James W. Silver, *Mississippi: The Closed Society* (New York, Harcourt-Brace, 1966), pp. 53–60; interview with R. Edwin King, July 22, 1986; "The Church and Race Relations," pp. 15–17, RG 75-01, box 45, folder 4, SRC Papers. The full text of the ministers' statement is printed in *Concern,* February 1, 1963, p. 16. See also W. J. Cunningham, *Agony at Galloway: One Church's Struggle with Social Change* (Jackson, University Press of Mississippi, 1980), and Neil McMillen, *The Citizen's Council: Organized Resistance to the Second Reconstruction, 1954–1964* (Urbana, University of Illinois Press, 1971), especially chaps. XII and XIII.

5. Interview with Warren McKenna, May 23, 1986; memo of Al Winham to Art Thomas, March 13, 1966, in folder entitled "White Mississippi—1966"; [Bruce Hilton], undated "Rough draft—contacts with white community"; Fred S. Lowry, "Notes on White Community Relations," March 13, 1966; items in box 6, Thomas Papers.

6. "The Mississippi Delta Ministry: The Planning Process," RG 77, box 7, folder 22, PCUSA Board of National Missions Papers, Presbyterian Historical Society; "Delta Project," undated handwritten memorandum; John M. Allin to Arthur E. Walmsley (and attached note, Walmsley to Paul Moore), July 17, 1964; Walmsley to Allin, July 21, 1964, items in folder entitled "Mississippi, 1964," Moore Papers; David Hunter to Allin, October 30, November 10, 25, December 9, 1964; Allin to Hunter, November 4, 16, 30, 1964; and Allin to Jon Regier, January 11, 1965; items in RG 5, box 16, folder 9, NCC Archives; Joel L. Alvis, "Racial Turmoil and Religious Reaction: the Rt. Rev. John M. Allin," *Historical Magazine of the Protestant Episcopal Church,* L (March 1981), pp. 83–96; *New York Times,* February 7, 18, 1965, unpaginated clippings in Bowie Papers.

On the opposition of Bishop Pendergrass, see especially "Delta Ministry" file, reel 158, NAACP Legal Defense Fund Papers; also "Statement About the Delta Ministry," April 28, 1966, Edwin King Papers, Tougaloo College, Jackson, Mississippi; undated, unsigned handwritten note to "Bishop Pendergrass"; Edward J. Pendergrass to Doctor R. H. Edwin Espy, August 27, 1965; unsigned "Response to letter of Bishop Pendergrass, dtd. 8-27-65"; items in folder entitled "White Mississippi—Methodists, 1964–65," box 6, Thomas Papers; B. F. Smith to Hodding Carter, Jr., March 10, 1966, in folder entitled "Correspondence: D-1966," Hodding Carter Papers, Mississippi State University; telephone interview with Jon Regier, October 28, 1986.

7. Arthur Thomas to Paul Moore, Jr., February 1, 1965, folder 42, box 12, Delta Ministry Papers, Atlanta; Sam J. Allen to Isaac Igarashi, February 12, 1965, folder entitled "White-Mississippi-Methodist, 1964–65"; Al Winham to Art Thomas, memo of March 13, 1966, folder entitled "White Mississippi—1966"; both items in box 6, Thomas Papers; Hilton, *The Delta Ministry,* p. 165; "Division of Christian Life and Mission: 1966 Askings for the Delta Ministry," in "Delta Ministry" file, reel 158, NAACP Legal Defense Fund Papers.

8. The successful efforts of white "moderates" to maintain political control in Mississippi after 1965 are discussed in Dittmer, "From Mississippi Movement to *Mississippi Burning,"* pp. 10–15, and Dittmer's unpublished Walter Prescott Webb

Lecture of 1991, "The Transformation of the Mississippi Movement, pp. 24–26. Some of these same "moderates," *as church leaders,* were among those publicly critical of the Delta Ministry in 1965 and 1966, even discussing their views with National Council officials at meetings in Atlanta and in Mississippi. Art Thomas to Hodding Carter III, May 6, 1965, in folder entitled "Hodding Carter, 1965," box 6, Thomas Papers; Nicholas von Hoffman, "Liberal Mississippi Paper Feuds With Delta Ministry," newspaper clipping dated July 28, 1965, and attached typewritten response of the Commisssion on the Delta Ministry, folder 9, box 43, SCLC Papers; and especially R. H. Edwin Espy to Owen Cooper, October 11, 1965; Espy to Jon Regier and Art Thomas, October 14, 1965; both items in folder 28, box 32, RG 4, NCC Archives. For Mississippi's "massive resistance" to black political empowerment after the passage of the Voting Rights Act, see Parker, *Black Votes Count,* chap. 2.

9. Garrow, *Bearing the Cross,* pp. 473–489; Carson, *In Struggle,* chaps. 13–16; Forman, *The Making of Black Revolutionaries,* chaps. 52–55.

10. Bryant George to Jon Regier, memo entitled "Evaluation Committee of the Delta Ministry," January 13, 1966; "Minutes, Meeting of Evaluation Committee, Mississippi Delta Ministry," January 21, 1966; "Membership List," Evaluation Committee, as of February 8, 1966; "Interviews at Greenville, Mississippi," April 21–22, 1966; "Report of the Evaluation Committee on the Mississippi Delta Ministry," May 16, 1966; all items in RG 5, box 16, folder 11, NCC Archives.

11. The chairperson of the ministry's board of directors protested the omission of African Americans from Mississippi from the evaluation committee shortly before the final report was made public. Paul Moore to Dale Fiers, May 18, 1966, folder entitled "Bishop Paul Moore," box 1, Thomas Papers. Lists of people who offered both written and verbal remarks to the evaluation committee and comments by the committee about the results are in "Report of the Evaluation Committee on the Mississippi Delta Ministry," May 16, 1966, pp. 3, 4, 5, 6, RG 5, box 16, folder 11, NCC Archives.

12. The General Board of the National Council fully endorsed the evaluation committee's work on June 2, 1966. "Actions of the General Board, National Council of Churches, June 2–3, 1966," RG 5, box 16, folder 11, NCC Archives.

13. "Report of the Evaluation Committee on the Mississippi Delta Ministry," May 16, 1966, ibid., pp. 6, 7–8.

14. Ibid., pp. 6, 7.

15. Paul Moore, Jr., "Report of the Delta Ministry to the Evaluation Committee of the General Board, June 1, 1966," p. 2, ibid.; Moore, "A Total Ministry," February 4, 1966, uncatalogued manuscripts, box 5, Thomas Papers.

16. "Background Material From Subcommittee on Overall Program of the Mississippi Delta Ministry," March 13–14, 1966, p. 2, RG 5, box 16, folder 11, NCC Archives.

17. Thelma Barnes, "Field Activities in Greenville (1964–65)," in folder entitled "Commission Meeting, October 1, 1965," box 3, Thomas Papers; A. Garnett Day, Jr., "'Justice Place' in the Delta," *World Call,* February 1966.

18. "Report and Evaluation—Hattiesburg, September 1964–September 1965," p. 13, in folder entitled "Commission Meetings," box 3, Thomas Papers.

19. "Background Material from Subcommittee on Administration of the Delta Ministry," February 28–March 1, 1966, pp. 1, 2, 2A–2D; Paul Moore, Jr., "Report of the Delta Ministry . . . to the Evaluation Committee of the

General Board, June 1, 1966," p. 3, both items in RG 5, box 16, folder 11, NCC Archives.

20. This was a connection established through the World Council of Churches early in 1964. Contributions from overseas in the first two years, almost $100,000 annually, were crucial to the ministry's continued existence. "Delta Ministry's Support," in "Delta Ministry" file, reel 158, NAACP Legal Defense Fund Papers; R. H. Edwin Espy to W. A. Visser t'Hooft, January 9, 1964; Visser t'Hooft to Espy, January 15, 1964; David R. Hunter to Espy, January 22, 1964; items in RG 5, box 16, folder 9, NCC Archives; *News,* February 7, 1967; *Delta Ministry Reports,* March 1967; both items in folder entitled "National Division: Delta Ministry," in offices of Board of Global Ministries, United Methodist Church (UMC), New York.

21. William A. Carhart to Arthur Thomas, January 18, 1966; Thomas to Carhart, January 20, 1966; Herman Ellis to Thomas, January 25, 1966; Stephen Feke to Jon Regier, March 18, 1966; items in folder entitled "Delta Budget, 1966," box 1, Thomas Papers; Feke to R. H. Edwin Espy, April 20, 1966; Thomas to Jon Regier, April 22, 1966; both items in folder entitled "Budget Memos," box 3, Thomas Papers; "Report of the Evaluation Committee on the Mississippi Delta Ministry," pp. 6, 7, RG 9, box 88, folder 6, NCC Archives; interview with Jon Regier, August 7, 1986.

22. Art Thomas to Jon Regier, April 22, 1966, folder entitled "Budget Memos," box 3, Thomas Papers; Thomas to Colin Williams, June 24, 1966, uncatalogued documents, box 1, Thomas Papers; Thomas to Harry Bowie, April 20, 1966, folder 49; Thomas to Al Winham, April 20, 1966, folder 49; Thomas to Ian Birch, May 4, 1966, folder 50; items in box 12, Delta Ministry Papers, Atlanta; "Report of the Evaluation Committee on the Mississippi Delta Ministry," p. 9, RG 5, box 16, folder 11, NCC Archives.

23. Bryant George to Kenneth Neigh, May 31, 1966, July 6, 1966; J. Edward Carothers to Kenneth Neigh, July 12, 1966; Neigh to Carothers, July 14, 1966; all items in box 6, Neigh Papers.

24. Arthur Thomas to Jon [Regier], July 6, 1966, folder 4; Regier to Thomas, July 13, 1966, folder 5; both items in RG 6, box 10, NCC Archives, Thelma Barnes to Paul Moore, Jr., July 11, 1966, folder 31, box 23; Warren McKenna to Moore, July 12, 1966, folder 42, box 12; Thelma Barnes to Mr. and Mrs. Malcolm Sillers, September 16, 1966, folder 32, box 23; items in Delta Ministry Papers, Atlanta; Colin W. Williams to Warren H. McKenna, August 12, 1966, in possession of author; telephone interview with McKenna, June 27, 1986. While living in England in 1957, McKenna took his trip to Communist China, and this caused considerable difficulty for him when he returned to the United States in the waning days of the McCarthy era. Although charges were made earlier and while he was in Mississippi that he was a Communist, there is no evidence to support such claims. Members of the evaluation committee raised the issue when McKenna was interviewed (perhaps in itself a case of red-baiting); McKenna stoutly defended himself against the questions. Significantly, the staff executive of the evaluation committee made a special point to secure a full review by the U.S. Justice Department of the loyalty status of all members of the Delta Ministry. "No evidence of disloyalty was revealed" of *any* staff person. Interviews with Warren McKenna, May 23, May 24, 1986; Anson Phelps Stokes to David Hunter, November 18, 1965, folder 9; "Background Material From Subcommittee on Overall Program of the Mississippi Delta Ministry," March 13–14, 1966, p. 12,

folder 11; "Report of the Evaluation Committee on the Delta Ministry," p. 3, folder 11, items in RG 5, box 16, NCC Archives.

25. The quotations are from Moore, "Report of the Delta Ministry, June 1, 1966," pp. 5, 6, RG 5, box 16, folder 11, NCC Archives. The decision of officials of the National Council in New York to retain Mt. Beulah is made explicit in "Goals for the Delta Ministry," attached to Jon Regier to Members of the Program Board of the Division of Christian Life and Mission, July 18, 1966, uncatalogued documents, box 1, Thomas Papers.

26. "Report of the Special Committee to Study the Relationship of the National Division to the Delta Ministry," in folder entitled "National Board: Delta Ministry," in offices of Board of Global Ministries, UMC; *Mission Memo* [Board of Missions, United Methodist Church], October–November 1966; *Christian Advocate,* October 20, 1966, p. 24; *World Outlook,* November 1966, pp. 568–569. The Women's Division of the United Methodist Church urged financial support of the ministry from its inception. From 1966 until the mid-1970s this group by itself provided the ministry with an annual appropriation of $30,000. *Journal,* Annual Meeting, 1975, Women's Division, UMC, pp. 333–336.

27. Moore's defense of Mt. Beulah in early June 1966 also stressed the need to recognize the new force of black power. See his "Report to the General Board, June 1, 1966," p. 6, RG 5, box 16, folder 11, NCC Archives.

28. Dittmer, "From Mississippi Movement to *Mississippi Burning,"* pp. 11–15, and "The Transformation of the Mississippi Movement," pp. 30–35, suggest the bittersweet political results for the MFDP and its allies in joining with whites in the Mississippi delegation to the 1968 Democratic convention. See also interview with Harry Bowie, June 29, 1989; "Citizenship Education Program," "Sunflower County," "Issaquena County," "Yazoo County," attachments to "Delta Ministry Annual Report, 1967," folder 32, box 3, Delta Ministry Papers, Atlanta; Rims Barber to author, July 9, 1988.

29. Rims Barber to author, July 9, 1988; interviews with Rims Barber, July 21, 1986, June 24, 1989; Roger Mills to Barber, September 26, December 4, 1968, reel 158, General Office Files, NAACP Legal Defense Fund Papers; Barber, "A Report to the Commission on the Delta Ministry, June, 1968," folder 2, box 4, Delta Ministry Papers, Mississippi State University; "Education—June to September," attachment to "Delta Ministry Annual Report, 1967," folder 32, box 3, Delta Ministry Papers, Atlanta.

30. The term "technician" was used to describe the work of the ministry by the writer of "Delta Ministry Report—1969," p. 1, RG 2, box 5, folder 1, NCC Archives; an example of coalition building is in Charles Horwitz, "Year End Report, 1969, From Hinds County Delta Ministry Project," miscellaneous documents, box 2, Thomas Papers; interview with Rims Barber, June 24, 1989. One of the first moments of recognition that the ministry's work had to change after mid-1966 is in "Report of the Evaluation Committee on the Mississippi Delta Ministry," p. 6, RG 5, box 16, folder 11, NCC Archives.

31. "Proposal for a Ministry Among the Residents of the Delta Area of the State of Mississippi," p. 5, RG 5, box 16, folder 9, NCC Archives; "Goals for the Delta Ministry Approved . . . July 7, 1966," p. 5, uncatalogued documents, box 1, Thomas Papers.

32. Owen Brooks to Greer Morton, December 26, 1967, folder 34, box 13, Delta Ministry Papers, Atlanta; "Report of the Delta Ministry, February 17–18, 1967," p. 6, RG 2, box 5, folder 1, NCC Archives; undated, untitled staff paper

[Delta Ministry, 1967], folder 6, box 4, Amzie Moore Papers, Wisconsin State Historical Society.

33. The futile search for industrual alternatives to the Delta's cotton culture is revealed in great detail in the correspondence of Alfred Winham, in folders 14 and 15, box 20, Delta Ministry Papers, Atlanta.

34. News release, Delta Ministry, September 7, 1965, folder 6, box 4, Amzie Moore Papers; "Facts About Delta Opportunities Corporation [1969]," folder 58, box 4, Delta Ministry Papers, Mississippi State University; fact sheet entitled "Delta Opportunities Corporation, March 6, 1969," folder 3, box 13, MFDP Papers.

35. "Memorandum," Owen Brooks to John F. Anderson (n.d.), folder 45, box 13; "Economic Development Programs," attachment to "Delta Ministry Report, 1967," folder 32, box 3; both items in Delta Ministry Papers, Altlanta; "The Delta Ministry Report, 1969," in folder entitled "Delta Ministry, April 1, 1969–March 31, 1970," Division of Homeland Ministries Archives, Disciples of Christ Historical Society, Nashville (hereafter cited as DHM Archives).

36. "Certificate of Incorporation of Delta Enterprises, Inc.," March 20, 1969, and attachments, in folder "Delta Enterprises," box 29, Interreligious Foundation for Community Organization Papers, Arthur L. Schomburg Library, New York (hereafter cited as IFCO Papers); "Delta Ministry Report–1969," p. 9, in folder entitled "Delta Ministry, April 1, 1969–March 31, 1970," box 5, DHM Archives; Tom Dent interview with Harry Bowie, May 28, 1978, Tom Dent Oral History Collection, Tougaloo College Archives; interview with Harry Bowie, November 6, 1989.

37. The quotations are in interview with Harry Bowie, November 6, 1989; see also Tom Dent interview cited in n. 36; *Delta Democrat-Times,* July 2, 1970, clipping; brochure entitled "Delta Foundation"; both items in folder 33, box 3, Delta Ministry Papers, Mississippi State University; "Delta Ministry—Economic Development," undated proposal submitted to National Council of Churches, in files of Harry Bowie, executive director of Delta Foundation, Greenville, Mississippi.

38. "Delta Ministry—Economic Development," undated proposal, Harry Bowie files, Delta Foundation, Greenville. Robert S. Browne to Charles Bannerman, October 26, 1970; and "Putting the System to Work," *NAM Reports,* July 29, 1974, pp. 9–11; both items in folder entitled "Delta Foundation," box 10, Black Economic Research Center Papers, Schomburg Library, New York. Comments on the Delta Foundation's activities in the 1980s are based on an untitled overview of the corporation's activities prepared for in-house use, in the office files of Mr. Harry Bowie, the executive director of the Delta Foundation, in Greenville, Mississippi, and Bowie to author, September 7, 1990.

39. Interview with Owen Brooks, July 14, 1986; interview with Harry Bowie, November 6, 1989; a brief description of MACE is in "Report of Activities" [1968], Citizens' Crusade Against Poverty, attached to Richard W. Boone to "Friends of the Crusade," February 28, 1969, in folder "Citizens' Crusade," box 4, Neigh Papers.

40. Interview with Harry Bowie, November 6, 1989; interview with J. Irwin Miller, May 29, 1990.

41. News release, Disciples of Christ Office of Interpretation, July 9, 1968; "Some Facts About Mt. Beulah," p. 1; both items in folder entitled "Mt. Beulah: Interpretations and Press Releases," box 8, DHM Archives.

42. Philip H. Young to Harry J. Lichy, April 29, 1970, folder entitled "Mt. Beulah," box 13, Neigh Papers. The perilous state of the physical plant at Mt. Beulah in Secember 1967 is revealed in Glen V. Carson to Kenneth G. Neigh, undated memo, Mt. Beulah folder, box 13, Neigh Papers. Carson, a property maintenance expert in the UPCUSA, concluded that "the Mt. Beulah plant is not suitable, now or as a base for future improvement, for the use as an educational institution of any kind."

43. In April 1970, Delta Ministry staff and supporters drove from Mississippi to the Disciples' headquarters in Indianapolis to discuss the lease termination directly with denominational officials. In addition 2,539 people signed petitions circulated nationwide asking that the campus be deeded to the Federation of Southern Cooperatives. This arrangement, seriously considered, failed because of lack of money. Edward McNulty to Kenneth Neigh, March 26, 1970; Neigh to McNulty, April 30, 1970; Philip H. Young to Harry J. Lichy, April 29, 1970; Young to Richard E. Murdoch, June 16, 1970; all items in folder "Mt. Beulah," box 13, Neigh Papers. The petitions are in an unmarked folder in box 9, DHM Archives. See also Roger A. Smith to Thomas Liggett, April 5, 1970; Liggett to Smith, April 9, 1920; both items in folder entitled "National Council Correspondence re: Mt. Beulah," box 9, DHM Archives. The closing of Mt. Beulah and the selling of the academy to the A.M.E. Church can be traced in notes of phone conversation, Russell Harrison and Jon Regier, February 16, 1971, in folder "Delta Ministry-NCC and UCMS re: Mt. Beulah Campus"; news release, June 23, 1971, in folder "Mt. Beulah: Interpretations and Press Releases"; and all documents in folder "Mt. Beulah: Bishop I. H. Bonner"; items in box 9, DHM Archives.

44. Frequent use of Mt. Beulah after 1966 as a statewide conference center, home for political workshops, and Head Start training center can be traced in *Delta Ministry Reports,* January 1967, p. 2; and all of the items in box 4, folder 35, Delta Ministry Papers, Mississippi State University; *D M Reports,* April, July, November 1967, June 1968, reel 11, microfilm edition of Fannie Lou Hamer Papers, Univerisity of Rhode Island.

45. Owen Brooks to Delta Ministry staff, March 3, 1970; Eddie Lucas to Amzie Moore, March 11, 1970; Jon Regier to Owen Brooks, March 11, 1970; all items in folder 7, box 14, Delta Ministry Papers, Atlanta; *New York Times,* March 7, 1971, p. 59; interview with Thelma Barnes, July 14; interview with Jean Phillips, July 17, 1986; interview with Sarah Johnson, July 17, 1986; Gail Noble, "The Delta Ministry: Black Power, Poverty, and Politics in the Mississippi Delta (unpublished M.A. thesis, Cornell University, 1969). Whether to maintain both statewide or local programmatic emphases of the ministry in a time of great budget stringency appears in Jon Regier to Arthur Thomas, January 14, 1971, and Thomas, "Report on the Delta Ministry," February 1, 1981, box 4, folder entitled "Mississippi Delta Ministry, January, 1971," Thoman Papers; Rims Barber to author, July 9, 1988.

46. Interview with Rims Barber, June 24, 1989; interviews with Harry Bowie, July 15, 1986, June 29, 1989; interview with Owen Brooks, July 14, 1986; interview with Roger Smith, June 29, 1989; Andrew Young to Martin Luther King, February 23, 1968, folder 23, box 150, SCLC Papers.

47. *Newsletter,* National Committee of Black Churchmen, October 1969, box 9, folder 11, Delta Ministry Papers, Mississippi State University.

48. Citations following refer to instances of great personal sacrifice by staff

persons to allow the ministry's work to proceed and to personal letters written after leaving Mississippi that reflected the community the ministry created: Paul Moore, Jr., to Thelma [Barnes], June 28, 1966, Barnes to Moore, July 11, 1966, folder 31, box 23; Billie [Wilmina Rowland] to Warren, Art, Larry, and Thelma, July, 1965, folder 4, box 5; Elizabeth to "family," November 21, 1965, folder 1, box 16; items in Delta Ministry Papers, Atlalnta; Gail Noble to Henry Parker, January 9, 1969, box 2, folder 63; Anne Pomeroy to Delta Ministry, June 9, 1969, box 3, folder 1; both items in Delta Ministry Papers, Mississippi State University.

49. "A Proposal for a Common Discipline for the Delta Ministry Staff," Appendix B attached to Jon Regier to Dr. R. H. Edwin Espy, "Progress Report on Delta Ministry," September 1, 1964, in folder, "Proposals on Delta Ministry: Basic Structure," box 3, Thomas Papers.

50. Ibid.

51. Arthur Thomas to John Fawcett, et al., April 28, 1965, folder 14, box 12, Delta Ministry Papers, Atlanta; interview with Warren McKenna, May 26, 1986; interview with Jon Regier, August 7, 1986; interview with Paul Moore, Jr., October 28, 1986; and especially Hilton, *The Delta Ministry*, pp. 157–159.

52. Interview with Rims Barber, July 21, 1986; and especially interviews with Fred Lowry, November 22, 1988; and with Bob Beech, October 12, 1989. Arthur Thomas seemed a partial exception to assertions that the ministry never exhibited public theological concerns. He made at least one attempt to reflect on the larger significance of the work of the ministry, in an unpublished essay written in the summer of 1964, just before the project in Mississippi began. Thomas, "The Movement and the Church," folder 22, box 1, Delta Ministry Papers, Atlanta.

53. In 1986 Cox confirmed the considerable impact new missionary structures like the Delta Ministry had on his thinking in the sixties. "In fact," he stated, "I still have a certain fondness" for such concerns. Harvey Cox to author, September 19, 1986.

54. Thomas Wieser, "Report on Conversations with the Staff of the Delta Ministry . . ," July 13, 1965; Walter Harrelson, "To the Members of the Southern Task Group on Race, WCC," November 23, 1965, and attachments; both items in undesignated manuscripts, box 5, Thomas Papers.

55. Interview with Bruce and Virginia Hilton, July 17, 1989; interview with Fred Lowry, November 22, 1988; interview with Robert Beech, October 12, 1989; interview with Roger Smith, June 29, 1989; John Else to Findlay, September 3, 1986.

56. Hilton, *Delta Ministry*, p. 157. A similar critique, stated in more general terms, is in John C. Bennett, "The Missing Dimension," *Christianity and Crisis,* September 29, 1969, pp. 241–242.

57. Owen Brooks to Arthur Thomas, May 23, 1974; program of the "Ten Year Celebration," June 10, 1974; both items in folder entitled "Hold," box 3, Thomas Papers.

58. *New York Times,* November 6, 1986, p. 31. A detailed and revealing study of the development of black political power in the Delta since the 1960s is in Minion K. C. Morrison, *Black Political Mobilization: Leadership, Power and Mass Behavior* (Albany, State University of New York Press, 1987).

59. Clayborn Carson's essay, "Civil Rights Reform and the Black Freedom Struggle," in Charles W. Eagles, ed., *The Civil Rights Movement in America* (Jackson, University Press of Mississippi, 1986), pp. 19–32, and his "Afterward" to Mary King's *Freedom Song: A Personal Story of the Civil Rights Movement* (New

York, William Morrow and Co., 1987), pp. 555–560, argue this point. See also Stephen F. Lawson's excellent "Freedom Then, Freedom Now: The Historiography of the Civil Rights Movement," *American Historical Review,* 96 (April 1991), pp. 457, 459, 464–467.

60. The writing on this topic by theologians from the mainline churches is very sparse. Robert Spike's *The Freedom Movement and the Churches* (New York, Association Press, 1965); *Civil Rights Involvement,* a pamphlet previously cited; and "Gospel, World, and Church," *Theology Today* (July 1965), pp. 163–172, are thoughtful, though very brief, attempts to define the church's mission in the context of the racial revolution. Spike's death in 1966 prevented his development of more systematic treatments of the subject, and few others followed in his footsteps.

61. Typescript of "The Rev. Andrew Young's Address to the Commission on the Delta Ministry, June 10, 1968," box 9, folder 2, Delta Ministry Papers, Mississippi State University.

6

The National Council of Churches and Racial Matters "At Home": Changing Circumstances, 1964–1969

Since the moment of its founding in June 1963, the National Council's Commission on Religion and Race had experienced an almost unbroken series of successes in its support of the black freedom movement. Two years later self-confidence and a strong sense of connectedness to national centers of decision making and public power were still manifest in the words and actions of ecumenical church leaders. The triumphalism that often accompanied national religious endeavors in the 1950s even now occasionally revealed itself. In March 1965, for example, in the aftermath of the brutal attacks by state and local police on black demonstrators in Selma, Alabama, the commission and national church leaders drew religious folk from across the nation to Washington to support a powerful new voting rights act proposed by the Johnson administration. On March 12 a delegation of these church people met with the president at the White House for over two hours, "discussing frankly the concerns of the country, and urging him [Johnson] to act decisively for the whole nation in the disgraceful business in Alabama." For two days thereafter Robert Spike and others continued in "frequent consultation" with the White House over the matter, and on Monday evening, March 15, 1965, Spike and Eugene Carson Blake, the chairman of the Commission on Religion and Race, were "guests of the President in his family box" as Lyndon Johnson spoke before a joint session of Congress proposing and urging passage of the Voting Rights Act.[1] Later in the year Edwin Espy, the general secretary of the National Council, responded to a request of the president for comments "on the achievements" of the Johnson administration after two years in office. Citing much of just-passed Great Society legislation, Espy concluded that these "policies and the concerns of the National Council of Churches have on the whole reflected parallel positions to a remarkable degree." Shortly Espy received from Johnson a personal note, thanking him for his "purposeful letter," and adding that "your support of what we have tried to do in the economic and social fields is encouraging."[2]

These incidents seemed to summarize the unprecedented involvement of the churches, especially in racial matters, in the public life of the country since 1963 and suggested that perhaps such actions had helped to maintain the mainstream churches' long-recognized "establishment" status. Spike's brief recapitulation for the Commission on Religion and Race of an event in which clergy advised the President of the United States concerning what soon became the Voting Rights Act of 1965 and Espy's circulation to staff members of his mutually congratulatory correspondence with Lyndon Johnson bespoke in subtle ways a certitude and self-satisfaction that flowed from "right" action. It was exhilarating—but the mood was not to last much longer.

During the famous Freedom Summer of 1964 the nation's attention seemed riveted upon Mississippi, but at the same time the first large race-related ghetto disturbances of the sixties in northern cities also occurred—in Harlem and in Rochester, New York, in middle and late July and in Philadelphia in August 1964. Alarmed by these developments, the National Council people sought ways to help in the aftermath. Although the riots in Rochester were severe—three people killed, dozens of businesses looted or damaged severely, disorder so great that the National Guard had to be called in—this city also presented unique opportunities for people hoping to bring about racial change.[3] It was a small place in comparison to New York City or Philadelphia; moreover, early versions of "high-tech" industries—Xerox, Bausch and Lomb, and especially Eastman Kodak—dominated the city's economy. Rochester thus possessed a large and well-educated middle-class, many of whom were the backbone of the mainstream churches in the city. Groups from these churches, the ecumenical Rochester Council of Churches, and especially a semiindependent subsidiary of the council, the Board of Urban Ministries, were prepared to participate actively in the struggles to resolve the city's racial problems. The difficulties seemed to be of relatively recent origin. Rapid migration of blacks for over a decade from the Deep South (that segment of the city's population more than quadrupled between 1950 and 1964) had created major housing and employment problems, which were key ingredients that helped to ignite the racial disturbances in the summer of 1964.[4]

The Commission on Religion and Race of the National Council of Churches assisted Rochester church leaders in working with Governor Nelson Rockefeller to end the riots and then immediately after in bringing to Rochester staff members of the Southern Christian Leadership Conference (Andrew Young, James Bevel, and Bernard Lafayette) to help initiate the search for solutions to the city's racial tensions. Thus well before the SCLC's better-known foray into Chicago in 1965 and 1966, Martin Luther King's people were making one of their earliest moves into a northern city. Early in August 1964, they preached about nonviolence to sizable crowds in African American churches in Rochester and initiated a brief voter registration campaign in the African American community, which, at best, met with indifferent success. Southern tactics and a heavy religious emphasis did not work, especially among the younger ghetto residents. By mid-August, Young, Bevel, and Lafayette had left.[5]

After much further discussion, local black and white church leaders sought out and eventually hired Saul Alinsky, the controversial community organizer from Chicago, to harness the energies of Rochester's African American community and thus also "the great army of bitter and hostile young unemployed [blacks] who constituted so much of the immediate problem" there.[6] Alinsky and his new protégés eventually focused on efforts to get Eastman Kodak Company, the dominant business in the city, to train properly and then to hire six hundred or more of these young people. Many were recent arrivals from the Deep South, largely unprepared to survive economically in a sophisticated urban setting like Rochester. Only after three years of complicated, frustrating, and frequently very tense negotiations were the job training and hiring arrangements achieved. Church people, both locally and through national religious organizations including the National Council of Churches, played important mediating and pressure-group roles throughout.[7]

The conflicts in Rochester which began in the summer of 1964 prefigured northern urban developments later in the decade. The initial riots anticipated the much larger and more destructive communal disturbances that broke out in the black ghettoes of Los Angeles in 1965, of Newark and Detroit in 1967, and in many cities following the assassination of Martin Luther King in April 1968. Franklyn D. R. Florence, a minister who became a leader of the local African American community after the riots, chiefly as president of FIGHT, the community organization Alinksy and his local allies nursed into existence, symbolized a new black leadership emerging nationally by the mid-sixties. A good friend of Malcolm X, Florence took strong, confrontational stands publicly, especially with Eastman Kodak, and often was rather cool in personal and professional relations even with local white supporters. In essence he and FIGHT were advancing a version of black power well before that concept surged into the national consciousness in mid-1966.[8]

Finally, the people in Rochester developed solutions to their problems that veered away from the programs used by the civil rights forces in the South. The chief proposal of the SCLC visitors in August 1964 was to initiate a voter registration campaign in the ghetto areas. It quickly died out. Under Alinsky and Minister Florence's leadership, the focus turned to urban renewal issues and job training and the hiring of unemployed young African Americans, especially by Eastman Kodak. The power of the vote was not viewed as terribly important. Instead, these early struggles with urban racial problems led inexorably to the need to confront basic economic issues in the ghettoes, like proper housing and the provision of meaningful, well-paying jobs. These fundamental *economic* concerns were increasingly the focus of national leaders of the black freedom movement throughout the last half of the sixties and became the central issue fought over for almost three years in Rochester.[9]

But Rochester also served as one of the few examples of relative success in dealing with racial conflict in a northern urban context, not only because of strong and effective black leadership, but also because of careful planning and organization in the black community (helped by Alinksy) and the persistent support of important groups within the white churches, both locally and nationally. This latter fact often did not exist in the late sixties.[10]

Only shortly before the troubles erupted in Rochester in June 1964 did officials of the National Council of Churches in New York begin to think about specific responses to racial issues in northern cities. It is revealing of the predilections of these northern liberals, and of the nation at large, that for so long public attention centered on the South and the struggle for equality there. From the outset the people in the National Council spoke about racial problems in the North as "complicated" and even "puzzling," which may help to explain why there was a reluctance to tackle them.[11] Race relations in the northern cities also lacked the starkness and clarity of purpose and action that seemed to characterize situations in the South, and the latter was much further away from northerners' doorsteps. Also, as was the case in Rochester, in many northern locations church agencies already existed designed to deal specifically with racial problems. For a national ecumenical body like the National Council of Churches, it was difficult sometimes to gauge when and how to help in a local situation without appearing heavy-handed or insensitive to people already at work. Throughout the nearly three-year struggle in Rochester, the National Council and its Commission on Religion and Race participated only if asked. Even so, instances occurred when lack of coordination caused problems.[12]

Late in 1964 and early in 1965, the Commission on Religion and Race tried to work more systematically with local church people in two northern cities, Detroit and Cleveland, in seeking solutions to the racial problems there. Investing $20,000 of their resources in each location and much of the time of a Commission staff member, after an initial flush of enthusiasm the two "pilot projects" lost momentum.[13] They were unable to surmount difficulties such as jurisdictional disputes with local church people, the growing reluctance of black community leaders to accept white-initiated proposals, and the fact that local white persons were unwilling to make even minimal changes in their racial attitudes and practices. A strongly backed voter registration campaign in Cleveland just prior to a citywide school board election affecting school desegregation failed miserably. In Detroit there was a more sophisticated effort to work with local church people on deep-seated housing problems experienced by blacks, but these efforts, too, did not produce many tangible, long-term results.[14] By early 1966, both of the projects had been discontinued.

These experiences enabled the commission increasingly to see that in northern cities the civil rights struggle had to "fan out ever more into complicated economic issues—employment and housing being important areas of this broader economic involvement." Inevitably, too, such economic concerns meant there had to be links with the federal antipoverty programs just then developing.[15] Thus from the end of 1965 onward, as these church people involved themselves ever more deeply in the knotted complexities of American racism, a shift in program emphasis occurred, from political to economic priorities. In Detroit and Cleveland these insights were not translated into successful programs; in Rochester, to a greater extent, they were. But the tight intermeshing of racial discrimination with the most basic economic institutions of our society was never again to be ignored or denied. If one recalls the work of the Delta Ministry in Mississippi, beginning late in 1966 the same sort of shift in priorities took place. At bottom the problems and issues were much the same, no matter what part of the country one was in.

The Commission on Religion and Race also faced other challenges at the end of 1965. Since the time of its founding in June 1963, one of its most unique and important characteristics was that it was directly responsible to the General Board, the chief policymaking body of the National Council of Churches. This meant that the commission bypassed all of the normal bureaucracy in gaining quick approval of its plans and programs. It was one way the National Council indicated to church people nationwide that the principal ecumenical body of mainstream Protestantism was serious in its support of substantive racial change. It might even be viewed as another indication of *kairos,* a temporary administrative arrangement necessitated by the "emergency" or crisis in national race relations that loomed so ominously, especially from 1963 on.

By 1965 mainline church leaders were realizing the inadequacy of the view that national racial problems were temporary. The issues were far more complex than people had supposed and could not be "solved" in two or three years. This understanding meant that eventually the commission had to be absorbed into the existing bureaucratic structure of the council. It would lose its special status and enhanced powers, but supposedly still serve as a powerful focus for race-related issues. But action of this sort seemed a tacit admission that the deep involvement of the council in the national racial struggle in 1963 and 1964 was not going to continue indefinitely.

In mid-1965 the first discussions regarding such a move took place. The plan that emerged from these discussions proposed a merger of the commission with the old Department of Racial and Cultural Relations, moribund since the establishment of the commission in 1963. The merged bodies were to be placed under Jon Regier, within the Division of

Christian Life and Mission. Regier had been a key figure in the establishment of the commission and a strong and consistent backer of the Delta Ministry (the latter was administratively always under his supervision). Still, these pending administrative changes sent a tremor of worry through members of the commission. At a meeting in September 1965 they expressed "strong concern" that in the new arrangements under Regier "the values and strengths of the present Commission on Religion and Race be secured."[16] But how? Absorption into the regular bureaucracy inevitably meant a blurring of focus and a lowering of commitments, and that was disquieting. These discussions, and the final implementation at the end of 1966 of the administrative changes that were the result, were another indication that a transition time in the work of the National Council on racial matters had arrived.

Robert Spike viewed this moment in just such a manner. At the September 1965 meeting of the commission, he announced that it seemed "the right time for the present director of the Commission on Religion and Race to take his leave." He resigned, effective January 1, 1966, to become the director of a new program to create Doctors of the Ministry at the Divinity School at the University of Chicago. This was to be an important new four-and-a-half year program of practical pastoral and advanced theological training designed to prepare students for newly emerging forms of ministry, especially in urban areas.[17]

The commission had affected racial issues nationally, both in and outside the churches, out of all proportion to its numerical size and financial backing. That fact was in many ways the result of Spike's presence as the executive director since its founding in mid-1963. At the time of that appointment he was not widely known outside his own denomination (United Church of Christ) and the network of national church executives in New York City. Nor was he thought of in church circles then as a nationally recognized "expert" on race relations.[18] Nevertheless Spike, along with the small but highly competent staff he gathered at the commission,[19] quickly demonstrated great administrative ability in marshalling on very short notice the large involvement of the mainstream churches in the March on Washington in the summer of 1963. He and the commission also evidenced considerable sensitivity to the rapidly evolving national political scene, playing a central role in securing powerful church backing for the great civil rights legislation of the mid-1960s (the Civil Rights Act of 1964 and the Voting Rights Act of 1965), and recognizing and supporting the most innovative efforts of the secular civil rights organizations, especially the work of the Student Nonviolent Coordinating Committee in Mississippi, beginning in the summer of 1963.

Still largely unrecognized yet also important was Spike's ability to articulate with intelligence and insight the theological and ethical meaning of the great racial struggle into which the nation had plunged. Unfortunately, at the time the audience for these musings and reflections was very limited, mostly the staff of the commission and a few others who may have heard him speak or who may have read his limited corpus of published writings on racial themes.[20]

But by 1966 Spike was almost uniquely prepared to begin to speak and write to national audiences, both churchly and otherwise, about the theological-ethical significance of the "American dilemma" of race. He had honed his skills in a daily crucible of practical decision making affecting directly many people's lives. Yet at the same time he had also written imaginatively and reflected deeply about these same activities, from the perspective of a trained theologian and ethicist. Perhaps now was the time to pursue a somewhat more contemplative life, to present his ideas to a wider audience and to help train a new generation of leaders in the churches. From the bits and pieces of evidence that remain from his days in Chicago, it is clear that Spike continued his activist life and involvement in racial concerns,[21] and that he was speaking and writing frequently about the need of the church to rethink both its theological base and its mission in the world.[22]

All the potential and promise of Spike's career following his years with the National Council of Churches came suddenly and tragically to an end in Columbus, Ohio, on October 17, 1966. His body was discovered in a guest room at the back of the new ecumenical Christian student center at Ohio State University, which he had helped to dedicate the day before. Spike had been murdered, his skull crushed by several blows from a blunt instrument, perhaps a claw hammer. His sudden death stunned the national Protestant church community and those who knew him within civil rights circles. There seemed no clear motive (robbery was not one since his wallet and wristwatch were discovered undisturbed in his room), and the murderer was never found.[23]

Subsequently there swirled about these events charges and counter-charges—of government complicity in Spike's murder because of his deep involvement in controversial activities in race relations, of a possible violent homosexual encounter that ended in the minister's death, of inadequate police investigation following his death. Spike's oldest son, Paul, provided the earliest and most forthright statements that government people, either directly or indirectly, played a role in Spike's death. A small group of national Methodist officials conducted a systematic review in 1980 of the available evidence on Spike's death and came to very similar conclusions. They and a number of Spike's co-workers now believe that probably he was assassinated.[24]

Some evidence available suggests caution in accepting this argument. At least one important official in the Johnson administration who knew him well did not place Spike in the top echelon of national civil rights leaders, and his FBI file does not indicate worries about him in any way equal to those raised about many African Americans in the black freedom struggle.[25] Moreover, the evidence we have regarding Spike's role, just before his death, in the efforts of church groups and others to reverse the Johnson administration's decision to end the funding of CDGM in Mississippi suggests that certainly he was a part of an intense political fight, but not threatening actions of sufficient import to cause government officials to want to kill him.[26]

Robert Spike was also bisexual. Evidence revealed at the time, especially by the Columbus police, seemed to suggest connections between this bisexuality and his death.[27] These extremely controversial charges have never been proven, but added to the defensiveness of national church officials and to charges of police impropriety in the aftermath of Spike's death.[28] In December 1966, William Minor, a sometime resident of Columbus, was arrested and confessed to the murder of Spike, but eventually was released on a legal technicality and a trial was never held.[29] Thus the actual murderer has never been determined, and we can only remain "agnostic" regarding the motivations for that individual to kill Robert Spike. What was reality at the time, however, was that the churches lost a major spokesperson for direct, vigorous involvement of mainstream religious institutions in the tangled national dilemmas of race. And Robert Spike's unexpected death also probably served as a blow to the continuation of the *kairos* moment in race relations that the churches had grasped so adventuresomely in 1963.

The churches' direct response to Spike's death furthered the tendencies toward ending the *kairos* moment. The known deep dislike of gay people by the Columbus police, and the prospect that a powerful backlash against the churches might set in if homophobic fears were added to racial fears, led religious leaders to engage in a "conspiracy of silence" of sorts following the murder. A vigorous, extended investigation into the causes of Spike's death was never pursued. And a curtain of quietness descended in church circles to blot out further public discussion of his work in the sixties. The homophobia still widespread today in American society was even more intense in the 1960s; in this instance mainstream Protestantism embraced all too willingly prevailing cultural norms and left a deceased national leader's reputation largely unprotected and undefended. It was not one of the liberal church's brighter moments.[30]

Six months before Spike left for Chicago another troubling issue manifested itself. At the June 1965 meeting of the commission, the executive director announced he had arranged a gathering on July 19 with "representatives of the Negro denominations" to discuss how best to create a "permanent Commission" within the overall structure of the National Council. Meetings with other minority groups were to follow. Immediately people present expressed "strong feelings" that the separate meeting on July 19 not be held. Instead, these commission members argued that "representatives of the Negro denominations [should] be included in the planning process from the beginning," and "more Negroes need[ed] to be involved in the whole planning process." Indeed, it was felt, the "leadership, talent and potential" of all minority groups were "not being utilized."

These were pointed and revealing criticisms, long harbored by minority persons on the commission. The National Council of Churches, even in the mid-sixties, was still managed and controlled by whites, although matters had improved somewhat from the almost total isolation J. Oscar Lee experienced as the token black staff person of the council in the 1950s. The commission itself, supposedly at the cutting edge of civil rights issues, until now had been directed by whites, although three members of the full-time program staff of eight in 1965 were African Americans, Anna Hedgeman, J. Oscar Lee, and James Breeden. Mrs. Hedgeman, especially, had publicly voiced her unhappiness with the racial insensitivities within the National Council and its member communions. Now for the first time in a formal meeting, several people were asking for more ongoing recognition and responsibility for blacks in the affairs of the commission and in the life of the National Council generally. The debate spilled over into the next meeting of the commission, held three months later in September 1965, an indication that to many of those involved the issues raised were quite important.[31]

In February 1965, Malcolm X had been assassinated in Harlem, not too far from the Interchurch Center. His acid-tongued criticisms of white society, including the churches, attracted much public attention both before and after his death. His willingness to state his views uncompromisingly in public made him a hero in black communities everywhere, a symbol of vigorous self-assertiveness that many blacks greatly admired. The squalid and worsening conditions of northern urban ghettos provided much justification for the criticisms of whites raised by Malcolm. The great urban communal explosion in Watts in Los Angeles in August 1965 profoundly underscored the social and economic problems existing in the ghettos and dramatized the frustrations of those who lived in these places. This general historical context,[32] added to the perceived slowness of the white leadership of the National Council to admit African Americans fully into their planning and decision-making circles, provided an explanation for the worries that surfaced so noticeably in the Commission on Religion and Race during the summer and fall of 1965. Although black power was not to come to full flower until almost a year later, these discussions in meetings of the commission pointed to a new self-consciousness among African Americans that was already at work. And perhaps the emergence of these new feelings and attitudes also tugged at Bob Spike, whispering that it was time to leave; in doing so he could create an opportunity for an African American to succeed him.

On December 12, 1965, the formal announcement of Spike's replacement appeared. Benjamin Payton, an African American minister from the Deep South, was young (only 33 at the time) and already seemed well fitted for the position he was assuming. Born in Orangeburg, South Carolina, he had moved north to secure advanced education at Harvard Divinity School, Columbia in New York City and at Yale (a Ph.D. in social ethics in 1963). For two years he taught at Howard University in Washington, then moved back to New York City in 1965 to become the director of the Office of Religion and Race of the principal citywide ecumenical organization, the Protestant Council of the City of New York. This job meant daily involvement in the network of national denominational and ecumenical church leaders that had informally developed in New York City in the 1950s and 1960s and that had provided so much of the national church leadership in the civil rights movement. Indeed, his office was located at "475"; as he noted later, "I just moved upstairs two floors," when the National Council of Churches hired him.[33] Payton already knew well those who were to select Bob Spike's successor and thus was ideally situated as a candidate for that job.

Payton was a long-time member of the National Baptist Convention, U.S.A., Inc., the largest African American denomination. In 1965 Payton's social activism (he was involved in the March on Washington and helped to organize a Freedom School in Mississippi) was strongly represented within his church, even though the denomination's leaders steadfastly refused to support officially the civil rights movement. Their position provoked such strong opposition from fellow-member Martin Luther King that eventually King and his allies had to leave the denomination; they formed a splinter group known as the Progressive National Baptists.[34] Payton stayed with the parent organization. His growing reputation as a national religious leader meant potentially he might help to draw further into the liberal ecumenical orbit an African American denomination that sometimes was hesitant about such matters. Thus both his civil rights commitments and his strong connections to the conservative but very influential black Baptists were probably viewed positively by people at the National Council of Churches and assisted further in his becoming Spike's successor.

Still the principal institutional advocate on racial matters for the National Council, the commission under Payton maintained important continuities with the past. The incorporation of the commission into the Division of Christian Life and Mission was finalized at the close of 1966. This was the end of a process that had been set in motion a year earlier and about which there was by this time little or no controversy. The shift in program focus of the council and the commission to urban areas principally in the North, so pronounced in 1965, continued, although with certain variations. Like his predecessor, Payton viewed economic issues as crucial to any realistic attempt to grapple with national racial issues. As he expressed it in his first formal comments to a major National Council assembly, "the civil rights movement [in 1966] seeks with its constituencies for some sign that the new legal definitions of equal rights will be made into flesh and blood realities. The *rights* which have been *couched in law are now being sought in life as practical social and economic matters.*" Thus a "major need" is for "a program of economic development to make civil rights real, in housing, employment, education and health care."[35] These words of Payton echoed in many ways those of his predecessor, but he suggested a difficult path of implementation. Probably influenced by

Anna Hedgeman, the old experienced politician from New York who had always been sceptical of the "pilot projects" in Detroit and Cleveland (because they were not connected closely enough to the existing power structures in each city),[36] Payton turned the commission toward a broader national focus.

Lyndon Johnson also influenced this move. In June 1965 at Howard University, the president, in a remarkable commencement address, urged the American people to build upon the new legal equality implicit in the Civil Rights Act of 1964 "to fulfill these rights" with a new wave of national legislation to aid minorities, especially blacks, long crippled by discrimination. Johnson also called for a national conference under White House sponsorship to make specific recommendations that could serve as the basis of a legislative agenda.[37]

In November 1965 the first planning sessions for the White House conference took place in Washington. Administration officials, strongly influenced by a new study by Daniel Moynihan (the now-famous "Moynihan Report"), then an under-secretary in the Department of Health, Education and Welfare, hoped to focus these sessions and eventually the conference on the black family and its alleged instabilities, traceable primarily to the crippling experience of slavery a century earlier. Civil rights groups were opposed, arguing that such an approach largely ignored ongoing *racial discrimination* as a principal cause of contemporary black family difficulties and that Moynihan's analysis downplayed the need to search more comprehensively within American society for solutions to the social and economic ills of the black community.[38] The Commission on Religion and Race of the National Council of Churches and other religious groups joined in these criticisms.[39]

Paying heed, Johnson jettisoned the Moynihan Report as a potential conference focus, yet also shaped the planning process more to his liking by narrowing the number of participants, relying on university social scientists as consultants and appointing in February 1966 Ben Heinemann, a Chicago businessman, as chairperson of the conference. Civil rights groups were not excluded, but their influence was not as great as at the outset.[40]

After Payton became the director of the Commission on Religion and Race in January 1966, he and the staff devoted much of their energies to organizing a large pre-White House conference in New York City. This gathering was to draft concrete proposals with the hope that they would be incorporated into the agenda of the national meeting, to insure that the focus of Johnson's conference remain on fundamental economic and social needs, and to begin a process "to help equal opportunity become a meaningful reality."[41] The White House affair was scheduled for June 1 to 2, 1966; thus to influence this meeting the New York preconference had to occur no later than early May. Four months was not a long time to mount such a large endeavor by a group as small as the commission, but the staff loyally, indeed enthusiastically, followed their leaader.[42]

One result of these activities was the termination of the last pilot project, in Detroit, begun in 1965. A request for monetary aid from the commission for a housing task force in part initiated and supported financially by the National Council was turned down. A staff member closely associated with the Detroit venture chided his cohorts, "we bear a major responsibility for at least providing the incentive" for certain new housing programs in the Motor City, and thus "cannot now say it was great fun and 'lots of luck.' . . . I feel strongly that we cannot abandon this relationship now."[43] His entreaties fell on deaf ears.

On May 10, 1966, the pre-White House conference convened in New York City. Attesting to the significance of the three-day gathering, Governor Nelson Rockefeller, Mayor John Lindsay, and Robert Kennedy, the junior senator from New York state, all addressed the 500-plus delegates. Kennedy, especially, proposed a comprehensive economic agenda to "fulfill the rights proclaimed in constitution and law," especially with the passage of the "historic" civil rights legislation of 1964 and the Voting Rights Act of 1965. The nation needed, he said, "to change every facet of our society; and that we begin in our urban ghettoes . . . which stand as a blight on our cities and a disgrace to our souls." He spoke of the primary need for jobs for the people of the ghettoes, created largely by the rebuilding of those very urban areas by their inhabitants. These efforts, and the ripple effects on education, social services, and business investment in the inner city, Kennedy believed, would help the people of the ghettoes "build a true community . . . a community able to manage and give direction to its own affairs, its own progress toward full participation in American life." He then charged the conference "to work toward the creation of mechanisms and structures to ensure that the control over our rebuilding effort rests, not in City Hall, and not in Washington—but in Harlem and East Harlem and Bedford-Stuyvesant."[44]

Payton and his staff were ready to do just that. Shortly before he joined the National Council, Payton and Seymour Melman, a professor of industrial engineering at Columbia University, prepared a long essay entitled "Metropolitan-Rural Development for Equal Opportunity," a blueprint for a national effort at social reconstruction, which underscored many of Kennedy's concerns. It focused on job training, housing, and health services; it made large cities or metropolitan centers, including surrounding rural areas, the focal point of the development process; it made clear the very large sums of money needed countrywide to be implemented (an estimated $43 billion over five years, beyond that part of the nation's wealth already committed to such activities); it proposed, beginning with the pre-White House conference in New York City, an ongoing "community organization process" of data collection and budget building to spell out in detail what was required to make the economic system of the nation "function equitably," and to put in motion "local groups of people . . . to get what they discover is needed."[45]

Although based largely on experience and data from the New York area, the Payton-Melman proposals were to be applied throughout the nation. Examined by critics and refined, the Melman-Payton essay served as a primary reference point for discussions at the New York City conference and was embodied in the recommendations the conference passed on to the planners of the White House conference, to be held three weeks later.[46]

The concerns of Robert Kennedy and of Payton and Melmon, especially the strong emphasis of all three upon grass-roots community participation in the planning and implementation of this reconstruction of metropolitan areas in decline, closely paralleled the ideas that, at almost exactly the same time, animated thousands of poor black people in their support of CDGM and the first Head Start programs in Mississippi. Kennedy, in words strikingly similar to what actually was practised for a brief moment in Mississippi, expressed it well. We must, he said, "help the people of the ghettoes build a true community," and to build such a community, "we will need—far more than in the past—to allow to the Negro and the Puerto Rican a far greater place in the councils which shape their lives." Kennedy also noted realistically that there would be "divisions and debate that are the price of giving the poor and the dispossessed a full opportunity to be heard." For him, though, it was clear that "we can and must afford" such a price. "It is time to make room at the table."[47]

Such hopes were not to come to pass, at least as these people envisioned it. We have seen how the Child Development Group's work was essentially destroyed, partly by people in Mississippi, but also by the Johnson administration in Washington, which supported the destroyers through the Office of Economic Opportunity, led by Sargeant Shriver, Robert Kennedy's brother-in-law. The results of the White House Conference on Civil Rights and its antecedents, which raised hopes that national leaders were going to confront racism directly and commit massive resources over an extended period of time to subdue it, were also disappointing.

In part the diversity of groups represented at the White House conference was so great that achieving a real consensus by the end of the two-day session (June 1–2, 1966) was all but impossible.[48] President Johnson spoke to the delegates the second night and ended the sessions in a glow of good feeling, but this was a brief papering over of disgruntlements and disagreements. For some the conference focused too narrowly on the problems of African Americans and ignored other minorities, notably Hispanics and Native Americans.[49] There was also strong opposition to Chairperson Heineman's refusal to allow resolutions to be proposed from the floor, which revealed considerable dislike of the administration's close "management" of the conference.[50]

But the most important problem that affected the gathering in Washington and especially efforts to implement the recommendations that came out of it, was an issue scarcely mentioned in the conference sessions—Vietnam. It had been almost a year since Lyndon Johnson had begun a massive escalation of American involvement in the Vietnam War. By the early part of 1966, significant grass-roots opposition had begun to develop and much more was to come. One important indication within religious circles came on December 4, 1965. On that date the General Board of the National Council announced its approval of a resolution, written by Eugene Carson Blake, then chairman of the Commission on Religion and Race, urging the Johnson administration to halt its bombing of North Vietnam "to create more favorable circumstances for peace negotiations," and to consider a "phased withdrawal" of its troops under United Nations supervision. The vote of the General Board was overwhelming—93 in favor, 10 opposed, with 6 abstentions. This was the first time in its history that the National Council of Churches had so openly criticized an American president for his conduct of a central aspect of American foreign policy, and it was the first critical statement on the Vietnam War by a major United States religious body. It was also far removed from the friendly exchanges between Robert Spike, Ed Espy, and the president just a few months and weeks earlier that we noted at the outset of this chapter.[51]

The council had been preceded in its criticism by Martin Luther King, one of the first major church leaders associated with the civil rights movement to express public opposition to the war. Although King's most famous sermon on the subject occurred at Riverside Church on April 4, 1967, he uttered his first public statements against the war in March 1965 and continued to express his views regularly thereafter.[52]

Anti-Vietnam sentiments did affect directly the White House Conference on Civil Rights. Just prior to the convening of the gathering, the Student Nonviolent Coordinating Committee, still the most militant of the civil rights organizations, announced that its representatives to the conference would not attend, as a protest against Johnson's policies in Vietnam.[53] An anti-Vietnam resolution was proposed on the floor of the convention by Floyd McKissick, the new director of CORE, but was brushed aside, further angering many of the delegates. And President Johnson exercised his penchant for sanctioning people who opposed him by making certain that Martin Luther King, Jr., who attended the conference, played little active role, primarily because of King's criticism of Johnson's Vietnam policies.[54] All of these activities also suggested the differences of opinion that continued to tear apart the national civil rights coalition and was another factor preventing a more friendly and unified response to Johnson among the groups at the White House Conference.

The rapid escalation of America's involvement in Vietnam beginning in 1965 most drastically affected the long-term prospects of the domestic social and economic programs that seemed to be emerging from the White House conference, the preconference gatherings like the one the

Commission on Religion and Race sponsored in New York City, and even from the offices of the Johnson administration in the guise of the Great Society. Although estimates of cost varied considerably, any realistic attempt to combat racism and poverty would require multiple billions of dollars to implement, and the federal government had to be both chief initiator of these programs and chief provider of funds. After 1965 that possibility became ever more remote as the Vietnam War absorbed the nation's resources—moral, intellectual, and economic—which might have been poured into the battle to overcome the deep-seated disabilities attributable to racial prejudice and discrimination.

This constituted a missed historical opportunity of truly tragic proportions. A quarter century has passed, and we now see more fully how the hopes still animating many civil rights supporters as late as mid-1966 were being dashed. But for church people and the hundreds of others involved in the national conference "to fulfill these rights" in June 1966, the portents of failure were already there, clearly in the air, yet another indication that the apparent successes of 1963, 1964, and 1965 in advancing race relations were almost at an end.

On June 6, 1966, four days after the end of the White House conference, James Meredith was shot from ambush on a road in northern Mississippi, as he walked a lonely, individual "march" to demonstrate to poor blacks throughout the state that they could vote freely under the new Voting Rights Act. Meredith was hospitalized, but the trek through Mississippi was continued by Martin Luther King, Jr., and other black civil rights leaders, who recognized the symbolic importance of doing so. In this second phase of the march, the words "black power" were first proclaimed for a major national audience, especially by Stokely Carmichael and his SNCC co-workers. Throughout the rest of the dangerous trip through the center of Mississippi, large crowds of local blacks roared approval of the phrase, expressing a new mood of black militancy, and most importantly, deeming it essential to "go it alone," without the support even of friendly whites.[55]

Reflecting the increasing frustration of African Americans nationwide that alliances with liberal groups outside their community were no longer moving the nation toward the elimination of poverty and an end to discrimination, the black power slogan caught on everywhere. Church people were no exception, and the Commission on Religion and Race again assumed a leadership role nationally. In early July 1966, Benjamin Payton convened a small gathering, consisting of the other black members of the commission, Presbyterian Gayraud Wilmore, and Rev. Henderson R. Hughes, a prominent A.M.E. minister in Harlem, in his office at "475," and they proceeded to create the National Committee of Negro Churchmen (changed later to "National Commission of Black Churchmen," reflecting accurately both the changing understanding of a community's public identity and the sexist nature of leadership in black as well as white churches). The NCBC, as it came to be called, was the principal mainstream ecumenical church group advocating black power concepts and strategies throughout the rest of the sixties.[56]

Payton and Wilmore, the primary creators of the NCBC, were well suited for such responsibilities. Both were deeply rooted within the African American churches, although in different and complementary sectors. As noted earlier, Payton was a member of the National Baptist Convention, U.S.A., Inc., the largest black denomination in the country. He left New York City in 1967 to become the president of Benedict College, an important African American college in the South, which was affiliated with Baptist conventions, both black and white. One of his colleagues on the Commission on Religion and Race noted recently Payton's "deep commitment to the black church," and that he helped to bring that church, through his work in the National Council's commission, "into the mainstream of ecumenical thinking, that it was not just an afterthought" for white ecumenical and denominational church leaders, as it had been previously.[57] The founding of the National Committee of Black Churchmen illustrates this point well.

Wilmore's roots were in the black segment of a predominantly white denomination, the United Presbyterian Church, U.S.A. This meant perhaps an earlier and more direct exposure to the white churches, but Wilmore was just as conscious as Payton, and in the later sixties even more vociferous in protesting, the indignities and discriminatory practices heaped upon blacks, especially from within the white churches. The reader will recall that Wilmore had been director of the United Presbyterians' Commission on Religion and Race since 1963, with offices at the Interchurch Center in New York. This provided him with a superb vantage point to observe at close range racial problems within his own denomination and to try and solve them. In addition, he was strategically placed to work often with his coequals in the National Council's Commission on race, and he did this regularly. Although not a graduate of McCormick Seminary, he had been there a number of times, especially in the 1950s, to receive special training for promising young denominational leaders, which exposed him to the theological and socioethical ideas that shaped the attitudes and actions of most of the young churchmen who were his peers at "475" in the sixties. But by the mid-sixties he, just as much as Payton, identified increasingly with black church people, both in his own denomination and in the larger world of American church life.[58]

In 1966 both men were sensitive and realistic interpreters of the black predicament. Seeking to explain the urban disturbances of 1965 and 1966 to a white audience in Ohio in August 1966, Payton emphasized that in the ghettoes

> because of the pressure under which they live, the people find their hearts bursting, themselves out of control, and the dam breaks. And they say, in this pitiful, anguished vocabulary, "We are here. We are real. The resources

of this country belong to us, just as they belong to the rest of the city. And we are tired of being pinned in, and we are tired of that noose of white suburbia around our neck—and we want out."[59]

With somewhat different emphases but with similar intent, Wilmore also commented on the urban disorders.

> The Black Church . . . is inseparable from the ghetto. . . . Whatever motivates the ghetto to peace-making or rebellion must motivate the Black Church. . . . Black clergy . . . did not condone the violence and criminal behavior of some of the street people, but they understood its [the disorder's] causes only too well and were caught up in it as leaders whose first impulse was to look to the safety and welfare of their people. [Thus] they met secretly with underground leaders, articulated demands to the press, argued with the politicians, and diverted police and national guard so that some of their folks could get out of the cordoned-off areas. . . . In Los Angeles, during the Watts outbreak in 1965, Black preachers formed an armed guard of men from their congregations to repulse a White motorcycle gang trying to invade their neighborhood in retaliation for the burning. Newark and Detroit Black clergy cooperated with the grassroots leaders of the rebellion in ways that would have made them vulnerable to prosecution even though they attempted to restrain the violence and turned their churches into shelters and feeding stations for those who had been burned out.[60]

These two quotations suggest how well the two writers understood and empathized with African Americans in the cities, and how angry they, too, were, about the conditions being endured. It is easy to understand why they were ready to respond to "black power!," to organize black church leaders in support of that slogan, and to develop interpretations of the phrase that were consistent with deeply held religious beliefs and long-established personal commitments within the institutional church.[61]

On Sunday, July 31, 1966, less than a month after its founding, the NCBC published a four-column statement on black power as an ad in the *New York Times* and then in the *Chicago Tribune*. Forty-eight black church leaders (Anna Hedgeman was the only lay person and woman included), representing both predominantly white mainline churches with sizable black constituencies and the largest predominantly black denominations, endorsed the statement and had their names printed at the end of it. Payton wrote the first draft of the text; he and Wilmore were members of a small group which revised that draft into its final form.[62]

Compared to the provocative slogans of Stokely Carmichael, the NCBC justification of black power did not advance a radical point of view. The writers were still integrationists—"we and all other Americans *are* one. Our history and destiny are indissolubly linked." They did not repudiate the civil rights movement entirely, and they urged fellow African Americans to work within the existing system to achieve the power that was rightfully and needfully theirs—"to have and to wield group power" just like "Jews, Italians, Poles, and white Anglo-Saxon Protestants." And they sought to use this "group" or "organizational" power to make "the rebuilding of our cities first priority in the use of our [national] resources." There were other hints that Benjamin Payton's and Seymour Melman's Metropolitan Development program from the New York pre-White House conference three months earlier had reappeared as a key part of the NCBC statement.[63]

But these black religious leaders were also moving toward new attitudes. They stressed that as African Americans

> we must first be reconciled to ourselves lest we fail to recognize the resources we already have and upon which we can build. We must be reconciled to ourselves as persons and to ourselves as an historical group. This means we must find our way to a new self image in which we can feel a normal sense of pride in self, including our variety of skin color and the manifold textures of our hair.[64]

Thus cultural and racial pride were entirely in order and should be encouraged. This was a major message of black power advocates in the middle and late sixties, and the NCBC was no exception.

This new organization was also challenging Martin Luther King, Jr., with its statement and later actions. The principal signers of the NCBC statement were *northern* black clergy. They represented a wide range of black church groups and thus were inherently ecumenical; King and his closest black advisors were mostly southerners and Baptists, although there were always ecumenical aspects to his work and that of the SCLC. Perhaps most importantly, the people in the NCBC were very sensitive to the problems of African Americans in the urban centers of the North simply because for years they had worked there. King was far less familiar with this environment and less able to deal with it, as exemplified in his northern campaign in Chicago in 1965 to 1966. The need for power in a highly diversified world of ethnic groups seemed realistic to northern blacks, more than creating a "beloved community" through nonviolence and a Christian love ethic. Thus the NCBC pointed to a division within the African American religious community which had existed since the Reconstruction era a century earlier, but was made fully evident to the general public from the mid-sixties onward only as the national black freedom struggle began to shift ground and focus fully on the North.[65] And by criticizing King and his approach to racial issues, the NCBC was also implicitly raising questions about the white religious community, so closely allied to King and so admiring of his techniques and personality.

Wilmore also noted later that the statement of July 1966 and the founding of the NCBC represented "the beginning of Black reflection on the racial situation in America independent of the White theologians and ethicists." Thus it was one starting point for a separate Black Theology, which emerged fully in 1969 and has been a major force in American theological studies since that time.[66] Although a historical movement that stands somewhat apart from our concerns here, it is another indication of the important changes that were taking place in black-white attitudes in the churches in the late sixties.

All of this meant that from the beginning there was blunt and painful public criticism of the mainstream white churches with which black people had been closely allied. In its first proclamation, for example, the NCBC noted that

> as black men who were long ago forced out of the white church to create and to wield "black power," we fail to understand the emotional quality of the outcry of some [white] clergy against the use of the term today. . . . [Indeed,] the Negro Church was created as a result of the refusal to submit to the indignities of a false kind of "integration" in which all power was in the hands of white people. A more equal sharing of power is precisely what is required [today] as the precondition of authentic human interaction.[67]

These were pointed and legitimate criticisms that needed to be made, and there would be many more assertions like them. Undoubtedly, too, there was a certain psychological liberation which occurred when black people felt the strength—personal "power"—to "tell it like it was" to whites, especially within the churches.

After July 1966, the NCBC became steadily more vigorous in its criticisms of whites and in joining those asserting that blacks should stand apart. On November 3, 1966, a solemn procession near the Statue of Liberty of 150 robed black clerics from twenty states ended with the reading of a public statement expressing concerns about the forthcoming national election and fears of a white "backlash." Early the following year the organization vigorously defended Adam Clayton Powell, Jr., against efforts in Congress to remove the powerful minister-politician from office because of a variety of alleged improprieties.[68] Most significantly, however, in September 1967, a national gathering of urban specialists called together by the National Council of Churches reached such an impasse of views that two caucuses formed, one white, one black. It was an unprecedented development, unknown previously in ecumenical circles, and reflected the growing polarization both in and outside the churches.[69] In all of these developments NCBC members, among the younger, best-educated clergy in the black churches, played key roles.[70]

Other events also eased the way toward these developments. Early in 1967 the Commission on Religion and Race disappeared into the NCC's bureaucracy, becoming a part of a new Department of Social Justice, which included five other special task forces of the council as well as the commission. Benjamin Payton was the head of this new agency, but he surprised his colleagues when in early May 1967, he resigned and left New York to become the president of Benedict College in South Carolina. For several months there was no permanent director.[71] Earlier fears that there would be a loss of focus and momentum on racial issues when the Commission on Religion and Race ended seemingly were now being realized.

The polarization that occurred at the church-sponsored urban conference in the fall of 1967 reflected in part the frustration of African American church leaders with the inability of the white churches, and especially the National Council, to mount an effective response to urban disturbances of increasing scope and intensity, extending from Watts in 1965 to Detroit in 1967. The National Council of Churches *did* react to these upheavals. It created in 1967 a so-called "Crisis in the Nation" program that was to encompass nearly all major departments within the council dealing with national domestic problems. But the diffuseness of this effort simply highlighted the leadership and programmatic difficulties of the council on racial issues that occurred after the demise of the Commission on Religion and Race. Although it existed for over two years, "Crisis in the Nation" ended up more a public relations ploy than a serious and realistic response to the great urban difficulties of the late sixties.[72] The National Committee of Black Churchmen sensed that fact, which only increased the members' feelings of alienation and the urgent need to develop new approaches to the problems of African Americans in urban areas.[73]

One very interesting ecumenical experiment did appear in the maelstrom of events that was the late sixties. On May 5, 1967, a small interfaith group, including Protestant ministers, Catholic priests, and a Jewish rabbi, held the first official meeting in New York City of the Interreligious Foundation for Community Organization (IFCO).[74] Its ecumenical origins made it relatively easy for IFCO, when relating to African Americans, to play down its sectarian or denominational religious connections. This was important in giving it credibility among the increasingly secularized young African Americans emerging as leaders in the ghettos under the banner of black power. At the same time the obvious involvement of mainstream church people in IFCO's organization and subsequent operation, it was hoped, would make it acceptable to the wealthy denominations as a place to commit large sums for grappling with racial problems in northern cities. Using money provided largely by the churches, IFCO's intent was to support financially as many as possible of the new African American community organizations springing up everywhere. Funding was to be carefully regulated, the end result of a detailed screening of proposals submitted by community groups. Essentially IFCO was to serve as a practical interlocutor or broker between whites and blacks who less and less were able to speak and act directly together.[75]

The first (and present) director, Lucius Walker, exemplified well the concerns of the organization. An African American, a native of New Jersey, and an American Baptist, Walker had a B.D. degree from Andover Newton Seminary in Massachusetts, and a master's degree in social work from the University of Wisconsin in Milwaukee. He had spent six years as the director of a "neighborhood house" in the black community of Milwaukee before coming to New York in September 1967.[76]

Walker quickly set out to modify certain traditional patterns of race relations that plagued even this new organization. The predominantly white executive board was altered by expanding its size (from 25 to 100 members) and inviting people from minority community groups to join.[77] Early efforts within the board of directors to limit the involvement of the organization in black power gatherings were strongly rebuffed.[78] Latino and Native American groups were encouraged to apply for money, thus theoretically expanding the number of minorities to be supported (although by far the largest number of grants still went to African American organizations).[79] These moves by Walker and his organization gave them additional credibility in the minority communities in response to the growing militancy and demands for autonomy from whites, yet did little to question openly IFCO's crucial, ongoing relationship with the mainline churches. Here were typical and revealing examples of the fine line IFCO had to traverse in order to maintain its unusual "brokerage" role between two potentially conflicting constituencies. And these activities also pointed to the lessened role of the National Council of Churches in race relations in 1968 and early 1969—not a single board member of IFCO was an official representative of that organization. The contrast with half a decade earlier, when the National Council occupied *the* leadership position among the liberal churches on racial issues, could not have been more sharply drawn.

In the charged atmosphere of the late sixties, IFCO projected deeply ambiguous images—striving for a considerable degree of autonomy from the predominantly white churches, yet never able to escape that influence because the churches were IFCO's funding source;[80] attractive to black community groups desperately in need of money, yet always a bit suspect because of its connections to the white church.[81] IFCO was trying to serve as a creative new means for the mainline churches to continue to affect race relations, yet it also might easily become a vehicle through which the black community, stirred by black power and a growing sense of anger and alienation from their former white allies, might turn and attack those very church groups with whom they had so long been associated. The great national liberal consensus between blacks and whites of the early and mid-sixties was falling apart, and the churches' portion of that consensus followed the same trajectory. IFCO's creation in part reflected that fact, yet also suggested an attempt by a few church people, white and black, to continue the struggle to bridge the gap between the races. There were huge risks involved; IFCO's early history also pointed to the volatile, inflammatory context into which its principal constituencies, black people and black community organizations and white churches, were moving. If someone struck a match in such a situation, a conflagration of unpredictable proportions and results might suddenly leap into being. Into this historical setting in April 1969 came James

Forman to proclaim the Black Manifesto, setting in motion a series of events that largely ended the mainstream Protestant churches' *kairos* of national racial activism. We must now focus our attention on that dramatic moment in time, exhibiting a special concern for the reactions to and results of the manifesto for the National Council of Churches and its supporters.

Notes

1. "Report of the Executive Director," NCC Commission on Religion and Race, April 1, 1965, pp. 2, 3, RG 6, box 47, folder 29, NCC Archives; "Meetings with Civil Rights Leaders, November 18, 1964–March 12, 1965," container 6, William Moyers Papers, Lyndon Johnson Library, Austin, Texas. See also Bill Moyers to Robert Spike, January 13, 1965; Lee C. White to "Bob," May 25, 1965; list of those invited to the signing of the Voting Rights Act, August 5, 1965; items in Name File, "Spike, L-R," White House Central File, container 483, Lyndon B. Johnson Papers, Johnson Library.

2. R. H. Edwin Espy to "Mr. President," November 22, 1965; Lyndon Johnson to "Mr. Espy," December 1, 1965; both items in RG 4, box 33, folder 15, NCC Archives.

3. Details of the riots and their immediate aftermath are in *New York Times,* July 25, p. 1; July 26, pp. 1, 41; July 27, pp. 1, 18; July 29, 1964, p. 40; *Rochester Democrat and Chronicle,* July 25, p. 1; July 27, p. 1; July 28, 1964, p. 1.

4. William C. Martin, *Christians in Conflict* (Chicago, Center for the Scientific Study of Religion, 1972), chap. 1; P. David Finks, *The Radical Vision of Saul Alinsky* (New York, Paulist Press, 1984), pp. 176–181; Sanford D. Horwitt, *Let Them Call Me Rebel: Saul Alinsky, His Life and Legacy* (New York, Alfred A. Knopf, 1989), pp. 451–456.

5. "Report of Bernard Lafayette," August 7–9, 8–13, 1964, to American Friends Service Committee, Chicago Regional Office, in files of David Garrow, loaned to the author; *Rochester Democrat and Chronicle,* August 10, p. 1B; August 12, p. 1B; August 14, 1964, p. 2B; P. David Finks, "Crisis in Smugtown: A Study of Conflict, Churches, and Citizen Organizing in Rochester, New York, 1964–1969" (unpublished Ph.D. dissertation, Graduate School of Union of Experimenting Colleges and Universities, 1975), pp. 30–32; Horwitt, *Let Them Call Me Rebel,* p. 456.

6. "Summary Report: Commission on Religion and Race, June 5, 1964–December 3, 1964," p. 5, RG 6, box 47, folder 31, NCC Archives; Finks, "Crisis in Smugtown," pp. 37–52.

7. The National Council of Churches' involvement in the later stages of the conflict, especially over the use of stock proxies at the 1967 meeting of the Eastman Kodak Corporation in New Jersey, is documented in RG 6, box 16, folder 25, NCC Archives. Martin, *Christians in Conflict,* provides important data on the participation of local churches in the struggle with Kodak. Other important analyses of the churches' role are in Finks, "Crisis in Smugtown," chaps. 1, 2, 4, 6–9, and Alexander Hawryluk, "Friends of FIGHT: A Study of a Militant Civil Rights Organization," (Unpublished Ph.D. dissertation, Cornell University, 1967), especially chaps. IV–VIII.

8. Finks, "Crisis in Smugtown," pp. 31–32, 47–49; Hawryluk, "Friends of FIGHT," pp. 61–63, 194–199, 201–204.

9. Brief summaries of that struggle are in Finks, *Radical Vision*, chap. 6; and Horwitt, *Let Them Call Me Rebel*, chap. 25.

10. "Eastman Kodak and FIGHT," Northwestern University School of Business Cases, 1967; "Why FIGHT?" pamphlet prepared by Presbytery of Genessee Valley; both items in Papers of Richard C. Brown, Rhode Island State Council of Churches, Providence; William C. Martin, "Shepherds vs. Flocks: Ministers and Negro Militancy," *Atlantic,* December 1967, pp. 53–59; David Hunter to Harold A. Bosley, June 14, 1967; Homer A. Jack to "Colleague," June 27, 1967, and attachment; both items in RG 6, box 16, folder 25, NCC Archives.

11. Minutes, NCC Commission on Religion and Race, June 29, 1964, p. 2, RG 6, box 47, folder 30, NCC Archives.

12. For the negative effects of a sudden intrusion in January 1967 by Spike's successor, Benjamin Payton, into the contest between FIGHT and Eastman Kodak, see *Rochester Democrat and Chronicle,* January 4, 1967, p. 2A; telegram, Benjamin Payton to Lewis Eilers, January 3, 1967; Eilers to Payton, January 9, 1967; C. E. Fitzgibbon to Marion B. Folsom, April 26, 1967; Folsom to R. H. Edwin Espy, April 27, 1967, Espy to Folsom, May 3, 1967, items in RG 6, box 16, folder 25, NCC Archives.

13. "Report of the Executive Director," Commission on Religion and Race, NCC, January 29, 1965, p. 4, folder 30; "Minutes," Commission on Religion and Race, NCC, April 14, 1965, pp. 2–5, folder 29; James C. Moore, "Report of the Director of Community Action: Pilot Projects in Northern Cities," Exhibit A attached to "Minutes," April 14, 1965; items in RG 6, box 47, NCC Archives.

14. B. Bruce Whittemore to Edwin Espy, February 23, 1965; "Minutes," NCC Commission Religion and Race, June 11, 1965, p. 5; Jay [James] C. Moore, "Progress Report of Detroit Pilot Project," Exhibit B attached to "Minutes," Commission on Religion and Race, NCC, September 24, 1965; James P. Breeden, "Progress Report on the Cleveland Project," Exhibit C; items in RG 6, box 47, folder 32, NCC Archives.

15. "Report of the Executive Director to the Commission on Religion and Race," p. 3, attached as Exhibit A to "Minutes," NCC Commission on Religion and Race, September 24, 1965, ibid.

16. "Minutes," NCC Commission on Religion and Race, September 24, 1965, p. 5, ibid.; "Report of the Executive Director," September 24, 1965, p. 5, ibid.

17. Ibid., pp. 4, 5; news release, Religious News Service, October 18, 1966, in folder entitled "The Rev. Dr. Robert Spike, Executive Director, CORAR," Washington office, NCC.

18. Spike's public utterances prior to 1963 were rather sparse and did not focus much on racial themes. See his address "New Dimensions of Mission," Christian Education Assembly, meeting as a part of the General Assembly, NCC, San Francisco, California, December 8, 1960, RG 2, box 3, folder 5, NCC Archives; "Mission in an Impacted Society," *Interchurch News,* February 1962, p. 5; *United Church Herald,* May 26, p. 20; August 18, pp. 6–7; September 22, p. 21; October 6, 1960, pp. 16–17; August 23, 1962, pp. 18–19. His first brief books, *In But Not of the World: A Notebook of Theology and Practice in the Local Church* (New York, Association Press, 1957) and *Safe in Bondage: An Appraisal of the Church's Mission to America* (New York, Friendship Press, 1960), devoted a combined total of five pages to the race issue. One of Spike's few early race-related essays, a long review of James Baldwin's *The Fire Next Time,* appeared in the *United Church Herald,*

May 2, 1963, pp. 16–18, one month before he joined the National Council of Churches.

19. The work of the commission was always viewed as a team effort. Just before he left, Spike characterized his colleagues and himself as "a diverse, sometimes disorganized, argumentative and passionately loyal clan, from whom I have relearned what agape really means, love experienced in commitment." "Report of the Executive Director to the Commission on Religion and Race," November 29, 1965, p. 1, RG 6, box 47, folder 29, NCC Archives.

20. See *The Freedom Revolution and the Churches* (New York, Association Press, 1965); *Civil Rights Involvement; Social Action,* xxxi (November 1964); *Presbyterian Life,* January 1, 1966, pp. 8, 37–38. The records of the Commission on Religion and Race in RG 6, box 47 and RG 11, box 6, NCC Archives and in box 15, Victor Reuther Papers, are essential sources.

21. On Spike's continuing activism after his move to the Midwest, especially as a mediator in the conflicts in the summer of 1966 between Martin Luther King, Jr., and Mayor Daley in Chicago and as a church lobbyist in support of the Child Development Group of Mississippi in the early fall of that year, see Garrow, *Bearing the Cross,* pp. 509–510, 511, 516; Alan B. Anderson, George W. Pickering, *Confronting the Color Line: The Broken Promise of the Civil Rights Movement in Chicago* (Athens, University of Georgia Press, 1986), pp. 248, 257, 260; Paul Spike, *Photographs of My Father* (New York, Alfred A. Knopf, 1973), pp. 199–204, 239–244; telegram, Walter Reuther to Sargent Shriver, October 5, 1966, folder 7, box 378, Walter P. Reuther Papers; "Final Report on the Child Development Group of Mississippi," October 10, 1966, reel 13, CDGM Papers.

22. Spike's analysis of the changed nature of race relations at the end of 1965, which forecast the breakup of the national civil rights coalition and offered convincing explanations of these developments, is in his "Fissures in the Civil Rights Movement," *Christianity and Crisis,* February 21, 1966, pp. 18–21. A small collection of Spike's sermons, speeches, and handwritten sermon outlines from the post-January 1966 period are in the Robert Spike Papers, Joseph Regenstein Library, University of Chicago.

23. *Columbus [Ohio] Evening Dispatch,* October 18, 1966, pp. 1, 6.

24. Paul Spike, *Photographs of My Father,* pp. 237–244; interview with Paul Spike, March 1, 1986; interview with Colin Williams, August 18, 1990; telephone interview with Jon Regier, October 28, 1986; interview with Robert Newman, November 20, 1990; interview with Paul Moore, Jr., October 28, 1986; "Summary of Findings: Robert Spike Murder Investigation," February 26, 1980 [panel of Methodist officials], in possession of Ms. Peggy Billings, Trumansburg, New York. A more tentative conclusion is in interview with Dean Wright, November 12, 1990.

25. "Spike is one of these quiet, anonymous, little guys who devotes his life to causes like this [improving race relations]." Bill Moyers to President Johnson, August 19, 1964, White House Central File, container 483, Lyndon Johnson Papers. On Spike and the FBI, see 57 pages of documents from FBI files, received under Freedom of Information Act (FOIA), request #265,737. On government surveillance of African American civil rights leaders after 1965, see O'Reilly, *"Racial Matters,"* chaps. 7, 8, 9.

26. Paul Spike, *Photographs of My Father,* pp. 240–242, provides important speculations concerning possible CIA involvement in his father's death. "Summary of Findings: Robert Spike Murder Investigation," pp. 3–5, is a similar, but

more specific and more convincing, explanation. See also interview with Colin Williams, August 18, 1990; telephone interview with Paul Moore, Jr., September 13, 1990; interview with Bruce Hanson, March 11, 1991.

27. *Columbus Evening Dispatch,* October 18, p. 6; October 19, 1966, p. 3; Richard O. Pfau, "Summary Re: Robert W. Spike Homicide," October 31, 1966, part of autopsy report attached to "Coronor's Report. Finding of Facts and Verdict," death of Robert W. Spike, October 17, 1966, Franklin [Ohio] County Coroner's Office, Columbus, Ohio.

28. The best summary and evaluation of these matters is in "Summary of Findings: Robert Spike Murder Investigation," February 26, 1980, p. 2.

29. On the investigation following Spike's murder, including the arrest of William Minor, see *New York Times,* October 18, p. 28; October 19, p. 92; October 20, p. 15; December 9, p. 30; December 10, p. 22; December 13, p. 15; December 17, 1966, p. 13. An evaluation of Minor's arrest, confession, and release, critical of the procedures followed by the Columbus police, is in "Summary of Findings: Robert Spike Murder Investigation," p. 3.

30. The principle periodicals of the mainline denominations offered no more than perfunctory recognition of Spike's death and assessments of his career. For example, see *United Church Herald,* December 1966, p. 9; *Presbyterian Life,* November 15, 1966, p. 27; *Christian Century,* November 2, 1966, p. 1330. An exception were the sensitive remarks in *Christianity and Crisis,* November 14, 1966, pp. 249–251. See also telephone interview with J. Martin Bailey, July 17, 1992; interview with Alice and William Wimer, August 18, 1992; "Summary of Findings: Robert Spike Murder Investigation," p. 2.

31. "Minutes," NCC Commission on Religion and Race, June 11, 1965, p. 6, RG 6, box 47, folder 29, NCC Archives. For Anna Hedgeman's views of the lack of racial inclusiveness in the churches, see her *The Trumpet Sounds: A Memoir of Negro Leadership* (New York, Holt, Rinehart, and Winston, 1964), pp. 175–176, and *Gift of Chaos,* pp. 100–101, 149–150; "Minutes," NCC Commission on Religion and Race, September 24, 1965, p. 2, box 47, folder 29, NCC Archives.

32. A good brief survey of race-related events in the mid-1960s is in Robert Weisbrot, *Freedom Bound: A History of America's Civil Rights Movement* (New York, Penguin Books, 1991), chaps. 6–8.

33. *New York Times,* December 12, 1965, p. 56; telephone interview with Benjamin Payton, June 4, 1991.

34. Telephone interview with Benjamin Payton, June 4, 1991; C. Eric Lincoln and Lawrence H. Mamiya, *The Black Church in the African American Experience* (Durham, Duke University Press, 1990), pp. 30–39; Branch, *Parting the Waters,* pp. 500–503, 504–507.

35. "Report to the General Board," February 23, 1966, p. 4, RG 6, box 47, folder 29, NCC Archives (italics in the original). See also "Resolution for Action by the Commission on Religion and Race: *Development for Equal Opportunity,*" March 16, 1966, RG 6, box 47, folder 29, NCC Archives.

36. Telephone interview with James Breeden, April 12, 1991; telephone interview with Benjamin Payton, June 4, 1991. In this interview Payton emphasized the deep influence Anna Hedgeman had on him while he was the director of the commission, and afterward.

37. *New York Times,* June 5, 1965, p. 1; the text of the speech is on p. 14.

38. A. Phillip Randolph, Morris Abram, and William T. Coleman to Benjamin Payton, November 10, 1965; Anna Arnold Hedgeman to Denominational

Race Staff, January 12, 1966; both items in RG 6, box 48, folder 7, NCC Archives; Payton's acute critique of the Moynihan Report is in an unpublished essay, "The President, the Social Experts, and the Ghetto: An Analysis of an Emerging Strategy in Civil Rights," with an important accompanying memo, Dr. William Ryan to "Anyone Interested," October 8, 1965, in RG 6, box 48, folder 6, NCC Archives. See also telephone interview with Benjamin Payton, June 4, 1991.

39. On November 9, 1965, Payton, then with the ecumenical Protestant Council of New York City, and Robert Spike had cosponsored a brief conference in New York that expressed early opposition to the Johnson administration's plans. This conference ended with a public statement, which was then "forwarded to the White House." Hedgeman to Denominational Race Staff, January 12, 1966, RG 6, box 48, folder 6, NCC Archives.

40. *New York Times,* May 22, 1966, p. 46. Interestingly, in February 1966, Robert Spike was appointed by Johnson administration officials to the planning "council" that prepared the agenda for the White House conference in June of that year. Clifford Alexander to the president, February 11, 1966, Name Files, White House Central File, container 483, Johnson Papers.

41. Benjamin Payton, "Introductory Remarks to the New York Pre-White House Conference on Civil Rights," RG 6, box 48, folder 6, NCC Archives.

42. Minutes, Pre-White House Conference Steering Committee, January 11, 1966, January 27, 1966, ibid.; Minutes, Executive Committee, New York Pre-White House Conference, February 19, 1966, March 3, 1966, ibid.; James Breeden to Denominational Race Staff and Related Staff Persons, February 17, 1966, folder 7, ibid.; Breeden to Payton, March 7, 1966, folder 7, ibid.; Anna Arnold Hedgeman to Payton, April 22, 1966, folder 7, ibid.

43. Jay Moore to Dr. Payton, January 17, 1966, RG 6, box 48, folder 6, ibid.

44. "Address of Senator Robert F. Kennedy, New York Pre-White House Conference on Civil Rights, May 11, 1966," ibid.; *New York Times,* May 12, 1966, p. 39. On the enthusiastic response of the conference organizers to Kennedy's remarks and participation, see Benjamin F. Payton to the Honorable Robert F. Kennedy, May 17, 1966; especially when compared with Payton to the Honorable John V. Lindsay, May 17, 1966, and Payton to the Honorable Nelson Rockefeller, May 17, 1966; both items in RG 6, box 48, folder 7, NCC Archives.

45. "A Strategy for the Next Stage in Equal Rights: Metropolitan–Rural Development for Equal Opportunity," February 25, 1966, RG 6, box 48, folder 7, NCC Archives. In August 1966, Payton suggested some of the ethical implications of this program in an address to a church group in Ohio entitled "Metropolitics: a Form of Christian Social Action," RG 6, box 48, folder 12, NCC Archives.

46. Attachment to James P. Breeden to Denominational Race Staff and Related Staff Persons, February 17, 1966; "Minutes," Executive Committee, New York Pre-White House Conference, March 3, 1966; Benjamin F. Payton to Lyndon B. Johnson, May 27, 1966, and attachment entitled "Resolutions and Recommendations . . . to the White House Conference 'To Fulfill These Rights,'" especially p. 7; all items in RG 6, box 48, folder 7, NCC Archives.

47. "Address of Senator Robert F. Kennedy . . . May 11, 1966," pp. 4, 5, folder 6, ibid.

48. The two thousand delegates were divided into fourteen categories, including 30 people from "Arts, Sports, and Entertainment," 150 from "Poor and

Grassroots Organizations," and even a mysterious "Miscellaneous" group of 100 participants. Revealingly, the largest groups invited were from "Business and Industry" (300) and "State and Local Officials" (400). One hundred religious leaders were included. Civil rights people were in a distinct minority, only 10 percent of those attending. Attachment to Berl I. Bernhard to James A. Linen, April 19, 1966, reel 1, Records of the White House Conference on Civil Rights, Law Library, Boston University. See also Harry C. McPherson to Charles Silberman, March 31, 1966, attached to Henry Siegman to Benjamin Payton, April 4, 1966, RG 6, box 48, folder 7, NCC Archives.

49. This was a major concern of the pre-White House Conference in New York, a "disservice" even to the "cause of the Negro," effectively "splitting off potential political support" in any effort to implement the proposals that came out of the conference. Benjamin F. Payton to Eugene Carson Blake, R. H. Edwin Espy, David Hunter, Jon Regier, Colin Williams, May 31, 1966, RG 6, box 48, folder 7, NCC Archives.

50. Ibid.; *New York Times,* May 25, 1965, p. 46.

51. *New York Times,* December 5, 1965, pp. 1, 6. The text of the General Board's statement is printed on p. 6, ibid.

52. Garrow, *Bearing the Cross,* pp. 394, 422, 425, 428, 429–430, 436, 437–439, 440, 443, 444–446, 472. The Riverside Church talk is reprinted in James M. Washington, *A Testament of Hope: The Essential Writings and Speeches of Martin Luther King, Jr.* (San Francisco, Harper's, 1986), pp. 231–244. See also Mitchell K. Hall, *Because of Their Faith: CAL-CAV and Religious Opposition to the Vietnam War* (New York, Columbia University Press, 1990).

53. *New York Times,* May 24, 1966, p. 28.

54. Garrow, *Bearing the Cross,* p. 473; Weisbrot, *Freedom Bound,* pp. 190–193.

55. Weisbrot, *Freedom Bound,* pp. 196–204. A recent study of the Black Power movement is William L. Van Deburg's *New Day in Babylon: The Black Power Movement and American Culture, 1965–1975* (Chicago, University of Chicago Press, 1992).

56. Hedgeman, *Gift of Chaos,* p. 150; Gayraud S. Wilmore, *Black Religion and Black Radicalism: An Interpretation of the Religious History of Afro-American People,* 2d ed. (Maryknoll, N.Y., Orbis Press, 1983), pp. 195–196; telephone interview with James Breeden, April 12, 1991; interview with Gayraud Wilmore, May 6, 1991; telephone interview with Benjamin Payton, June 4, 1991. On the history of black ecumenism generally in the United States, see Mary R. Sawyer, "Black Ecumenism: Cooperative Social Change Movements in the Black Church," unpublished Ph.D. dissertation, Duke University 1986.

57. Telephone interview with James Breeden, April 12, 1991. See also telephone interview with Benjamin Payton, June 4, 1991.

58. On Wilmore's early life and activities in the Presbyterian church, see McCloud interview with Wilmore, part I, tape 857, Presbyterian Oral History Collection. On his connections with McCormick Seminary, see Findlay interview with Wilmore, May 6, 1991. On his eventual ambivalence toward white church people, reflecting opposition to their continuing racism yet a necessity to remain "connected" with them, see "Identity and Integration: Black Presbyterians and Their Allies in the Twentieth Century," in Coalter, Mulder, and Weeks, *The Presbyterian Predicament,* pp. 109–133; his *Black and Presbyterian: the Heritage and the Hope* (Philadelphia, Geneva Press, 1983); interview with Wilmore, May 6, 1991.

59. "Metropolitics: A Form of Christian Social Action," August 10, 1966, pp. 2–3, RG 6, box 48, folder 7, NCC Archives.

60. Gayraud S. Wilmore and James H. Cone, eds., *Black Theology: A Documentary History, 1966–1979* (Maryknoll, N.Y., Orbis Press, 1979), pp. 15–16.

61. One must be reminded that "black power" was a catchword susceptible of a variety of understandings. It was not the simple tocsin to revolution and violence the average white American believed it to be. A brief discussion of this point is in Weisbrot, *Freedom Bound*, pp. 204–206, 216, 222–236. See also Van Deburg, *New Day in Babylon*, chaps. 1, 3–6.

62. *New York Times*, July 31, 1966, p. E5; Hedgeman, *Gift of Chaos*, pp. 150–152; Wilmore and Cone, *Black Theology*, p. 17; telephone interview with Benjamin Payton, June 4, 1991.

63. *New York Times*, July 31, 1966, p. E5. The entire statement has been reprinted in Wilmore and Cone, *Black Theology*, pp. 23–30.

64. *New York Times*, July 31, 1966, p. E5.

65. Sawyer, "Black Ecumenism," chaps. 2, 3; Wilmore, *Black Religion and Black Radicalism*, pp. 197–198; interview with Wilmore, May 6, 1991. On the black church in northern urban centers since World War I, see Wills, "An Enduring Distance," in Hutchison, *Between the Times*, pp. 184–186; Lincoln and Mamiya, *Black Church in African American Experience*, chap. 6.

66. Wilmore and Cone, *Black Theology*, p. 18.

67. *New York Times*, July 31, 1966, p. E5.

68. "Summary of CORR Activities in 1966," RG 6, box 48, folder 12, NCC Archives; *New York Times*, November 4, p. 29, November 6, 1966, part IV, p. 7; "The Powell Affair—A Crisis of Morals and Faith," February 1967, pamphlet in RG 6, box 48, folder 12, NCC Archives. See also Charles U. Hamilton, *Adam Clayton Powell, Jr.: The Political Biography of an American Dilemma* (New York, Atheneum, 1991), chap. 20.

69. Wilmore, *Black Religion and Black Radicalism*, pp. 198–199; Wilmore and Cone, *Black Theology*, pp. 18–19. In agony over these divisions, one small group of white conferees sought admission to (and thus full identification with) the black caucus, but were turned away—an indication of the new level of self-confidence and militance black church people demonstrated, and the new reality white church people had to face. Wilmore and Cone, *Black Theology*, p. 19.

70. On the social characteristics of the NCBC membership, see Sawyer, "Black Ecumenism," pp. 153, 155. Sawyer estimates that at its peak in the last year or two of the sixties, the NCBC had "some 1200 members" and that 40 percent came from black groups in predominantly white denominations, the rest from the predominantly black churches (p. 155).

71. Minutes, Department of Social Justice, National Council of Churches, April 14, 1967, pp. 1–2, May 8, 1967, p. 2, RG 6, box 2, folder 35, NCC Archives. Gayraud Wilmore was Payton's temporary replacement, briefly assuming responsibility for the NCC agency as well as the comparable organization within his own denomination. Interview with Wilmore, May 6, 1991.

72. On negative assessments of the "Crisis in the Nation" program by officials of the National Council, see David Hunter to Thomas Hook, October 7, 1969, RG 5, box 19, folder 19; Hunter to R. H. Edwin Espy, December 29, 1969, RG 4, box 35, folder 2; and especially Earl D. C. Brewer, "A Report and Evaluation on the Crisis in the Nation Program," (preliminary draft) [March] 1969, pp. 2–6, RG 4, box 35, folder 3; all items in NCC Archives. On other documentation of the

inadequacies of the "Crisis in the Nation" program, see "Crisis in the Nation" [budget figures, 1968, 1969], RG 5, box 14, folder 27; Forrest C. Weir to R. H. Edwin Espy, August 13, 1968, RG 5, box 14, folder 28; David Hunter to Weir, August 19, 1968, RG 5, box 14, folder 28; William F. Haase to Concerned Staff and Denominational Representatives, June 21, 1968, RG 5, box 14, folder 28; Gerald E. Knoff to Paul E. Bergman, June 4, 1968, RG 5, box 15, folder 2; Charles S. Spivey, Jr., to R. H. Edwin Espy, April 16, 17, 1969, RG 4, box 35, folder 2; all items in NCC Archives.

73. For example, see J. Metz Rollins [then executive director of NCBC], "Statement on the 'Crisis in the Nation Program,' for presentation to the General Board [of the NCC], May 1–2, 1969," RG 4, box 35, folder 2, ibid.

74. "Minutes," organization meeting, Interreligious Foundation for Community Organization (IFCO), May 5, 1967, IFCO headquarters, New York. The group had been incorporated, becoming "a legal reality" in December 1966, but it took another nine months to complete essential organizational details. "IFCO: A Status Report—1968," p. 1, in folder entitled "IFCO Status Report," box 27, IFCO Papers, Schomburg Library.

75. An early outline of the philosophy and procedures of IFCO are in "IFCO: A Status Report—1968," p. 1, IFCO Status Report folder, box 27, IFCO Papers.

76. Ibid., p. 9; "Minutes," IFCO, June 13, 1967, IFCO headquarters.

77. "Minutes," IFCO Board of Directors, December 11, 1967, IFCO headquarters; "IFCO: A Status Report—1968," p. 6, IFCO Status Report folder, box 27, IFCO Papers.

78. "Minutes," Board of Directors' meeting, July 19–20, 1967, in IFCO headquarters.

79. On the sociopolitical characteristics of the groups supported by IFCO, there are suggestive data in "IFCO: A Status Report—1968," Appendix C, IFCO Status Report folder, box 27, IFCO Papers, a detailed listing of grant proposals made by community organizations to IFCO through 1968; "Projects Funded by the Interreligious Foundation for Community Organization (IFCO), September 1967–April 1969," in folder entitled "James Forman," box 15, Neigh Papers; and "IFCO Funded Projects: September 1967–October 1969," in folder entitled "IFCO at the Forefront of the Crisis . . . ," box 43, IFCO Papers.

80. In its first year of operation, IFCO allocated grants totaling "close to $1 million" to thirty-eight "urban and rural projects across the country" from money made available by the mainstream churches. *IFCO News,* November 1968, pp. 2–3, in RG 5, box 18, folder 30, NCC Archives. Also during 1967 IFCO received $107,000 to cover its administrative costs; all but $4,000 of that total came from four mainline Protestant denominations—the Presbyterians, the Episcopalians, the Methodists, and the United Church of Christ. The Roman Catholics, the American Jewish Committee, and the American Baptists each contributed $1,000. "Minutes," Interreligious Foundation for Community Organization, October 15, 1967, IFCO headquarters. As late as December 1970, the executive director noted "IFCO has failed to develop a black source of income." "Summary of Executive Director's Report to the IFCO Board of Directors," December 9, 1970, in box 43, IFCO Papers. See also "Income Summary, Inception to March, 1970," attached to *Report of IFCO, April, 1970,* in folder "IFCO—Annual Rept's," box 18, Ralph Smeltzer Papers, BHLA Archives.

81. From the outset, members of IFCO noted the absence of any support from

the predominantly black churches. Some speculated this was because of the organization's close connections with the most powerful mainline white churches. "IFCO: A Status Report—1968," p. 5. See also "Minutes," IFCO Board of Directors, December 11, 1967, June 11, 1968, IFCO headquarters. Yet IFCO also worked closely with the National Committee of Black Churchmen, far more militant on political issues than the black denominations. "Minutes," IFCO Board of Directors, October 17, 1967, p. 3, IFCO headquarters; *IFCO News,* November 1968, pp. 1–2, in RG 5, box 18, folder 30, NCC Archives. The reluctance of the predominantly black churches to support IFCO probably stemmed as much from the latter's friendliness toward black power, and the dislike of that fact by some of the national leaders of those churches, as from IFCO's friendliness with the white churches. See *New York Times,* November 4, 1966, p. 29.

7

The Black Manifesto and Its Aftermath: The End of an Era

In 1968 the United States experienced terrible internal discords over racial issues (new ghetto rebellions and seeming threats to public safety posed by radical groups like the Black Panthers) and over the war in Vietnam (the aftermath of the Tet offensive, which included Lyndon Johnson's surprise decision not again to seek the presidency). Once again people felt the personal shock of assassinations of national leaders (Martin Luther King, Jr., in April and Robert Kennedy in June). And in July, during the national convention of the Democratic party in Chicago, police beat dozens of demonstrators in the streets, as television news cameras recorded the spectacle. "The whole world is watching," chanted young people as they were clubbed to the ground. And the world looked on, aghast. Yet throughout this year there were small groups in the churches and elsewhere who struggled to discover or invent new ways to transcend terrible events like these. In race relations these efforts sometimes led, ironically, to further explosions.

As early as June 1968, Lucius Walker and his staff in IFCO began to think concretely about the broad economic implications of their work in race relations. They had come to see the close interrelationship between community organizing (primarily a political activity) and economic development within the black community, of "community organization as a necesary precondition for black economic development." Similar ideas were sprouting in the Deep South as the Delta Ministry and its allies, moving beyond voter registration, sought to experiment with new economic structures—first handicraft cooperatives and then small industrial ventures—to serve as the rudiments of a new economic base for Mississippi's impoverished rural black folk. A principle concern in both rural and urban areas was that these economic functions "be responsible to the black community," that local African Americans have a large measure of direct control over these new activities.[1]

Acknowledging the need for further exploration of the subject, in

September 1968 IFCO authorized up to $50,000 from its annual budget to plan and implement a nationwide conference on economic development in the black community and encouraged its staff to begin "holding conversations with other groups which should be involved in planning and co-sponsoring such a conference."[2] Following the election of Richard Nixon in November 1968, and the new president's enunciation of a major effort to encourage "black capitalism" in the ghettos, the conference planning assumed a new urgency, to "help counteract" the tendency of government officials "to plan economic development . . . *for* rather than *with* members of the black community." Instead IFCO intended "to enable minority groups in urban and rural areas to develop cooperative, self-determining programs in their own communities."[3]

By April 1969 the National Black Economic Development Conference, as it came to be known, had attracted as cosponsors over twenty black community development organizations, and funding extended well beyond IFCO's financial support, including black corporations, private individuals, and major industrial and labor interests in Detroit. As the time for the conference neared (April 25–27), prospective participants also began forming into special interest caucuses, reflecting the African American community's many-sided concerns—people interested in southern rural land use as well as northern urban development, or those who felt the prime focus of the conference should be how to create more jobs for African Americans rather than new black business enterprises. Members of the Nixon administration "from several levels" also attended. Thus a wide range of ideological positions were represented, from nationalist separatists to conservative African American business people. Six hundred participants showed up, instead of the planned for four hundred, suggesting the unusual degree of interest and excitement the conference generated.[4] IFCO was a key enabler throughout. Walker and his staff had conceived and largely planned the conference; Walker became the conference chairperson and oversaw the daily program. And IFCO's sizable monetary contribution early in the planning process was crucial in enabling the gathering to occur at all.

At the end of the second evening (April 26) James Forman, executive secretary of SNCC earlier in the sixties and still connected to that organization, was scheduled to give a major address to the conference. Forman presented his now-famous Black Manifesto to the evening gathering, demanded that it be adopted as the official program of the conference and that a permanent organization be established to implement the proposals contained in the manifesto. The sharpness of his attack upon a major white institution such as the church, the justness of his criticisms, the size of his demands—$500 million in "reparations" from the churches—and the relative familiarity to many of the delegates of the program he proposed, made Forman's address very compelling. The delegates present, numbering a little over a third of the total conference attendees, quickly endorsed this unexpected development.[5] The event, largely unnoticed at the time in the larger black and white communities, became the starting point for a series of clashes between whites and African Americans in the churches that would exacerbate tensions and help to bring to an end the era of deep involvement of the mainline religious groups in national racial matters. And Forman's slashing criticisms of the churches and sweeping demands for reparations brought into public prominence once again a fascinating though somewhat quixotic man. Strongly influenced early in life by relatives who were black Baptists and Methodists and by Catholic nuns and priests in parochial schools he attended, now years later he suddenly emerged as a powerful secular critic of America's religious establishment, viewed by many in the largely white churches as a far more disturbing prophet in their midst than Martin Luther King, Jr., a few years earlier.[6]

The manifesto that Forman made public on April 26 was almost two separate documents. The first part was a lengthy introduction of generalizations and exhortations reflecting Forman's (and some of the delegates) radical political and economic views. The SNCC leader still exhibited a certain idealism, although quite different from that of former allies from the early sixties in the mainline churches. The manifesto stated, for example, that although

> we talk of revolution[,] which will be an armed confrontation and long years of sustained guerilla warfare inside this country, we must also talk of the type of world we want to live in. We must commit ourselves to a society where the total means of production are taken from the rich people and placed into the hands of the state for the welfare of all the people . . . and that must be led by black people, by revolutionary blacks who are concerned about the total humanity of this world.[7]

It was a rather straightforward Marxist analysis, but statements like this in the introductory section soon were cited by white church people as ample justification for the churches to reject the manifesto out of hand. Much later Forman recalled he had been reluctant from the outset to make public the introduction, but had been overruled by his close associates. That turned out to be a major tactical mistake.[8]

Not until Forman had presented almost half of his talk were the churches mentioned specifically. He was unsparing then in his criticisms, expressing sentiments many blacks both within and outside the churches shared—that Christians, "have been involved in the exploitation and rape of black people since the country [the United States] was founded. The missionary goes hand in hand with the power of the [capitalist] states." Thus even though church people had created the conference and "done a magnificent job of bringing us all together," he said, new leadership was needed. We [Forman and his supporters] "must say to the planners of this conference that you are no longer in charge. . . . We are going to assume power over the conference and determine from this moment on the direction in which we want it to go."[9] Yet the planners of the conference were still very much among those in charge, for Forman had no real organization of his own to implement the manifesto.[10] And ironically he needed support from some of the very white church people he was attacking, for two crucial reasons—their organizational connections, which hopefully would lead to very large sums of money over which they seemed to have some control.

The Black Manifesto also contained a very important second section, practical and more moderate in tone, and quite specific in its demands. It demanded $500 million in "reparations" from "the white Christian churches and Jewish synagogues" because these churches "have a tremendous wealth and its membership, white America, has profited and still exploits black people." As blacks, asserted Forman, "for centuries we have been forced to live as colonized people inside the United States, victimized by the most vicious, racist system in the world." Now was the time to begin to receive some recompense for that fact, money to help finance a southern land bank for blacks, to establish four black-controlled publishing houses, "the most advanced" television network possible, a black university to be located in the South, a black think tank, or "research skill center," and funds to establish a "National Black Labor Strike and Defense Fund."[11]

Although the demand for $500 million from the churches in reparations was new and breathtaking in scope, the programmatic section of the manifesto that followed reflected more fully the thinking of the conference in workshops held before Forman spoke. The proposals were not unfamiliar or even terribly revolutionary. Indeed, the most militant delegates, chiefly nationalist black separatists, cast many of the negative ballots against the manifesto after Forman spoke because his program contained no hint of the creation of a separate black state somewhere in the South.[12]

At the end of the gathering in Detroit, a permanent Black Economic Development Conference was created (known thereafter as "BEDC," or simply "bed-cee") with Forman as its head and with a program in mind, yet also possessing almost no money and an unknown and inexperienced staff. In the next few months, Forman proceeded to carry his demand for reparations directly to most of the mainline churches in a series of widely reported public confrontations. These actions were fully in tune with, and added to, the sense of public tumult that pervaded so much of American life at the end of the sixties.

Perhaps the most famous of these "visits" of Forman was the first, which took place on Sunday, May 4, 1969, at Riverside Church in Morningside Heights in New York City, just across the street from both the National Council of Churches' Interchurch Center and Union Theological Seminary.[13] The three institutions seemed almost the epitome of mainstream Protestantism. The fact that one of Riverside's principal benefactor's was the family of John D. Rockefeller and that the church was located on the edge of Harlem were also important symbolic points that were not lost on Forman and his supporters. Despite pleas from the senior minister, Ernest Campbell, not to do so, Forman chose to inter-rupt the principal Sunday service to read the manifesto and to place specific economic demands upon the church, including "unrestricted use" of the church radio station and the handing over of "sixty percent of the yearly income from all church stock, property and real estate." Was this to be viewed as a symbolic parallel to the nailing of "Ninety-five Theses" to the church doors at Wittenberg in 1519 by an earlier rebel against existing authority? Many of the worshippers that Sunday did not think so. Dr. Campbell, his assistants (the congregation was to observe communion that day), and a sizable part of the congregation left as For-man spoke, although about 500 of those attending remained to hear the new speaker. Soon after the church secured a legal restraining order to prevent disruptions in the future by this "modern day prophet."[14]

Quickly thereafter Forman confronted most of the other mainstream church authorities. By the end of May he had placed his demands before the United Church of Christ, the United Presbyterian Church, U.S.A., the Lutheran Church in America, the American Baptist convention, offi-cials of the United Methodist Church, and the presiding bishop of the Episcopal Church. A visit on May 9 to the chancery offices of Cardi-nal Terence Cooke, Roman Catholic Archbishop of New York, was brushed aside.[15] These challenges could be mounted quickly and with great dramatic effect in part because so many of the national church offices were in New York City. Thus ironically the concentration of national leadership of the churches in a single urban center, which in earlier years helped greatly in shaping church policies and tactics of direct involvement in civil rights activities, in 1969 became a key point of vulnerability, increasing the frequency and then heightening the visibility of attacks upon the churches by Forman and others.

For almost a year prior to May 1969, the educational and religious institutions centered in Morningside Heights in New York City had been in a state of upheaval, including student riots and occupation of buildings at Columbia University, police "busts" of students, mass opposition to the Vietnam War and to a generally perceived insensitivity of the institu-tions there to the needs and rights of the citizens of Harlem, who lived everywhere in the area. Union Seminary was similarly affected (many of its students participated in the events at Columbia), and in addition the seminary was riven by controversies over the selection of a new president and the restructuring of its curriculum, to be done, it was hoped, with direct and considerable student participation.[16]

Forman's dramatic appearance at Riverside Church in early May 1969 must be viewed within this immediate environment of turmoil and un-certainty.[17] It was a part of an almost seamless web of heated public debate, rude and sometimes violent confrontations, and extraordinary, theatrical public displays of great passion and emotion. Moreover, the issues Forman and the manifesto symbolized resonated deeply with the daily concerns of many of the people who lived and worked in the area. It seemed almost inevitable that this man's protest against the deep complicity of the churches in the racism that permeated American society would spread quickly, often without his direct assistance.

Thus on Monday morning, May 12, 1969, just a week after Forman's interruption of the weekly service at Riverside Church, black and white students of Union Theological Seminary occupied the school's main building and demanded that the seminary Board of Trustees support the manifesto, give $100,000 out of the school's budget for the following year to BEDC, and then go on to raise another $1 million for Forman's organization. In response the faculty of the seminary voted to raise $100,000 for "black development," the board of trustees decided to invest $500,000 of the institution's endowment in "black enterprises," and the board agreed to try and raise $1 million "for projects to be operated in Harlem under seminary auspices" and to secure personal gifts to a fund "to be administered by a committee of the seminary's black alumni, faculty, students, and board members."[18] Although not entirely unsympathetic to the student supporters of the manifesto, these responses by the Union Seminary faculty and trustees were decidedly moderate in tone; no funds, for example, were placed immediately and directly under Forman's control. The seminary was setting precedents in its responses to pressure about the manifesto that would be followed in a rough sort of way by a number of other similarly challenged church groups.[19]

The occupation at Union Seminary was quickly followed by similar moves across the street at the Interchurch Center. On May 14 supporters of Forman occupied the offices of the National Board of Missions of the United Presbyterian Church, then (aided by students from Columbia and Union Seminary) extended the occupation the following day to include the four floors rented to the Board of Missions of the United Methodist Church. By the first week of June either Forman or his representatives had also staged sit-ins in the offices of the National Council of Churches, the United Church of Christ, and the Reformed Church of America in different areas of the nineteen-story Interchurch Center.[20] Part of the motivation in these instances was to coordinate activity in New York with Forman's appearances at the respective national church assemblies being held at the same time elsewhere in the country.

By early June the occupations at "475" seemed to be hardening into longer-term affairs and on June 9 there was a one-day work stoppage in the entire building by those in sympathy with Forman and BEDC.[21] The continuing disruption of offices throughout the center posed enough of a dilemma that on June 13 the trustees of the Interchurch Center and several of the denominational tenants whose offices had been occupied took the first legal steps to secure, first, a temporary restraining order and then a permanent court injunction against the demonstrators. Church officials refused to discuss issues further with Forman until he left the building. He did so during the evening of June 18.[22] The injunction was never issued, but the temporary restraining order was, and the shock of that legal maneuver for a brief time divided the church groups in the Interchurch Center even more deeply than before. As one participant put it shortly after the restraining order went into effect, the tensions seemed "like the walls of a skyscraper."[23]

On June 19 the National Council convened an unprecedented exercise in participatory democracy in the Interchurch Center's chapel. Ed Espy and other top officials discussed before typists and secretaries (and many outsiders from the area) the council's participation in the steps leading to the issuing of the restraining order and the preparation of the injunction. A vote of employees, both professional and clerical, at the end of the meeting asked that the restraining order and the pending injunction be dropped. This vote underlined the growing recognition, as one NCC official put it, "that the legal route was a dead end for institutions that believe in moral suasion."[24] Forman also made an unscheduled appearance, surrounded by the media, and appealed for support, and outside the chapel in the wide ground-floor entranceway to the building the Poor People's Theatre performed "Beautiful Dreamer," a tribute to Martin Luther King, as an endorsement of Forman's challenge and in protest of the proposed injunction.[25]

In several ways the chapel gathering thus influenced Espy and others to begin the process that eventually led to canceling the restraining order and never implementing the court injunction. In the short run, the National Council of Churches had largely avoided a major legal confrontation with Forman, which could have led to very uncertain consequences. But in addition, whether they liked it or not, the mainstream churches were now caught up fully in the wild, often unrestrained public feelings unleashed by the profound issues agitating the nation at the end of the sixties. That was a daunting fact, another powerful indication that the liberal cultural hegemony that had existed since the 1930s even in the churches was coming rapidly to an end.

For the most part, church people across the nation did not like what they saw of the spectacle taking place in New York City, in national church meetings elsewhere, and occasionally even in their local churches. James Forman had challenged many cherished notions and beliefs of these people, both as churchgoers and as Americans generally, and they reacted almost viscerally as they communicated with their leaders. Letters pouring into the National Council offices in New York were dotted with words like "blackmail," "extortion," and fears of Forman's "philosophy of violence." One writer believed that Forman's views as expressed in the manifesto "appear as anti-Christian as anything he seeks to correct." Another, urging total rejection, summarized much of the widespread feelings—that "the acceptance of this manifesto in any form will constitute an endorsement of its spirit, its methods, its forms of deciding culprits, and is totally foreign to the Christian Church and [its] present intended mode of functioning."[26]

At the heart of much of this intense dislike was the reaction of people to the introductory theoretical portion of the manifesto, with its radical critique of America and its churches and its clear revolutionary overtones. These passages set off powerful cultural signals that were quite enough to stymie much serious consideration of the rest of Forman's arguments. Immediately people could associate this man with long-held fears of Marxism and communism, now greatly heightened by the Vietnam War and America's massive involvement there. Links also were possible between Forman's church sit-ins (which at no time provoked physical attacks either against him or against his opponents) and the violence that had plagued public life for several years in the form of great urban riots, massive public demonstrations against the Vietnam War, and widespread police-student confrontations on college campuses.[27]

A thinly veiled racism also broke into the open at times as people vented their feelings. "Well, I say, this tiny minority of empty-headed, brassy, egotistical 'spokesmen' (or who seem to think they are) like Forman . . . are disgusting to me and I find myself tending to reject *all* the black plans." Or, "I fail to see where we owe the blacks anything whatsoever for past injustices. . . . They should be treated fairly at all times but WE DON'T OWE THEM ANYTHING." Or, "If they [African Americans] are seeking reparations and condone all kinds of violence to get it then why do we not seek the same type of consideration for all of the senseless killing and riots promulgated by the black race? Detroit, Watts, and many others?"[28] While most of the writers were more cautious and restrained than this, the close association of violence with African Americans, the rejection of any sort of compensatory aid for them, and exaggerated stereotypes all reflected potent racist images and feelings that remained widespread in the nation and greatly inhibited careful, critical thinking about the crisis over the Black Manifesto.

In late May 1969 Gallup pollsters tested the feelings of everyday Americans about the manifesto. Ninety percent of the sample opposed the payment of reparations by the churches, only 4 percent approved. Ninety-two percent of all *churchgoers* were opposed, only 2 percent approved. However, there were important differences by race. Fifty-two percent of blacks opposed reparations and 21 percent favored them, but a very large "no opinion" vote (27 percent) can be construed as hesitation on the part of many blacks to reveal to whites their sympathy for Forman's proposal.[29] Still, according to the poll a majority of blacks disliked the reparations principal sufficiently to express opposition openly to it. This finding underscored noticeable divisions within the black community, both religious and secular, over the manifesto, especially between older, conservative church and civil rights leaders and the younger, militant clergy, such as those in the NCBC.[30] Gallup's statistics also powerfully reinforced what letter writers to the National Council were saying, that many white people in local churches were strongly opposed to making concessions on reparations, the central demand of the manifesto.

Many of the communicants with the council made it clear that if the churches endorsed Forman even partially, their response would be to invoke a familiar and highly effective tactic of supporters of voluntary groups—to withdraw economic support and personal commitments from the National Council. This was a very real threat to the council and the rest of the national church structures. Church leaders, especially, fretted over this point. A Methodist Conference official in Tennessee with an "able Negro bishop as our episcopal leader" foresaw "the tenuous support line for the National Council" and all general church agencies' fiscal security "brought into serious question" if the idea of reparations were "accepted as a valid principle." Others, like the national finance chairperson of Church Women United, observed that for the National Council to "continue helping minority people" at all "they must be able to raise money from their constituents at the 'grass roots.'" A need to exercise caution was the clear implication.[31]

Just as vexing to white church officials at "475" and elsewhere was the fact that, despite the qualifications just noted above, a significant number of black church leaders, some of them close associates for years, quickly endorsed the Black Manifesto. Black women with long-established ties to their white sisters in the old ecumenical group, United Church Women (now renamed Church Women United) did not hesitate to express themselves. In late June 1969, the head of the A.M.E. Zion Women's Home and Foreign Missionary Society wrote to Margaret Shannon, the executive director of Church Women United, these powerful and unequivocal words:

> As a member of the Black Community with personal experiences as a black woman; as one who has shared the many gruesome experiences of the members of my church for approximately forty years; as the wife of an A.M.E. Zion Pastor, and as the past Executive Secretary and incumbent President of the Women's Department of my church, having had intimate conversations and experiences with women in all parts of the Nation, *I know reparations are due.*[32]

The National Committee for Black Churchmen also spoke out forcefully. On May 5, 1969, the day after Forman's first visit to Riverside Church, the NCBC expressed publicly its backing of the manifesto, and two days later the gist of the same statement was approved and then announced publicly by the NCBC's Board of Directors, meeting in Atlanta. Moreover, on May 9 the executive director of the NCBC, J. Metz Rollins, a leading black Presbyterian minister, went personally with Forman to confront Roman Catholic officials for the first time at the chancery of the Archbishop of New York.[33]

The NCBC's public statement backing the manifesto suggested again that they were people to be reckoned with. Once more they observed that "the white churches and synagogues undeniably have been the moral cement of the structure of racism in this nation, and the vast majority of them continue to play that role today." And, the document went on, these churches *"are* capable, out of their enormous corporate assets, to make some reparation for their complicity in the exploitation of blacks." In so doing, argued these black church leaders, "they will demonstrate to other American institutions the authenticity of their frequently verbalized contrition and of their faith in the justice of God."[34] These last words were like arrows driven straight at the moral sensitivities of national white church leaders, who quickly would read the phrases and have to ponder how to react to them.

The fullest expression of the attitudes and feelings of the militant African American church leaders regarding the manifesto emerged from the mind and pen of Gayraud Wilmore in late June 1969 in an essay entitled "The Church's Response to the Black Manifesto." This was at the very moment when officials of the National Council of Churches embarked on a long, agonizing process of fashioning a formal response to Forman and his supporters, and in part Wilmore expressed his views in public as a way of influencing that process.

Wilmore began by exploring the deep attraction of black power for him and other African American church people. He wrote about the "special guilt" the American churches carried because of their active participation in the national system of racism. The indictment was quite specific since as a national official of the United Presbyterian Church he had been able to observe for several years and in great detail the discriminatory practices of his own denomination and the churches generally.

> Many of the laymen who sit on the governing boards of wealthy white congregations are the absentee owners and managers of the corporate and political structures which have kept black people in deprivation and powerlessness. Many of the homeowners who refuse to sell to black buyers and effectively keep them from moving into white neighborhoods are members of fine suburban congregations. . . . Many white churches own thousands of acres of land in the South, where black sharecroppers, desperately in need of land, are being forced off into the already crowded urban ghettoes. White churches make purchases of thousands of dollars from discriminatory businesses and contractors and yet refuse to join Project Equality which uses church purchasing power to open up jobs for black folk.[35]

It was situations like these that helped to shape the special contours of African American experience,

> formed in the matrix of psychological and physical suffering, segregation, discrimination and the ever-present remembrance of a previous condition of involuntry servitude. Out of this condition has come . . . a type of human being whose sensibilities and perceptions, religious and secular, are rarely identical with those "born and raised white" in America.[36]

Many whites, Wilmore argued, had ignored these facts and thus by implication believed them to be unimportant or "invalid." Quite the contrary, because of this experience blacks probably possessed a "certain depth and richness" in their lives, a "certain passion for justice" that was special among all Americans. And it was because black power and its religious concomitant, black theology, sought "to reclaim" the "something of value" in "black humanity and the black church" that they had become so attractive to African Americans. Malcolm X, for example, became a model and a guide for black church people as well as for secular African Americans and several times Wilmore cited him approvingly.[37] Thus he concluded that the rise of the black power movement after 1966, with its emphasis upon black solidarity, pride, and self-determination, "completed the destruction of integrationism as the dominant ideology of the black community." In 1969 it was time for white churchmen "to face this fact unblinkingly. The quest for racial integration . . . *has come to an end.*"[38]

Wilmore then tackled the emotional (to whites) question of reparations. The concept was a widely understood idea, sanctioned even in the Bible, and Wilmore offered numerous examples of the United States' implementation of it, especially at the end of World Wars I and II (implicitly by force as one of the victors' demands over the vanquished). Even the GI Bill at the end of World War II, he argued, was "reparational legislation," although qualitatively different from the examples provided from the field of international affairs. Shrewdly and accurately he also noted that Ernest Campbell, the senior minister at Riverside Church, in his formal reply to James Forman's challenge, had accepted the principle of reparations and even sketched out a theological justification for it. And finally he suggested that it was entirely possible for the mainline churches to pay the $500 million reparations "bill" that the Black Manifesto had created (again his experience as a national church administrator enabled him to speak with considerable specificity), although he did not demand a specific timetable for payments.[39]

Throughout Wilmore grounded his concerns in a theological perspective. Insistently he took a prophetic stance. His view of Forman, for example, differed mightily from that of white coreligionists in the mainline churches:

> This is not the first time God has called upon the wrath of those outside of the church to summon it to repentance and obedience. The great wealth that churches have accumulated may have become a spiritual liability. Rather than help men and women to destroy the dehumanizing, demonic structures which cripple them, most church funds have been used simply to enhance the welfare of the churches and their members. The time may be at hand for the cleansing of the Temple as our Lord accomplished it. The time may be here, as the Scriptures warned, for "judgment to begin in the household of faith." It well may be that for all his vehemence and rudeness, James Forman is being used by God to declare to the churches "this night your soul is required of you; and the things you have prepared, whose will they be?" (Luke 12:20)

And speaking more generally about the nature of the church's mission in the world, and its relation to the crisis that began with the proclamation of the Black Manifesto, Wilmore asserted:

> The church seeks to make "human life more human" as the essential meaning of the Gospel of Jesus Christ. That means working with God in the world to bring to naught the things which are and to bring into existence the things which do not exist. (I Cor. 1:28) And that program, as revolutionary as it is and has always been, starts from the assumption that love, human compassion, and a sense of sharing in the sinfulness and weakness of the world are relevant to the struggle.[40]

This was a Christian "prophetic stance," which probably never motivated Forman personally but which suffused Wilmore's writing and actions, his powerful criticisms of the mainstream churches accompanying his endorsement of the manifesto, and his biting (to some people controversial) view of the secular bearer of the manifesto as a contemporary sign of God's intervention into, and caring for, the world.[41]

But Wilmore also moved beyond the hurling of prophetic thunderbolts at his fellow religionists. He was a realist, and a significant portion of his essay tried to deal with that fact. He acknowledged that Forman's advocacy of the use of violence and guerilla warfare, if necessary, over an extended period of time and the latter's plan to extend the power of the state to "total control" of the entire society, black and white, were a "break with . . . realism." He also urged his white readers to pay much less attention to the "rhetoric" (there was much debate over the accuracy of this assessment) of the revolutionary/radical words of the introduction and more to the broader intentions of the manifesto. He ended by saying that the mainstream churches could "safely assume" they could "endorse the programs [of the manifesto] without necessarily embracing the more extreme parts of the ideology and tactics of the preamble." In effect Wilmore was acknowledging, as Forman did later, that the preamble should have been toned down considerably in order to secure the white cooperation that was essential to implement the manifesto in any realistic way.[42]

The ambivalent, inconsistent signals that Wilmore was conveying to white church people of prophetic thunderbolts *and* moderation reflected the dilemma in which even the most vehement churchly black supporters of the manifesto found themselves. They were prepared to "tell it like it is" to the white churches of the latter's complicity, and guilt because of that complicity, in the national system of racial oppression, but they also realized that African Americans had to rely heavily on the very people they were criticizing if the vicious cycle of human degradation had any hope of being broken.[43] A system of dependency still existed that black church people understandably disliked intensely, but found difficult to end completely, even when white friends were in charge. It was a terrible, and sad, irony to endure.

The National Committee of Black Churchmen (of which Wilmore was an important leader) and the Interreligious Foundation for Community Organization, key groups engaged in efforts both to pressure the churches and to provide acceptable ways for them to act, moved quickly following the proclamation of the manifesto to create a specific context to ease the churches along the way. Almost immediately African American ministers, chiefly from the NCBC, joined the governing board of the Black Economic Development Conference, still only in embryo and struggling to secure enough money to become a viable organization. By early July 1969, Forman had become "Director of Field Services" of BEDC, responsible chiefly for fund raising under what was known as the Black United Appeal. A young minister, Calvin Marshall, pastor of an A.M.E. Zion church in Brooklyn and a member of the NCBC, replaced him as the executive director.[44]

IFCO, with its many connections with the mainline denominations, was in the best position to serve as an intermediary between the white churches and their black critics. Once again IFCO sought to perform the delicate balancing act that always seemed to have been its role. At a special meeting on May 6, 1969, two days after Forman's visit to Riverside Church, the board of directors of IFCO directly endorsed the *programmatic* aspects of the manifesto (but not the introduction), stated that any proposals for funding from the Black Economic Development Conference would be "considered a priority," and urged the predominantly white churches to "come up with the basic sums [$270,000] to launch the activities of the Conference Steering Committee" and to designate specifically gifts that went to the conference. Undesignated funds awarded IFCO could be directed to BEDC, but only if the latter group applied through the normal grant-making channels and competed with all other applicants for money—an important qualification. At the same time the governing board of IFCO moved to create a distinct division between themselves and BEDC. At the May 6 meeting it urged that "no staff member serve on the Conference steering committee" and a few days later stated that "the Board [of IFCO] must accept the Conference as an autonomous entity and must deal with it on its own terms. The National Black Economic Development Conference has its own agenda, and IFCO has its own agenda, that of funding community organizations."[45] It became widely understood that IFCO, with a solid track record of careful initial examination and overseeing of grant proposals and credibility in both the black and white communities, could become a major means through which the predominantly white churches might funnel large sums of money, to be distributed to BEDC (perhaps) and certainly other, largely secular, black community organizations throughout the country.[46]

At least four options eventually developed that leaders of the predominantly white mainstream churches could follow in responding to the monetary demands of Forman and his supporters. The simplest was to reject all the demands outright, as did the Roman Catholic hierarchy, the Southern Baptists, most Jewish groups, and conservative mainstream Protestant denominations such as the Dutch Calvinist Reformed Church in America and all the Lutherans except the American Lutheran Church.[47] But for the mainline churches who were most active in the civil rights struggles of the sixties, the issue was more complicated. Many of the leaders of these groups—American Baptists, United Methodists, United Church of Christ, Episcopalians, United Presbyterians, Disciples—accepted in principle at least the reparations argument, although they also often were shocked and offended by the confrontational tactics and rhetoric of Forman and his allies. They wanted to do *something;* but they were cautious, especially knowing the powerful negative feelings of their local constituencies, the ultimate possessors of the "moneybags" of the denominations. By mid-June 1969, a month after Forman's visit to Riverside Church, the patterns of response were becoming clear, as several of the denominations held their annual national assemblies where such decisions were to be made.

Even though the young black church leaders of NCBC cajoled and threatened and urged their white coreligionists to provide money for BEDC, only pennies for that organization were ever forthcoming. Fearful of revolutionary utterances, most of the white churches turned their backs on Forman and his closest supporters. These same people were ignorant of or unwilling to listen to those who pointed to the perhaps less offensive programmatic aspects of the manifesto. They also ignored the fact that black church people had modified considerably Forman's influence in the organization that grew out of the manifesto. By the end of the summer of 1969, less than $25,000 of the $270,000 deemed necessary to operate BEDC for a year had been raised from church sources, black and white alike.[48] Bereft of significant long-term economic support, the Black Economic Development Conference gradually withered away.

Instead, the most socially conscious mainline churches chose one of two paths, or combined the two approaches. The most liberal solution was to give substantial, "undesignated" amounts of money to IFCO, and then to allow that organization to distribute the gifts through its normal grant-making procedures to all sorts of community organizations, religious and secular, within the African American community. By March 1970 the American Baptists, the Episcopal Church, the Lutheran Church in America, the United Church of Christ (formerly Congregational), the United Methodist Church, and the United Presbyterian Church had contributed a combined total of over a million dollars to be administered by IFCO. After 1970, as the immediate impact of the manifesto disappeared and the general conservative thrust of the nation continued, this support dropped off noticeably, but even in 1975 IFCO still received almost half a million dollars from outside sources, mostly the churches, to support its operating expenses and its grant-making functions.[49]

Even more attractive than giving unrestricted sums to IFCO was to fund directly the activities and projects of the rapidly developing "black caucuses" of the mainline churches, or projects and groups already sponsored by a denomination. Since 1966 the black power movement had spawned not only a major ecumenical black church organization in the form of the National Committee of Black Churchmen, but also black caucuses in several of the predominantly white denominations. Since the end of the Civil War these churches—principally Methodists, Episcopalians, Presbyterians, Congregationalists, Baptists, Disciples—had gradually developed small groups of African American members, principally but not exclusively in the South, worshipping mostly in all-black congregations (another indication of the deeply rooted racism of the white churches). These black church groups were in addition to the much larger and more powerful all-black *denominations,* such as the National Baptist Convention, U.S.A., Inc.; the African Methodist Episcopal Church; and the African Methodist Episcopal Zion Church.[50]

Thus the black power movement almost immediately led to the creation of black caucuses within the predominantly white churches. Black power provided a strong sense of identity instead of the constant ambiguity of being "neither members in an independent [black] church nor full participants in a truly inclusive church." By the time of the manifesto in 1969, nine such caucuses had been formed, including a significant group within the Roman Catholic Church.[51]

One of the largest of these caucuses, Black Methodists for Church Renewal (BMCR), crystallized within the United Methodist Church in early February 1968. It was led by James Lawson, an early proponent of nonviolence and a nationally recognized civil rights leader until the mid-sixties. The shift in his views from early to late in the decade were another indication of the major changes that had taken place in relations between blacks and liberal whites.[52] Similar developments in the Episcopal Church led to the rapid disintegration and demise in 1970 of the Episcopal Society for Racial and Cultural Unity (ESCRU), a widely recognized interracial group which flourished throughout the early and mid-sixties, in turn to be replaced by an Episcopal Union of Black Clergy and Laity. In the United Presbyterian Church the Presbyterian Interracial Council, a powerful force within the denomination earlier in the sixties, disappeared as Black Presbyterians United was founded in 1968 and grew rapidly thereafter.[53] These caucuses and others like them confronted the white leadership of the mainline denominations with sit-ins, strikes, and demands for financial support that paralleled closely the activities of Forman in New York City and elsewhere. In some instances the whites reacted negatively; in other instances they responded with support although never as fully as their black critics desired.[54]

Nevertheless, these were in-house struggles, which to the people in leadership positions were far preferable to having to deal with a secular black radical like Forman and the Black Economic Development Conference. Still, as one black Methodist noted, the support that did come "represent[ed] 'hand outs' from white folks." Paternalistic relations continued, even with white liberals, and it was galling to blacks to have to endure it all yet another time. IFCO and its brokerage system provided a partial way out, but not many of the whites were able to see their way to embrace that option. Thus when the Methodists' national Board of missions rejected the demands of their black caucus, despite a "passionate plea" by Jim Lawson for the board "to begin taking major risks for the black community as a testimony to a renewal [*sic*] attempt at Christian witness," people in the meeting were reported "either very near tears or openly weeping with frustration over the recalcitrance of one of the Church's most 'progressive' and 'liberal' Boards."[55]

The charged atmosphere of this meeting was replicated often in the many church gatherings that discussed James Forman's proclamation in the summer and fall of 1969. As we have already seen, the National Council of Churches was no exception, although their final response differed in interesting and significant ways from other efforts of the mainstream churches. Because it was the overarching ecumenical body of those churches, its public actions were always powerfully symbolic. Thus for many people its decisions about the manifesto would be especially significant and influential. Trying to weigh carefully the competing demands upon their sensibilities, the leaders of the council took what seemed to be an unusually long time to make a reply. And when they did, their reaction could not exactly parallel those of individual denominations since the National Council lacked the large institutional endowments and the vast potential for annual fund-raising from local churches that the denominations possessed. Yet despite these inherent financial weaknesses (which critics often did not fully appreciate), ultimately the NCC was able to devise one of the most creative and potentially useful responses to the manifesto.

One should recall that James Forman had approached the National Council with his demands on May 2, 1969, two days *before* he first publicly indicted the white churches at Riverside Church. On May 2, officials of the NCC asked for more time to consider the manifesto, until June 23, when the General Board next met.[56] Forman agreed to this postponement. Unable in June to resolve the deep conflicts that by then existed, a "Committee of 16" was appointed by the National Council's executive board to consult more fully with Forman and his supporters and to report back to the board with specific recommendations. In several meetings during the rest of the summer intense discussions occurred inside the executive board, recapitulating on a small scale the tempest over the manifesto then sweeping through all of the mainline denominations.

Two of the participants, James Laue, a social-psychologist from Harvard, and Grover Hartman, head of the council of churches of Indiana, able to think coolly and carefully on the spot about these complex and confusing events, came closest to summarizing the issues that underlay the deep divisions. First, the predominantly white religious groups were "offended by the rhetoric and revolutionary/Marxist ideology [in the manifesto], fearful of constituent reaction back home, . . . and concerned about the future of current organizational programs in race, social justice and human relations."[57] Yet there also seemed to be "broad agreement" among the church officials at the Interchurch Center that the manifesto, "unacceptable as its ideology might be," had drawn attention "forcefully" to an "iniquitous situation" against which "all too little progress had been made." African Americans in the meetings reportedly had said: "We have been saying [these things] to you quietly for a long time and, by and large, you have not listened. Now James Forman . . . has made you listen. This is a step in the right direction." Among these church people, Forman the rude prophet had succeeded at least partially in his role.[58]

There was also a growing recognition that African Americans should be able to conceive and manage their own programs, even if that seemed to verge on separatism. In essence, what minorities were urging was to share *power,* real power, with their white brothers and sisters. Only reluctantly and under great pressure did white church leaders come to understand fully the blacks' demands. And they did so largely because highly respected national black church leaders, like Edler Hawkins, past moderator of the United Presbyterian Church; Dr. John Williams, a prominent member of the conservative National Baptist Convention, U.S.A., Inc.; Dr. M. L. Wilson, president of the Council of Churches of New York City; and especially Andrew Young, who came to New York to participate in the deliberations, stood shoulder to shoulder with the younger militants in the NCBC.[59] Thus it was reported, that "whenever the idea was advanced of channeling money to Black agencies with strings attached, the cry was raised, 'This shows your lack of confidence. It declares that to you we are still "boys."'" Thus for the National Council of Churches to "maintain relevance" it was necessary "to shear off any semblance of white paternalism and permit Black churchmen to act as they see fit. . . . This independence of action is essential to the [African Americans'] full acceptance as mature persons which is the foundation of meaningful integration."[60]

At least some of the white religious leaders had come to see that full personhood is ofttimes vindicated and enhanced when *institutional* power is shared with the powerless. This is most likely to occur when the powerless press the powerful so hard that, very reluctantly, institutional power relationships are altered. Church people were no exception in this regard. Ironically the manifesto was creating for liberal church persons in the North dilemmas similar to those the civil rights movement had created for southerners—the likelihood of loss of some control of institutional power.[61] There were analogies between the manifesto and CDGM in the questions both raised about power in society, the need to share it, and how to go about that sharing. In both instances African Americans secured only partial victories. And that fact was highly instructive concerning the tenacity and subtlety with which racial prejudice maintained its hold upon the American psyche and American institutions.

On September 11, 1969, the General Board (the principal governing body) of the National Council of Churches formally approved a "Response . . . to the Black Manifesto." It rejected the "extremist" ideology of the manifesto, yet accepted "as prophetic" its "call to repentance." It also asked for $500,000 to be pledged by the council's member denominations, to be given to and administered by either IFCO or the NCBC. The council made no mention of support for the Black Economic Development Conference.[62] In its general outlines, this statement of the National Council did not depart substantially from the positions taken by the most forward-looking of the mainline church groups. But the council's own response to the financial demands of the manifesto differed from those of the denominations, and we must now examine that specific reaction in some detail.

From July 1969 onward there emerged a concern that the council should try to create long-term instruments of support for the African American community that could harness the immense capital resources of the churches, such as mortgage-free real estate, the denominations' pension funds, and endowments of local churches, national denominational boards, seminaries, and even church-related and secular colleges. A year earlier, as a part of the "Crisis in the Nation" program, the council had created a committee to try and secure funds from the member denominations for "ghetto community development." By September 1968, the committee had to admit failure, unable to secure denominational cooperation and noting that the National Council's own resources in this regard were "virtually exhausted." The committee recommended to the General Board its own termination.[63]

With the memory of this recent failure at ghetto involvement still fresh in people's minds, and with the manifesto demanding even more urgently that action be taken, in the formal response of the National Council to the manifesto in September 1969 the General Board requested that a program be developed by appropriate agencies of the council to "make available to disadvantaged groups funds from the churches and other sources in the order of tens of millions of dollars to be used . . . for social and economic development."[64] Out of these somewhat vague, bureaucratic phrases emerged a new program of investments that no other mainline church group had thought it possible to create.

Arthur Flemming, the president of the National Council, believed strongly that the resolution of the board could be actualized, and he moved immediately to begin that process.[65] By the end of September 1969 a small group with a ponderous title—the Project Committee on Minority Group Social and Economic Development—had been established and two "task forces" placed under it, one to develop mechanisms to *acquire* funds, the other to consider how to *disburse* funds. The task forces met in New York on October 4 to begin their work.[66]

The acquisition task force, composed of legal and financial experts as well as church officials and minority representatives, was particularly active at the outset. By the middle of November, the planners had developed concrete proposals for an "economic development structure" to aid minority communities. They began with certain assumptions or theories about how this development might take place. It should occur "on a continuum," beginning with community organizations where direct grants like those awarded by IFCO would be most helpful, through support, by means of longer-term loans, of basic industrial needs such as skills training for workers and managerial and technical assistance, to large scale funding of businesses and other enterprises through substantial capital investments.[67]

This was perhaps an overly schematic analysis—activity at each level probably would occur simultaneously in different locations—but it made clear the essential components of the process. Especially significant were the *structures* to be created to provide grants, loans, and capital investments. First, there was to be a foundation, controlled by minorities at both the board and staff level, which would provide "grants and loans to local groups" for both community and industrial development. Clearly viewing IFCO as a model, it would receive money "in the form of donations and grants from both individuals and institutions," serve as a "conduit" for "institutional lines of credit to local [community] groups," and facilitate the use of low interest financial guarantees then available from the Federal Small Business Administration.[68]

Second, and more important, there was to be established a mutual fund, managed by "reputable investment professionals" who engaged only in "clean" investments. That is, "criteria of a moral or social nature would be used in the selection of [the] portfolio." The fund was to be promoted within church circles and in other institutions "as a new vehicle for investment" for "endowments[s], pension funds, etc." The new mechanism would "guarantee an adequate (in most cases more than present) return," on investment. In addition some of the annual "surplus" (profits) were "to be placed in the foundation, thus constantly increasing *its* grant potential."[69]

This proposal anticipated by almost a decade the rise in the 1980s of the "socially responsible" mutual fund.[70] Its "clean" portfolio also reflected both the early flutterings of the environmental movement and the national effort to end investments in corporations doing business in South Africa.[71] Conceived toward the end of a long period of national prosperity that would soon end, the planners probably were too optimistic about the profit margins they would have to maintain over the long term to implement their ambitious social goals, yet also allow the fund to remain attractive to investors. Still, legal and management specialists dealing with large-scale investments who met early in November 1969 to discuss with church people an early outline of the foundation and fund "generally agreed" that in both process and purposes the proposal "was unique and exciting."[72]

In late January 1970, an interracial group from the National Council of Churches traveled to Boston and met with the top officials of the Putnam Management Company, a nationally known and respected investment management company. One knowledgeable participant from the council noted that Putnam "actually runs 8 Mutal Funds (Conservative to Go-Go Leverage)," The Putnam People agreed to set up and manage the new fund, to institute a "buddy system" to include African Americans "at all levels of the Fund's operation" in order to "learn the business," and to begin to develop the "clean" aspect of the fund, reportedly "a new experience" for Putnam's managers and "as far as they knew, for any fund" then in existence.[73]

In addition, on January 27, 1970, representatives of the NCC, BEDC, IFCO, NCBC, and the Southern Christian Leadership Conference met to begin planning in detail how money from the foundation and the fund would be disbursed within minority communities. The inclusion of the SCLC (again, Andrew Young was its representative) was a further move toward moderation, probably intended to reassure potential investors that African American friends of the mainline churches would play a major role in establishing the critera for, and the process of, disbursement. Significantly, a suggestion within the National Council executive committee to add representatives of the more conservative NAACP and the Urban League to the disbursement group was turned aside.[74]

By the first week of March 1970, the project had gathered such momentum that in meetings with the Putnam Management people lists of white and black "potential trustees" of the mutual fund were discussed in detail, all the legal work in setting up the fund and the foundation was being assumed *"at no cost"* by Patterson, Belknap, and Webb, a major law firm in New York City, and there was much consideration of how best to announce the fund to the public through major national news sources. Especially revealing was the report of Robert Potter, a lawyer from Patterson, Belknap, and Webb, of exploratory meetings with trustees of Harvard and Yale. The group reasoned that if Harvard, Yale, Princeton, and Union Theological Seminary (their first targets) committed endowment monies, then the fund would have "tremendous prestige" with these institutions "already on board" when it went "into an aggressive [public] sales process." Potter and Richard Cutler, a major official from Putnam, whose contacts were "fantastic" and "a godsend for the fund," were to be given three months' leaves of absence from their organizations to do the "initial sales work" with "law firms and the trustees from the above mentioned educational institutions."[75] In an extremely shrewd and sophisticated manner, the National Council and its allies were trying to make certain, as one of the participants put it, "that when the foundation and the mutual fund are announced it [they] will not be an idea but a very imposing fact."[76]

In November 1969, one of the principal church facilitators of the entire project estimated that it would take approximately seven months for all of the legal hurdles to be cleared to bring the new mutual fund into being, including clearance of the plans by the Federal Securities and Exchange Commission. In late July 1970, a mere one month behind that originally conceived schedule, the final approval from the SEC was about to occur, and that same church facilitator informed others in the National Council that the "actual public sale of the Fund will commence on or about January 1, 1971."[77] The herculean efforts to create a truly innovative nongovernmental institutional response to America's racial problems seemed about to be crowned with success. Suddenly, however, the dense archival paper trail vanishes, and not another written word appears about the entire project. Like some mysterious ghostly ship sailing into a fog bank and disappearing forever, the Project on Minority Group Social and Economic Development simply ceased to function before it ever legally existed!

From the memories of some of the participants, tapped twenty years later, at least the rough outline of what happened can be reconstructed. At the very moment that the Minority Group Project was about to be realized, the Putnam Management Company was being "taken over" by another, larger money management company in New York, Marsh and McLennon. As the process of merger proceeded, all investment activities of Putnam were certain to be scrutinized very carefully, and risky ventures of any sort would be viewed with great caution. Simply put, the Minority Group Project presented considerable risks and was axed.[78] Apparently even the Putnam people developed strong doubts about the lack of sufficient capitalization that characterized the mutual fund aspect of the project. The SEC required $100,000 in start up funds for any proposal it approved, and it was clear that this amount was obtainable.[79] But the Putnam officials really wanted more collateral to be pledged.[80] Their nervousness was greatly increased by the fact that their contacts on the Harvard Board of Overseers raised questions about the ability of that university legally to commit portions of its endowment portfolio to an investment fund not managed and controlled by the Harvard Corporation. And finally there was the concern that in such a fund as the National Council of Churches had proposed the profit margin would not be substantial enough to satisfy clients like Harvard, who had to achieve substantial earnings each year. Combining these worries with the "climate of the merger" with Marsh and McLennon, the Putnam Management Company backed off and the entire enterprise collapsed.[81] Ironically this program to secure aid "in the tens of millions of dollars" to support the daily lives of America's minorities failed largely because it was too far ahead of its time, certainly for the perdominantly white churches throughout the country who would had to have been its prime supporters.

Although not of its own making, the failure of the large financial scheme of help for minority communities envisioned by National Council officials in late 1969 and 1970 reflected general tendencies then in the churches regarding race relations. Everywhere there were signs of disruption and decline in the old coalitions and friendships between whites and blacks in the churches. In September 1967, responding to the challenges of the black power movement, the Episcopal Church had authorized the creation of a General Convention Special Fund, with an initial budget authorization of three million dollars, to be expended in development programs in minority communities. Controversial from its inception, in October 1970 opposition from bishops and local church people led to major restrictions on the functioning of the fund. Three years later it disappeared entirely in an internal bureaucratic merger. Partly as a result, the presiding bishop, John Hines, from the beginning one of the strongest supporters of the Special Fund, resigned, three years before the end of his normal twelve-year regime. Hines was replaced as presiding bishop by John Allin, well-remembered in these pages as the Bishop of the Diocese of Mississippi.[82]

In 1971 the National Board of Missions of the United Presbyterian Church and that denomination's Council on Church and Race (originally the Commission on Religion and Race), since 1963 bulwarks of support for African American empowerment, received a comeuppence of sorts from opponents in the denomination. Just prior to the General Assembly held in June, the council, with money supplied by the Board of Missions, made a grant of $10,000 to the legal defense of Angela Davis, soon to be tried as an accessory in an attempted escape of prisoners, and the killing of the trial judge, from a courtroom in California. Citing the fact that Ms. Davis was African American, a woman, and a publicly acknowledged Communist, the Presbyterian officials justified their grant as money to help insure her a fair trial.

The uproar that ensued within the church expressed overwhelming grass-roots opposition to the grant, deeply agitated the General Assembly, and continued unabated after the assembly adjourned in mid-June, 1971.[83] Although the Council/Board of Missions action was not repudiated (proposals to this effect finally were voted down at the General Assembly), the national gathering of the church did officially communicate to the Council on Church and Race "serious questions concerning the propriety" of its grant toward Davis's defense.[84] This rebuke was yet another indication of the deepening opposition in all the mainline churches to the continuing efforts of some leaders to reach out across racial lines. Unfortunately, these acts attempting to testify to the need for justice and racial reconciliation so jangled sensitivities threatened by radical ideologies and the new racial assertiveness that chasms between church people were widened significantly rather than narrowed.

Then from November 30 to December 5, 1969, less than six months after the tension-filled weeks of confrontations at the Interchurch Center in New York, the National Council of Churches in its triennial General Assembly in Detroit experienced an unprecedented series of divisions and debates among its own people. There were floor demonstrations, heated disagreements between the delegates, and a series of "happenings" by a dissident group known as "Jonathan's Wake" (a play on the name of the eighteenth-century American theologian Jonathan Edwards) that were reminiscent of the secular antics of Ken Kesey's "Merry Pranksters" or Abby Hoffman and the Yippies disrupting the New York Stock Exchange. As one of the participants aptly stated of the gathering, it was "beyond my powers to describe it verbally."[85]

A young college student giving up his draft card as a protest against the Vietnam War pleaded to be put under the protection of the assembly. After a long and emotional floor debate, the young man's request was rejected. Immediately a member of Jonathan's Wake startled delegates by pouring red paint, as an "act of conscience" against the war and as "injustice to people goes on," over the tables and papers of the leaders of the council, seated in an imposing, establishment-type line across the front edge of the stage of Cobo Hall. (One member of the protesting group apologized later for the paint splashed on Arthur Flemming, the presiding officer.)[86]

Twenty years after her first involvement in the National Council of Churches as a national leader of United Church Women, Cynthia Wedel was elected president of the council. She was the first woman to secure this office. This happened in spite of great pressure for her to withdraw in favor of Rev. Albert Cleage, the first *African American* ever to be nominated and the first person to challenge from the floor an official nomination of the council.[87] James Forman also appeared again and argued that the NCC should be disbanded so that the Manifesto could be fully honored. And African American delegates vocally made known their disappointment over the defeat of their candidate for president.[88]

Despite their success in the presidentail contest, 150 women rose from their seats and remained standing in support of a passionate speech by Peggy Billings of the Methodist Board of Missions, who criticized women's continuing discrimination in an ecumenical church dominated by "male, white-skinned clergy over 40." She went on, "we have just begun to organize, but you will hear from us until you are sick of this theme."[89] This action in part surely reflected a rapidly rising female self-consciousness that was crystallizing everywhere in the nation. But it also represented the boiling over of long-held resentments of women who had served faithfully for years within the National Council's ranks but, like blacks, felt they had never been recognized adequately or been allowed to share power properly with the white males who still ran the organization. Cynthia Wedel's election as president was a sign of change, but it did not occur soon enough to prevent the "unladylike" demonstration in Detroit. Interestingly, the principal ecumenical women's group, United Church Women, had pointed the way to these events in 1969. A major reorganization of the National Council begun in 1965 had downgraded the women in the council's structure and produced new restrictions that curtailed their prized sense of independence. As a result, on September 26, 1969, United Church Women, now renamed Church Women United, withdrew from the National Council and resumed their autonomous existence, much as it had been before 1950.[90] The connections between this action and what transpired in Detroit two months later seem quite clear. And thus it appeared that all the strains and stresses tearing American society apart in the late sixties were present and being stirred into the smoking cauldron that was the council's six days in Detroit.

Throughout 1969 and in the years immediately following, local church people reacted strongly to events like these by lowering contributions to the National Council in particular and to church benevolence generally. The cutbacks were widespread and continued throughout the 1970s. For example, the National Council announced in December 1972 a proposed budget for the following year of $13,800,000. This was in contrast to a similar budget figure in December 1969 of just under $18,000,000. The falloff was approximately 25 percent. Although the decline in income began before the manifesto affected the council, the tendencies were continued and accelerated after 1969. "Fiscal stringency is clearly a fact of contemporary life in the NCC," lamented an executive board member in September 1970. A two and one-half million dollar drop in income during 1970 began a particularly painful period of adjustment. And declines generally in local church giving to benevolences continued throughout the rest of the 1970s.[91]

Thousands of mainline churchgoers during those same years either left the churches or became inactive. Declines in membership in the mainline denominations began in the mid-sixties after almost a century of steady increases. Declines in church *attendance* extended back to the mid-fifties when the statistical peak in the postwar religious revival was reached.[92] But these losses accelerated in the 1970s and 1980s. The causes of this membership decline have been widely studied and commented upon by scholars and journalistic pundits, but racial attitudes have seldom been suggested as a factor shaping those massive shifts in religious practice.[93] At least for the late sixties and early seventies, that factor should not be ignored.

By 1970 the *kairos* moment of the sixties in race relations had disappeared for the National Council of Churches and for the mainline denominations, and *chronos* once again had taken over. Liberal racial policies severely curtailed or reversed, retrenchment of staff and programs dealing with racial issues, and the emergence to national prominence in the 1970s of the evangelical churches, generally more conservative about or simply uninterested in racial matters—all made the end point of *kairos* clear. This was probably inevitable since it is difficult to sustain over a long period of time the personal and institutional enthusiasms that initially spark large movements for social change.

But the mainstream churches' involvement in the black freedom movement of the 1960s was especially vulnerable because it was largely a commitment that began at the top of the church hierarchies and worked its way downward (if at all) rather than developing as a massive grass-roots movement, as was the case within the black community. The commitment of predominantly white religious groups toward the solution of racial problems was primarily an elitist effort initiated largely by ministers and church bureaucrats. This seems to be a surprising, rather unexpected source for social innovation and change, but if unexpected then it was quite biblical. Moreover, elite agents of change are not entirely unusual in countries that are heavily bureaucratized, as is true of the United States and all other modern technological societies.[94]

Elitist leadership especially characterized the National Council of Churches. Almost by definition ecumenism suffers from sufficient grounding in the local churches. But leadership on racial questions in the denominations also centered in their national social agencies and home mission boards. The people who led those agencies, and their colleagues in the National Council of Churches, were well prepared—because of their knowledge of current social problems and because they possessed a moral perspective that was especially relevant to the race issue—to act decisively once they secured the authority to involve the churches directly in the great national struggle over race. For a short time in 1963 and 1964, leaders in the National Council and other mainline church groups were able to draw their local constituencies along with them in support of such events as the March on Washington and especially the intense and prolonged lobbying for the Civil Rights Act of 1964. These were especially successful activities, in part because of this close identification of leaders and grass-roots supporters.

The deep church commitments made in Mississippi during that same time and continued for a decade through the Delta Ministry began to suggest the difficulties of sustaining elite-initiated programs. Local churches became more cautious and began to resist the continuing political and economic demands placed upon them. These difficulties were greatly increased in the late sixties as the voices of former black allies both in and outside the churches became more independent and at times more strident, and as their requests for support escalated. The Black Manifesto and the responses to it, from both the black and white religious communities, revealed a strong grass-roots opposition, yet also the desire of *some* of the national church leaders to respond to the economic demands of the manifesto. The attempt of the National Council of Churches to create a multimillion dollar "socially responsible" mutual fund, accompanied by a black-controlled foundation to funnel profits into the African American community, was a good example of how connections with the banking and legal communities in New York and Boston could be translated into a highly imaginative instrument for social change. Yet one wonders if the planners from the National Council were not too optimistic throughout about the possible success of that enterprise. For they were never able to test precisely whether denominations and local churches would commit their endowments and other investments at a time when national support among whites on racial issues had declined substantially. In this instance, the National Council of Churches' leadership position did not assure success because their relationship to their own followers was uncertain.

The ending of the *kairos* also seemed to be one among many indications of the closing of an era, extending well back into the nineteenth century, when the "mainline," "mainstream," or "oldline" denominations were seen as an informal yet definite Protestant "establishment." The gradual demise of that establishment took place over much of the twentieth century. As we have already noted, only recently have historians begun to study that process systematically in any detail.[95] In retrospect one can view the involvement of the churches in the civil rights movement of the sixties as a last hurrah of sorts of the establishment. It was a revival of the Social Gospel, which had become the social creed of establishment Protestants in the early twentieth century. The leaders of the participating churches were nearly all ecumenical Protestants, another key manifestation of mainline Protestantism since just before World War I. An establishment dominated by white males and a moderately liberal sociopolitical viewpoint regarding public affairs were bound to be placed under severe stress by national developments in the middle and late sixties. The picture of a line of figures on a stage in Cobo Hall in Detroit in late 1969—leaders supposedly in control of the General Assembly of the National Council of Churches—challenged again and again by African Americans, women, youth, Native Americans, Vietnam protestors, and others drove the point home that establishment Protestantism was disintegrating.[96] The continued functioning of the National Council of Churches today suggests that after 1969 changes were made successfully, but those adjustments were indeed painful.

The most thoughtful of white church people who began their prolonged involvement in racial matters in 1963 ended the decade chastened, perhaps more realistic, and probably much less hopeful about the prospects of solving soon the nation's racial problems. In 1970 the shape of the battlefield was much different and far less inviting. But their religious commitments kept them from ultimate despair and cynicism. Not long before he died, Robert Spike articulated many of these feelings in his final official words to the National Council of Church's Commission on Religion and Race. He began by quoting William Morris, the late nineteenth-century English visionary and poet:

Men fight and lose the battle, /
and the thing that they fought for /

comes about in spite of their defeat, /
and when it comes /
it turns out not to be what they meant, /
and other men have to fight for /
what they mean under another name. /

Superficially, mused Spike, the words of Morris seemed "terribly pessimistic," even a "hopeless kind of philosophy." But in reality, he concluded, these phrases were "realistic," and "grimly true." The long-term results of the battles for social change "are never in the hands of the [immediate] contenders." Spike continued:

> There are always forces and factors more powerful than the precise dreams of the reformers. And the human capacity for sin is boundless. Pride and vanity and triviality are giants never really brought low. . . . [But] the human spirit, molded by the plan of God, is more indomitable than that. What is asked of us is obedience to the moment, every new moment. God will take care of the centuries.[97]

When it came to race relations in the United States, black Christians had always tended to assume an attitude not unlike that articulated by Spike late in 1965. But whites had seldom paid much attention—until the 1960s. Early in that decade Gayraud Wilmore, who became well known to many white church people a bit later, wrote words that could easily have started with Spike's affirmations, but added on insights and emphases about race relations that only a black person in America could have developed. Perhaps a "rapproachment" between white and black Protestants can occur "in the next few years," Wilmore said, but only if

> white Protestants have finally realized the truth of Richard Wright's affirmation that "the ties that bind us are deeper than those that separate us." ("Look at us and know us and you will know yourselves, for *we* are *you,* looking back at you from the dark mirror of our lives.") . . . [Within such a context, Christian brotherhood] will then mean something profoundly human and incisively political; it will mean standing with and for one another in the exasperating and bewildering realities of secular life. This is what the new Negro—and many "new" white Christians—want from the church.[98]

In the 1960s the National Council of Churches and many individual white mainstream Protestants, pressed yet supported on many sides by black people, had made a beginning, but only a beginning, at realizing Gayraud Wilmore's vision of true Christian brotherhood. But armed with Robert Spike's belief in the necessity of the long view of history, and his faith in the ultimate power of God, perhaps sometime soon they would try again to make "black and white together" a living reality. The historical record of their struggles in the 1960s toward such an end deserves to be remembered, as an essential precondition of any effort at reconstruction in the future.

Notes

1. The quotations are in "Minutes," IFCO Board of Directors, September 9–10, 1968, pp. 7, 8, IFCO headquarters, New York City. For the first explicit references to IFCO's interest in economic development projects focused on "community organization" and "cooperative" enterprises rather than "the individual entrepreneur," see "Minutes," IFCO Board of Directors, June 11, 1968, p. 2, IFCO headquarters.

2. Ibid., June 11, 1968, p. 8; "Minutes," IFCO Executive Committee Meeting, September 9, 1968, p. 2, in IFCO headquarters.

3. "IFCO and the BEDC," undated working paper [probably written by Lucius Walker], in folder entitled "IFCO/BEDC Relationship," box 37, IFCO Papers, Schomburg Library. For further confirmation of the defensive strategy against Nixon's "black capitalism" proposals, see interview with James Forman, March 11, 1991; news release, Religious New Service, December 5, 1968, in folder entitled "NBEDC, Detroit, April 25–27, 1969," box 41, IFCO Papers.

4. "The Truth and Consequences of Advocacy," August 1969 [report prepared for the Board of National Missions, UPCUSA], p. 8, RG 4, box 34, folder 21, NCC Archives. See also Lucius Walker to Charles Spivey, April 16, 1969, folder 14; Walker to Doreen Graves, April 18, 1969, and attached program of National Black Economic Development Conference, folder 14; both items in RG 6, box 35, NCC Archives. Walker recalled much later that Nixon's people pressed so hard to come that he "finally quit taking phone calls from them," but because there was no "litmus test for attendees," eventually they were admitted. Interview with Lucius Walker, July 29, 1991.

5. "The Truth and Consequences of Advocacy," August 1969, p. 8, RG 4, box 34, folder 21, NCC Archives; interview with Robert Chapman, September 12, 1991. On why the liberal white churches were vulnerable to Forman's attack, see *New York Times,* May 7, 1969, p. 27.

6. Forman spoke about religious influences in his early life in his autobiography, *The Making of Black Revolutionaries,* pp. 20–29, 546–547. His discussion in the autobiography of the manifesto and its attempted implementation is disappointingly brief (pp. 543–551).

7. "Manifesto to the White Christian Churches and the Jewish Synagogues and All Other Racist Institutions in the United States of America, . . . delivered and adopted by the Black Economic Development Conference in Detroit, Michigan on April 26, 1969," pp. 4, 5, attached to Minutes, Executive Committee, General Board, NCC, June 23, 1969, RG 3, box 4, folder 12, NCC Archives. The manifesto was reprinted in Wilmore and Cone, *Black Theology,* pp. 80–89.

8. Interview with James Forman, March 11, 1991.

9. Forman, "Manifesto," p. 3, RG 3, box 4, folder 12, NCC Archives.

10. On this issue, see Cleveland Sellers, *The River of No Return: The Autobiography of a Black Militant and the Life and Death of SNCC* (New York, William Morrow, 1973), p. 262.

11. Forman, "Manifesto," pp. 7–8, RG 3, box 4, folder 12, NCC Archives.

12. On conference proposals that closely paralleled those of Forman, see "Statement of the League of Revolutionary Black Workers to the National Black Economic Development Conference," RG 6, box 35, folder 14, NCC Archives; on the southern landbank, see "A Proposal for a Southern Land Bank Demonstration Project," in folder "Black Economic Research Center, 1969–70," box 33,

IFCO Papers; on voting by black separatists on Forman's proposals, see "The Truth and Consequences of Advocacy," August 1969, pp. 8–9, RG 4, box 34, folder 21, NCC Archives.

13. On May 2, 1969, Forman met for the first time with the General Board of the National Council of Churches to discuss the manifesto and its demands, but this turned out to be a brief meeting that postponed until June 23, 1969, a full consideration of the document. "A Chronicle of the Black Manifesto Debate in National Religious Bodies as of August 21, 1969," in folder "Black Manifesto," in files of Barbara Campbell, Women's Division, Board of Global Ministries, UMC, New York (hereafter cited as Campbell files); Jack Fisler, "Summary of Denominational Visits & Responses," May 15, 1969, RG 5, box 13, folder 23, NCC Archives.

14. *New York Times,* May 5, 1969, pp. 1, 37; James Forman to the Board of Deacons and membership of Riverside Church, RG 5, box 13, folder 17; Fisler, "Summary of Denominational Visits and Responses," RG 5, box 3, folder 23; items in NCC Archives. On the perceived parallels between Forman and earlier Christian rebels and prophets, see "Statement of the Board of Directors of the National Committee of Black Churchmen," May 7, 1969, in folder "Denominational Responses," box 37, IFCO Papers; and Forman's own words and actions, reported in the *New York Times,* May 7, 1969, p. 26.

15. Fisler, "Summary of Denominational Visits and Responses," folder 23; Forman to The Most Rev. John E. Hines, May 12, 1969, Forman to Ben Herbster and Howard Spragg, May 14, 1969, folder 17, and "Summary of Demands Made to American Baptist Convention," May 20, 1969, folder 17; all items in RG 5, box 13, NCC Archives.

16. Handy, *History of Union Theological Seminary in New York,* pp. 273–280.

17. It should also be stressed that throughout May and June 1969 there were demonstrations supporting the manifesto and its demands in churches and at national church gatherings, in many places other than New York. See especially mimeographed, undated "Chronology," pp. 9, 10, 11, 12, 14, 16, 17, in folder entitled "Respond," box 41, IFCO Papers.

18. Untitled memo of occupying students, 10:00 A.M., Monday, May 12 [1969]; "Resolution Passed by the Faculty at a Faculty Meeting Thursday, May 15"; "Response of Union Seminary Directors to Demands Made by Students," May 20, 1969; items in file entitled "Other Responses," box 37, IFCO Papers; "A Chronicle of the Black Manifesto Debate in National Religious Bodies as of August 21, 1969," in folder entitled "Black Manifesto," pp. 1–2, Campbell files; Handy, *History of Union Theological Seminary in New York,* pp. 280–282.

19. On the implementation later in 1969 of commitments concerning the Black Manifesto by the board of trustees of Union Theological Seminary, see folder entitled "Union Theological Seminary," box 7, Black Methodists for Church Renewal Archives, United Methodist Center, Dayton, Ohio (hereafter cited as BMCR Archives).

20. "Chronology," undated, mimeographed, pp. 7, 8, 12, 17, 18, 20–21, in folder entitled "Respond," box 41, IFCO Papers; Tracey K. Jones to Council of Secretaries re Events at "475," July 14, 1969, pp. 1, 2, folder entitled "Black Manifesto," in Campbell files.

21. Copies of some of the flyers and memos generated at the Interchurch Center concerning the Forman occupations and the strike held on June 9, 1969, are in RG 4, box 34, folder 18, NCC Archives.

22. Tracey K. Jones, Jr., to Council of Secretaries, July 14, 1969, in folder entitled "Black Manifesto," Campbell files; "Chronology" [mimeographed, undated], pp. 12–24, in folder "Respond," box 41, IFCO Papers; John Coventry Smith to Commission Members, June 19, 1969, entitled "Chronicle of events at '475,'" in folder entitled "James Forman," box 15, Neigh Papers; interview with R. H. Edwin Espy, September 2, 1988.

23. Harriet M. Spangler to Bruce K. Wood, RG 4, box 34, folder 17, NCC Archives. A copy of the restraining order is in RG 4, box 34, folder 18, NCC Archives.

24. *New York Times,* July 12, 1969, p. 74.

25. This account follows closely that of Betty Thompson in "A View from 475," *Engage,* July 15, 1969, p. 13. A somewhat different version is in interview with R. H. Edwin Espy, September 2, 1988. Espy described the meeting in the chapel as a "happening" and felt that the vote at the end "sandbagged" him since there were no criteria for voting eligibility and everyone in the room participated, many of whom had no regular connection with the Interchurch Center. On the effect of the chapel meeting on the restraining order, see R. H. Edwin Espy to All NCC Staff, Twelve Noon, June 19, 1969, RG 5, box 13, folder 16, NCC Archives.

26. For a sampling of such opinions, see Mrs. Theodore I. Wells to Office of Administration [NCC], June 27, 1969, folder 16; Mary L. Reifer to Dr. Edw. Espy, June 28, 1969, folder 16; Herman W. Bansemer to Arthur Fleming, July 7, 1969, folder 16; Bruce K. Wood to R. H. Edwin Espy, May 15, 1969, folder 17; Sam N. Varnell to Espy, June 4, 1969, folder 17; John T. Lundy to Espy, May 26, 1969, folder 17; items in RG 4, box 34, NCC Archives. An especially vehement critic was Francis Harmon, a wealthy, long-time supporter of the National Council who lived near the Interchurch Center and who personally tried to stir widespread public opposition to the manifesto. See especially RG 4, box 34, folder 16, NCC Archives.

27. Such explicit linkages of feelings and attitudes are to be found in Bruce K. Wood to Espy, May 15, 1969, folder 16, ibid.; A. Dale Fiers to Espy, May 29, 1969, folder 16, ibid.; Raymond Shaheen and Genevieve Huiess to Espy, July 2, 1969, folder 16, ibid.; O. K. Armstrong to Espy, September 18, 1969, folder 16, ibid. For more general discussion of the themes mentioned here, see David W. Levy, *The Debate Over Vietnam* (Baltimore, Johns Hopkins University Press, 1991); and Todd Gitlin, *The Sixties: Years of Hope, Days of Rage* (New York, Bantam, 1987), especially chaps. 12–17.

28. Kendall Redfield to National Council of Churches of Christ, June 28, 1969, folder 16; Evelyn M. Reed to the National Council of Churches, June 24, 1969, folder 17; Herman W. Bansemer to Dr. Arthur Flemming, July 7, 1969, folder 16; all items in RG 4, box 34, NCC Archives.

29. George Gallup, *The Gallup Poll: Public Opinion, 1935–1971* (New York, Random House, 1972), vol. III, p. 2200.

30. Bayard Rustin called the demand for reparations "preposterous" and characterized Forman as "hustling" or "begging." Roy Wilkins was more circumspect but also critical. *New York Times,* May 9, p. 44; May 13, 1969, p. 32; One of the more extreme statements came from J. H. Jackson, president of the National Baptist Convention, U.S.A., Inc., who asserted in late June that the manifesto was a "message for the destruction of the United States" and threatened to pull his denomination out of the National Council if the latter group acceded to

Forman's demands. *New York Times,* June 29, 1969, p. 21. See also *New York Times,* July 7, p. 35; August 2, p. 30; and especially July 21, 1969, p. 41; Joseph Gomez to R. H. Edwin Espy, July 8, 1969, RG 5, box 13, folder 16, NCC Archives.

31. E. A. Eldridge to R. H. Edwin Espy, May 26, 1969, folder 17; Mrs. Walter B. Driscoll to Dr. Arthur Flemming, July 9, 1969, folder 16; both items in RG 4, box 34, NCC Archives. See also Esther E. Prevey to Espy, July 8, 1969; Mrs. Theodore I. Wells to Office of Administration [NCC], June 27, 1969; Mrs. Charles N. Schlenker to National Council of Churches, July 2, 1969; Robert M. Blackburn to Edwin Espy, May 14, 1969; R. H. Huenemann to Edwin Espy, September 16, 1969; items in RG 4, box 34, folder 16, NCC Archives; news release, November 17, 1969, "Excerpts" from statement of Bishop Roy H. Short, pp. 3–4, box 76-55, folder 1349-7-1:17, files of General Board of Church and Society, UMC, Methodist Archives.

32. Emma B. [Mrs. James W.] Watson to Margaret Shannon, June 24, 1969, in folder entitled "CWU and the Black Manifesto, Spring–Summer, 1969," box 3, CWU Papers. See also Phyllis Bedford to Margaret Shannon, July 3, 1969, box 3, CWU Papers.

33. "Statement: Ad Hoc Black Caucus—May 5, 1969"; "Statement of the Board of Directors of the National Committee of Black Churchmen," May 8, 1969; both items in RG 5, box 13, folder 17, NCC Archives; "Chronology," mimeographed, undated, p. 5, in folder entitled "Respond," box 41, IFCO Papers.

34. "Statement of the Board of Directors, NCBC," May 8, 1969, p. 1, RG 5, box 13, folder 17, NCC Archives.

35. Gayraud S. Wilmore, Jr., "The Church's Response to the Black Manifesto," June 23, 1969, p. 5, in folder entitled "Respond," box 41, IFCO Papers.

36. Ibid., p. 3.

37. Ibid., pp. 3, 4–5. For a recent analysis of Malcolm's relationship to American church people, both black and white, see James H. Cone, *Martin and Malcolm in America: A Dream or a Nightmare* (Maryknoll, N.Y., Orbis Press, 1991).

38. Ibid., pp. 3, 4. Italics in original.

39. Ibid., pp. 5–7, 15–16. Ernest Campbell's response to the Black Manifesto is reprinted in a collection of essays edited by Robert S. Lecky and H. Elliott Wright, *Black Manifesto; Religion, Racism, and Reparations* (New York, Sheed and Ward, 1969), pp. 127–132. A very useful analysis of the manifesto, especially the reparations issue, is in Max L. Stackhouse, "Reparations: A Call to Repentance," in folder with the same name, box 43, IFCO Papers. See also "Black Reparations: Two Views," reprinted from *Dissent,* July–August 1969, pp. 317–320, in Reparations folder, box 43; Lucius Walker, Jr., "A Case for Reparations to Black America," no folder, in box 39; both items in IFCO Papers.

40. Wilmore, "The Church's Response to the Black Manifesto," pp. 7, 11, in folder entitled "Respond," box 41, IFCO Papers.

41. There were others in the African American religious community who spoke publicly in much the same vein as Wilmore. See Andrew White [Executive Secretary, Division of Christian Education, A.M.E. Church], "Interpretive Notes on the Black Manifesto to the Churches," July 1, 1969, RG 4, box 34, folder 23, NCC Archives; "Suggested Guidelines for A.M.E. Zion Churches," August 1, 1969, in folder entitled "Black Manifesto"; and *Journal,* 2d Annual Meeting, Board of Missions, UMC, October 23–31, 1969, p. 32; both items in

Campbell files; and especially telegram, Ralph David Abernathy and Andrew J. Young to R. H. Edwin Espy, June 22, 1969, RG 4, box 34, folder 23, NCC Archives. There are similar perceptions from a Jewish observer in Albert Vorspan, "How James Forman Lost His Cool but Saved Religion in 1969," *Christian Century,* August 6, 1969, p. 1042.

42. Wilmore, "The Church's Response to the Black Manifesto," pp. 10, 13; in folder "Respond," box 41, IFCO Papers; interview with James Forman, March 11, 1991.

43. For comments recognizing this delemma by important Methodist observers, see "Going the Second Mile," *Together,* August 1969, p. 13.

44. "Minutes," Steering Committee, Black Economic Development Conference, July 11–12, 1969, pp. 6–8, RG 6, box 35, folder 14, NCC Archives, are especially revealing, but see also "IFCO and BEDC," p. 7, in folder entitled "IFCO/BEDC Relationship," box 37, IFCO Papers; "The Truth and Consequences of Advocacy," p. 9, RG 4, box 34, folder 21, NCC Archives. Marshall's attitudes are partially revealed in his essay, "The Debacle of Berkeley," November 26, 1969, in folder entitled "Miscellaneous—NBEDC," box 43, IFCO Papers.

45. Minutes, Board of Directors, IFCO, May 6, May 11, 1969, IFCO headquarters.

46. As early as May 7, the national press began to learn about IFCO. On that day the staff writer of the *New York Times* who reported on religious topics noted IFCO's decision the preceding day to "endorse the goals of the black manifesto," but to "stay at arm's length from Mr. Forman and his tactics," and concluded that these actions "may in the long run prove crucial" in enabling IFCO to serve as a "broker" in both the black and white communities. *New York Times,* May 7, 1969, p. 27. See also Kenneth G. Neigh to "All Pastors and Ministers of the United Presbyterian Church," May 7, 1969, in folder "Kenneth G. Neigh, May 7, 1970," box 5, Neigh Papers; "The Truth and Consequences of Advocacy," August 1969, p. 9, in folder entitled "The Board of National Missions [PCUSA] and IFCO," box 43, IFCO Papers.

47. "The Interreligious Foundation for Community Organization (IFCO) and Its Finances," *The Presbyterian Layman,* October 1976, pp. 5–6 (I am indebted to Lucius Walker for this very important source); "Chronology" [undated], pp. 11, 20, 27, in folder "Respond," box 41, IFCO Papers.

48. By August 1, 1969, BEDC actually had received $3,500 from the students of Union Theological Seminary, $15,000 from the Washington Square Methodist Church in New York City, and $1,000 from an interdenominational group of black clergymen in Philadelphia. "IFCO and BEDC," pp. 6, 7, in folder "IFCO/BEDC Relationship," box 37, IFCO Papers. In January 1971, IFCO ended its role as an administrator of money designated specifically for BEDC because of "repeated failure to cooperate with the administrative procedure IFCO follows in all grant relationships." Lucius Walker to Calvin Marshall, January 4, 1971; see also "Information Memo," January 17, 1971; Lucius Walker to Gordon Verplank, January 29, 1971; all items in folder entitled "Black Economic Development Conference," box 31, IFCO Papers.

49. The estimate of money collected between the summer of 1969 and March 1970 is approximate since figures for gifts are drawn from public reports from IFCO, which represented total sums collected between 1967 and March 1970. "IFCO and Its Finances," *The Presbyterian Layman,* October 1976, p. 5. See also

"The Board of National Missions [United Presbyterian Church] and the Inter-religious Foundation for Community Organization, August, 1969: II—A Full Financial Statement," in folder entitled "The Board of National Missions and IFCO"; "Application for Funding," IFCO to General Convention Special Program of the Episcopal Church, [no date] in folder entitled "GCSP Proposal"; both items in box 43, IFCO Papers. In 1975, IFCO received in gifts from all sources $457,044. *The Presbyterian Layman,* October 1976, p. 5.

50. Lincoln and Mamiya in *Black Church in African American Experience* do not systematically examine these groups, but see pp. 65–67, 124, 159, 298–300 for helpful comments.

51. Ibid., p. 67; *NOW* [newsletter of Black Methodists for Church Renewal], July 1, 1968, p. 6, box 8, BMCR Archives; Wilmore, "Church's Response to Black Manifesto," June 23, 1969, p. 1.

52. Cain Felder, "A Status Report of the Black Methodists for Church Renewal," May 5, 1969, pp. 4–5, in folder entitled "Executive Director's Report, May 5, 1969," box 2; James Lawson to All Members of the Board of Directors of BMCR, July 8, 1968, in folder entitled "Minutes—Board of Directors, Philadelphia, PA, August 30, 1968," box 1; both items in BMCR Archives.

53. On the decline of ESCRU and the emergence of the Union of Black Clergy and Laity, see Minutes, Board Meeting [ESCRU], November 15–17, 1968, pp. 1–2, in folder "Minutes of the Board, May–November, 1968," box 7; *Newsletter,* ESCRU, December 15, 1968, folder 36, box 8; September 14, 1969, pp. 1–2, folder 36, box 9; June S. Crowley to ESCRU Members, November 4, 1970, folder 36, box 10; items in ESCRU Papers, Martin Luther King Center; *NOW* [newsletter], July 1, 1968, p. 6, box 8, BMCR Archives. On Black Presbyterians United, see Gayraud Wilmore, "Identity and Integration: Black Presbyterians and Their Allies," in Coalter, Mulder, and Weeks, *The Presbyterian Predicament,* pp. 124, 125–126.

54. On the angry, agonized debates between the Black Methodists for Church Renewal and several of the national boards of the United Methodists, see news releases, May 27, May 30, 1969, General News Service, files of General Board of Church and Society, UMC, folder 1349-7-1:17, Methodist Archives; *NOW,* August 25, 1969; October 10, 1969; December 15, 1969; items in box 8, BMCR Archives. On the BMCR's financing, see Cain Felder to Members of the Board of Directors, Black Methodists for Church Renewal, July 4, 1969, in folder entitled "Executive Director's Report, June 4, 1969," box 2, BMCR Archives; *Journal,* 2d Annual Meeting, Women's Division, Board of Missions, UMC, October 25–31, 1969, pp. 5–6, Campbell files. On similar debates among Episcopalians, see Minutes, Board Meeting [ESCRU], June 20–21, 1969, folder entitled "Minutes of the Board, January–November, 1969," box 7; *Newsletter,* ESCRU, September 14, 1969, pp. 1–2, folder 36, box 9; both items in ESCRU Papers.

55. For detailed and moving accounts of the debates over whether to fund the Black Economic Development Conference with Methodist and Episcoplian funds, see *Newsletter,* September 14, 1969, pp. 1–2, ESCRU Papers; *Newsletter,* BMCR, December 15, 1969, pp. 2–3, box 8, BMCR Archives. The "handouts" remark is in Cain Felder to Members of the Board . . . , July 4, 1969, in folder entitled "Executive Director's Report, June 4, 1969," box 2, BMCR Archives.

56. A detailed account of the meeting on May 2, 1969, is in "Report on the Meeting of the General Board of the N.C.C.," attached to Edward D. Grant to R. H. Edwin Espy, May 13, 1969, RG 4, box 34, folder 15, NCC Archives.

57. Confidential Memorandum of James H. Laue to Arthur Flemming, et al., entitled "Report of Observations at 475 Riverside Drive, July 13–15th [1969]: The Churches and Black Reparations," p. 3, RG 4, box 34, folder 23, NCC Archives. See also Robert Torbet to David R. Hunter, May 21, 1969, RG 5, box 13, folder 16, NCC Archives.

58. Grover L. Hartman, "Reflections on the National Council of Churches' Response to the Black Manifesto: Background and Interpretation," September 19, 1969, RG 5, box 13, folder 22, NCC Archives. Apparently there were connections between these conclusions and Gayraud Wilmore's essay, "The Church's Response to the Black Manifesto," which was circulated among those who participated in the discussions in the summer of 1969. Hartman to Chief Executives of State . . . and City Councils, July 23, 1969, p. 2, in folder entitled "Governing Board Resumés, 1967–1983," Grover L. Hartman Papers, DePauw University. See also similar reflections of Methodist Bishop Roy H. Short, in news release, November 17, 1969, General News Service, UMC, folder 1349-7-7:17, files of General Board of Church and Society, Methodist Archives.

59. Grover L. Hartman, "Reflections on the National Council of Churches Response to the Black Manifesto," p. 1, RG 5, box 13, folder 22, NCC Archives; Hartman to Chief Executives of State . . . Councils, July 23, 1969, p. 3, folder, "Governing Board Resumés, 1967–1983," Hartman Papers. As a former staff member at the Interchurch Center, Andrew Young still exerted unusual influence within the National Council of Churches. The telegram he and Ralph Abernathy sent to the council on June 22 defending much of Forman's action ("a crude but determined prophet to plague us to repentance") and joining in the chorus of African American criticism ("the churches have long been guilty of a lack of stewardship as institution[s]") was a major factor in drawing Young directly into the discussions in New York City. Telegram, Ralph Abernathy and Andrew Young to R. H. E. Espy, June 22, 1969, RG 4, box 34, folder 23, NCC Archives.

60. Hartman, "Reflections on the National Council of Churches Response to the Black Manifesto," pp. 1, 2, RG 5, box 13, folder 22, NCC Archives. A near-paraphrase of these views is in David Hunter to John S. Lyles, October 21, 1969, RG 5, box 13, folder 16, NCC Archives. Hunter was Espy's administrative assistant.

61. A lengthy and important discussion of this issue, especially as it applied to the mainstream churches during the summer of 1969, is in the *New York Times,* July 27, 1969, pp. 1, 54. See also, from a thoughtful African American perspective, the mimeographed remarks of Robert Browne at an Interchurch Center Teach-In, June 25, 1969, in folder entitled "National Black Economic Development Conference," box 41, IFCO Papers.

62. "Response of the General Board of the National Council of Churches to the Black Manifesto," adopted by the board, September 11, 1969, RG 2, box 5, folder 1, NCC Archives; Grover L. Hartman to Chief Executives of State . . . Councils, September 1969, pp. 2–3, in folder, "Governing Board Resumés, 1967–1983," Hartman Papers.

63. "Report," Investment Committee for Ghetto Community Development, Agenda Item no. XXI, General Board meeting, January 21–24, 1969, pp. 7–8, in folder entitled "Mutual Funding Plans, NCC," Robert Chapman Papers, St. Phillip's Episcopal Church, Brooklyn, New York.

64. "Draft Proposals re: Finding," Committee of Sixteen, July 10, 1969, RG 4, box 34, folder 21; Minutes, Committee of Sixteen, July 21, 1969, pp. 2–3, RG 4,

box 34, folder 21; "Reponse of the General Board . . . to the Black Manifesto," September 11, 1969, p. 2, RG 2, box 5, folder 1; all items in NCC Archives.

65. One key observer asserted eventually that Flemming was the "conceptual father" and "primary enabler" of the project. David R. Hunter to Arthur S. Flemming, February 6, 1970, RG 5, box 13, folder 24, ibid.

66. A preliminary "idea session" with J. Irwin Miller and a small interracial group of church leaders occurred on September 17, 1969. David R. Hunter to Edler Hawkins, et al., September 15, 1969, ibid. Much of the meeting of the acquisition task force on October 4 was also devoted to brainstorming. Notes of Jim Liebig, Acquisition Task Force, October 4, 1969; "Meeting of the Task Forces on Acquisition and Disbursement . . . at LaGuardia Airport Holiday Inn," October 4, 1969, pp. 1–2, both items in folder entitled "Mutual Finding Plans, NCC," Chapman Papers.

67. Jon Regier, "Background and Present Status of Economic Development," November 11, 1969, RG 5, box 13, folder 24, NCC Archives. A more detailed description and analysis of both the development theories behind the proposals, and the structures of implementation envisioned, are in Frank White, "Report from Task Forces on Social and Economic Development to the Program Committee of the National Council of Churches," attached to Frank White to David Hunter, October 23, 1969, RG 5, box 13, folder 24, NCC Archives.

68. Regier, "Background and Present Status of Economic Development," November 11, 1969, ibid.

69. Ibid. Italics added. A detailed outline of the Mutual Fund concept, including an example of a possible Prospectus for the Fund, is in Frank White to NCC Project Committee re: Economic Development Report and meeting, November 22, 1969, ibid.

70. There is no critical, comprehensive history of the movement toward socially responsible investing in this country. Pax World Fund, established in 1970 by Quakers and Methodists, was the first clearly designated socially responsible mutual fund. Its plan to avoid investments in weapons or defense-related industries was obviously tied to the Vietnam War. But not until the early 1980s did the movement spread and secure national attention. See Alan J. Miller, *Socially Responsible Investing: How to Invest With Your Conscience* (New York, Simon and Schuster, 1991), chap. 1; Ritchie P. Lowry, *Good Money: A Guide to Profitable Social Investing in the 90's* (New York, W. W. Norton, 1991), pp. 19–20, 22–36, 57–70, 120–122, 136–138; Council on Economic Priorities, *Research Report,* (February/March 1991), pp. 1–4; telephone interview with James Liebig, April 20, 1990.

71. In late 1965 and early 1966, national church groups sparked the first efforts to withdraw funds from banks in New York City providing large loans to South Africa. College and seminary students, national religious leaders including Reinhold Niebuhr, and the missionary boards of several of the denominations participated. After a long internal debate, in June 1968 the directors of the General Board of the National Council of Churches rejected a proposal that the council withdraw major deposits from City Bank of New York. The financial administrators of the council carried the day, instead of the social activists of the Division of Christian Life and Mission. In November 1977 the council finally began to remove some of its deposits from New York banks involved in South Africa and urged its member denominations to do the same. RG 4, box 36, folder 9 and RG 5, box 17, folder 8, NCC Archives; Handy, *History of Union Theological Seminary*

in New York, pp. 268–269, 343–345; telephone interview with Timothy Smith, October 21, 1991; *New York Times,* November 11, 1977, p. 6.

72. Frank White to David Hunter, re Meeting at Patterson, Belknap and Webb and Future Developments, November 3, 1969, RG 5, box 13, folder 24, NCC Archives.

73. Frank White to David Hunter and Jon Regier, February 3, 1970, ibid.; Richard Cutler to Robert S. Browne, February 13, 1970, ibid.

74. Richard Cutler to Robert S. Browne, February 13, 1970, ibid.; David R. Hunter to Arthur S. Flemming, February 6, 1970, ibid.

75. Frank White to David Hunter and Jon Regier, March 9, 1970, ibid.

76. David R. Hunter to Tracey K. Jones, March 20, 1970, ibid.

77. Frank White to David Hunter, November 3, 1969, ibid.; Frank White to L. Brininger, D. Hunter, J. Regier, E. Espy, B. Hanson, July 28, 1970, ibid.

78. Telephone interview with James Liebig, April 20, 1990; interview with Richard Cutler and Natalie Grow, February 14, 1991.

79. Frank White to L. Brininger, D. Hunter, J. Refier, E. Espy, and B. Hanson, July 28, 1970, RG 5, box 13, folder 24, NCC Archives.

80. Interview with Cutler and Grow, February 14, 1991. Cutler, at the present time a senior vice-president at Putnam Management Company, now believes, given the experience with "socially responsible" mutual funds in the 1980s, that the fund envisioned in 1970 needed a capitalization of approximately 25 to 30 million dollars.

81. Ibid. In this interview Cutler pointed out that today it is common practice for educational institutions like Harvard to place substantial portions of their endowment portfolios into specialized investment funds, especially functioning outside the United States in the international capital markets, which of course even a large investor like the Harvard Corporation does not control.

82. David S. Summer, "The Episcopal Church's Involvement in Civil Rights: 1943–1973," unpublished S.T.M. thesis, University of the South, 1983, pp. 60–68, 87–91, 96–112; John L. Kater, Jr., "Experiment in Freedom: The Episcopal Church and the Black Power Movement," *Historical Magazine of the Protestant Episcopal Church* (March 1979), pp. 67–81.

83. One official noted that the volume of mail sent to the key leaders of the denomination was "altogether without precedent," and that it was "overwhelmingly negative about the grant." *Presbyterian Life,* July 15, 1971, p. 16. A representative sample of letters is printed on pp. 16–19. Hundreds of letters and petitions from individuals, local churches, and presbyteries are included in the archival boxes related to the case at the Presbyterian Historical Society in Philadelphia. These papers are not open presently to scholarly examination. See also folder entitled "Why Angela Davis?" box 5, Neigh Papers.

84. Good summaries of the debates at the General Assembly, and a helpful official statement from the Stated Clerk of the church about the case are in *Presbyterian Life,* July 1, pp. 21–25, and July 15, 1971, pp. 20–21, 36. See also Wilmore, "Black Presbyterians and Their Allies" in Coalter, Mulder, and Weeks, *The Presbyterian Predicament,* especially pp. 126–133.

85. Grover L. Hartman to Chief Executives of State, Metropolitan, County, Area, and City Councils, December 1969, in folder entitled "Governing Board Resumés, 1967–1983," Hartman Papers. See also "Joy Box with No Joy: The N.C.C. at Detroit," December 17, 1969, *Christian Century,* pp. 1601–1605.

86. NCC News Release, December 3, 1969, RG 2, box 5, folder 15, NCC

Archives; *Detroit News,* December 4, 1969, p. 16A: Hartman to Chief Executive . . . City Councils, December 1969, in folder "Governing Board Resumés," Hartman Papers.

87. One seasoned participant noted that a moderate African American might have swayed the delegates and been elected. Andrew Young had agreed to be nominated, but was rejected by the militant African Americans, especially in the NCBC, who were sponsoring Cleage. *Christian Century,* December 17, 1969, p. 1602.

88. *Detroit News,* December 4, 1969, p. 10D.

89. Hartman to Chief Executive . . . City Councils, December 1969, in folder "Governing Board Resumés," Hartman Papers; National Council of Churches News Release, December 1, 1969, RG 2, box 5, folder 15, NCC Archives; *Detroit News,* December 5, 1969, p. 8c.

90. Brereton, "Women as Subordinated Insiders," in Hutchison, *Between the Times,* pp. 162–163; "Minutes," Enlarged Executive Committee, Church Women United, September 25–26, 1969, p. 10, and attached Exhibit C; Richard L. Morgan to Dorothy Nossett, November 14, 1969, items in folder "Church Women United—1969," box 3, CWU Papers.

91. News release, NCC General Assembly, December 2, 1972, RG 2, box 5, folder 35, NCC Archives; Grover L. Hartman to Association of Council Secretaries, September 1970, p. 3; Hartman, "Review of National Council of Churches General Board Meeting," June 20–21, 1970; Hartman to Chief Executives . . . City Councils, September, 1969; items in folder "Governing Board Resumés," Hartman Papers; Loyde H. Hartley, "Inflation and Recession Hit Local Church Budgets," in Constant H. Jacquet, Jr., ed., *Yearbook of American and Canadian Churches, 1981* (Nashville, Abingdon Press, 1981), p. 260.

92. On relevant trends in church membership, see Jacquet, *Yearbook, 1976,* pp. 254–255, and *Yearbook, 1975,* pp. 264–265; Peggy Ann Leu Shriver, "Do Americans Believe in the Church?," *Yearbook, 1979,* pp. 255–258. On church attendance since the 1950s, see *Yearbook, 1978,* pp. 256–257.

93. For example, Wuthnow, *The Restructuring of American Religion,* devotes only three pages to a direct consideration of the civil rights movement; Roof and McKinney, *American Mainline Religion,* offers four pages of comment about race and the churches, most of it a statistical description of the racial make-up of American Protestantism. Milton J. Coalter, John M. Mulder, Louis B. Weeks, eds., *The Mainstream Protestant "Decline": The Presbyterian Pattern* (Louisville, Westminster/John Knox Press, 1990), an important case study of a single denomination, omits any consideration of racial issues. James Davison Hunter, *Culture Wars: The Struggle to Define America* (New York, Basic Books, 1991), also largely ignores race as a defining concern.

94. On the need to recognize the contributions of small but highly influential elites to the racial revolution of the sixties, see Neil McMillen's review of Hugh Davis Graham's *The Civil Rights Era: Origins and Development of National Policy,* in *Reviews in American History,* June 1991, p. 283. On a parallel, race-related movement to create new forms of urban training and mission within the mainline churches, which flourished in the 1960s and declined in the 1970s, see George D. Younger, *From New Creation to Urban Crisis: A History of Action Training Ministries, 1962–1975* (Chicago, 1987).

95. See Introduction, pp. 4–5.

96. News release, National Council of Churches, December 1, 1969, RG 2,

box 5, folder 15, NCC Archives; *Detroit News,* December 2, p. 3. On the image "of a deeply entrenched Establishment" projected by "the long imposing row of officials on the platform" in the assembly meetings, see Alton M. Motter to R. H. Edwin Espy, December 16, 1969, RG 2, box 5, folder 13, NCC Archives.

97. "Report of the Executive Director to the Commission on Religion and Race," November 29, 1965, p. 7, RG 6, box 47, folder 29, NCC Archives.

98. Gayraud Wilmore, "The New Negro and the Church," *Christian Century,* February 6, 1963, pp. 170, 171.

SOURCES

The principal manuscript materials on which this book is based are the National Council of Churches Archives, housed at the Presbyterian Historical Society in Philadelphia. A massive archival resource consisting of over eight hundred linear feet of material, the papers were arranged by professional archivists who also prepared a detailed guide, which immensely facilitates use of the collection. The largest portions of the collection cover the activities of the National Council of Churches in the decade of the 1960s, but there are significant materials dealing with the 1950s and even some important records of the Federal Council of Churches reaching back well into the 1940s. The collection covers a wide range of topics related to many aspects of the churches' involvement in American life and in missionary activities overseas since World War II. Given the quality and importance of the collection it is still underused by historians.

The Presbyterian Historical Society also contains other important manuscript materials relevant to this study. Especially useful have been the archival records of the several boards and commissions of the United Presbyterian Church, U.S.A., that were most directly involved in racial matters in the sixties. This includes the papers of the Commission on Religion and Race of that denomination (not to be confused with the Commission on Religion and Race of the National Council of Churches) and the office files of the National Board of Missions. These papers have been well organized and annotated with detailed guides by the excellent staff of the Historical Society. These collections are further supplemented by important papers of individual Presbyterian leaders in the racial struggle of the sixties, especially those of Eugene Carson Blake, a leading ecumenicist and eventually the general secretary of the World Council of Churches. The important papers of Kenneth Neigh, the executive director of the Board of National Missions throughout most of the decade of the 1960s, are nearby at Princeton Theological Seminary.

Another research center of great importance to this study is the Martin

Luther King, Jr. Center for Non-Violent Social Change in Atlanta. Here are housed several of the principal archival collections documenting the central events, figures, and organizations of the civil rights era, all of which impinge upon this study. At the center are the papers of Martin Luther King, Jr., from 1963 to his death in 1968, the files of the Student Nonviolent Coordinating Committee and the Mississippi Freedom Democratic Party, and the papers of the Southern Christian Leadership Conference. In addition, the center has manuscript holdings that make it possible to examine in great detail the activities of church people in the Deep South, especially in Mississippi, throughout the 1960s. This includes over half the office files of the Delta Ministry; the papers of Arthur Thomas, the first director of the ministry; the papers of Thomas Levin, the principal founder of the Child Development Group of Mississippi; and the records of the Episcopal Society for Racial and Cultural Unity, an important interracial group of clergy and lay people who throughout the sixties pressed for changes in racial practices within their denomination and the larger society.

Archival material at several spots in Mississippi also provided crucial information. About 40 percent of the manuscripts of the Delta Ministry have been deposited in the Special Collections Office at Mississippi State University. The archives of Tougaloo College near Jackson also yielded important materials, especially in the papers of Charles Horwitz and R. Edwin King, two members of the Delta Ministry, and in taped interviews with Owen Brooks in the Tom Dent Oral History Collection. At the University of Southern Mississippi in Hattiesburg, I examined two boxes of materials of the Mississippi Sovereignty Commission, which are a part of the Paul Johnson Papers and crucial for any understanding of white opposition to the movement in Mississippi.

Scarcely less important are the manuscripts available at the Wisconsin State Historical Society in Madison, Wisconsin. That institution's Social Action Collections cover many aspects of the activism of the sixties and in a number of cases were directly relevant to my work. I found valuable the papers of the Highlander Center, Myles Horton's innovative educational home in Tennessee; a small collection of the papers of Harry Bowie, another Delta Ministry staff person; and especially the central files of the Child Development Group of Mississippi from 1965 to 1967, with which the Delta Ministry worked so closely. There is an excellent directive to all of these materials and many others, entitled *Social Action Collections at the State Historical Society of Wisconsin: A Guide* (Madison, State Historical Society of Wisconsin, 1983). Robert Beech also has promised to give the Historical Society his personal papers (although at present they are still in his possession in Bovey, Minnesota). This collection offers a priceless view of church activities, especially those of the Delta Ministry, in Mississippi in the mid-sixties.

There are also significant archival sources in Washington, D.C., primarily in the Manuscript Division of the Library of Congress. This includes the massive collection of the records of the NAACP, a small but very important set of office files and correspondence of the Leadership Conference on Civil Rights, and a most revealing "Log" (a daily diary of sorts) of Stephen Horn, the principal legislative assistant to Senator Thomas Kuechel of California, the Republican floor leader in the Senate during the extended debates over the Civil Rights Act of 1964. Especially important to this study were the relevant files of the Washington office of the National Council, which were made available by the then and current director of that office, James Hamilton.

Archival centers of several of the mainline denominations also possess valuable materials documenting church involvement in the racial struggle of the sixties. The Presbyterian Historical Society is the premier repository in this regard, but there are important materials concerning the hub of operations of the Delta Ministry at Mt. Beulah in Edwards, Mississippi, in the Division of Homeland Ministries papers at the Disciples of Christ Historical Society in Nashville. The national Methodist Archives, located at Drew University in Madison, New Jersey, contain the papers of Church Women United, a key constituency in the National Council of Churches from 1950 onward, and important official records of the Methodist agencies involved in racial issues. The official files of Black Methodists for Church Renewal, located at the United Methodist Church Center in Dayton, Ohio, offer a clear view of one of the most important denominational black caucuses that developed in the late sixties. The Church of the Brethren national office files and the papers of Ralph Smeltzer provided documentation throughout this study and are at the Brethren Historical Library and Archives in Elgin, Illinois. The papers of the Board of Homeland Ministries of the United Church of Christ at the Amistad Center at Tulane University in New Orleans, are filled with significant materials regarding race relations, in the sixties and earlier.

Finally, there are manuscript collections available at research centers scattered elsewhere in the country that contain important materials related to this study. These include the Victor and Walter Reuther papers in the Labor History Research Center at Wayne State University in Detroit, which are crucial in documenting many of the civil rights ventures in which National Council of Churches' people got involved; the Martin Luther King, Jr. and Howard Thurman Papers at Boston University; the National Catholic Conference for Interracial Justice Papers at Marquette University in Milwaukee, a very helpful source in revealing Catholic involvement in the racial struggles of the sixties; the Southern Regional Conference Papers at Atlanta University, which possess material on the activities of Will Campbell in the late fifties; the Papers of Bishop Paul Moore at the Cathedral of St. John the Divine in New York City, which highlight the civil rights activities of an influential Episcopalian; the Rogert Spike Collection at the University of Chicago, a distressingly small but important set of manuscripts written by a central figure in this study; the files of the Interreligious Foundation for Community Organization at the Schomburg Library in Harlem, absolutely essential for understanding the churches' response, both black and white, to the Black Manifesto; the Field Foundation Papers at the University of Texas, useful in documenting the final stages of the fight over the refunding CDGM in late 1966; and the Grover Hartman Papers at DePauw University in Indiana, a small but highly revealing source documenting the National Council's reaction to the Black Manifesto.

Oral history interviews and recollections gathered recently with many of the participants in the events of the sixties also constituted an important source for this study. The majority of these interviews were taped and detailed indexes of the interviews were prepared. Transcripts of these interviews would have been very costly and time consuming; detailed indexes seemed a reasonable alternative, and that procedure was followed. A number of interviews were conducted by telephone; most of these conversations were not taped (for those that were, permission of the interviewee was secured beforehand) but detailed notes were made both during and immediately after the discussions. These notes have been placed with the indexes. The handwritten indexes, notes of telephone interviews, and the tapes eventually will be deposited in a public archive, probably the Presbyterian Historical Society, so that interested persons can have access to them (if for no other reason than to check my documentation!). Listed below are the names of the people interviewed, the dates of interviews, and a clear designation if the interview was conducted by telephone. Also appended are the few oral interviews conducted by persons other than myself and their source.

Aronson, Arnold	January 9, 1986
Bailey, J. Martin	July 17, 1992
Barber, Rims	July 21, 1986; June 24, 1989; telephone, August 16, 1989
Barnes, Thelma	July 14, 1986; July 18, 1986; July 24, 1986
Beech, Robert	October 12, 1989; October 13, 1989
Billings, Peggy	Telephone, February 27, 1991; telephone, September 26, 1991
Blanchard, Eric	March 12, 1991
Breeden, James	Telephone, April 12, 1991
Bowie, Harry	July 15, 1986; June 29, 1989; November 6, 1989
Brooks, Owen	July 14, 1986; telephone, July 6, 1989
Calkins, H. Bruce	Telephone, Januray 18, 1989
Caplan, Marvin	Telephone, March 28, 1985; January 9, 1986
Carter, Hodding, III	June 13, 1988
Chapman, Robert	September 12, 1991
Cobb, Charles, Sr.	November 22, 1988

Cutler, Richard	Telephone, February 11, 1991; February 14, 1991 (with Natalie Grow)
Espy, R. H. Edwin	September 2, 1988 (A.M.); September 2, 1988 (P.M.)
Flory, Margaret	Telephone, May 11, 1987
Flemming, Arthur	February 15, 1988
Forman, James	March 11, 1991
George, Bryant	October 23, 1989
Greenberg, Polly	September 27, 1989
Grow, Natalie, with Richard Cutler	February 14, 1991
Guyot, Lawrence	June 13, 1988; September 28, 1989
Hamilton, James	March 15, 1985; January 9, 1986
Hall, Clarence	July 18, 1986
Hanson, D. Bruce	August 1, 1984; July 26, 1985; February 15, 1988; telephone, November 23, 1990; March 11, 1991
Hayes, Curtis	January 14, 1991
Hilton, Bruce and Virginia	July 16, 1989; July 17, 1989
Hilton, Virginia	May 31, 1991
Hood, Robert	April 7, 1990
Horwitz, Charles	July 27, 1989
Hoyt, Phyllis	August 5, 1985
Hudson, Winthrop	Telephone, March 9, 1991
Hunter, David	February 16, 1989
Johnson, David	October 15, 1990
Johnson, Sarah	July 17, 1986
King, R. Edwin	July 22, 1986
Kushino, June	April 9, 1985
Lee, J. Oscar	March 22, 1990
Leventhal, Melvin	October 9, 1990
Liebig, James	Telephone, April 20, 1990
Lowry, Fred	November 22, 1988
Luker, Ralph	January 4, 1989
McKenna, Warren	May 23, 24, 26, 1986; telephone, June 27, 1986
Miles, Matthew	October 9, 1990
Miller, J. Irwin	May 29, 1990
Miller, Roberta	June 30, 1989
Moore, Paul, Jr.	October 28, 1986; November 25, 1986; telephone, September 13, 1990
Moses, Robert	Telephone, January 27, 1989

Mudd, John | August 3, 1989
Neigh, Kenneth | October 30, 1989
Newman, Robert | November 20, 1990; telephone, November 21, 1990
Oniki, Gary | October 9, 1989
Payton, Benjamin | Telephone, June 4, 1991
Phillips, Jean | July 17, 1986
Pratt, John M. | June 16, 1985; telephone, February 25, 1991
Ramage, David | October 9, 1989
Regier, Jon | August 7, 1986; telephone, October 28, 1986; telephone, February 8, 1987; telephone, December 28, 1987; telephone, August 29, 1989; telephone, June 20, 1990; telephone, August 25, 1991
Scott, Marshal | October 9, 1989
Smith, Roger | Telephone, October 13, 1986; June 29, 1989; telephone, January 15, 1991
Smith, Timothy | Telephone, October 21, 1991
Spike, Paul | March 1, 1986
Stone, Robert | Telephone, January 22, 1989
Taylor, Richard | June 18, 1985
Thelwell, Michael | May 22, 1990
Walker, Lucius | September 22, 1989; December 27, 1989
Walmsley, Arthur | March 24, 1987
Watkins, Hollis | June 27, 1989
White, Herbert | Telephone, September 5, 1991
Williams, Colin | August 18, 1990
Wilmore, Gayraud | May 6, 1991
Wimer, Alice and William | August 18, 1992
Wright, Dean | November 12, 1990

Other Interviews

Campbell, Will D. | Oral history with Will Davis Campbell, vol. 157, 1980, Mississippi Oral History Program, University of Southern Mississippi, Hattiesburg, Mississippi.
Dent, Tom | Interview with Harry Bowie, May 28, 1978; interview with Owen Brooks, August 18, 1978; Tom Dent Oral History Collection, Tougaloo College Archives, Jackson, Mississippi.
McCloud, J. Oscar | Interview with Gayraud Wilmore, December 23, 1981, tapes 857 and 858, Oral History Collection, Presbyterian Historical Society, Philadelphia.

The religious and secular press often reported in detail and commented perceptively about the central events and people discussed in this book. Only the most helpful of these publications can be noted here. *Presbyterian Life* and the *United Church Herald,* general periodicals of two major mainstream denominations, offered bellwether judgments and information from within the heart of "establishment" Protestantism. In the fifties and sixties, *The Christian Century* was (and still is) the most widely read ecumenical Protestant weekly in the United States. I examined carefully files of all three publications covering the two decades of my study, and the files of *Christianity and Crisis,* another important ecumenical journal for most of the 1960s. *The New York Times,* with its incomparable index, detailed coverage of daily events throughout the country, and a superb reporter, Claude Sitton, located in the Deep South for several years, remained an invaluable asset to historical research concerning race relations in the fifties and sixties. Also helpful for developments in Mississippi because of its relatively moderate stance on racial affairs throughout the sixties was the Greenville, Mississippi, *Delta Democrat Times.* I used both daily newspapers extensively, especially concerning events in the 1960s.

Finally, photographic materials related to this project need to be noted. Especially important is the Ken Thompson Collection in the offices of the Board of Global Ministries, United Methodist Church, at the Interchurch Center in New York City. Thompson was the official photographer of the NCC's Commission on Religion and Race. The 2,000 prints and negatives are compromised somewhat by the lack of captions. There are also important photographs in the office of Sarah Vilankulu in the National Council of Churches headquarters in New York concerning many aspects of the civil rights era, and at the Presbyterian Historical Society, in Record Group 301.7, box 45, folder 28, related to the early Head Start program in Mississippi. Two of the "minister-counselors" who were in Mississippi in the summer of 1964 and earlier shared pictorial materials as well as their remembrances. Donald McCord of Oak Park, Illinois, allowed me to copy his invaluable collection of 200 Kodachrome slides, and Simon A. Stone, of Jerseyville, Illinois, sent me an 8-mm film of picketing and demonstrations in Hattiesburg, Mississippi, which I copied on videotape. John Mudd of Cambridge, Massachusetts, helped me obtain two documentary videotapes which illuminate the early history of the Child Development Group of Mississippi. All of these materials will be deposited at the Presbyterian Historical Society.

INDEX